THE
DALLAS MYTH

The publication of this book
was assisted by a bequest from
Josiah H. Chase to honor his parents,
Ellen Rankin Chase and Josiah Hook Chase,
Minnesota territorial pioneers.

THE
DALLAS MYTH

The Making and Unmaking
of an American City

HARVEY J. GRAFF

UNIVERSITY OF MINNESOTA PRESS

MINNEAPOLIS • LONDON

Published by the University of Minnesota Press
111 Third Avenue South, Suite 290
Minneapolis, MN 55401–2520
http://www.upress.umn.edu

Library of Congress Cataloging-in-Publication Data

Graff, Harvey J.
The Dallas myth : the making and unmaking of an American city / Harvey J. Graff.
p. cm.
Includes bibliographical references and index.
ISBN 978-0-8166-5269-3 (hc : alk. paper) — ISBN 978-0-8166-5270-9 (pb : alk. paper)
1. Dallas (Tex.)—History. 2. Dallas (Tex.)—Social conditions. 3. City and town life—Texas—Dallas—History. 4. Dallas (Tex.)—Race relations. 5. Dallas (Tex.)—Economic conditions. 6. City planning—Texas—Dallas—History. I. Title.
F394.D2157G73 2008
976.4'281206—dc22
2008003684

Printed in the United States of America on acid-free paper

The University of Minnesota is an equal-opportunity educator and employer.

15 14 13 12 11 10 09 08   10 9 8 7 6 5 4 3 2 1

This book is for Jill Milling (1946–2001),
my student and friend,
and my teacher about many things,
including Dallas and Texas.

CONTENTS

PREFACE:

FINDING MYSELF IN DALLAS

Finding myself in Dallas called into question everything I thought I knew about cities. In this sprawling space, simply staying oriented was a constant challenge. The popular proclamation that Dallas was free from the constraints of history provoked me, as a social and cultural historian, to excavate its past and explore the city as a material and ideological construct. In the process, I uncovered a Dallas that its white, middle-class residents preferred to ignore, especially its marked racial-ethnic segregation, class inequality, and undemocratic polity. Through the ironies and contradictions inherent in historical development, the shining televised images of downtown and North suburban Dallas generated their own negations, the neglected wastelands of South and West Dallas. Seeing the city as a fractured mosaic, rather than through the partial view of the privileged, transforms the questions we ask. If Dallas is America writ large, or perhaps America taken to extremes, what challenges do the patterns generated by its growth pose for us in the twenty-first century?

This project began in 1975 when I accepted a faculty position at the University of Texas at Dallas (UTD), which despite its name is located not in the city but in Richardson, a sprawling suburb sixteen miles north of downtown. By upbringing and choice, I was—and still remain—a "city boy." I grew up in Pittsburgh, went to college near Chicago, and did graduate work in Toronto. Comfortable with large and anonymous but traditionally urban places, I was entirely unprepared for the culture shock that moving to Dallas engendered. Over two decades, I struggled to understand

Dallas both as physical place and as cultural and political economic space. I was unable to recognize in Dallas what most appealed to me in older cities. I was disconcerted by how Dallas presented itself on the ground and was represented in the discourse that filled the air: as the self-proclaimed exemplar of "new," "Sunbelt Cities," with downtown rapidly eclipsed by suburbs and exurbs and a growth machine directed toward seemingly endless expansion. My perceptions of difference and feelings of estrangement propelled me to come to terms with Dallas.

The place presented serious obstacles to comprehension. We bought our first car within two days of our arrival. My wife Vicki and I moved into an apartment and townhouse complex at the intersection of two major expressways, I-75 and 635, about five miles from campus and a dozen miles from downtown. It felt like we were living in the middle of nowhere. Once, when Vicki was walking down the service road from the supermarket carrying a single bag of groceries, a motorist stopped and asked if she needed help. Although I often felt lost, assistance in orienting myself to Dallas's grand scale was not forthcoming. I found Dallasites' explicit lack of interest in their city's history as disconcerting as its automobile-driven spatial decentralization.

Returning from two years away in 1981, we renegotiated our relationship with the city, resettling in "Old" East Dallas, an early twentieth-century neighborhood near downtown. I commuted to UTD's suburban campus, while Vicki took the bus to her downtown office. Relocating our everyday lives to a place I recognized as urban helped a great deal. Still, much about the city remained hard to grasp. I never imagined that I would stay in Dallas for so many years.

I struggled to understand Dallas historically as well as politically and culturally, seeking a clearer accommodation with a city that was unlikely to feel like "home." Living well *within* the city, finding its historic footprint, comparing it to other urban places, and tracing the continuities and discontinuities in its patterns of growth helped. In time, I gained insight into Dallas's urban forms and distinctive ways, enlarging some of my definitions, parameters, and expectations and shedding some biases along the way. The late urban historian Eric Monkkonen enjoyed teasing me by reiterating that Dallas really *is* a city.

I was drawn into the history of Dallas through engaging in a variety of public as well as academic activities that challenged existing frameworks methodologically, interpretively, and organizationally. One layer of this project's grounding is my own and others' research into primary historical documents and artifacts; another is the reinterpretation of the stories Dallasites tell themselves; and a third entails different ways of seeing—literally and metaphorically—Dallas as place and space.

I owe my initial interest in the city's past to the promptings of others. I received many requests to speak before community groups, join advisory boards, and contribute to local historical and cultural efforts. Over the years, I participated in projects of the Dallas Historical Society, Historic Preservation League (now Preservation Dallas), Dallas Public Library, Texas Committee for the Humanities, Black Dallas Remembered, Dallas's Texas Sesquicentennial Committee, North Texas Phi Beta Kappa, and Southern Methodist University's William P. Clements Center for Southwest Studies. From the late 1970s through the mid-1980s, I drafted the brochures that accompanied each structure and space designated a landmark by the City of Dallas. From 1981 to 1996, I initiated and led a Dallas-area Social History Group, with participants from local universities, that continues today. I learned a great deal from all these associations.

From 1975 on, UTD students in my courses took the city as the setting and subject for research and completed masters theses and PhD dissertations on topics in its history. As I felt more solid ground under my feet, I began to tackle certain aspects of Dallas's past. I seriously contemplated organizing a major quantitative history project on the city, but other commitments and research interests intervened.[1] With support from UTD and in collaboration with two graduate students, Alan R. Baron and Charles Barton, I organized an inventory of the major documentary resources and published *Dallas, Texas: A Bibliographic Guide to the Sources of Its Social History*.[2] Alarmingly, but not surprisingly, given the general lack of interest in local historical research, we found records in dangerous states of deterioration; much had already been lost or destroyed. Public as well as private records were at risk. No local institution solicited donation of the treasure troves of personal and family documents or institutional records and memorabilia. We did what we could to encourage more complete and careful relocation and cataloguing. Happily, the Dallas Public Library, long the major custodian of Dallas's documents, has now been joined by African American and other ethnic and local history collections. Area universities, especially the University of Texas at Arlington and Southern Methodist

University, have developed more local interests. Public records are also getting better care.

In the early 1980s, in an effort to enliven the history curriculum, stimulate research, and extend my own knowledge, I began teaching undergraduate courses on Dallas history. The first class was especially memorable. We started with a bus tour of central Dallas and some of the older urban districts. For many of my undergraduates, even some who had grown up in the area, this was their first trip downtown. Driving through residential neighborhoods, students were surprised by the quantity and apparent quality of older houses in the city and asked with interest, "How much do houses cost around here?" Classes met in the Texas and Dallas History Collections of the Dallas Public Library and at the Dallas Historical Society in the Hall of State in Fair Park. Local experts and celebrities, including political columnist Molly Ivins, were eager to talk with the students. Out of this especially stimulating set of experiences, students produced excellent research papers that we archived at Dallas Public Library.

Before long, I started a graduate seminar on Dallas in an interdisciplinary Arts and Humanities doctoral program. This advanced course considered theory and method, conceptions of space and place, and different constructions of history, memory, and the past. Paying close attention to contemporary currents in historical, social-scientific, and humanistic thinking, the course moved from the once "new" social history toward emerging approaches in cultural studies and engaged with renewed interest in cities as human constructs of space and place and in the play of political economics in everyday life. A number of fine papers and a steady stream of theses stand among the results.

Ironically, my quest to understand Dallas began at a new university with relatively few connections—beyond technology and business—to the city of Dallas past or present. It intensified when I relocated to the inner city. But I was busy with other projects, and not until the mid-1990s was I finally convinced by my associates, colleagues, and students to write a book about Dallas. Completing this book has taken longer and proved much harder than I expected.

In the spring of 1998 we moved to San Antonio, Texas, a city very unlike Dallas that has made its history central to its identity. A much poorer and less pretentious place than Dallas, with a strikingly different racial and ethnic composition, San Antonio has a stronger and more cohesive social fabric and sense of a shared public space. Less fearful of the potential for conflict arising from cultural and social mixing, perhaps because it was already a minority-majority city, San Antonio nourishes a more inclusive public life. Its residents take pride in its past and are active in its preservation and commemoration. The annual fiesta draws participants from both the Hispanic and Anglo communities, although it partakes of the theme park commodification of history evident at the Alamo and Fiesta Texas (formerly Six Flags Over Texas). Offering a strikingly different object and angle of vision, San Antonio stimulated me to think more about the relationships among past, present, and future in contemporary urban life, about the play of place and space, about the future of American cities, and about the uses and abuses of the past. Can cities preserve the integrity and authenticity of the culturally diverse histories they display and equitably share the economic returns they yield? Can difference be promoted with dignity? Can their many pasts inform and instruct the leaders and residents of such different places as San Antonio and Dallas?

Other events that demanded my attention enlarged my perspective. I was elected president of the Social Science History Association for its twenty-fifth anniversary year, and awarded the Doctor of Philosophy *honoris causa* by the University of Linköping, Sweden. For three years, I served as historical advisor to the Chicago Historical Society's Teen Chicago project, which taught teens to collect, interpret, and display the stuff of history, focusing in particular on the experiences of Chicago's young people throughout the twentieth century.

We moved back to the "Rustbelt" in 2004, when I became the first Ohio Eminent Scholar in Literacy Studies as well as Professor of English and History at Ohio State University. In Columbus, now the fifteenth largest U.S. city, we live surrounded by students in an older residential area seven blocks from my office on a huge campus around which the city of Columbus has grown during the past one hundred years. It is entirely possible that I had to leave, first Dallas and then Texas, in order to complete this book.

As a comparative urban social and cultural historian, I feel strongly that the past and the present reciprocally interrogate and inform each other. A more comprehensive, comparative, and critical historical perspective on cities that remain deeply divided by class and racial-ethnic inequalities enables us to envision and move toward a more inclusive, equitable, humane, and democratic future.

ACKNOWLEDGMENTS

This book has been long in the making, so I am indebted to an extensive list of institutions and individuals. First are the many students in my graduate and undergraduate courses on the history of Dallas, American and comparative urban and social history, public history, and theory and practice in research. Although they often did not know how much I was learning from their questions, my students taught me a great deal.

There is no single repository for the sources of Dallas history. Only recently have local libraries and historical societies actively sought to collect basic materials documenting the city's history and make them accessible for researchers. Major gaps still exist, especially for the study of ordinary people and racial-ethnic minority groups. Given the paucity of material, I am especially grateful to these libraries and institutions and their helpful staff: Texas and Dallas History Collections, Dallas Public Library (thanks in particular to Gerald Saxon, Marcelle Hull, Wayne Gray, Lucille Boykin); Dallas Historical Society (thanks to John Crain, Peggy Riddle); University of Texas at Austin Center for American History; Texas State Library and Archives Commission; University of Texas at Arlington Library Historical Collections (thanks to Gerald Saxon); University of Texas at Dallas Library and Archives (thanks to Vicki Bullock, Ellen Safely); and the University of Texas at San Antonio Library (thanks to Sue McCray, Charley Thurston).

For intellectual, financial, and material assistance and supports large and small, I acknowledge my home universities during the period in which xvi

ACKNOWLEDGMENTS

this book was conceived, researched, written, and revised: the University of Texas at Dallas; the University of Texas at San Antonio; and The Ohio State University. UTD and UT–San Antonio awarded me research leaves. Special thanks to Dennis Kratz, Dean of the College of Arts and Humanities, and Hobson Wildenthal, Provost and Academic Vice President at UTD. Ohio State assisted generously with the costs of manuscript preparation and of copies and permission fees for the photographs and maps. At OSU, Valerie Lee saw to it that my position provided me with the professional scholarly resources I needed, and Cheryl Frasch enabled me to use them.

Other Dallas institutions and individuals with whom I collaborated on extracurricular and sometimes curricular projects enhanced my understanding of Dallas and Texas. In particular, I thank Bob Ray Saunders, Rob Tranchin, Bill Zeeble, and Karen Denard at KERA public radio and television; at the *Dallas Morning News,* Steve Blow, Victoria Loe Hicks, Rena Pederson, and David Dillon; at the City of Dallas, Weiming Lu, Tom Niderauer, Leif Sandberg, and Jack Luby; at UTD's Bruton Center for the Integration of Geographic Information Systems, Spatial Analysis, and Exploratory Data Analysis in Social Sciences, Brian Berry, Paul Waddell, and Paul Jargowsky; the Dallas Institute for Humanities and Culture; and two Texans who were institutions in their own right, Molly Ivins and A. C. Greene. Key issues were illuminated by the speakers in the North Texas Phi Beta Kappa–Dallas Public Library urban culture lectures series: Tom Bender of New York University, Mike Frisch of the State University of New York at Buffalo, and John McDermott of Texas A&M University.

Among the many students who assisted me over the years, I acknowledge Patricia Hill, author of *Dallas: The Making of a Modern City,* who now teaches history at San Jose State University in California; John Stilwell, Melinda Poss, Steve Hamlin, Darrell Baird, Richard Rome, Tony Fracchia, Chris DeBritain, Mohamed Taherzadeh, Evelyn Montgomery, Jan Forrester, Alan Baron, and Charles Barton, all at UTD; Stacy Noll at UT–San Antonio; and Rachel Clark, Kim Thompson, Cate Crosby, Kate Curry, Kate White, Kelly Bradbury, Michael Harker, Susan Hanson, Shawn Casey, and Lindsay Dicuirci at Ohio State. Jill Milling, Sally Ramsey, and Cathy Civello merit special mention for their patient but firm teachings about many things Texan. The premature deaths of Jill and Sally leave this work without the bracing and corrective responses they would have provided.

A number of colleagues, some with little interest in Dallas history, attended to my mind and spirits over the years, especially during the Dallas years: Gerald Soliday, Dan Orlovsky, Michael Wilson, David Weber, Ted Harpham, Bob Bradley, Paul Peretz, Ric Hula, and Paul Monaco. In San Antonio, Woody Sanders, Char Miller, and David Johnson stepped in. My newer colleagues at Ohio State provided strong support and expressed more interest than either they themselves or I expected.

At Ohio State, Sonya Huber-Humes worked on the manuscript, and geography graduate student Paul Hoeffler prepared several of the maps. The staff of the Humanities Information Services scanned a number of images that illustrate this book. I was assisted with photographs and maps at the Dallas Public Library by Michael Miller, Jane Soutner, and Beth Andresen; at the Dallas Historical Society by Rachel Roberts, Susan Richards, and curator Alan Olson; at the Texas State Library and Archives Commission by John Anderson; at the Dallas Chapter of the American Institute of Architects by Larry Good, of AIA and Good, Fulton, and Farrell, and Jenny Lorenz; at the *Dallas Morning News* by David Woo; by Elissa B. Kenny and Donald J. Sanders of Southwestern Life Insurance Company; by Darwin Payne; and by Eric Anderson. Advice on maps and mapping came from Paul Jargowsky and Ron Briggs at UTD, Stuart Murchison of the City of Dallas, Bob Fairbanks at UT–Arlington, Michael Phillips then at UT–Austin, and Darwin Payne at SMU. After I moved, Tony Fracchia helped to keep me informed about Dallas.

Urban historians and friends contributed in many ways. I thank in particular Michael B. Katz, Jan Reiff, and the late Eric Monkkonen. Fellow students of Dallas history Patty Hill, Royce Hansen, Kay Ofman, and Michael Phillips shared ideas and sources and responded to various calls for help. Patty, Michael, and my friend and fellow urbanist Paul Mattingly gave the manuscript critical constructive readings that influenced its final form.

From many presses and editors came much advice, some of it good and useful, some of it interesting but impossible to follow. To my initial surprise, several shied away from publishing work about Dallas and Texas, others from avowedly different approaches to the conventional ones. Among the most receptive editors, special recognition and thanks go to Peter Agree, editor in chief at the University of Pennsylvania Press, and Pieter Martin, editor at the University of Minnesota Press. They both understood and appreciated *The Dallas Myth* in the ways that I intended. Peter Agree's grasp of this book's approach to "reading" a city and his comprehension of its comparative dimension have made it a stronger work. At the University of Minnesota Press, Andrea Patch, Laura Westlund, Rachel Moeller, and freelance editor Deborah A. Oosterhouse and indexer Sallie Steele turned my manuscript into a book.

Michael Frisch, a longtime friend and colleague in urban history and public history, gave the manuscript a reading that valued my innovative, experimental methods of reading cities and writing about them. He combined his praise with a firmly critical but always constructive recognition of the problems in the sprawling manuscript and made specific suggestions for revision. His professional and personal support is very important to me and to the revision of this book.

One of Mike's most valuable recommendations, which also came from Peter Agree, led me to Grey Osterud, fellow social historian and now full-time editor and adviser extraordinaire. To an extent rarely found in my experience, Grey blended probing critical readings, blunt criticism, accurate identification of problems, perceptive advice for redrafting, a focus that always embraced both the forest and the trees, and care for the author. Her attention remained firmly with editorial goals without ever losing sense of what I tried to do in this book—not always an easy task. Grey is also a font of general publishing advice, from form and format to illustrations and negotiations, as well as unwavering professional and personal support.

The last words of gratitude, not for the first or the last time, go to Vicki Graff, Harrison in the Dallas years, and McDonald in San Antonio and Columbus. They know why, more or less.

INTRODUCTION

Dallas was and is a city at the crossroads, both metaphorically and materially. It began as a rough settlement at the intersection of two major land routes, turned itself into a railroad junction, and now operates a huge airport. At first, the crossroads that generated Dallas was geographic. The city was founded in 1841 where overland routes from north and south, east and west met. Despite the impossibility of developing a navigable passage down the Trinity River to the Gulf of Mexico, the river crossing rapidly became a point of contact and communication. By 1860, four stagecoach routes with numerous connections converged there. In the 1870s town boosters captured two railway lines. The city grew as an entrepôt and processing center for a prosperous agricultural region. Putting politics into the service of economic expansion, Dallas incorporated, first as a town and then as a city, and seized the county seat.

Despite incessant claims that "Dallas had absolutely nothing" to stimulate its development because it was entirely deficient in natural resources and geographical advantages, the historian James Howard observes that "the physical surroundings of Dallas have exerted a telling influence on the city's economic and social growth."[1] Dallas "was the pivot in the richest region in America in regard to four prime commodities—wheat, cotton, cattle, oil."[2] The metropolitan power of St. Louis led some residents "to acquire an overwhelming desire to make of Dallas a metropolis in every sense of the word." Looking to other cities and fashioning itself on their model is a central theme in Dallas's development. Contrary to myth, "the

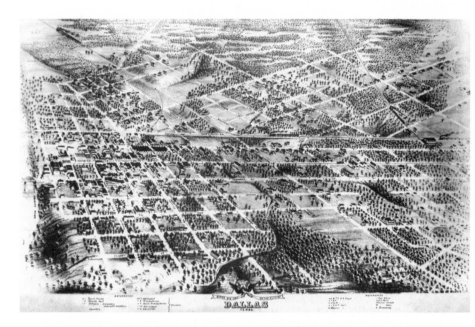

FIGURE 1. In this bird's-eye view, Brosius pictured Dallas from the southwest just before its first commercial boom. From the collections of the Texas/Dallas History and Archives Division, Dallas Public Library; printed by permission of the Dallas Historical Society.

FIGURE 2. Town to city: Giraud depicted the city's expanding commercial center and sprawling residential districts in this bird's-eye view from 1892. From the collections of the Texas/Dallas History and Archives Division, Dallas Public Library.

circumstance of its being an inland city has supplied an added incentive for Dallas to be zealous in developing lines of land and later air transportation." "The city's location near the boundary of East and West Texas has afforded it an opportunity to act as a balance-wheel between these two sections of the state," or between sections of an ever-larger region and perhaps the nation. Dallas's profitable agricultural economy "laid the ground-work for the growth of Dallas into a regional center of commerce and finance."[3]

As Dallas grew, its economy shifted. In 1947, John Gunther observed, "primarily it is a banking and jobbing and distributing center, the headquarters of railways and utilities; it is the second city in the United States in Railway Express business, the fourth in insurance, the fifth in number of telegrams."[4] Justin F. Kimball, long the chief superintendent of Dallas's public schools, foresaw the next transformation in 1953: "Just now Dallas sits at the crossroads of the western air world, where the great air highways cross east and west, north and south. The cities of Texas, notably Dallas . . . sit at the gate of Latin-American commerce."[5] In the comparative rankings featured in Dallas's characteristic discourse, Dallas/Fort Worth International Airport is the third busiest airport in the world. It carries a heavy volume of freight traffic and, with a land area the size of Manhattan, enjoys ample room for expansion.

In addition to its descriptive usage, "crossroads" appears frequently in discourse about Dallas. This symbolic usage signals the recognition that the city faces a significant challenge, an opportunity or a threat, a moment of decision. Today, more common than geographical images of the city "at the crossroads" are such temporal phrases as "on the threshold," "at the brink," "on the edge," "on the verge," "at the moment of truth," "poised" or "reaching for greatness," variously defined. At times, the challenge lay in avoiding controversy, unwanted consequences, public embarrassment, failure, or disaster.[6] A city "at the tipping point" is a city at risk, paralyzed by fear of falling.[7] The shift from a metaphor of the city at the crossroads to the city on the brink signifies Dallasites' discomfort with their city's internal diversity and its uncertain place in the world, as well as its substitution of myth for history and its long-term avoidance of democratic decision making. Only recently have Dallasites imagined their city as at a crossroads in time, facing a choice between one course of development and another. A sense of manifest destiny, pressure for unanimity of opinion, and the power of the ruling oligarchy prevented—or relieved—Dallasites from conceiving of alternatives and confronting the choices before them. This book aims to remedy that problem, restoring human agency to the story of the city's making and offering a political-economic perspective within which all of its citizens may consider its future.

WRITING DALLAS HISTORY

The Dallas Myth: The Making and Unmaking of an American City proposes a historical approach to a city that has often obliterated and denied its own past. An experiment in historical thinking, historical interpretation, and historical writing, and in interdisciplinary scholarship, *The Dallas Myth* interweaves the perspectives of urban social and cultural history, historical geography, and political economy. It builds on recent research conducted by historians and political scientists, yet the account it constructs differs significantly from the revisionist histories that others have offered. Most importantly, it draws on cultural studies to suggest an original, integrative "reading" of the city that connects the material to the rhetorical and ideological domains. This book is neither a narrative urban biography that personifies the city as the main actor in its own history nor a topical analysis of the forces, groups, and ideologies that have shaped this place over time, although indebted to both those forms. To paraphrase a chorus that recurs throughout the paeans to progress that pass as histories of Dallas, this book is "different."

What is most striking about Dallas is not its difference from other U.S. megalopolises, but rather its exaggeration of features that many contemporary cities share: spatial decentralization; preoccupation with economic and geographic expansion to the exclusion of the environment and quality of life; the assumption that business elites are best fitted to define the common interest; the erosion of civil society, open debate, and political opposition; the absence of shared public space; the increasing spatial segregation of racial-ethnic groups and their stratification along lines of class and power; and the transformation of culture into a commodity to be purchased, repackaged, and sold. In Dallas, these features of urban development existed almost unopposed for a half-century or more, so the cityscape starkly reveals the strange new world they made. This understanding emphasizes the simultaneous making and unmaking of a major American city.

Deconstructing this notion of a self-made city free from the constraints of place and the past and constructing a more grounded, bounded account of its configuration in space and time is by definition a critical undertaking. The ironies that pervade this work signify a certain skeptical distance from Dallas's core myths, but the analysis offered here resonates with the themes that define Dallasites' stance toward the future. This book is offered as a contribution to public reflection as citizens of Dallas and comparable cities elsewhere face the legacies of the past and undertake their cities' reconstruction.

FACING HISTORICAL AND SPATIAL LIMITS

Dallas is an unusually revealing city to probe critically at the end of the American Century. Known for its bold, even excessive claims of greatness, Dallas is associated with comparatively recent events, especially the Kennedy assassination, the Dallas Cowboys football team, and the television series *Dallas,* whose cultural meanings are deeply ambivalent. Outside the city, Dallas's pride, aggressiveness, disregard for law and order, sheer newness, and ostentatious prosperity are all derided. At home, these qualities are regarded as badges of distinction. Dallas is both criticized and envied, or even loved and hated. "Big D" swaggers, proliferating images for itself and projecting a powerful identity. When examined closely, however, these images are stunningly weak and profoundly confused. McCombs and Whyte captured this quality as early as 1949, commenting that "the stranger leaves feeling as if he has been suspended in a vast hyperbole."[8] As a place, Dallas lacks clear identity. It exhibits deep insecurities that strain its public promotion and contradict its private pride.

Dallas is difficult to read and almost impossible to grasp. Compared to other major American cities, even those shaped by automobile-fueled sprawl, it is not a particularly legible place. Spatial disorientation is so common an experience, even among longtime residents, that city planners make jokes about directional signs located downtown that point to downtown. "Lost in Dallas" would be amusing if it were not so deliberate in this city without edges. There is no "city as a whole"; fractured along lines of class as well as race and ethnicity, the cityscape is composed of a myriad of noncommunicating fragments. The near-invisibility of this characteristic, at least to the privileged, is a measure of the degree to which it distorts Dallasites' vision.

Dallas shrilly asserts that it is a unique city with "no limits," "no reason to be," and "no history." This credo serves to magnify leading Dallasites' accomplishments. Although Dallas is hardly unique among major American cities in making such self-serving claims, it is unusual in the frequency of the repetition. Dallas is distinguished by the degree to which claims of exceptionalism combine to form a narrative of the city's growth that almost completely substitutes for a history and an inclusive vision. Mythology and ideology undergird distorted and incomplete conceptions of the city and obscure its actual physical construction and social configuration. The myth of a city with no past and no limits and the ideology of growth for the sake of private and corporate profit shape the scope and activity of many local educational and cultural institutions, the workings of urban governance, and major physical development and redevelopment projects. Dallas offers a special opportunity to explore the question of what it means to claim proudly that a city has no history.

What is excluded from these tellings of the Dallas story is often as important as what they say. Untold stories include the high costs of Dallas's success in terms of racial, social, and geographic inequality, limited public political arena and access to power, and a tradition of quick resort to violence. Belief in Dallas's autonomy from regional, national, and world conditions has had damaging consequences for many well-to-do as well as poorer Dallasites. These complications simultaneously derive from and exacerbate Dallas's and its suburbs' incomprehension of themselves as parts of a larger whole. That limited and distorted vision underlies the confusion of Anglo North Dallas with all of Dallas and its environs and explains the long-term neglect of African American South Dallas and Hispanic West Dallas. In many ways, Dallas's history is a "tale of two cities." Obscured and ignored is the rich diversity of many Dallases, not a single homogeneous one. These are stories of the inextricably linked, dialectical relationships among the ideological and material forces that have propelled the city's simultaneous making and unmaking.

Despite its claim of being "a city with no history," the mythology of Dallas's century and a half of development and the ideology that is built upon it form a historical and urban developmental discourse. Learning that history can be marketed profitably, Dallas recently rediscovered—or invented—certain parts of its past without perceiving any need to revise its narrative. The discourse of a "can-do" city whose "business is business" substitutes powerfully but inadequately for other modes of understanding. Not only are these elements too thin to bear the weight of more than rhetorical promotion, but they are challenged, qualified, and contradicted by deeply rooted historical patterns.

Among many questions raised by this evasion of history is whether Dallas is a southern, western, southwestern, or—as this work argues—a southern midwestern city. Dallasites have a long-standing fantasy of transforming their landlocked city into a river port by making the often barely traceable but flood-prone Trinity River navigable to the Gulf of Mexico or adding a "Festival Harborfront" to downtown Dallas by digging a big hole and filling it with water in the style of Richard Rouse, who redeveloped derelict wharves in Boston and Baltimore into shopping precincts. The monumentally scaled Dallas/Fort Worth International Airport is repeatedly proclaimed the city's "port." Many urban and suburban theme park elements have come to mark the Dallas landscape. Developers and manipulators of Dallas images struggle to give a city with no functional center an urbanity it never had, with a lively downtown surrounded by residential neighborhoods. The central contradictions of Dallas's urban development, historically as well as more recently, inseparably but confusingly intertwine myth and ideology with actual patterns of urban historical development, together making and unmaking the city.

Dallas has a history, largely unwritten, and only recently of interest locally. From its founding, Dallas followed the path of a frontier crossroads, developing into a growing market town serving a prosperous and expanding agricultural hinterland. With the acquisition of political functions and town status in the 1850s and 1860s, the Civil War–era boom, and the capture of two railroads in the 1870s came accelerated growth of population and attendant economic, political, and cultural institutions. Its active, politically and economically astute, and adventurous entrepreneurial class employed a skilled workforce and drew on a fertile hinterland to achieve regional dominance as a commercial city. Dallas's principal ahistorical or antihistorical narrative slights the significance of these foundations by turning them into prehistory or teleology, as Dallas followed its foreordained destiny toward urbanity. The history is far more important than those glosses permit. Neither Dallas's present or possible futures nor a usable understanding of how the city moved from its rude founding to its current metropolitan status is comprehensible without an awareness of its historical course. The usual emphasis on the period from the 1930s or World War II to the present excludes too much of the city's shaping.

On the one hand, Dallas has the familiar history of a successful commercial city, albeit with some major wrinkles and twists. Typically, its story features great personalities from town founder John Neely Bryan to promoter and city builder Robert L. Thornton. But no less significant are its urban origins and original founding as a town; its long-term domination of and by the market and its major institutions and players; traditions of political and economic machinations that include stealing the building blocks and prizes of urban development and metropolitan status, from the railroads to the Federal Reserve Bank, Texas State Centennial, and major corporate headquarters; traditions of elite political reform; contradictory relationships to government funding; exclusion of disadvantaged groups from a share in the polity and economy; socially, culturally, and economically irresponsible actions and failures to act by political leaders; and narrow definitions of the scope of public action along with a confusion between the public and the private. There are some surprises in this strong, successful, and common pattern of city-building that challenge typical Dallas images and narratives: the extent of manufacturing and labor organization; social and cultural diversity; political conflicts and clashes of visions; and the major role of governmental spending.

But on the other hand, Dallas is different. The differences that undergird popular images of Dallas as distinctive and distinguished also contradict some of the central images and lessons derived from positive tellings of the Dallas tale. Key examples include the "Dallas Way" of elite organization, exclusive control of formal politics, and exercise of power; the nature of urban growth under that hegemonic political-economic regime; intolerance of ideological or cultural diversity; quick recourse to violence and tolerance of right-wing extremism; exceptionally limited access to political and economic power; and the underdevelopment of cultural and educational institutions as well as civil society more generally. Although the Dallas Way is usually identified with the Dallas Citizens Council from the mid-1930s through the 1960s, its ideology, provenance, and power predate and postdate that period. Truly exceptional for any large American city are Dallas's creation and reproduction of self-perpetuating elites that maintained their hegemonic power with scant criticism or challenge until the Kennedy assassination and even afterwards. The extent of private domination of the public sphere raises major questions about the American urban polity in the twentieth century. The myth of a disinterested leadership class concerned only with the public interest stands out, as do questions about the relative contributions of proclaimed growth and prosperity as compared to actual urban and economic growth in establishing and maintaining political hegemony.

The Dallas Myth: The Making and Unmaking of an American City explicates the intricate interrelationship between the mythology and ideology of Dallas's rise and achievement and the creation, operation, and maintenance of local growth and its centers of power. Here the fear of history and its replacement by mythology and the ideology built upon it are especially telling. The *new* Dallas tales that this book begins to tell pivot to an unprecedented extent on factors of race, class, ethnicity, gender, geography, and power. Dallas's very real achievements have come at great human, environmental, cultural, and political costs. Repairing the urban fabric, constructing a more inclusive community, opening the polity to democratic representation, allowing space for diversity and dissent—these are the tasks that Dallas's past bequeaths to the present. They are also, significantly, imperatives that face most American cities in the twenty-first century, caught in the crosscurrents of globalization and democratization.

ORIENTING OURSELVES IN DALLAS

More like a choreography than a chronology, this book is organized in two movements that when taken together are analogous to the interrelated processes of making and unmaking the city. The first is deconstructive—pulling apart Dallas's images and discourse (chapter 1), scrutinizing its myths and ideology (chapter 2), and analyzing their powerful internal contradictions. The second is reconstructive—exploring Dallas's political economy from the points of view of the rich and powerful (chapter 4) and the disinherited and marginalized (chapter 5) and tracing the configuration of power built on the ground (chapter 6). The pivotal chapter in between (3) outlines principles for writing a pluralistic and comparative history of the city that are only incompletely realized in this volume but set an agenda for collaborative work and offers a working chronology of Dallas's development. The final chapter (7) examines Dallas at the turn of the twenty-first century, following the belated "coming of democracy," when citizens had to reckon with their differences and recognize their city's tenuous place amid a globalizing economy.

This critical history was written in a constructive spirit, not a negative one. Dallas needs to confront its past, and comprehend its present through the lens of its past, if it is to understand itself in time and to imagine and work toward a different future. Dallasites must stop seeing their city as separate and different, but rather situate it in American urban history, in order to understand and take control of the destructive forces they have set in motion and redeem their city's democratic promise.

If acknowledging limits enables Dallasites to recognize their diversity, redress segregation and inequality, and overcome their social and spatial fragmentation, then the crises the city now faces will have done salutary work. This book contributes to that end by anchoring Dallas in space and time and situating it in relation to other American cities, probing the human and environmental costs of its sprawling growth, and illuminating the collective agency that, despite the myth of destiny and the hegemonic ideology of elite control, underlies civic choices and enables democratic decision making. That could contribute to "remaking" the city.

PART I

SEARCHING FOR DALLAS

chapter 1

Locating the City:
Three Icons and Images of "Big D"

DALLAS IS . . . THE BIG D . . . DALLAS, TEXAS!

Texas's Democratic governor, the late Ann Richards, summed it up expansively: "You can't think of Dallas without thinking big. Dallas is a city of big buildings, big business, big ideas and people with big hearts. . . . all part of what makes Dallas so special and so . . . Dallas."[1] So Dallas? Both the size and the self-referential character of this image are telling. Big seems to know no boundaries in the place that calls itself "the city with no limits." Yes, Dallas *is* big. Texas-sized. A fifty-two-foot tall "Big Tex" statue welcomes visitors to the State Fair in Dallas's Fair Park. The huge Dallas/ Fort Worth International Airport sprawls between the city and its closest rival, connecting the landlocked Metroplex to the world. Images and icons of Dallas declare their size, yet fail to distinguish the city from other places or silence its self-doubts. Veteran Dallas and New York newspaperman Stanley Walker observed in 1956, "Dallas has many times listened to the half-concealed slurs and catty innuendoes, born of envy, from other Southwestern cities. Many Texans regard Dallas as a mite 'uppity.'" The worst offense, in Walker's eyes, was to impugn Dallas's sophisticated style and cosmopolitan aspirations by branding it a "Yankee" city. He boldly asserted: "It is not merely 100 per cent Texan. It is, to revive a word that unfortunately has fallen into disuse, truly Texanic."[2] Truly Texanic? Dallas stimulates slurs in response to its shameless self-promotion and excessive image-mongering. Such sensitivity to outsiders' opinions is a hallmark of insecurity, provoking

3

defensive delusions of grandeur. In 1996, journalist Mark Stuertz inflated the city's scale from Texas-sized to world-class: "There is a dynamic to Dallas that touches its very core: an individualistic, swashbuckling spirit of daring free enterprise and success coupled with Texas geniality. . . . But Dallas is more than a bastion of commercial know-how. . . . Dallas is poised to enter the next century as one of the most important metropolitan areas in the country, if not the world."[3] This glowing prose proclaims Dallas's dream of itself as a powerful engine of prosperity propelled by free-market energy and can-do gumption. But the desire to assert this "swashbuckling spirit" alludes to everything that threatens to deflate this image.

Widely recognized images circulate and accumulate, but fail to cohere or to give the city a distinct identity—at least one that it wants to claim. Think of Dallas. What images come to mind? What are their sources? To what ends do they work? Toward what composite image of the "Big D" do they move? Most images of Dallas mirror other major so-called "new cities," especially in the South and West: images of glass-encased skyscrapers glinting in the heat of a southwestern sky. The exercise also arouses images that stand apart and differ, not only in scale but also in the mix of positives and negatives, attractions and repulsions, and what the promotional pundits like to call the "essence," "soul," or "spirit," the identity of the place.[4]

Images of Dallas are confused and contradictory, containing both the rudeness of the western frontier and the nouveaux riches of oil, real estate, and high tech. Dallas displays the full spectrum from down-home southern hospitality to the glimmering sophistication of Neiman Marcus and the Dallas Opera, from BBQ and Tex-Mex to nouvelle americaine and haute cuisine. Styles of sociability circle from warm, welcoming friendliness through arrogant gaucherie and pretentious standoffishness back to graciousness. Right-wing extremism meets democratic populism; firearmed violence mixes with Good–Ol'–Boy (and Gal) fraternalism; virulent racism encounters ecumenical evangelicalism. Powerful politicians and financiers like Ross Perot, standing in boots and cowboy hat, evoke a rural landscape and a sprawling urban agenda. In and around Dallas, Ford pickups and Lexuses are tied up in a massive traffic jam.

Major social, economic, and cultural contradictions lie at the heart of this uncertain identity, created and compounded by Dallas itself. U.S. cities tend to turn inward with "an almost paroxysmal gaze on themselves," says the Italian critic Marco D'Eramo. "American cities demand to be perceived and studied from a certain angle that would be impossible for a European metropolis. . . . You feel constrained to regard cities in the United States as though they were individuals or, rather, individual subjects of history."[5] The inward-looking visions of Dallas, which aspires to call itself "America's city," unintentionally shed light on the very American dreams, fears, and conflicts that have channeled themselves in peculiar paths through this place. The region's population growth, relative "youthfulness," open prairie spaces, entrepreneurial orientation, rush for development, identification with mass marketing, and exuberant urge for promotion made it a late twentieth-century incarnation of the American Dream, displaying the lures and fruits of upward economic mobility. At the same time, Americans'

FIGURE 3. From city to metropolis: After World War I, the central business district was rapidly growing up and out. Fairchild Aerial Survey, Downtown, 1923. From the collections of the Texas/Dallas History and Archives Division, Dallas Public Library.

FIGURE 4. Metropolitan expansion: After World War II, the city center attained new heights, fueled by railway and road networks connecting it to the metropolitan region and beyond. Bird's-eye view, Downtown Dallas, 1950. From the collections of the Texas/Dallas History and Archives Division, Dallas Public Library.

deep ambivalence about the temptations, illusions, and dangers of the big city, amounting at times to antiurbanism, pervades Dallas culture. An uneasy awareness of the environmental, political, and social costs of growth is coupled with a sometimes spoken fear of failure. Most importantly, yet rarely acknowledged, the dream is shadowed by the persistence and reproduction of economic and racial-ethnic inequality.

The wealth of Dallas has flowed to points north on its compass, to neighborhoods and separate cities with revealing names such as Highland Park, while the West Dallas barrio and the South Dallas slums have suffered malignant neglect. In following this pattern, separating predominantly white suburbs from brown and black inner-city residential districts by a shiny downtown and encircling the urban core with freeways, Dallas resembles many American cities. Yet here, too, Dallas goes to extremes. Dallas is one

of the most spatially segregated cities in the United States, with large disparities in income and other indicators of class position among the populations
of its distinct districts, which are defined above all by race and ethnicity.
Statistical indexes of dissimilarity reveal patterns that exist on the ground,
but the majority of Anglo Dallasites seldom see these other citizens at home.[6]
In a segregated city, the poor and marginalized are relegated to peripheral
areas devoid of businesses and other attractions that would draw outsiders,
invisible to even those denizens of the suburbs who work downtown. To
Hispanic and African American Dallasites, however, their subordination
is a matter of everyday experience as they gaze at the glittering skyline
from below.

FIGURE 5. Metropolitan expansion: Early suburbanization formed elite enclaves that
incorporated as "the Park Cities" separate from the City of Dallas. Fairchild Aerial
Survey, Highland Park, growing westward, 1923. From the collections of the
Texas/Dallas History and Archives Division, Dallas Public Library.

FIGURE 6. Metropolitan decentralization: Later suburbanization and population deconcentration spawned new towns beyond Dallas's boundaries. Aerial view of new housing development in Plano, 1971. Plano once ranked among the nation's most rapidly growing suburbs. *Morning News* Collection, December 20, 1971. From the collections of the Texas/Dallas History and Archives Division, Dallas Public Library.

Dallas is the capital of the realm of urban and suburban theme parks, with their mélange of varied and conflicting claims and representations.[7] In a postmodern world, the distinct and isolated residential enclaves within and beyond Dallas's boundaries—Anglo suburbs of North Dallas capped by super-suburban Plano, underdeveloped and predominantly African American South Dallas, and Hispanic-dominated West Dallas—also resemble theme parks, with different residential populations, modes of entry, lifestyles, and life chances. (To be sure, the representation of Hispanic, Asian, and African Americans in suburbs is also growing.) Both within Dallas and in comparison with other places, the clash of similarity and difference

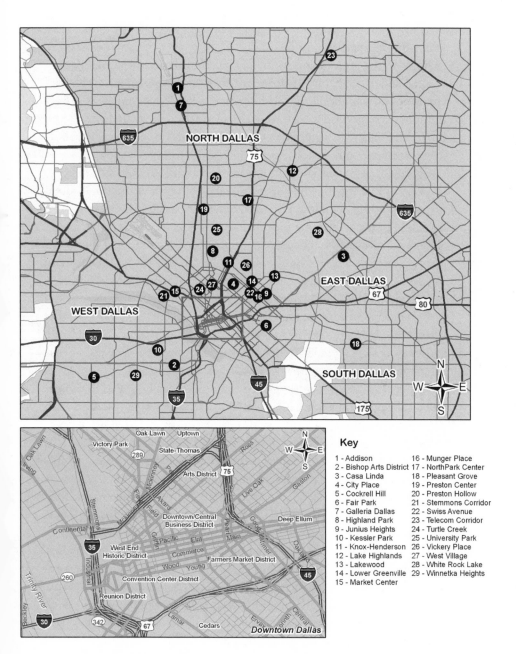

Map 1. Dallas neighborhoods and districts, 2006. Data from ESRI, U.S. Census Bureau. Drawn by Paul Hoeffler.

fuels and complicates the proliferation of images by which we locate, read, and confront the city.

Both on the ground and in the imagination, Dallas is peculiarly fragmented and disorienting. Those accustomed to navigating more coherent cityscapes find its illegibility disconcerting, even disturbing. This discussion of "reading" Dallas and other urban places follows the tradition of interpretation and design initiated by Kevin Lynch in his landmark book, *The Image of the City*. Lynch's innovation was to "concentrate especially on one particular visual quality: the apparent clarity or 'legibility' of the cityscape. . . . the ease with which its parts can be recognized and can be organized into a coherent pattern. . . . Legibility is of special importance when considering environments at the urban scale of size, time, and complexity."[8] Almost a half-century of additional urban transformation and numerous attempts to make sense of its causes and consequences teaches us how hard this task can be.[9] On the one hand, as sociologist Sharon Zukin observes, we do not "have spatial images of the built environment that would adequately describe the landscape of 'metropolitan deconcentration'—neither urban nor suburban—in which most Americans live."[10] On the other hand, as literary critic Alexander Gelley emphasizes, however useful and powerful the metaphors, cities are not simply "texts" to be read in the modes of literary criticism, nor is "reading" a city really like reading a text. In Gelley's view, "The problem we face in articulating this notion is that space is both the framework of our analysis (the schematic construct we require as operators of relation, as indicators of placement) and the topic of the analysis (objects and places)."[11] To place ourselves in the cityscape, we must scrutinize our geographical positioning system as well as our environment.

Promoters and critics alike typically view Dallas as an uncomplicated and relatively transparent city, though they disagree about whether that is a positive quality.[12] From the perspective offered here, however, the city's opacity is more apparent and important. So, too, are fundamental, long-standing challenges to Dallas's sense of identity and security. Those complications connect Dallas's present to its past in significant ways. Relentless boasting and incessant self-promotion camouflage weaknesses in public identity, deep insecurities, and confusion over what a city should do and how private and public come together to form a "city that works." Awareness of the relationships among history, image, and identity contributes to a reorientation in how we understand not only Dallas but also American and twenty-first-century cities more generally. The lessons may be as big as the Big D, reluctant as the city's leaders seem to be to learn them.

THREE ICONIC IMAGES AND THE "PROBLEM" OF DALLAS

Locally, nationally, and internationally, three iconic images—the Kennedy assassination in Dealey Plaza, the Dallas Cowboys football team, and *Dallas,* the television show—dominate views of the city, attracting other images and myths and organizing them into ideological statements. Often stark but not always simple or stable, these images reveal multiple and variable meanings when we shift our gaze critically from past to present and back again toward Dallas's possible futures.

Plying familiar images in close association, Dallas Mayor Ron Kirk declared in 1997, "To many people around the world, Dallas *is* defined by three things: the Kennedy assassination, the Dallas Cowboys, and an internationally popular television show."[13] The mayor countered these marks of Dallas's dubious distinction from other cities by reciting in statistical staccato the overblown, equally familiar stuff of city boosting: Dallas's population exceeds one million, making it the United States' eighth largest city.[14] The second largest convention city in the United States, it is Texas's top visitor destination, with more restaurants per capita than New York City and more shopping centers per capita than any other American city. From this recital, without mentioning his own election as Dallas's first African American mayor, Kirk skipped lightly to the city's changing demographic composition: "Dallas also is a diverse city, with a rapidly growing Hispanic and African-American population."[15] This account of Dallas is remarkable mostly for its unremarkability; it entirely fails to engage the powerfully defining images that form its starting point.

Mayor Kirk's view, like those of his predecessors, unquestioningly accepts the media-driven definition of a prominent city by a presidential shooting and the public trauma that followed, its longing for redemption by a professional sports team with its thrill of victory and agony of defeat, and its fabulous and infamous fortunes propagated internationally by a weekly prime-time TV soap opera. With respect to the power to define the city, he added the obligatory populist, individualist cliché: "Dallas is also defined by each of us every day." Kirk did not explain *how* these images came to define Dallas or explore what it *means* for a city to be so defined. Although Kirk acknowledged a multiplicity of popular visions of the city, he was not concerned with the ways in which this mode of defining Dallas shapes and is shaped by varied interests competing for dominance. Nor was he concerned with the ways in which Dallas residents share or dissent from this definition of their city.

Although he was addressing the Dallas Historical Society, not the Chamber of Commerce or Visitors Bureau, Kirk did not adopt a historical perspective. None of these three defining phenomena predates 1960. Dallas's 120-year history prior to the Kennedy assassination and the advent of the Cowboys does not figure at all. That is no more astonishing than the claim that the city is "defined" by a television soap opera that caricatures, melodramatizes, and sometimes ridicules consumerist, amoral, and competitive culture, or by an assassination that long shamed and scarred the city, garnering for it the reputation of an outcast hotbed of extremist violence. Identifying Dallas with a professional sports team seems to pale in comparison, although the city was never a cowboy town (as if that mattered). Other major cities, such as Miami, Houston, and Los Angeles, are identified by their sports teams, but none goes as far as Dallas's association with the Cowboys, despite the fact that the benefits to the city's economy and image are of questionable value.[16] Powerful contradictions go dangerously unexamined in the simple equation of Dallas with three defining frames.[17]

Despite some observers' contention that, as the end of the twentieth century approached, the mayor and the city were "at last" confronting Dallas's problems, definitions like Mayor Kirk's indicate the opposite: a failure to examine the city of Dallas critically, situating its current difficulties, dreams, and dilemmas and its development over time in social-historical perspective and political-economic context; and an attempt to substitute for that salutary self-scrutiny the repetition of a narrow range of well-publicized images and rhetorical gestures. The most striking feature of these frequently recirculated images is precisely their lack of clarity, reflection, and secure sense of identity.

Dallas's "big three" defining images are ambiguous and contradictory, though powerful. Separately and together, they often do useful political and cultural work for the city. Yet careful analysis of their internal construction and public reception and of their complex interrelationships reveals that they express and embody intense ambivalence. Rather than defining Dallas in the sense Mayor Kirk intended, these images provide valuable entry into the "problem" of Dallas: for all its prominence and image promotion, Dallas is an unusually illegible, ill-defined, and insecure city.

Kirk's 1997 definition of Dallas reflects continuities rather than progressive changes in the associations that city boosters hope to promote. Selective forgetting and remembering, especially of the largest images, occurs very slowly.[18] A special Gallup Poll commissioned by the *Dallas Morning News* on the twentieth anniversary of the assassination in 1983 identified the same three images: the Cowboys (listed by 28 percent as first association, another 10 percent as second); the Kennedy assassination (17 percent, 6 percent); and the *Dallas* TV show (11 percent, 10 percent). "Nothing or don't know" was the third largest response (13 percent) when only first associations are selected, but when first and second associations are combined it was most frequent (37 percent). For those seeking to improve the city's image, these results were inauspicious.[19]

The *Dallas Morning News* fooled no one in stressing the ascendancy of the Cowboys over the assassination and the recent rise of the TV series. Both team and TV series undeniably attracted national and international attention to Dallas, some of it distracting from assassination associations but some of it reminiscent and reinforcing. Indeed, in both policy and ideology, investment in and propagation of images is part of the "Dallas Way": a mode of concerted action, an ethos, and a strategy for practicing and circumventing politics and manufacturing consent. The Dallas Citizens Council, active from the 1930s onward in superelectoral steering of the entire ship of the city, held the Dallas Way to be an implicit and explicit code for furthering its interests, creating a kind of civic hegemony that defined the interests of Dallas at large. *Dallas,* the television series, drew upon this Dallas Way as a base for its fictions, although the fictional nature of this show was often lost on Dallas residents.

Local commentators engaged in a form of exaggerated primitive realism with respect to the prime-time soap opera. For eleven years the TV *Dallas* portrayed "a city of the future, the capital of the Sunbelt—clean, bright, moneyed, crazy for commerce and competition . . . the Dallas of the Super Bowl champion Cowboys." In *Texas Monthly,* Steven Reddicliffe declared, "*Dallas* captured the mood. It was the first TV show that was really about money and that had a money man—J.R.—as its central character. Dialogue was rich with business and legal lingo. Viewers were offered a crash course in the oil industry."[20] A writer for *The Met,* a local weekly, expounded: *Dallas* "captured the spirit of that success for outsiders and newcomers alike. . . . The Ewings were nouveau riche. . . . [They] tried their damnedest to make a good—or at least a powerful—impression. When *Dallas* was getting big, Dallas was also sculpting its own image—seeking out a distinctive skyline, crowning its football squad 'America's Team,' cashing in on, for all it was worth, the flash of the city."[21] The program's long run at home and great attraction abroad indicate that it tapped into certain contradictory yet appealing images of the city, and even the nation. *Dallas,* lest we forget, was not reality TV. Neither its makers nor its sponsors intended it to appear like a documentary, nor did most of its viewers see it in that way.[22] Irony often fused with parody, if not with social commentary.

Those who accord great and unambiguous cultural power to media images miss the oblique connections of conflicts—love and hate, positive and negative reactions—and underestimate the viewing public's ability to discriminate among them. Association and identification are not always positive contributions, nor is popularity a sure sign of health. With no hint of satire, one local journalism professor tried mightily to salvage the series for positive ends: "Though the show portrayed Dallasites as having a lot of qualities that were negative, people didn't think of Dallas in a negative way. Certainly there was a grain of truth in the representation of the flashy, glamorous, superficial narrow-mindedness of some of the characters. All those things, though they aren't good, changed the way much of the world looked at Dallas, because the lasting image of this city had been of the Kennedy assassination."[23]

The TV *Dallas's* popularity depended on the existence of a hated and only partially rehabilitated postassassination Dallas, which lent the limited credibility the series required. The characters—J.R. Ewing, an oilman and the son of a rancher; his feuding family, including his envious younger brother and his murderous mistress and sister-in-law; and a cast of ruthless and untrustworthy business friends and foes—were caricatures styled by popular stereotypes of Texas and Dallas. J.R.'s blatant disrespect for the law and personal integrity as well as the brutal clashes of cartoonish evil and good over all things large and small fit popular images of Dallas at least as much as they changed them. *Dallas,* the TV series, broadcast the city's image worldwide but did not enhance it except by comparison to its previous infamy.

In 1984, *Dallas Times Herald* columnist Jim Schutze suggested that "the business about the TV show and what it had done for or to the city's image is a two-edged sword." "On the one hand, it probably isn't possible now to visit the New Guinea bush country without bumping into somebody who wants to know how J.R. is doing. . . . On the other hand, they certainly seem to have us typecast. Ironically, as the gulf between rural and urban Texas widens—and nowhere is the gap more noticeable than in Dallas—the show seems to have stuffed a Stetson on our head, clamped a bourbon in our hand and told us to give the folks out there a great big gap-toothed smile. . . . But the first words of qualification escape our lips— 'Well, you know, Dallas really is a more complicated place than the show may indicate'—and our listeners inwardly cringe and tell themselves: 'Oh no. A booster.' Which is understandable, too. In fact, we may really be too sensitive, even to the point of being boring (God forbid). For all the dangers of typecasting, the truth is that the show has spread the city's name far and wide, has made the link with the Kennedy assassination less immediate, and has hit at least one nail on the head in describing us. The show portrays Dallas as a center for full-bore the-more-the-merrier free enterprise capitalism."[24]

In 1987, Dallas boosters sought to capitalize on the series' image of the city in order to promote tourism. In an article titled "Is Dallas the 'Dallas' of TV Fame, or Is It Something Better?" Jim Schutze again caught the contradictions. As the head of the advertising agency that designed the campaign explained to him: "When you talk about Dallas outside the city and state, all they know is the show and the Dallas Cowboys. . . . So the ad campaign uses the Lorimar soap opera, *Dallas,* as a jumping off place." Schutze agreed: "The soundtracks of the TV ads all include versions of the theme from the show. You have to get the folks' attention. They do know about the show. So that much seems to make sense." But, Schutze continued, the ads themselves featured characters in cowboy costumes talking "about how different Dallas is from the image of it portrayed by the show (they cut away to some sophisticated Dallas scenes). And I'm thinking, 'Hey, I like that; this is a clever idea.' But the last line of the voice-over says, 'If you liked the show, you'll love the city.' Which doesn't make any sense. Either the ad is saying that the city is not like the show or that the city is indeed like the show. But it says both. Which doesn't make sense."[25]

In 2006, preparing for the soap opera's reincarnation as a movie, Dallas's public officials launched a successful campaign to persuade 20th Century Fox to "Shoot J.R. in Dallas"—seemingly unaware of the slogan's echoes of the Kennedy assassination. According to the *Dallas Morning News,* the mayor and the head of the Dallas Film Commission backed "a task force aimed at sweetening the pot for 20th Century Fox" and got "the private sector involved in offering alternative perks to the filmmakers." The editorial page asked provocatively:

> Through cinematic history, Dallas has served as a stand-in for Detroit, Los Angeles, 23rd-century Washington, D.C., 1950s Little Rock, rural Nebraska, even An Nasiriyah, Iraq.
> But can Dallas be *Dallas?*
> City officials insist that it can.

Explaining the subsidy that Dallas offered the Hollywood company to lure it from competing sites, the editorial continued: "Officials estimate that the film would result in $30 million for the local economy, to say nothing of new jobs and free publicity."[26] This strategy, deliberately blurring the lines between Dallas and *Dallas* as the city strives to imitate fiction, comports with the blending of public and private investment to ensure that profits from the film go to Dallas rather than its rivals. Both are as telling as they are typical. "Shoot J.R. in Dallas"?

The image propagated by the television series, along with other, more deliberate attempts to reshape city images, cannot be understood without acknowledging the profound effect that the Kennedy assassination has had on the city's psyche. The series fit well within the terms of the public relations campaign mounted by Neiman Marcus CEO and liberal civic leader Stanley Marcus shortly after the assassination to promote the idea that "there's a lot right with Dallas."[27] Marcus's effort portended a whole series of campaigns aimed at creating alternative images, manufacturing new identities, and generating renewed growth and development for the city.

Big D has operated under the grip of a firm belief that a new image can create a new reality. Writer Lawrence Wright looks back on growing up in Dallas in the 1950s and 1960s, recovering contradictory responses to the assassination, shaped locally by Dallas's origin myths and recent transformation, on the one hand, and externally by reactions to Dallas's aggressive self-promotion, on the other. This juxtaposition reveals how fragile yet dangerous these influential images of Big D were. Wright relates: "What distinguished Dallas from the other cities of the new world (this was the legend we told ourselves) was that there was no reason for its existence. . . . And because there was finally no reason for Dallas, there was anxiety among its citizens. It might all disappear tomorrow. . . . Dallas was a fire that might go out at any time. To keep it alive the citizens advertised it far and wide, and even to ourselves; it was 'Big D, my oh yes!', the city that works, et cetera. We were blowing on the coals."[28]

The coals, if not the city, smoldered in the wake of the events of November 22, 1963. The myths, images, and rhetoric of Dallas turned into shrill whines, meaningless repetition, silences, and denial. The seeming strength of city images metamorphosed into signs of public insecurity and a profound weakness of identity. Silence and denial incensed many outside Dallas, primed to heap censure and abuse. In the end, it did not matter if "Dallas killed Kennedy." Dallas provoked strong, negative reactions, and Dallasites were angry and afraid. Hinting at other myths, Wright continues:

> Dallas killed Kennedy; we heard it again and again. Dallas was "a city of hate, the only city in which the President could have been shot." . . . But Dallas had nothing to do with Kennedy's death. The hatred directed at our city was retaliation for many previous grievances. The East hated us because we were part of the usurping West, liberals hated us because we were conservative, labor because we were anti-union, intellectuals because we were raw, minorities because we were predominantly and conspicuously white, atheists and agnostics because we were strident believers, the poor because we were rich, the old because we were new. . . . no other town would ever know the opprobrium Dallas had endured. . . . It's no wonder Dallasites were defensive and angry. And yet behind our anger was the fear that there must be a whisper of truth in the lies people were telling about our city.[29]

Images and myths undercut each other's foundations. If the assassination's aftermath was a test, Dallas did not fare well.

After the assassination, and even before, it seemed to some that Dallas was "a logical place for something unpleasant and embarrassing to happen."[30] The assassination caused some to search for distracting, therapeutic transference at home and distracting, impressive success outside. Many Dallasites turned to another big image, however incommensurate, to repair the damage: the Dallas Cowboys football team. Dubbed "America's team" by an NFL Films producer, not by the team or Dallas leaders, or so the sometimes questioned story goes, the team reflected glory on Dallas. Serious questions remain about the extent to which the Cowboys were consciously fashioned from the mid-to-late 1960s into an image designed to erase the stain of the assassination and contribute to the resurrection and rehabilitation of the city. The effort seemed to work, up to a point and for a time. In the attempt, the team was joined with another myth and image-in-the-making, postassassination Dallas reconstructed as a more open, progressive, and dynamic environment for civic, political, cultural, and economic life.

Engaging in myth-making by repetition and exaggerated spinning of images, *Dallas Morning News* editorial writer Henry Tatum retrospectively claims the legacy of the triumphant Cowboys for the city and its business leaders, strategically elevating the status of a phoenix-like Dallas rising out of its 1963 ashes. Tatum proposes, in hindsight (the best way), that the team was part of an explicit narrative plot: "Dallas wasn't the city that killed John F. Kennedy. It was the home of the Dallas Cowboys. And as long as those silver helmets with blue stars kept winning, the harsh memories of Nov. 22, 1963, were pushed further into the background." Without mentioning particular connections, Tatum asserts: "The business leadership looked to the Cowboys to restore this city's reputation. And for the most part, the strategy worked." Tatum concludes, "Dallas needed to have America's Team. So that is what the Cowboys became to adoring fans."[31]

Tatum's ode to the magical Dallas Cowboys and the revival of their all-American city is mediocre poetry and even less persuasive argumentation. Many accepted the identification of Dallas with the Cowboys and at least implicitly endorsed this symbolization of a "new," improved, or vindicated Dallas. That a football team in time proved inadequate to sustain that image and perform that political and cultural work is no more surprising than the fact that leaders and promoters seized and depended on that image, a foundation too thin to carry the great weight of a city in need.

The critical portrayal of the Cowboys and of Dallas culture in Peter Gent's 1973 novel, *North Dallas Forty*, caused a stir nationally and aroused scandal and umbrage locally. Written by a former player, it dispelled the mystique surrounding the coach, management, and players, offering matter-of-fact descriptions of drug and alcohol abuse, out-of-control behavior, and homosexuality among the athletes.[32] Gent's frank descriptions of racism, sexism, violence, crass materialist display, dangerous driving, and hypocrisy in Dallas were equally controversial and unpopular in many quarters of the city. *North Dallas Forty* confronts and uses the city of Dallas, physically and ideologically, descriptively and mythically, in ways that few other Dallas novels do, playing these elements off against each other.[33]

Gent's game on the page is composed of a certain measure of realism, without overly abundant affectations of fiction *noir* or limiting authorial self-consciousness. Humor, sometimes mixed with sarcasm and a touch of cynicism, is deployed effectively. Gent's Dallas is oversized and full of its own myths. Although unabashedly critical of Dallas, the portrayal is neither wholly negative nor unrelieved. The city is a striking presence in the novel:

> The view of downtown Dallas, although not awe inspiring (no view of Dallas could inspire awe), was still impressive. I read the lighted message on the north side of the CRH Building. The entire north and south sides of the building contained banks of lights used to spell out messages to the city. Tonight letters twenty stories high spelled out POW, part of a community-wide campaign to get involved in the Southeast Asia war. The war ranked third in community importance behind the Texas-Oklahoma Football Weekend and [football team owner] Conrad Hunter's acquisition of one more good white running back.

Another telling passage treats the geography of racial politics with wry humor:

> South Dallas blacks aren't a deprived ethnic group, they're a different civilization living in captivity. Just blocks from the phenomenal wealth of Elm and Commerce streets, South Dallas was a hyperbole. A grim joke on those who still believe we are all created equal. There isn't even a real struggle for equality. Equality with what? The white man? No, he's crazy. The blacks seemed to be waiting, watching, knowing they would always be getting fucked. They took solace in the dependability.[34]

Deplored by Dallas boosters at the peak of the Cowboy's success, Gent's portrayal of the team—if not of its city—eventually hit home.

No one else in Dallas anticipated the inevitable fall of the Cowboys. Tatum recalls: "When Dallas' financial collapse coincided with the Cowboys' talent collapse in the mid-1980s, many became convinced this city really couldn't succeed without the team. The fortunes of the two would be linked forever." New owner, coaches, and stars, and three Super Bowl wins in four years in the 1990s "did nothing to dissuade [sic] that theory" when the city experienced "an impressive financial recovery" at the same time. "When Steve Bartlet assumed Dallas' mayorship in November 1991, he announced that Dallas should become 'America's City.' Not a bad idea, since 'America's Team' already plays football here," opined the *News*.[35] But, sensing a seismic shift, Tatum retreated from the Cowboys of the 1990s, whose "victories didn't seem as sweet" because of the team's bad behavior and scandal off the field: "In a city where a positive image seems to be everything, the team's outlaw reputation was becoming an embarrassment." With as many as six players suspended for drug or alcohol abuse and rumors of worse, "Dallas no longer could turn to its favorite NFL team for a publicity boost."[36]

In the wake of another brouhaha after the coach was caught carrying a gun in his flight bag, the *New York Times* thundered under the headline "Outlaw Cowboys": "There is a swagger about the Cowboys that seems to say this team does not have to bother about the rules."[37] Whether intended or not, this national censure evoked an assassination-era image of Dallas as out of control, precisely the shadow image that "America's team" was seen as repudiating. Despite its aggressive self-promotion, Dallas has long sought, indeed depended on, the legitimating approval and praise of authoritative outsiders. Criticism of Tom Landry's Cowboys as too homogeneous and contained was not often associated with another much-criticized assassination-era characteristic, the homogeneity and containment of the citizenry, or at least the middle-class whites who counted.[38]

As usual in pursuit of the city's advantage, the *Dallas Morning News* searched for a silver lining. On the op-ed page, Henry Tatum belatedly adopted a consoling, if patronizing and hypocritical, practicality: "It may not be realistic to expect much more from professional athletes than a good performance on the court or playing field. . . . Multimillion dollar salaries have a way of doing that to talented young people who seldom have been told no." Tatum spun a new myth of a mature Dallas whose "destiny [is] no longer tied to Cowboys." "So, there just might be something positive emerging," he suggested. "For the first time in more than 35 years, Dallas finally can realize its fortunes don't rise and fall on the success of the Cowboys. . . . Dallas decided that success of this city didn't hang in the balance while a spiraling pass hung precariously in the air. . . . City leaders can take it from here."[39]

The image of the Dallas Cowboys lost much of its sparkle. *Sports Illustrated*'s Peter King quoted "one Texan" as saying, "If this is America's team, then woe is America." *Dallas Morning News* sports reporter Kevin Sherrington moved to the Sunday op-ed pages to ask "Are the Cowboys ruining our lives? Team is embedded in Dallas' psyche; Cowboys help to shape Dallas' identity."[40] Although the Cowboys are relocating from suburban Irving to Arlington, which offered greater enticements, despite Dallas's effort to lure them "home" to a proposed new "Victory" stadium downtown, the Cowboys and Dallas will not easily or cheaply separate or divorce. Regardless of the precise geographic location of their playing field, the city's fortunes remain tied to the Cowboys' star.

The event whose long shadow the Cowboys eventually displaced has itself receded over time. Dallas came to terms with the Kennedy assassination by removing it to a safe distance as an occurrence that took place in the past. Commemoration seemed to contain it in history, allowing Dallasites to stop reflecting on what share of responsibility or guilt their city justly or unjustly bore and treat the event much as the rest of the nation did. After almost a quarter century, the Sixth Floor Museum commemorating President Kennedy and his death in Dallas was built, with an unendorsed Conspiracy Museum nearby. On the assassination's thirtieth anniversary in 1993, the Dealey Plaza site of the shooting was dedicated as a National Historic Landmark.[41] The histories of these monuments attest to Dallas's difficulties in facing history and itself.

In what Jim Schutze called a gesture "to prove we're past the guilt thing," Dallas allowed key portions of Oliver Stone's 1991 film *JFK* to be shot in Dallas, including the grassy knoll in Dealey Plaza. But much of the film was removed, literally as well as metaphorically, from the site of the shooting. My favorite personal experience was the day that the block in East Dallas on which I lived was closed to traffic—without notice, a violation of the city code—so that it could stand in as background for another part of town, Oak Cliff. The City Manager's Office understood my concern about the need to inform residents, but not my comments about the neglect of historical accuracy involved.[42] That criterion had little or nothing to do with the motivating sense that the advancement of the city required promotional and entertainment uses of history, however contradictory or confusing. The movie's plot, too, played fast and loose with local facts, taking liberties even with popular conspiracy theories. In the filmed version of the conspiracy, Dallas law enforcement officials were only bit players in a vast scheme to prevent the President from withdrawing U.S. troops from Vietnam. As *Time Magazine's* review put it: "So, you want to know, who killed the President and connived in the cover-up? Everybody! High officials in the CIA, the FBI, the Dallas constabulary, all three armed services, Big Business and the White House. Everybody done it—everybody but Lee Harvey Oswald."[43] And everywhere but Dallas. Dallas itself appeared like the hapless dupe Oswald, accidentally becoming the scene of the crime.

The refusal to reckon with the longer-term and contemporary significance of its history—most directly, with the propensity toward extremist violence that appears as the countermyth of the city's vaunted civility—prevents Dallas from admitting and reflecting on its past, as well as displaying it more constructively and instructively. The long delay and powerful opposition to a memorial to John F. Kennedy and an assassination museum are not exceptional, but typical of the city. As Dallas struggled with the place of the assassination in its past, present, and even its future, at stake in the continuing battle is the history that remains and the history that is expressed.

For some Dallasites, controlling the real and potential damage to the city that followed the assassination meant erasing all signs of that event, regardless of any question about collective culpability. This "see no evil, speak no evil, hear no evil" revisionism took many forms, including Mayor Erik Jonsson's monument building and Goals for Dallas and Stanley Marcus's promotion of cosmopolitanism.[44] Influential leaders proposed imploding the Texas School Depository Building from which Oswald allegedly shot the President rather than maintaining so visible a mark of Dallas's shame or blame. The building's future was in question for years before it was reborn as the Sixth Floor Museum, a development that long met resistance and criticism.[45]

The Book Depository recently had its own upbeat revisioning, its top floor turned into an art gallery. Under the headline, "Mixing Tragedy with Art in Dallas," the *New York Times* reported on March 3, 2003, that the gallery displayed traveling photography shows such as Andy Warhol's silk-screen portraits of Jacqueline Kennedy. A building formerly at risk of demolition is now in demand: "The gallery is also available for rent, and it has become popular for corporate dinners and receptions. Guests are free to wander down the open staircase and view artifacts of the assassination." While some found this adaptive reuse in good taste, "Others admit to mixed feelings. 'I attended a reception there for a departing city judge,' said Wick Allison, the publisher of *D,* a Dallas magazine. 'It's a really nice space but also a truly weird place to have a reception with people drinking and guffawing and making jokes.'"[46] Attempting to remain relevant and adding to its appeal in the aftermath of 9/11, the Sixth Floor Museum announced that it would mount a new exhibit on five key American traumas: President Lincoln's assassination, the attack on Pearl Harbor, the Kennedy assassination, and the bombing of the Murrah Federal Office Building in Oklahoma City, culminating in the attack on the World Trade Center.[47]

Many Dallasites, some of them influential, saw no need to remind citizens or visitors of its scars by erecting a public monument to Kennedy. Mayor R. L. Thornton declared on December 4, 1963: "I've heard people talking about erecting a monument in their sadness. For my part, I don't want anything to remind me that a President was killed on the streets of Dallas. I want to forget."[48] Famed architect Philip Johnson designed the memorial, but this brought little comfort. Widespread sentiment at home and abroad insisted that Dallas had an "obligation" to construct a public shrine and place for prayers and devotion.[49]

Seven years passed before the memorial was built on the west side of downtown, its $200,000 cost paid for privately with donations from more than 50,000 people. Standing two hundred yards from the assassination site, the monument is composed of four thirty-foot-high concrete walls, standing slightly off the ground. The north and south ends have narrow openings. An 8- by 8-foot granite slab inside is inscribed with Kennedy's name. Philip Johnson stated that the open tomb is "an empty space to memorialize a person. . . . I wanted a place that didn't have a roof. You'd go in and it wouldn't be a memorial at all. It would just be . . . the silence of the sky and you, a place to be quiet with yourself."[50]

The abstract, unadorned structure has not inspired all its viewers, to say the least. As the *Dallas Morning News*'s Henry Tatum put it, "The memorial always has delivered a mixed signal to the people of Dallas and the millions who have come." Johnson's intentionally simple and quiet space seemed "somewhat stark to many visitors." Perhaps the structure was not grand enough for its historical work, or to meet viewers' expectations; lack of funds precluded a more monumental memorial. Lack of support locally led to occasional suggestions that it be torn down. The granite weathered poorly. After a man with a history of mental illness vandalized the walls with spray paint, more than a year passed before the memorial was restored at a cost of $80,000. The vandalism, claimed Henry Tatum of the *Dallas Morning News,* "provided a wake-up call for those who long ago decided that the downtown site was nothing more than an obligatory response to world scorn following the assassination."[51]

In June 2000, the memorial was rededicated, its luster returned, thirty years to the day after its initial dedication. The audience was estimated at two hundred persons. With sweeping historical revisionist spirit, *Dallas Morning News* editorial columnist Tatum proclaimed: "Dallas finally comes to grips with its past," an assertion contradicted by the size of the crowd. Tatum's statement may be part of a larger revisioning and representation of Dallas, yet his main message said more about the Kennedys than about Dallas's relationship to its past. The concluding sentence of Senator Ted Kennedy's open letter to the people in this community sounded simple enough: "It means a great deal to know the citizens of Dallas County loved him, too." But Tatum spun it into a message for a Dallas now presumed to be forgiven: "For those who were here 37 years ago to witness the bleakest day in Dallas' history, the words finally brought relief and ended the wondering."[52]

In the Dallas Way, Tatum rhetorically revised the city's relationship to its recent and current history. He claimed that the rededication gave Dallas "a chance to pay its respects without the guilt that seemed to fuel everything during the 1960s. Even the rededication allowed local leaders to speak more honestly about the death of the president and the turmoil that followed." That strange and self-serving assertion allows the *Dallas Morning News* editor to move from Ted Kennedy's statement "It means a great deal to know . . ." to words meant to help construct a new Dallas: "a city that finally has come to grips with its past."[53]

Less than three years later, during redevelopment of the Dallas County Plaza, some proposed removing the memorial entirely. With great economy, the *Morning News* summarized: "Moving the memorial, which was engineered into the parking garage below it, would be difficult. Then try explaining why Dallas, given its ignoble history of Kennedy-bashing just before the assassination, would dare touch the monument that showed this city mourned, too."[54] The director of the Sixth Floor Museum alluded to the possibility of a national scandal, and fear of criticism and censure, combined with technical problems, ruled.

Proclaiming that "anything that took so much fortitude to build ought to stay where it stands,"[55] the *Dallas Morning News* lauded Dallas in as many ways as it could, calling the construction of the monument a "big step" past the old Dallas desire to exonerate the city from blame: "the memorial is a tribute not just to President Kennedy but to Dallas. Its construction . . . represented a first tentative acknowledgement . . . yes, this terrible event happened here." The *News* then empathizes with the city: "There's no clue there to the misery and ambivalence Dallas experienced . . . and the unflinching candor it took to memorialize an event so many wanted to forget."

The passage of forty years has blunted some of the pain, and "We're comfortably removed from that terrible defensiveness, that itching private fear that the nation and the world blamed Dallas. . . . The memorial did not erase that fear, but it signified endurance and acceptance. It's as much a statement about Dallas."[56] In a monumental sleight of hand, not destroying a memorial signifies coming to terms with the event it commemorates. Dallas claims forgiveness and absolves itself from responsibility, setting aside shame and pain. As the newspaper admits, the statements are really about Dallas, and the city's approach to history is at least as much about forgetting as about remembering.[57]

IMAGE AND IDENTITY

No city can be defined by a television soap opera and a professional football team, or even an assassination. The power of these "big three" images obstructs the more difficult and important work of wrestling with Dallas's history and identity. Yet these icons are at least as much consequence as cause of the "problem" of Dallas. Dallas's leaders have long sought to produce and promote a visible, marketable, and consumable identity for the city through the fabrication and dissemination of images.

Although image making and marketing is a thriving enterprise in many cities across the United States and internationally, Dallas is more prone than most other urban places to rely on the proliferation of images as a substitute for identity. Even more problematic, Dallas's visual, verbal, and material images are remarkably incoherent: multiple, blurred, and inconsistent. In contrast to other "new" as well as "old" cities, Dallas willfully neglects its own urban history, in part out of fear of what reckoning with the past might mean.[58] Through its overreliance on images, as well as through their incoherence and the illegibility of the cityscape itself, Dallas inadvertently but transparently exposes its insecurity and problematic identity.

Willie Morris, writing in *The New Republic* in 1964, observed that Dallas employed "every possible means of institutional power in pursuit of its 'image.'" After the Kennedy assassination, Dallas became "perhaps the most mistrusted city in the Western world, and object of scorn, comedy and myth."[59] *Life* magazine reporter Robert Wallace pointed out that the city's long-standing preoccupation with projecting its image had backfired: "Dallas . . . clamors for honest attention, but its own booster-minded press reads as though nothing unpleasant ever occurs in the city. Nonetheless the image of Dallas is enormous—'Big D,' *Giant*—and like a shadow in the slant of sun is larger than the thing that casts it."[60] The shock of the assassination prompted others to vilify Dallas as an extremist haven, a violence-prone city of hate. In reaction, city leaders intensified their determined invention and propagation of positive, even pristine images. Wallace's observation about Dallas culture still holds true today: "A man must be either a booster or a knocker. Anything else than strident patriotism is apt to be viewed as subversive."[61]

Four decades' struggles against the assassination's infamy have exacerbated, not diminished, the difficulty of defining Dallas's identity and the propensity to proffer images instead of substance. The press is no less booster-minded, and no more aware of the dark shadows that such grandiose pretenses cast. The *Dallas Morning News,* since the 1980s the city's only daily, refracts and magnifies the anxieties, dreams, and fears of the city. As Dallasites discuss Dallas, they create a fictional construct that we must also employ—although self-consciously and critically—to take part in the conversation. Dallas boosters speak about Dallas as if it were a living thing. The conceit is so powerful because no one exposes the image as an illusion. Indeed, concern for protecting the city's image trumps serious self-criticism. In October 1997, the *Dallas Morning News* admonished: "Regardless of whether scandals are becoming more commonplace, critics say, they should be regarded as more than an image problem for Dallas."[62] City leaders have yet to take this salutary advice.

These tendencies to self-magnification and sensitivity to criticism from those who could be deemed outsiders are longstanding and deeply rooted features of Dallas culture. The city's tendency to promote itself through the proliferation of images began long before the Kennedy assassination damaged its reputation. Writing in 1945, at the height of the city's wartime prosperity, Herbert Gambrell, Southern Methodist University history professor and director of the Dallas Historical Society, described both Dallas's oversized self-images and others' strong reactions against them. In Gambrell's view, "present-day Dallas is characterized by such traits as aggressiveness, promotionalism, opportunism, investmentism (which is a sort of civic merchandising); and that it chooses its civic objectives after shrewd forecasts of the probable direction of economic and social winds. The first third of Dallas's century of history shows that these traits are not new. They are the traits that transformed a muddy-river settlement into a city."[63]

Right from the start, Gambrell maintained, the city's founders adopted an entrepreneurial model for urban growth and governance, with a peculiar combination of aggressive self-fashioning and strategic adaptation to changing market conditions. He added three more characteristics: "*Self-appreciation:* a consciousness of its own worth and shrewdness (Outsiders sometimes mistake this for arrogance); *Superiority complex:* an unexpressed but not carefully concealed feeling of superiority over other Texas cities, which would have made it difficult in 1872 (or 1945) for Dallas to win a popularity contest; *Competitive determination of civic objectives:* the very human desire to want something more keenly if someone else is trying to get it."[64] To put the point in the postwar psychosocial vernacular, its superiority complex covers a deeper inferiority complex. Gambrell's list captures the contradictions as well as the continuities in Dallas's self-image: despite, indeed, because of its self-centeredness, the city looks uneasily toward those it sees as rivals.

The same combination of self-regard and sensitivity to criticism appears, after the assassination, to express a deep insecurity about Dallas's identity. Writing in *Fortune* in 1964, Richard Smith noted the city's insularity: "In general, Dallasites looked upon their city as the center of the universe. 'Dallas as a city,' wrote native son John William Rogers, 'never sees any but its own newspapers and follows nothing but its own activities. . . . Its life is lived in terms of itself.'"[65] The *Dallas Morning News* pointed to the connection between isolation and insecurity: "In an odd way, for a city that has long been accused of excessive boosterism, a recent Dallas woe seems to be a lack of true confidence. Perhaps it's because sitting out in the middle plains, Dallas has only itself to focus upon. The city's shortcomings thus can become magnified."[66] In a *Texas Monthly* essay on why "Houston Is Better Than Dallas," journalist Harry Hurt III poked serious fun of the city's pretensions: "it is like Dallas to try to use such aliases ["Metroplex"] to pass itself off as something it is not, for Dallas basically is insecure. It is simply not happy with what it is. From the beginning, the whole conception of Dallas was cockeyed."[67] In this reading, the "cockeyed" conception of Dallas lies not only in its entrepreneurial self-creation but also in its location in the middle of nowhere. Throughout its history, Dallas has tried "to pass itself off as something it is not," fearful that skeptics within and outside the city would point out that its images were predicated on false pretenses.

Dallas author Lon Tinkle, writing in 1965, worked to transform admitted liabilities into unrecognized advantages and to buy time for the city to grow up. The city's trademark, he proclaimed, was "the image of growth." "But in the case of Dallas the change is happening to a city which has not yet grown into a personality of its own, unlike Rome or Paris. . . . Dallas has no woods to hem it in as it sparkles in the clear south-western sunlight. No mountains wall it in, lakes do not limit its expansion, docks and wharves do not narrow its boundaries."[68] This "scenic handicap" is also an asset. The city's very immaturity, Tinkle averred, "may allow Dallas a swifter and freer growth in the engineered cities of the Space Age. It may even be a spur, just as ambition and need are for a poor youth. . . . Dallas must grow into itself, whereas most other cities face the problem of having to grow out of themselves into something other, something new."[69] Tinkle's boundless optimism draws on the city's freedom from natural limits and the absence of history, which also figures as a constraint. His expression, however, draws more on semantic sleight of hand as he provides a rationalization for the persistent problems of an insecure identity.

If geography dictates or shapes identity, then Dallas has good reason to be confused. Many people are surprised to discover in an atlas that Dallas is more centrally located than western or southwestern. In its own and others' figurative positioning, Dallas appears as southern, western, southwestern, midwestern, or south-central. Sometimes Dallas's locations come in the form of multiple sitings, a reasonable if inconsistent approach, since cities' orientations and external connections do change over time. Herbert Gambrell deemed Dallas "sort of Mid-Western," hardly a popular identification in 1945 and even less so today. Most promoters attached it to the south, west, or southwest, seeking to gain the allure associated with these regions but risking geographic and cultural disorientation. For a time in the 1970s and early 1980s, the term "Sunbelt" seemed to serve all ends, but that fad seems to have run its course. Dallas's historical location in the southern Midwest is the city's best-kept secret. That "middle plains" explains much about its culture, including its desire to evade the reputation a midwestern identity carries.[70]

Even locating Dallas within Texas is tricky: the South is said to end in East Texas and the West to begin at Fort Worth, with Dallas sited awkwardly in between. "Texas is so big that people in Brownsville call the Dallas people Yankees, and the citizens of El Paso sneer at the citizens of Texarkana as being snobs of the effete east," says the *Texas Almanac*.[71] Reminding us that history and culture help to construct geography and that these matters are subject to controversy, Houston newspaperman Lynn Ashby, who grew up in Dallas, quipped, "the rest of Texas has a certain wonderment if Dallas is really part of Texas, or sort of Wall Street West, tassel-loafers on the Trinity. Is it Bowie and Charolais or brie and chardonnay?"[72] As if in reply, John Gunther reports, "'Dallas is rich and beautiful,' a Texas friend told me, 'but it isn't Texas.' What he meant is that it is not 'west' Texas. For Dallas, though Fort Worth is only a metaphorical stone's throw away, no more connotes longhorns and coyotes than do[es] Columbus, Ohio."[73]

Location is both literal and metaphorical. As Dallas places itself ambiguously on the continent, it declares an ambivalent relationship to the rest of American society, epitomizing its dreams but seeking to avoid its failures and evade its nightmares. Questions about Dallas's history, geography, and insecure identity intertwine with political economy and culture in the making and remaking of the city. Taking these questions seriously means examining the patterns and processes, as well as the myths, of its growth, including the great disparities among its districts and the marked inequalities among its residents. It means probing terms and meanings, calculating costs and benefits, and acknowledging limits.

In his inaugural address in June 1995, Mayor Kirk announced his vision of Dallas as "the capital of the American Dream" and "the capital city of

NAFTA and the Americas,"[74] an idea the *Dallas Morning News* endorsed in its description of Dallas as "an international city ready to trade."[75] Kirk proclaimed, "I think Dallas has the potential to be the next great city in North America. . . . Dallas is sitting on an economic volcano."[76] This metaphoric language inadvertently expresses not only the hope for explosive growth but also the exciting and disturbing city politics of the late 1980s and 1990s, following what one press pundit called the belated arrival of "democracy" in Dallas via city council restructuring, greater representation of African Americans and Hispanics, and unprecedented neighborhood activism. Whether echoing the tremors of the recent past or forecasting the shocks of the future, it is startling that the mayor employed an image of Dallas as an erupting volcano, implicitly but forebodingly endangered by its own pent-up energies and unrestrained expansion.

Associating Dallas closely with the American Dream echoes the city's founding as a trade settlement for a rich agricultural region. In this formulation, and materially, the course of the city's history is tied inseparably to the growth of the region and nation, and now to globalization.[77] For Dallas, like the nation, this quest distorts history into a preordained, manifest destiny, present at its creation. Both city and nation swell with tales of imperialistic conquests, Darwinian struggles for survival by the fittest, triumphs of the favored, missions of the ordained, the driven, the entrepreneurial. Both face unceasing threats large and small to survival and success, from within and without, and must be ever vigilant and defensive, suffering confusion over their identities and uncertainty about their security. Faith and arrogance, with little sense of humor or self-criticism, combine to preclude reconsideration of the quest or alteration of their path. Both Dallasites and Americans often find ourselves without the guidance offered by a complex look at history or the security provided by a clear sense of identity.

Similarly, Dallas provides a vision for "the American city," equally bold, partial, and contradictory. Dallas epitomizes the triumph of enterprise over nature, surmounting the limitations of its resources and making something from nothing. In its approach to city planning and its avoidance of the constraints that meaningful city plans necessarily entail, Dallas resembles many cities that grew up and out in the twentieth century. The city reaped praise in national media from the 1920s through the 1950s.[78] A century and a half of unlimited growth has brought serious challenges to Dallas, as for Texas and the United States. The city triumphant expresses a spirit of expansion in all dimensions; devotion to business; political stewardship by economic leadership, which blurs the boundaries of the political, public, and private domains; domination by the market and the rule of laissez-faire, except when deemed not in the city's best interest; and an ideology of material success eventually trickling down to all deserving citizens. With no sense of contradiction, Dallas also embraces ideals of antiurbanism, the desire to grow without facing the problems development brings, and the wish to be a great metropolis without the conflicts that burden other cities' histories.[79] Dallas spins and then weaves together the threads of nature and conquest, geographical advantage and liability, entrepreneurial dominance and elite domination, economic acumen and politics of stealth, high technology and hard labor, capital and culture, monumental and vernacular, haves and have-nots, leaders and led into a cloth so uneven that its ragged and unfinished underside, whenever glimpsed, belies its surface beauty.

The insecurities arising from geopolitics and economics are reinforced by the city's signal absence of a popular or serious cultural tradition of its own. Unlike many other prominent cities, Dallas has no signature song, film, novel, or stage play.[80] Some Dallasites claim signature status for "Big D," written by Frank Loesser for the Broadway musical *Most Happy Fella*. While the chorus spelled out the city's name—"Big D, little a, double l, a, s"—the lead sang:

And that spells Dallas
I mean it with no malice—
But the rest of Texas looks a mess
When you're from big D.

In my view, "Big D" lacks the recognition value and iconicity of a signature song. It has not proved as popular as songs like "Chicago" or "New York, New York," nor has it held its popularity over time and been embraced by new audiences.

Dallas has another lively tradition of songwriting that will never be recognized officially or publicly acclaimed: songs that bash Dallas or celebrate its underside. "Deep Ellum Blues," one of the most famous songs about Dallas, portrays the sexual commerce that once took place in that district.

Well if you go down to Deep Ellum, put your money in your shoes
Women in Deep Ellum got them Deep Ellum blues.

Chorus
Oh sweet mama, your daddy's got them Deep Ellum blues.
Oh sweet mama, your daddy's got them Deep Ellum blues.

Once I had a girlfriend, she meant the world to me
She went down to Deep Ellum, now she ain't what she used to be.
[Chorus]

Jimmie Dale Gilmore's "Dallas" is a leading example of the anti-Dallas song:

Well, Dallas is a jewel, oh yeah, Dallas is a beautiful sight.
And Dallas is a jungle, but Dallas gives a beautiful light.
Dallas is a rich man with a death wish in his eye . . .
A rich man who tends to believe in his own lies.

When songwriters, including prominent artists, take on Dallas, they express ambivalence or worse, as well as celebrating the city.[81]

Dallas lacks distinctive, let alone distinguished writing, fiction or non-fiction, about itself. One exception serves to prove the rule: Doug J. Swanson's trio of detective novels is set in Dallas *(Big Town, Dreamboat,* and *96 Tears).* A *Dallas Morning News* reporter strained to see Dallas as a distinct and shaping presence in these novels: "As much as any human being in the Flippo series, Dallas is a central character in the books, but with a twisted and clever reflection of its vaunted self-image as the ultimate city of money and deals. Everybody has a hustle here. Even low-life criminals are upwardly striving in Mr. Swanson's Dallas." The reporter failed to see that almost any other city could be substituted, and that the characteristics he describes as typically "Dallas" are ubiquitous. Swanson, who is also a *Dallas Morning News* reporter, repeated the familiar Dallas refrain in chorus with Sam Howe Verhovek: "'Dallas is not an artistic place—it's a business place,' Mr. Swanson says, and the pervading sense of money's importance may give his desperate, scrambling characters a greater edge. 'You're expected to come here and work and make your money and be a productive citizen and be conservative, and all that. . . . So I think maybe the contrast here is stronger.' . . . At the same time, none of the action takes place in corporate board rooms or the conference areas of luxury hotels." Dallas boosters' metaphors are ubiquitous; so are the stereotypes in which Dallas is decried. But Dallas is never distinctively described.

Swanson himself was not quite convinced of Dallas's role in his fiction. When asked whether Dallas serves as a "natural place" in which to set a crime novel or movie, he replied: Dallas "doesn't have mountains. It doesn't have the ocean. It doesn't have a forest. It doesn't have a desert. . . . It's not New Orleans. It doesn't create the natural mood for plots of intrigue. But it does have this outsized quality. Everyone, I think, has some idea about Dallas. It might be the city that killed Kennedy, it might be the TV show, it might be the Dallas Cowboys. But they've heard about it." Almost poetically, the report on Swanson's novels ends, "Dallas will remain the setting for his Flippo novels, including one built around Flippo's relationship with an 'assassinologist,' who gives tours of Dealey Plaza in his 1963 Lincoln convertible, playing a radio broadcast of the shooting of President Kennedy."[82] Life and art do sometimes imitate each other, even if the relationship provides little clarification.

Dallas's research, educational, and cultural institutions have produced few serious studies of the city. As its would-be historians simultaneously lamented and celebrated its past, its history is missing the stereotypical ingredients of traditional histories: great public men, great battles, great events, great disasters.[83] Dallas's best-known characters, prior to Tom Landry and Ross Perot, are the outlaws Bonnie and Clyde. Dallas seeks to escape its past, evading rather than facing the violence, lynching, and Ku Klux Klan activities that scar its history, and desperately denying the divisions of race and ethnicity that circumscribe the lives of its residents today.

Dallasites do not trust their own judgment culturally or intellectually. Outside experts are consulted for their opinions and advice, and then condemned as effete snobs who look down on businesslike Dallas. World-famous architects and planners are picked to design its monuments, and then criticized for the resulting structures' failure to fit into their surroundings. Journalist, author, and local historian A. C. Greene explains:

Artistically, Dallas doesn't believe in itself. "If it (or he or she) is any good, what is it (or he or she) doing here?" Opinions on cultural matters must be imported to be valued. Dallas believes what others say about Dallas, but not what it says about itself. . . . By the same token, Dallas doesn't accept history. . . . Dallas leadership resists history. . . . They're scared to death the term "historic" is going to hinder them from demolishing some structure they own. The greatest hindrance to Dallas' future as a center of creativity is the community's zeal to make everything pay off, to demand the arts be run "like a business," which is the highest encomium Dallas confers. . . . Dallas hasn't matured to the point where it can use history to chart cultural growth, and find no basis for local culture other than alien myth and legend. Consequently, Dallas is more defined by outsiders than from within the community, becoming to a great extent what others say it is.[84]

Struggling for identity, Dallas is less chameleon-like than Greene posits. Its insularity joins with an inconsistent striving to be different from other cities and to emulate them, all at the same time.

FIGURE 7. Skyline, 1999. Photographer: Damon Winter, *Dallas Morning News.* Printed with permission.

A key marker of the city's lack of clear identity is the absence of powerful images and symbols of itself that are recognizable and accepted at home and beyond. Dallas's hallmarks, "growth" and "progress," do not lend themselves to visualization. The city's contemporary financial, real estate, and high tech–based economy does not offer vivid, concrete images any more than its role as a center of finance and distribution for a regional economy based on cotton and oil did. Dallas may buy or borrow images—a herd of sculpted bronze steers in Pioneer Park, signature buildings by world-famous architects, fine and lesser arts and entertainment districts—but none creates a clear identity for the city. Dallas obsessively attempts to fill this void with bold statements and grand constructions reminiscent of other major metropolises.

In 1976, Bill Porterfield remarked in *The Book of Dallas* that the city's "foremost symbol is the downtown skyline."[85] The reflecting glass and steel skyline that the introduction to the TV show *Dallas* made famous, focusing visually on Reunion Tower and the adjacent Hyatt Hotel, became an icon for the series, but no more than a photo-op for the city. Most photographic images of Dallas adopt one of two conventional perspectives: downtown photographed from a distance as skyline or horizon, sometimes stylized in outline or abstraction, or shot from slightly above, to express the density, solidity, and architectural diversity of the core; or aerial photographs of the apparently boundless geographic spread of the built environment, with roads, housing, offices, and shopping centers stretching out beyond the edges of the frame.[86] These two images more often clash with each other like stereotypical urbs and suburbs than compose a whole. Neither point of view accords much distinction to Dallas when compared to other major cities. And both leave out vast portions of the population: those who identify with neither downtown nor suburbia, but with the marginal southern and western sections of the city.

Visual images play a significant role in the construction of cities, giving rise to real competition over cityscapes, especially skylines and skyscrapers. Boundaries and edges are equally important, although less often acknowledged. Psychologist and theorist James Hillman intriguingly addresses the problem Dallas has with images. "Images provide limits," he observes, and by conceiving of itself as "a city without limits" Dallas may be unable to imagine or reflect on itself. "No limits means no image. . . . The absence of both external and internal natural borders leaves a city without those obstacles and hindrances that force reflection."[87] Hillman identifies the underlying connection between Dallas's self-definition and its lack of integrating images. Metaphorically and physically (perhaps metaphysically, too), the city's failure of imagination is another face of its ceaseless self-promotion. The proliferation of disparate images does not meet the need for "external and internal natural borders." With this "absence," images grow and spread, out of control physically and cognitively, in an endeavor to signify progress and growth.

In a particularly telling effort to manufacture an image for the city, Dallas's leaders attempted to replicate an image from the past. From the 1930s through the 1950s, Dallas had a logo: Pegasus, the flying horse that revolved atop the Magnolia Building.

> As the headquarters of the Magnolia Oil Company (a predecessor of Mobil Oil), this 29-story landmark tower symbolized the growing influence of oil in the city's commercial activities. When completed, the Magnolia Building was the 16th tallest skyscraper in the U.S. and the tallest south of Philadelphia. It remained the tallest building in Dallas until World War II. In 1934, the Flying Red Horse, J. B. McMath, signmaker—a 30-foot high red neon revolving sign—was erected atop a 50-foot tower on the building's roof. "Pegasus" quickly became the city's unofficial trademark and has remained one of the most endearing features of the Dallas skyline.[88]

Pegasus was white at first, made of a quarter-mile of fluorescent glass tubing; later the winged steed was colored neon red. Reputed to be visible from the air as far away as Waco, it was used by pilots as a beacon for finding Dallas. This singular figure was a local and tourist favorite, frequently reproduced on postcards showing scenes of the city.

Now a replica of the original Pegasus sits in the shadow of taller buildings, hoisted onto its perch during a New Year's Eve party for forty thousand Dallasites as 1999 turned into 2000. A project to propagate Pegasus as the city's public art symbol followed, in large part by littering the landscape with hundreds of copies.[89] By April 2001, "Dallas Soars!" was advertising for sponsors to pay from $3000 to $8000 per Pegasus and seeking local artists to decorate two hundred fiberglass copies by the end of summer. "It's bringing more vision to our public arts program, it's a wonderful cultural tourism initiative and it's just plain fun. What better symbol

FIGURE 8. Magnolia Building with Pegasus, architects Alfred C. Blossom (New York), Lang and Witchell, built 1921. The revolving red horse was a Dallas landmark for decades. Much later, when it was obscured by taller buildings, Pegasus was proposed as an icon for the city. Photographer: Doug Tomlinson. From *Dallasights: An Anthology of Architecture and Open Spaces* (Dallas: American Institute of Architects, Dallas Chapter, 1978); reprinted with permission.

to have throughout the city than a soaring Pegasus?" declared Clayton Henry of the city's cultural affairs commission.[90] Peter Max came to town to paint a horse. By late fall 2002, 106 horses "stampeded" downtown Dallas; other replicas, officials unconvincingly claimed, were victims of September 11th's effect on budgets. Dallas Soars! declared the project a great success.[91] But the anticipated boost to the city's image and tourist revenues failed to materialize. The *Dallas Morning News's* Tom Sime reported that the Pegasus Project not only fell short of its goals but also absorbed several hundred thousand dollars of arts funding.

> At best, the project will break even. So it raises more questions than funds. Is this kind of gimmick really needed to generate interest in local arts? Couldn't the city push cultural tourism by promoting what's already here, instead of generating a herd of 150 pound tchotchkes for corporate self-promotion? Or by buying artists' own work, rather than forcing them to paint someone else's? Will tourists appreciate the sight of a horse in wire-rims and penny loafers next to downtown's John Neely Bryan log cabin? And was it Sept. 11 that deflated the project, or was it just a foolish idea in the first place? More important, could the thousands of dollars spent to create each of the big, winged baubles have been raised to actually support an arts organization needing money to pay actors, dancers, musicians, or creditors?[92]

Dallas's image makers refused to let Pegasus die. A $4 million proposal for eight hundred tourism signs included the winged horse as a recurring icon. Architectural designer John Bosio enthused, "This could become a standard for all of Dallas. This can have a significant impact on the image of downtown." How visitors would interpret the multiplying signs remained mysterious. The *News's* Tony Hartzel quipped, "Take heart, identity- and directionally challenged residents."[93]

The museum of Dallas under construction in the Old Red County Courthouse will display an old copy of the original Pegasus that long adorned a Mobil gas station. As for the Pegasus painted by Peter Max, the *Morning News* reported on May 7, 2003: "After a few months in the public eye, the high flying Pegasus disappeared, eventually landing in a Florida salvage yard. Last week, it popped up on eBay, with an opening bid of $1000." Attracting only three bidders, it went unsold.[94] Apparently, the attempt to create image, identity, and history with a cast-off corporate logo did not result in additions to Dallas's cultural bottom line.

A second example of Dallas's image and identity confusion concerns an existing work of public art. Dallasites justifiably are proud of their distinctive city hall building, whose most striking element is a broad slanted face of glass peering down onto the street. On the twentieth anniversary of its 1977 opening, architectural writer David Dillon proclaimed: "As a feat of engineering and symbol of a youthful city on the make, it is hard to beat." "The building is a byproduct of post-Kennedy-assassination Dallas, when the city was struggling to change its image as a backwater of bigotry and violence. Mayor Erik Jonsson focused on rebuilding its civic institutions,

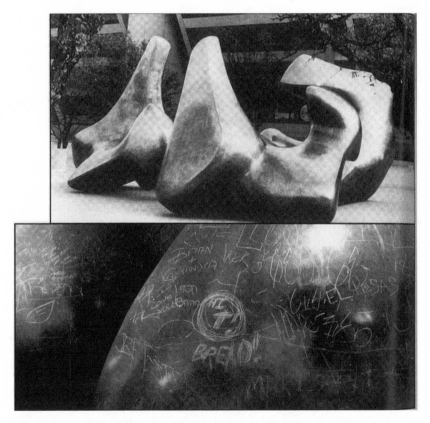

FIGURE 9. Henry Moore's *Dallas Piece*, vandalized, City Hall Plaza, 1996. Photographer: Darwin Payne. From Darwin Payne, *Big D: Triumphs and Troubles of an American Supercity in the Twentieth Century* (Dallas: Three Forks Press, 1995); reprinted with permission.

starting with City Hall, and hired an up-and-coming architect, Mr. Pei, to design it."[95] On its great plaza sits the "Dallas piece," Henry Moore's largest outdoor sculpture, a gift from an anonymous benefactor to the people of Dallas.

As the *Dallas Morning News* relates, "for some, the Moore sculpture is nothing more than a smooth surface for carving girlfriends' initials—or worse—relieving themselves." Criminal destructiveness is only part of a larger problem; as the *News*'s headline screams, "Vandalism of Henry Moore Sculpture also Defaces Dallas." The story raises long-standing questions about the nature of Dallas and Dallasites:

> Restoration of Mr. Moore's sculpture cannot restore the missing Dallas pride that has allowed this travesty to occur. Other cities display important outdoor works of art without the constant threat of vandalism. Why should it be happening in Dallas? . . . In many ways, the Moore sculpture reflects the maturation of Dallas from a railroad crossing . . . to an international center of commerce. When people are allowed to trash such an asset in the heart of the city, Dallas' reputation is defaced as well.[96]

In outrage and confusion, the collectivity that encompasses this place and its people is conflated with a nonrepresentational sculpture. Neither the image nor the "Dallas piece" itself can bear this burden. Dallas's pride becomes one with a handsome hunk of polished stone. However ironically and contradictorily, Dallas's inferiority to other unnamed cities is reaffirmed. The image of Dallas "defaced" confirms symbolically and materially the city's problems of image, identity, and insecurity.

Behind Big D's Texas-sized appearance and its vaunted pride, images less clear and positive, identities less secure and superior, sit uncomfortably with the city's legendary self-promotion and others' critiques of it. In "reading" Dallas, we contend with *many* Dallases, rather than a singular, homogeneous place that promoters pitch and sell. The problem of Dallas's preoccupation with images is neither new nor a consequence of the assassination.[97] The challenges the city faces—despite its desperate efforts to avoid confronting them—are a central part and product of Dallas's history. Defining the city by the "big three" icons, replicated logos, or imported monuments does not stem fears of falling or failing. Since the 1990s, as during the 1930s, Dallas has worried publicly about its future.[98] Pervasive anxiety makes it difficult for Dallas to reject, revise, or even laugh at self-definition through the Cowboys and the TV series. Dallas still lacks a widely shared collective identity. The consequences long have permeated the city's polity and economy as well as culture and society.

DALLAS DISCOURSE

In Dallas, verbal discourse is clearer and works more powerfully than visual images to proclaim an identity for the city. Dallas discourse is a distinctive way of speaking and writing about the city past and present employed mainly by Dallasites. (For a lexicon of Dallas-speak, see Figure 10.) It embraces most types of writing, nonfictional and fictional (though these are often difficult to distinguish), and most uses of rhetoric: modes, genres, tropes, style, diction, and vocabulary. Dallas discourse is peculiarly marked by hyperbole, paradox, and contradiction. In verbal constructions of Dallas, as in its visual images, promotion tends to substitute for description, aspiration for realization. Here, too, Dallas proclaims itself a "city with no limits."

Language is power. Sharpe and Wallock put it simply: "Our perceptions of the urban landscape are inseparable from the words we use to describe them and from the activities of reading, naming, and metaphorizing that make all our formulations possible."[99] Critical approaches to language make these functions visible, as Paul Bové explains: "The 'self-evident' and 'commonsensical' are what have the privilege of unnoticed power, and the power produces instruments of control. . . . Discourses and their related disciplines and institutions are functions of power: they distribute the effects of power . . . [which] must always be seen as 'a making possible.'"[100] In Dallas, dominant interests and institutions have, with considerable though imperfect success, camouflaged contests for power. The vocabulary, metaphors, and associations of Dallas-speak are seldom questioned, treated as if their meanings were transparent, and accepted as hegemonic. Dallas discourse draws on the language of sports and competition, especially winning and losing, rising and falling, securing or failing to achieve its great destiny; at times it takes on apocalyptic overtones. This eminently serviceable and flexible vocabulary has proved enormously influential, cognitively and in practice, imaginatively and materially.

The perspective of geographers Chris Philo and Jerry Kearns on "The

Names

Big D
A great city
America's city
Dallas is different
Metroplex
The city by the Trinity
Southern, western, southwestern, or midwestern
World-class, international, cosmopolitan

The City in Action

The can-do city, the city that works
The city with no limits
The city with no reason to be, no reason to exist
The Dallas Spirit
The Dallas Way
Growth, progress, momentum

Dallas, Inc.

The business of Dallas is business
The city as enterprise
The city that's run like a business

Dallas Past

Dallas as destiny
City with no history
"Dydamic men," "Yes and No Men"
"Dydamic days"

Dallas's Future in Prospect

Destined for greatness, reaching for greatness, poised for greatness
On the verge, at the edge, on the brink, at the threshold, at the moment of truth
City at the crossroads

FIGURE 10. A lexicon of Dallas-speak.

Promotion of Cities" is helpful in understanding the contours and uses of Dallas discourse: "Selling places is now a well-known feature of contemporary urban societies," they observe, recognizing political economy as one crucial context. Although addressing contemporary Anglo-American developments, their words also apply to Dallas over the long period of its rise to prominence: "Places are not so much presented as foci of attachment and concern, but as bundles of social and economic opportunity *competing* against one another in the open (and unregulated) *market* for a share of the capital investment cake (whether this be the investment of enterprise, tourists, local consumers or whatever). In this discourse places do indeed become 'commodified,' regarded as commodities to be consumed and as commodities that can be rendered attractive, advertised and marketed much as capitalists would any product."

The transformation of place into product pivots on the revisioning of space in word and image. Discourse of difference and similarity creates and constructs, re-creates and reconstructs Dallas and elsewhere:

> For places the idea is not so much that they be genuinely different from one another but that they harness their surface differences in order to make themselves in a very real sense nothing but "the same": to give themselves basically the same sort of attractive image—the same pleasant ensemble of motifs (cultural, historical, environmental, aesthetic) drained of anything controversial—with basically the same ambitions of sucking in capital so as make the place in question "richer" than the rest. . . . writers of promotional literatures find themselves extolling the supposedly "unique" qualities of supposedly "unique" places using an actually quite universal vocabulary of "better, bigger, more beautiful, more bountiful" and so on.[101]

For this heady competition, Dallas discourse seems unusually well crafted. The "lexicon of Dallas-speak" illustrates the workings of this process with respect to nicknames and synonyms, the city as successful business corporation, and claims to uniqueness. The production and circulation of images of difference and similarity work alongside the visual symbols of Big D to attempt to project Dallas to a high rank among metropolitan centers.

Simultaneously, as this exploration of Dallas's weak yet multifarious images has demonstrated, that very advantage can be seriously limiting. Geographer David Wilson refers to "the power of locally grounded metaphors" that "fashion social reality and . . . legitimate a dominant growth discourse and uneven development in the city." He describes their functioning: "These metaphors . . . contribute to an everyday consciousness—already steeped in decades of pernicious power relations, to be sure—that powerfully transforms, via a wealth of signifiers, a process that is negotiable, political, and contestable into an unproblematic neutral object."[102] In sum, discourse takes the outcome of historical struggle as a fait accompli and elevates it into an uncontestable, unquestionable presupposition, turning what is into what must be. Not only does this move obscure the contests for power that shaped the city in the past, but it forecloses public debate in the present.

In the lexicon of Dallas-speak, metaphors of growth and greatness serve effectively as a means of promotion, intended both to attract newcomers and to reassure insiders. At the same time, they function to conceal the process of choosing between alternative courses of action, to allow those in power to imagine their interests as synonymous with "the city as a whole," and to erase the many other people who are adversely affected by the decisions made by the few. This vocabulary and syntax take the present as leading inexorably to a future that is more and more of the same, without counting the costs or imagining other goals. Dallas-speak constitutes the material and ideological geography of the city. By scrutinizing it carefully, becoming aware of its contradictions as well as its limits, we can begin to imagine another way of looking at this place in time.

Constructing a City with No Limits

"Dallas is different": this refrain recurs in Dallas discourse as if difference were a state of being and not a claim that must constantly be touted and promoted by comparisons with other places. City boosters' persistent solicitation of support for this assertion of Dallas's exceptionalism suggests underlying questions about their sense of security and identity, lest the city's distinctiveness be erased or disparaged when measured against other cities and common patterns of urban growth. Claims of Dallas's differentness prove slippery when scrutinized, dissolving into multiple and often disconnected forms of uniqueness. Examining these claims requires an approach to cities in general and to Dallas in particular that emphasizes the basic constructedness of urban places and the play of similarities and differences among them.

We begin with a multilayered notion of cities that embraces physical constructions (built environments) and mental constructs (images and ideologies). People's views of the city are grounded in the particular locations they inhabit and the cultural perspectives they espouse. So there are many Dallases: not only distinct social, material, and geographic sections but also multiple images, ideologies, and historical experiences of the city, all competing for prominence and dominance.[1] The shape of the city shifts depending upon where people stand. The situated nature of perspective is fundamental both to the material construction and the cognitive or perceptual experience of place, especially in urban form. Different residents as well as observers view, understand, and regularly contend with different places all called Dallas. Diverse and contradictory experiences make a mockery of singular, homogeneous images of the city. No less important, the city's physical form and its imagined forms—both of which are sites of struggle—clash at many turns.

Claims of Dallas's difference and its constructedness appear everywhere, often as a pair. In "What Makes Dallas a Different City," journalist and local historian A. C. Greene writes, "Dallas, do not forget, was *created*, purely and simply. . . . It sprang from people's minds."[2] Elsewhere Greene writes, "Dallas has been the work of people—led since birth by a citizenry that believed a golden destiny was assigned the place where they lived. . . . This may sound like romantic nonsense, or the boosterism that characterized dozens of other western cities, but it has been a Dallas reality and must be accepted as a determining factor in the city's story."[3] In a postassassination autopsy of Dallas published in *Fortune,* Richard Smith remarked, "The city is really an enormous heavier-than-air machine that has got off the ground and been maintained in permanent flight by the efforts of its business leaders. Without those efforts the city would have experienced only scrub growth, for there was essentially no reason for Dallas' existence."[4]

Despite the divergence between Greene's affirmation of a democratic destiny and Smith's attribution of historical agency to business leadership, the two perspectives converge in the self-consciously constructed character of Dallas. The seemingly disparate dimensions of Dallas come together in the "construction" of a "city with no reason to exist" that also "has no limits," a city "destined for greatness" from its beginning that also has "no history." As Greene concedes and others who assert Dallas's definitive differentness concur, in its self-proclaimed inventedness, Dallas may be more like other cities than different from them. Compared with other cities, however, Dallas achieves distinction through endlessly reiterated claims of its uniqueness, the promotion of an ideology of growth, and the deliberate creation of a lexicon of discourses, myths, and visual symbols to explain its development. Ironically, in attempting to be different, Dallas strives to repeat the features of other major metropolises: historically, in acquiring status-giving and wealth-generating assets, architecture and planning, institutional development, political reform, and professional sports teams; and today, in downtown redevelopment, grand arenas and concert halls, arts and entertainment districts, "historic" districts, international airports, huge shopping malls, suburban "urban" centers, and professional sports teams. Rather than distinctive, this development is often mimetic, transplanting prestigious elements from other cities into a jumbled, ill-assorted landscape.

James Donald outlines a dynamic, multidimensional view of cities that blends distinct physical and conceptual perspectives: "To put it polemically, there is no such *thing* as a city. Rather *the city* designates the space produced by the interaction of historically and geographically specific institutions, social relations of production and reproduction, practices of government, firms and media of communication. . . . *The city*, then, is above all a representation. . . . I would argue that the city constitutes an *imagined environment*."[5] In the singular, "the city" appears as an invention that can mystify the social relations through which it is constituted. Sharon Zukin elaborates this active conceptualization of city construction:

> In a narrow sense, *landscape* represents the architecture of social class, gender, and race relations imposed by powerful institutions. In a broader sense, however, it connotes the entire panorama that we see: both the landscape of the powerful—cathedrals, factories, and skyscrapers—and the subordinate, resistant, or expressive vernacular of the powerless—village chapels, shantytowns, and tenements. A landscape mediates, both symbolically and materially, between the socio-spatial differentiation of capital implied by *market* and the socio-spatial homogeneity suggested by *place*. . . . Landscape also represents a microcosm of social relations.[6]

Materially and ideologically, Dallas landscapes are fractured along lines of class, race and ethnicity, culture, and power. Different lives are lived in what Zukin terms the "microcosm of social relations," different spaces within a place.

More than most places, I argue, Dallas is an invention, an imagined environment, mythologized and promoted in singular images. At the same time, it is fragmented and plural, a complicated and divided landscape. As Donald and Zukin remind us, constructions and representations are often difficult to read and sometimes deliberately obscured, marked by lies, errors, distortions, exaggerations, anachronisms, projections, and exclusions. Hana Wirth-Nesher's gloss on the situation of literary "modern urbanites" applies no less to Dallas's residents and observers: "Cities promise plenitude, but deliver inaccessibility. As a result, the urbanite, for better or for worse, is faced with a never-ending series of partial visibilities, of gaps. . . . The city dweller inevitably reconstructs the inaccessible in his imagination. . . . But the effect of inaccessibility differs with each city dweller. . . . The metropolis is rendered legible, then, by multiple acts of the imagination; it is constantly invented and reinvented."[7]

Together Donald, Zukin, and Wirth-Nesher suggest why and how constructs of cities are developed and diffused and gain recognition and hegemony, despite at least implicit conflicts among these constructs. Some conflicts are expressed in age-old dualisms of the city: good or evil, civilized or anarchic, public or private, collective or anomic, enriching or impoverishing, and always either rising or falling. By definition and usage, city constructs promise salience, clarity, and inclusiveness, often in the form of visible images or symbols that are relatively easy to hold in the mind's eye, reproduce, and communicate to others. Yet coherence often entails oversimplification and stylization, which verges on caricature. City constructions are necessarily built on partiality or bias, exclusions, and oppositions that generate conflicts unless continually repressed. Central to their cultural work is the claim of being more accurate, complete, and compelling than competing constructions. In practice, however, neither "truth" nor completeness is the primary task or the sole test of a city construct, a point often missed by those who write about Dallas past or present.

In Dallas, myth and ideology substitute for other kinds of knowledge, including historical research and searching criticism. As mental maps of the city that rationalize and naturalize its construction, they take the place of shared memory, collective experience, and understanding of the dynamics of change. At the same time, they preclude dissent, obstruct debate, and delegitimize alternative or opposing views, in part by providing a limited lexicon as a vehicle for discourse.[8] Historian John Findlay explains:

> Geographers have pointed out that urbanites tend to identify with a city at two different levels. . . . On one level, they identify with the city as an abstract whole and attach themselves to a symbol—such as its name, slogan, or chief landmark—that encapsulates the larger complexity. . . . On the second level, urbanites become familiar with those specific locales within the metropolis where they spend their time. To utilize Rapoport's terms . . . "users" gain a sense of control over the built environment by "taking possession" of those parts of it that are most relevant to their lives.

Findlay observes, "Mental maps screened out many aspects of city life and deepened the gulf between the social worlds of urbanities whose orbits did not intersect."[9] In the making of city constructs, some individuals' and groups' mental maps count more than others, not only as representations of the existing landscape but also as designs embedded in city plans. Those maps that won contests for power and authority are accepted as "normal" by many residents, while other residents feel alienated from those abstract images and dispossessed even in their familiar locales.

Dallas constructs weave complex relationships among citizens, dividing the city, concealing internal conflicts, and blurring history and myth. More than most major cities, I contend, Dallas's history plays a complex role in the formation of its mythology. While its origin myths are ahistorical, even antihistorical, they were constructed and reconstructed in specific historical contexts and do cultural work to rationalize the trajectory of Dallas's development as heroic and ordained, if not inevitable.

CONSTRUCTING DALLAS'S ORIGIN MYTHS

Other places have histories; Dallas has a record of economic expansion. Dallas's primary mythologies occupy the place usually accorded historical narratives, ascribing the city's growth to either impersonal economic factors or self-made business elites and simultaneously erasing and inscribing the relations of power that demonstrably shaped the city's development. In *City of Quartz*, a stunning exploration of Los Angeles, Mike Davis frames a connection that also holds for Dallas: "It is hard to avoid the conclusion that the paramount axis of cultural conflict . . . has always been the construction/interpretation of the *city myth*, which enters the material landscape as a design for speculation and domination (as Allan Seager suggests, 'not [as] fantasy imagined but [as] fantasy seen')."[10] Myths have high value, culturally, politically, and economically, so constructing and disseminating myths is a crucial historical struggle. Medieval cultural historian Gervase Rosser writes that constructing city myths gave people "a shared urban identity, located on common ground" but also a vocabulary for the struggle for power, and "the effect of these urban myths was not merely to reflect the cultural and social *status quo*, but to transform it."[11] The process of myth-making marks the key moments of Dallas history from its founding.

Having "no reason to exist," being "a city with no limits," fulfilling Dallas's "destiny," equating city survival and growth with the functions of a port, defining urban development as synonymous with expansion, and conducting "the business of the city like a business": all these planks in the platform of Dallas mythology present themselves as declarative historical statements regardless of their veracity, consistency, or completeness. These myths stimulate actions and policies that propel Dallas's development in the direction of those goals and expectations: continuous, even accelerating growth; local immunity from national and global economic currents; domination by the "free" marketplace; the equation of private profit with public benefit; and rule by exceptional business leadership. In Dallas, city myths masquerading as history enjoy almost uncontested rule.

Dallas is hardly unique in either the substitution of myth for history or the shaping influence of strong mythologies. The origin and resurrection myths of other major U.S. cities are more familiar to outsiders than Dallas's: the Dutch purchase of the island of Manhattan from Native Americans for trinkets of trivial value; Mrs. O'Leary's cow igniting the Great Chicago Fire that cleared the ground for a metropolis; Atlanta's rise from the ashes of the Civil War and Phoenix's from the desert; and Los Angeles as a magic land producing mass entertainment and an all-consuming suburban utopia. Myths of region include the "Mason-Dixon line," Midwest as "heartland," and the conjoined decay of the "Rustbelt" and advent of "Sunbelt" cities. None of those common examples features a city myth as locally prominent, singular, or powerful as Dallas's. Indeed, denizens of these places often laugh at these myths as the delusions of outsiders; Los Angeles as "Tinseltown" and Atlanta as "the city too busy to hate" are acknowledged locally as mythical images. In Dallas, the dominant myths remain confused with history and retain their shaping power; in the prevailing view, Dallas is fundamentally autonomous, self-formed, and separate from larger currents of history.

The responsibility for this curious cultural circumstance rests in part with Dallas's promoters, including business elites and the media, and Dallas's historians, who have too often been content to salute rather than scrutinize city myths. The first histories of Dallas were written by prominent citizens, journalists, or local "men of letters" who valued the telling of a good story but who were no less concerned with promoting their city.[12] Current historians suffer from an equally debilitating though opposite agenda as they seek to "disprove myth" with the "facts" in pursuit of the "true" story. Important as it is to establish the limits of myths, propose alternative narratives, and offer causal explanations, persistent origin myths are too important simply to be disproved and dismissed. An overly narrow and misconceived search for fact as opposed to myth excludes the enormous power of myth in making history.

Historian Patricia Hill has demonstrated that the prevailing myth of Dallas's history—great men making a great city out of nothing but sheer willfulness—was elaborated amid the difficult political-economic conditions of fear and crisis during the 1920s and 1930s and read back into Dallas's past.[13] The city "with no reason to exist" foreshortened the chronological and historical span of Dallas's development and obscured key contexts of its founding. The city's first origin myth, "Dallas as destiny," emerged during the mid-nineteenth century and remained influential for a century. Indeed, contemporary critiques of the second myth tend to return, however unconsciously, to the first. In his recent brief history of Dallas, Michael Hazel asserts, "In the last half century, a popular myth has arisen that Dallas is an 'accidental' city, one with no obvious reason for being. . . . Dallas's location, its natural resources, and even its climate have all played key roles in its development. . . . The history of Dallas is really a story about how individuals capitalized on the city's natural assets, especially its geographic centrality in a rapidly developing transportation network, to create a major city."[14] This tale omits the colorful characters who created "the city with no reason to exist," conflating it with an "accidental city" and ascribing agency to timeless, impersonal geopolitical factors. More troubling is this account's implicit endorsement of "Dallas as destiny," with a nod toward great civic and economic leaders redolent of the very myth avowedly being challenged. It entirely fails to expand the scope for Dallas history to embrace a larger active population and a more complex conception of historical change. Two seemingly contradictory myths of Dallas's origin can coexist and contribute toward a unitary vision of the city's rise to greatness.

However misleading these myths may be, over a century or more dominant groups have wielded them to promote public consent and exert significant influence in the shaping of Dallas. The most important questions about social and cultural myths address their uses and abuses and their social consequences, not merely their truth or accuracy. Raymond Williams, the key theorist of cultural Marxism, recognized myths as "an account of origins" and "an active form of social organization."[15] Historian William McNeill elaborates, "Myth and history are close kin inasmuch as both explain how things got to the way they are by telling some sort of story." Origin myths rationalize the way things are as the way they have to be and serve to reproduce the status quo. "Without such social cement no group can long preserve itself," McNeill concludes.[16]

The view of Dallas as "destined for greatness" by the combination of the natural advantages offered by its geographic location and the entrepreneurial vigor of the city's founders was planted in the historic soil of the first generations of Dallasites. Looking back on two generations of Anglo urban settlement, the 1892 *Memorial and Biographical History of Dallas County, Texas* proudly embraced and inflated that early history, proclaiming "It has been the pleasure of a few of these pioneers to behold their little village nestling on the east banks of the Trinity transformed into a most magnificent city . . . the metropolis of the Southwest."[17] Claiming a central location and commercial development comparable to Chicago's, Dallas's early narrators mythically—and at that time quite improbably—pointed to a grand future stated in the imperative: the city "must gradually expand into more mammoth proportions." The 1892 *History* quoted one prominent citizen who prophesied a metropolitan hinterland encompassing "the Territories and States to the north and northwest of us . . . and the imperial domain of Mexico" all looking to Dallas "for raw materials and manufactured products as well, thus making it a veritable New York for all this portion of the continent."[18] The business of urban boosterism produced and circulated images of a place's potential that promoted its economic development. The hype that enveloped Dallas could be a liability as well as an asset, however. Some newcomers had their hopes dashed when they actually confronted the place. In 1844, John Billingsley from Missouri found on his arrival that his "imaginary town had vanished," with his expectations only "one of my air castles that was destined to fall to the ground."[19]

According to the 1892 *History*, the advent of railroad connections was the definitive event that foretold Dallas's destiny:

> The future for Dallas as a great city in the Southwest first dawned upon the citizens when the two great railroad lines, the Missouri Pacific and the Houston & Texas Central arrived and intersected each other in the then small town of Dallas, in 1872. This was the beginning of that most marvelous growth. . . .

Being centrally situated as it is, without any strong commercial competitors near by, and in one of the most fertile sections of the country in America, and being the commercial, manufacturing and distributing center of Texas . . . it is but natural for it to attract attention.[20]

Lawyer John Milton McCoy moved to Dallas from Indiana in 1870. In letters to his family, McCoy's initial subdued descriptions and disappointed expectations shifted to prophetic myth-making as he recorded the intertwining of everyday realities with great hopes and disorderly growth with both pastoral and urban visions. In December 1871, he wrote, "Dallas is improving very rapidly. The prospects now are very flattering indeed. . . . The people are crazy, talking of Dallas being the Indianapolis of Texas for a railroad center." In April 1872, he predicted, "Within a year from now, Dallas will be quite a city."[21]

As the railroads arrived in July 1872, McCoy's promise of progress erupted in hyperbolic splendor and gendered mythic terms:

Dallas is to be grinned at no longer as a one horse town. It has put away its petticoats and donned yesterday a new pair of "britches" with pockets and a cigar in its mouth, and is no longer a boy—a full man in feeling, strides and gas. Talk about your Baltimores, New York and Philadelphia and leave Dallas out of the ring if you dare. Baltimore is no more of a "Hub," New York is no more of a "Street" and [a] Philadelphia lawyer isn't any sharper in his own estimation than Dallas, Dallas, the Hub Dallas, the crescent of the southwest, Dallas the bright spot of the Lone Star, Dallas the coming City of Texas, the center of the grand Eldorado of the South.[22]

The list of older cities to be envied, mimicked, and rivaled, along with the litany of slogans, became persistent features of Dallas boosterism.

Taken as description, McCoy's enthusiasm is misplaced. By 1880, the city's population barely exceeded ten thousand. This was no Baltimore, Philadelphia, or New York, let alone El Dorado. Read as a stanza evoking Dallas's presumed destiny—a myth in service of the past and the future—McCoy's flight was more than fancy. It was foundational and transitional, mythically shaping and promoting images, ideologies, and visions, just as the city of Dallas was itself building, albeit on a less exalted scale.

In 1893, looking to the future with nary a glance at the past, Dallas's *Souvenir Guide with Directory* took flight into prophetic vision:

Amazed, [the dreamer] beholds . . . a landscape beauteous with thrifty farms, and luxuriant crops . . . netted with railways, telegraph and telephone lines . . . and navig'ble streams . . . and above all, the *City of Dallas* near by, with its tall spires and smoking factories, mammoth stores and beautiful homes, where the shrill whistle of the steamers Harvey and Dallas, foretells of that halcyon time, when the metropolis shall send her products, at water rates, to the seaboard and the world. . . . Great enterprises and boundless public spirit were stamped on every feature of the city. Enterprise and industry have achieved results as startling as the wave of the magician's wand, and in this atom of time has sprung up, as if it were by magic, a city with a population of 61,855 souls. Nor had the march of development slackened, but the watch-word is still "Onward!" and Dallas is ranked among the largest and most progressive cities of the South.[23]

FIGURE 11. Launched in 1892, the snagboat *Dallas of Dallas* is shown trying to clear out a raft on the Trinity River. The boat was broken up in 1898. From the collections of the Texas/Dallas History and Archives Division, Dallas Public Library.

FIGURE 12. Thousands celebrated when the steamboat *Harvey* arrived in Galveston from Dallas in 1893. From the collections of the Texas/Dallas History and Archives Division, Dallas Public Library.

The 1894 *Souvenir Guide* presented its mythic message as transitional. Dallas's road to success through industry and enterprise was confidently asserted. But this great commercial potential could be realized only with the development of water transportation: "As a manufacturing and industrial center, Dallas presents superior advantages. Its geographical location will soon be able to give it a water route, via the Trinity river, to the sea, thus affording her greater facilities for the transportation of her products, than any other section in the great Southwest."[24] However long awaited, Port Dallas never materialized. The dream of a water route linking the city to the sea persisted, essential as it was to contemporary notions of urban dominance.

In 1894, the lack of waterway and port was a problem to be solved practically through engineering. From the very founding of permanent white settlement, visions of Dallas's development had been endowed with the prospects of a port. John Neely Bryan's original site sat at a ford on the Trinity River. Ferry service preceded bridge building. For decades, plan followed plan to transform river and city together. In 1868 *Job Boat No. 1,* the first steamboat to travel from Galveston to Dallas, took more than seven months for the journey. In 1893, the *H.A. Harvey* reached Dallas from Galveston in sixty-seven days. But, owing to low water levels and numerous snags that regularly stranded even shallow boats, regular trips were never achieved.

The future so confidently anticipated in 1894 failed to materialize. As the mirage of a port evaporated, leaving a landlocked city, the myth of Dallas had to change as well. Yet even today, Dallas boosters remain enthralled by certain aspects of this first myth, continually hatching schemes to "improve" the riverfront. The image of a recreational park along the river has taken the waterway's place in contemporary dreams of urban planning and city boosting. Grand designs tend to ignore the stubborn combination of recurrent flooding and inadequate supplies of fresh water that presents the low-lying city with pressing practical problems today. In the 1980s, planners semiseriously proposed turning downtown Dallas into a festival harborfront similar to Richard Rouse's developments in Boston and Baltimore by digging a huge ditch beside the site of the Farmers' Market and filling it with water.[25] Other dreams for developing the Trinity waterfront seek to crown the meandering, often dry riverbed with soaring bridges designed by famed architect Santiago Calatrava, an extravagant but appealing solution to a nonexistent problem. Copying other cities in order to achieve distinction is as self-defeating as imagining the Trinity as a navigable waterway. Dallas has taken definite steps toward realizing this dream, taking bids for Interstate highway bridges and proposals to develop the waterfront and rechannel the river into a Trinity Lake near downtown.[26] Now, as then, Dallas's boosters and mythmakers believe that to be without a waterway diminishes the city.

Gradually, over a period of several decades, an alternative mythic construction crystallized and gained hegemony in Dallas. The second origin myth emanated from the first in two ways: the dream of a port obscured the historical significance of a trade and exchange center and the railroads in the making of Dallas, and its dissolution portended ill for the city's imagined future. As faith in the mythic complex of "Dallas as destiny" ebbed amid the economic instability and political turmoil of the early twentieth century, the second origin myth emerged: Dallas had "no reason to exist." A significant revision, if not outright contradiction, of the previous origin myth, the second began to eclipse the first as the city's business leaders sought to restore confidence and impose their own vision of social order and urban development in the 1930s. If Dallas in fact lacked the physical means to create a navigable waterway to the Gulf of Mexico, then, it was reasoned, the city lacked any natural and historical basis for urban development.

In the newer construction, the city's successes came despite having "no reason to be" in terms of nature, geography, and history, an origin story that magnified the achievements of Dallas's leaders. The second myth was even more misleading and inaccurate, but no less powerful than the first as an explanation for the city's growth and a rationale for its extension. The rise and progress of a city with "no reason to exist" emphasized the exceptional determination, power, and skill—as well as sheer good luck— of Dallas's business and civic leaders and their human agency in triumphing over other cities with greater natural advantages. This origin myth charted the coalescence of a self-conscious group of political-economic titans as self-proclaimed fact, legend, and legacy. It simplified the story, substituting a shiny new myth for the failures of the old as chronic disappointments and stubborn contradictions were repressed, even deliberately forgotten. This ideology generated images and rhetoric well suited for promoting the city on the national stage and for maintaining elite hegemony at home.

Before the mid-1930s, Dallas's elite was not the cohesive, well-organized class that it became during that crucial decade. The creation of the new myth of Dallas's development was part of the social and cultural process of leadership or dominant class formation, a topic still in need of detailed study.[27] What we know about the city's political history suggests that this second origin myth exaggerates, at least in retrospect, the hegemonic power of the elite whose rule it rationalized.[28] The cast of central characters includes G. B. Dealey of the *Dallas Morning News,* banker and four-term mayor Robert L. Thornton, city building bankers Nathan Adams and Fred Florence, theatre chain owner Karl Hoblitzelle, and, later, mayor and Texas Instruments founder J. Erik Jonsson and Stanley Marcus of Neiman Marcus, the city's signature department store. These men—for it was *men* who had their hands on the levers of corporate power[29]—stood closest to the major modes of communication, from the Dallas dailies to national financial and cultural publications. The ideological thrust from this construction of the origin myth was powerful in its simplicity and appeal, and it was attractive to local and national audiences eager to have their images of the American urban dream, the "self-made" upwardly mobile city, confirmed and polished. Here, too, Dallas sought to be—or at least to appear to be— "America's city."[30]

Holland McCombs and William F. Whyte of *Fortune* magazine breathtakingly drafted the second myth's classic crystallization in 1949:

> Properly, it never should have become a city. Founded for no ascertainable reason, in 1841 on a flat piece of blackland soil that grew nothing much but cotton, Dallas was set astride no natural routes of trade. . . . There was no port nearby. Beneath the city were none of the raw materials—the oil, gas, and sulfur—that made other Texas cities rich. . . . The climate in summer is practically unendurable. Yet there Dallas stands—its skyscrapers soaring abruptly up from the blackland like Maxfield Parrish castles, and so wildly, improbably successful that the stranger leaves it feeling as if he had been suspended in a vast hyperbole. It is the Athens of the Southwest, the undisputed leader of finance, insurance, distribution, culture, and fashion for this land of the super-Americans. . . . Everything in Dallas is bigger and better. . . . And in all of these things, it is, finally, a monument to sheer determination. Dallas doesn't owe a thing to accident, nature, or inevitability.[31]

In this commonsensical but erroneous understanding of urban history and economic development, Dallas's many natural advantages and its founding and growth as a crossroads city were disregarded. The absence of a water port and natural resources such as oil or minerals was seen as evidence that there was *no* reason for the city to become a successful metropolis, ignoring the presence of railroad connections and the proximity of a vast prairie suited to the extraction of cotton and oil. The leap from destiny to willful decision was made in a single bound: Dallas "is what it is . . . because the men of Dallas damn well planned it that way."[32]

Dallas's second creation myth was distributed in colorful copy, regularly quoted and widely reproduced. It became a truism: "Most cities are born out of geographic good fortune. They're located at natural seaports or along waterways. But Dallas was born out of nowhere, shaped out of dreams."[33] Although clearly related to the material making of the city, this process of construction assumed a quasi-autonomous existence.

The *Fortune*-telling by McCombs and Whyte in 1949 is the most famous manifesto of the city's second creation myth, but many versions were distributed from the 1920s to the present. The dramatic transformation of Dallas origin myths is already visible in a 1925 promotional guide, which differs markedly in ideology, vision, and discourse from the 1894 *Souvenir Guide* and 1892 *Memorial and Biographical History.* These compendia were printed for sale in the marketplace or published by subscription as "mug books" loaded with names and capsule biographies, family histories, and pictures of "pioneer settlers." The 1925 guide, sponsored by the Republic Bank, is less specific about people and place, exemplifying an emerging genre of publications distributed widely by city financiers in hopes of inducing new and growing business to locate there. "The remarkable rise of Dallas . . . is still more remarkable when the fact is considered that Dallas is an inland city with no great natural waterway or unusual advantage except the fertility of the soil in the surrounding territory. The growth of the 'Metropolis of the Southwest' can only be attributed to the spirit and industry of its inhabitants and to their unbounded faith in the future of their city."[34] This orientation to the future made no reference to the past and Dallas's "history as destiny"; progress is asserted as an achievement based on nothing more—and demanding nothing less—than absolute faith in the city as enterprise.

This radical revision of the mythic narrative of Dallas's development took place under particular historical conditions during the 1910s, 1920s, and 1930s. According to historian Patricia Hill, "The elite that matured in the 1920s and consolidated its power with the formation of the Dallas Citizens Council in 1937 put an abrupt end to . . . internecine feuding. . . . It relied on civic boosterism, control of the media, the mythology of frontier capitalism, prejudices and fears of the largely native, white population, and brutal repression to isolate and marginalize those who challenged its hegemony." Hill explains, "A series of bitter conflicts in the years following World War I convinced a new generation of business leaders that Dallas's commercial growth was threatened by the unruly nature of urban affairs."[35] The sources of turmoil included real and perceived problems in the structure and conduct of local government; the prominence and popularity of the Ku Klux Klan, which enjoyed some elite support; growing community support for organized labor, social democrats, and socialists, along with progressive concerns about social welfare, social reform, and social justice;

a visible urban popular culture with interracial contact and prominent African American contributions, particularly in music and entertainment; and anxieties about proper orderly public behavior suitable for a city striving for regional economic and cultural domination and seeking national recognition. Inseparably connected to these troublesome issues were rising concerns about the physical city, pivoting around the control of growth and civic beautification, planning, zoning, public health and related reforms, transportation, institutional and infrastructural development, and other long-term goals.[36]

The Great Depression heightened fears and made the quest for stability and growth at home and national recognition an even greater priority. The formation of the Dallas Citizens Council, bringing together the "dydamic" businessmen who held the power to say "yes and no" to any public proposal, neatly tied up elite control of the city. Dallas leaders' coup in securing the city's selection as host of the 1936 Texas Centennial Exposition—despite the fact that Dallas had not even existed in 1836—represented a political triumph and promotional success. R. L. Thornton, Dallas promoter without peer, led both efforts with strong support from Dealey and his *Dallas Morning News*. The Centennial, it was said, introduced Texas, and Dallas, to the nation.[37]

Reflecting on this triumph in 1956, journalist Stanley Walker related the complications, his ironic humor and unself-conscious biases telling perhaps more than he intended. Dallas, he said,

> lacks spectacular landmarks. No Golden Gate. No Pike's Peak. No romantic ruins such as the French Quarter of New Orleans, and no picaroon to match Jean LaFitte. The Trinity [River] falls somewhat short of the Hudson. No desert, and, therefore, nothing to compare with Phoenix or Palm Springs. . . . Poor old Dallas! The Indians who once lived at the Three Forks were simple agriculturists, pleasant dullards, far removed from the history-making Sioux. Few desperadoes except such as the repellent Clyde Barrow and Bonnie Parker. . . . Even the Dallas poets, doing their best, were under an extreme handicap because bluebonnets do not flourish in the Dallas countryside. No Alamo. No San Jacinto. No Hornsby's Bend. Even the founder of Dallas, John Neely Bryan, although he had many excellent qualities and was in part at least a spiritual brother of the dynamic Men of Vision who were to come later, fell somewhat short of greatness and was sadly deficient in flamboyant qualities.[38]

Without natural or historical claims to distinction, Dallas had to stake its claim on other grounds.

Walker narrated Dallas's quest to host the 1936 Texas Centennial Exposition, romantically transforming the Dallas delegation's success at negotiation and strong-arming into glorious myth even as he comments on a humorous irony: Dallas didn't exist in 1836. But no matter: "Ridden by an inferiority complex, gnawed by vague feelings of guilt, apologetic for their presumption—they did their best. . . . They won. It was one of the finest and most characteristically audacious things any group ever did for Dallas." Walker neglected to mention how many millions of dollars Dallas leaders offered up to secure the Fair.

FIGURE 13. Dallas County Courthouse with John Neely Bryan cabin, ca. 1936–42. From Maxine Holmes and Gerald D. Saxon, eds., *WPA Dallas Guide and History* (Denton: Dallas Public Library and Texas Center for the Book, University of North Texas Press, 1992).

Redefining the origin myth, Dallas's leaders in effect remade the city, giving it as well as themselves a renaissance or rebirth. As Thornton put it, "The
charge against Dallas was that we had no history. My reply was: The people
in general weren't looking for history—they could find it in books and museums. What they wanted was progress. I pointed out that while we didn't
have any history in Dallas, we had all the other ingredients."[39] With his distinctive down-home directness, Thornton declared, "I believe it can safely
be said that Dallas all along through its growth and progress has been truly
a man- and woman-made city, where men were as patriotic to city as to
country, where men pushed forward, where leaders died in the harness as
city builders."[40] The equation of business elites with city leaders and the
conflation of civic loyalty with patriotism made faith in "the city as enterprise" akin to evangelical religion, which was broadly and deeply rooted in
the culture. *Fortune* and other national media expressed this view in more
erudite, extravagant prose and broadcast it to the nation and beyond. Elements of Texas scale, wealth, and audacity neatly blended with notions of
Dallas sophistication, which competed with less positive images of violence,
enforced homogeneity, and narrow conservatism. The gloss on Dallas's public image concealed and repressed as much as it proclaimed and enforced.

With this telling shift in city myths came revisions of Dallas's dominant
ideology, images, and rhetoric. Progress was the key plank in the elite's ideological platform for the city they claimed as their own. If Dallas had no
reason to exist and no history, then its great achievements depended mainly
on its leaders.[41] A city without any geographical grounding becomes "a city
with no limits," constructed by a kind of agency that knows no bounds. A
city with no limits is also a polity whose rulers are not accountable to its
citizens. As this lexicon of Dallas developed, the construct of "a city with
no reason to exist" licensed elite-dominated growth and legitimated the
presumption that, unfettered, this "can-do" metropolis had only its future
to preserve. To a gospel of progress thus framed, as Thornton decreed, history held little interest. This ballad of Dallas's epochal self-creation appears
across all genres of writing about the city, from the pens of historians who
might be expected to know better to those of journalists, memoirists, promoters, and literary folk.[42] "No reason to be" supplies grist for even more
mills than "Dallas as destiny," in part because it is so flexible and adapt-
able in legitimating actions, reactions, and inactions, and in underwriting
narratives of city struggle and triumph.

More than half a century after Thornton's dictum, the *Dallas Morning News* trumpeted: "This City Was Built of Nowhere on Pure Guts, Sweat and Determination. When We Stand Together, There's Nothing We Can't Do."[43] In this version of the mythology and ideology of Dallas's origins, the *News* loses sight of the stuff of history—its framing contexts, the discipline of time, space, and human possibilities—as well as historical facts that contradict such stories.[44] Working to "free" Dallas from its actual history, both myths—the historical determinist and the antihistorical determinist— ignore, abuse, and attempt to replace history.

At the beginning of the twenty-first century, as at the end of the nineteenth, landlocked Dallas still lacks a waterfront, despite the prophetic visions and practical plans of its promoters. The first origin myth, of Dallas as destined for greatness, went aground on the shoals of shallow water, as well as the rising demands of a perceived "urban crisis" in the early twentieth century. The second creation myth, of Dallas as a city with "no reason to exist," still demands that Dallas move heaven and earth to construct itself in the image of waterfront greatness, or at least as a simulacrum of a world-class port. Promoters dream of a watery theme park and bridges soaring over nothing. The recurrence of this dream suggests that when this kind of history repeats itself, tragedy returns as farce.

The direct contribution of the second origin myth to city building seems more negative than positive: efforts without results, costs without returns, expectations without satisfactions, and political neglect of social and economic inequalities despite a century and a half of "wet dreams." According to the myth, if Dallas's leaders keep trying—and citizenry and polity gratefully accept their efforts—greatness will follow, even if an array of racial, ethnic, legal, educational, economic, and physical problems still threaten the city.

THE POWER OF MYTH IN THE CONSTRUCTION OF DALLAS

Dallas's ahistorical origin myths generate curious distortions, as well as outright denials, of its history. The dominant myths are echoed in popular books, magazines, and media treatments that trivialize and caricature what fragments of history they include.[45] As A. C. Greene recognizes, "Dallas overlooks history by claiming it has none. Its leaders and planners tend to accept this simplification at face value, confusing history and nostalgia." Beyond that confusion lies a real fear of history, which underwrites insecurity: "Dallas is a self-made society with lingering frontier doubts of its own worthiness," Greene observes.[46] Associating the myth of a city with "no reason to exist" with the claim that Dallasites are "heirs to a rugged frontier tradition," *D Magazine* founder Wick Allison posits another element of civic insecurity in Dallas's topography: "Because every newcomer to Dallas is so immediately unimpressed with our natural terrain, or lack of it, that an explanation for the existence of a boomtown in the middle of it seems improbable; only the cliché suffices."[47]

Despite their criticism of certain common Dallas beliefs, both Allison and Greene accept ahistorical and reductionist explanations of Dallas's development that in effect deny the city a history of its own.[48] Instead of history as the word is usually understood, Greene enthuses, "Dallas has exuberance. . . . call it class or call it put-on. Both terms miss the mark, by and large. I will use *excitement* because it avoids setting up standards." This spirit of self-promotion "is undefinable; it can be maddening—but it is all the history Dallas has."[49] Refuting that origin myth serves Dallas little better. "The present-day Dallas mythology, which maintains that the city came out of nowhere and had no real reason for being, simply ignores the inevitability of Bryan's choice," asserts William McDonald in a book sponsored by the Dallas Historical Society.[50] In this formulation, sweeping notions of inevitability undercut the stated import of historical origins. History is displaced again, replaced by a belief in inescapable destiny.

Regardless of which myth commentators choose, the slogan remains: Dallas has no history. For more than a century, promoters have claimed that Dallas is a "young city," still growing up, insufficiently mature or complete to have a history.[51] To many, the slogan means that historical reflection must wait while Dallasites busily pursue progress. This stance neglects both the difference that placing the contemporary city in historical perspective might make to Dallas's development and the contribution that understanding the history of Dallas might make to Americans' comprehension of our urban history from the nineteenth century to the present.

As myth substitutes for history, Dallas's origins are obscured.[52] With geographic advantages, location at a crossroads, and connections east and north as well as west and south, Dallas was born urban. Its white American founders had great dreams of commercial and real estate development, envisioning their city as an engine for the development of its agricultural hinterland and as a node in a national urban network. Dallas shared in the mid-nineteenth-century pattern of ambitious town foundings across the Midwest and West, characterized by frank boosterism and fierce competition.[53] Dichotomous portrayals of rural versus urban, commercial, or industrial lose sight of formative interrelationships. Comparison among cities was the name of the game, promoting salutary emulation and a drive toward distinction, as well as bankruptcy and failure for some towns. Always a city of migrants, Dallas rhetorically moves itself back and forth between the South, the Southwest, and the West as occasion and promotion require, while denying its historically formative location in the southern Midwest. Although it has always been intricately tied to the region, nation, and world by transportation and communications and their technologies, by financial and commercial as well as cultural connections, Dallas projects an image of political-economic autonomy.

In the light of myth, a single hue and a sense of linear progress and prosperity dominate the Dallas canvas, instead of a multifaceted history of struggles, advances and steps backward, with varied contributions from diverse persons who differ by gender, race, ethnicity, class, chances for success, and luck, pluck, and influence. A narrowly cast representation of commerce and the conspicuous consumption of its rewards appear as the stuff of Dallas. Neiman Marcus, image-maker par excellence, long stood as a major symbol of Dallas to those outside the city and to many Dallasites as well, combining wealth and style with a more or less respectable dose of Texas scale and hype.[54] Typically, Dallas is identified with only one part of its population and its geographic region: well-to-do, primarily Anglo, middle- to upper-class North Dallas.[55] African Americans and Hispanic Americans find no place in most representations, and South and West Dallas are marginalized or forgotten, except when entangled with racial and ethnic conflicts that cannot be repressed. The effort in the mid-1980s to prevent the publication of journalist Jim Schutze's book *The Accommodation: The Politics of Race in an American City* owing to fear that it would blemish Dallas's image is but one sad example of this repression.[56]

Dallas's origin myths contribute, materially and rhetorically, to the city's making and shaping. I consider the consequences of the substitution of myth and ideology for history in two distinct, but interconnected, dimensions: persistent patterns and recurrent problems in the construction of the

urban fabric, along with the anxieties that great expectations inevitably generate; and the curious propensity to invent a new past in a place from which
history has been banished.

City myths inspire and shape urban development projects and serve as
active facilitators of city construction, both discursive and physical. Dallas's two major myths spurred growth, whether seen as inevitable or willful. Transportation via rail, road, and air, if not water, is the most salient
example spanning the city's history. In the railroad era, Union Station served
as Dallas's port to the world; now Dallas/Fort Worth International Airport has taken over that role. The myth of Dallas's destiny stimulated the
city's advance as marketplace and service center for a rich and developing
hinterland, from processing, manufacturing, and distribution to finance,
administration, marketing, and an endless stream of services, as the key
commodities shifted from cotton to oil and high technologies.

Here, as elsewhere, federally funded interstate highways built to facilitate intercity transport promoted the decentralization of residential and
commercial development, leapfrogging what edges the city once had and
drawing the surrounding prairies into the intracity web. The shift from a
myth that focused the destiny of the city on its role as a central place to a
myth that projected the city outward in space by an act of will enabled
promoters to seize the opportunities for profitable expansion offered by new
modes of transport.

The myth of self-creation helped Dallas's boosters to attract or capture
migrating people, businesses, and other organizations, with major waves
of corporate arrivals in the 1940s and the 1970s–80s. Both myths authorized Dallas's entrepreneurs and city builders to aim high and legitimated
the triumphs they achieved through questionable means, as by stealth and
purchase they secured such trophies as railway terminals, a regional branch
of the Federal Reserve Bank, a Ford auto plant, and an aircraft manufacturer. In Dallas, as elsewhere, competition was never as free as it was imagined to be. The city myths prompted Dallasites to seek—though often
tardily and incompletely—the varied social and cultural accoutrements of
a metropolis.

Dallas residents who buy into the prevailing ideology see the city as approaching metropolitan, even cosmopolitan, "greatness," playing a role central to its state, region, nation, and then the world. Measuring Dallas against
other cities that excel on all these scales, city builders compile a wish list

of institutions and amenities that they presume greatness requires. "A great city needs a great _____" is the familiar refrain, plastered on billboards and broadcast in campaigns, as if these imported improvements are the ingredients of distinction. Examining the process of constructing Dallas reveals characteristic approaches to city building that shed light on how the origin myth and ideology of growth shape and limit development, creating visible distortions that the powerful refuse to acknowledge but cannot avoid.

In historical perspective and political-economic context, the process of city building in Dallas exhibits these key characteristics: development by stealth and purchase, inducing major assets to locate in Dallas by persuasion, subsidy, or outright theft; development by denial, malign neglect, and destruction of the city's environment, topography, and history, including both the material city and the city of memory; development by mimesis, imitating or appropriating planning, structural, design, and stylistic elements deemed unmistakably urban from other cities; and development by monumentalism, concentrating on major visible structures and centralized institutions to the neglect of basic infrastructure and public services, fragmenting the city and producing unequal returns for different districts and groups. Together, these approaches to city building produce a pastiche that lacks coherence and fails to distinguish Dallas from other cities, generating an anxiety-inducing gap between its aspirations and achievements and profound alienation among its residents.

Despite grand predictions, economic growth did not accord Dallas the cultural or economic standing of a national center by the 1920s or an international metropolis by the 1980s, and disappointment predictably followed. Jealousies intermingled with insecurity as Dallas's "city envy" found newer and bigger targets. Escalating chronologically from regional to national and international scales, the cities that Dallas boosters have sought to rival extend from such midwestern centers as St. Louis, Kansas City, and Chicago to Sunbelt cities such as Atlanta, Miami, and Los Angeles, as well as such continental stars as San Francisco and New York, Toronto and Vancouver. Houston, San Antonio, and Fort Worth are longtime, too-close competitors, taken alternately as objects of envious emulation and as targets of efforts to create factitious distinctions between Dallas and these historically different Texan places.[57]

Sweeping popular conceptions of predestined or willfully projected urban growth create expectations that are almost always impossible to meet. In creating great expectations without providing any means to achieve them, Dallas's origin myths heighten fears of falling short or failing. Pervasive insecurity gives rise to overstatements and defensiveness that often turns aggressive. These myths were designed in part to combat fears of failure, yet their repetition only raises the stakes. Uncritical faith in unfettered destiny or unchecked entrepreneurial agency leads to frustration and conflict, especially when widely diffused myths assume the form and function of ideological belief. The ceaseless promotion of Dallas, especially by business elites and the media, has generated a widespread conviction that the city's very existence depends on constant growth and Dallas is immune from national economic downturns. Bust never follows boom in Dallas, it would appear. When recession strikes, or political conflict flares, Dallas promoters express surprise and dismay. Even investors do not expect Dallas to be buffeted like other cities, and speculation uncushioned by hedging can lead to financial losses.[58] The unfounded notion that Dallas is exempt from the downside of the economic trends its elite promotes, such as the globalization of manufacturing and information technologies, only exacerbates its insecurity.

The promised rewards of urban development have never been shared with the majority of Dallasites.[59] Overwhelmingly, these benefits come to North Dallas and the suburbs, but much less often to South or West Dallas, reinforcing the historical geography of this divided city and exacerbating long-standing political-economic inequalities. Dallas-style economic development has often meant supplanting dependence on one major economic engine with dependence on another. The benefits of diversification are neglected, and the vital importance of manufacturing to Dallas's economic development is obscured. Industries that helped to build Dallas include agricultural implements and machinery, motor vehicles, munitions, aeronautics and aerospace, and clothing; even today, a substantial if partially undocumented garment trade employs a large, casualized workforce. Recognizing the centrality of finance, marketing, and other services to Dallas's economic past and present means placing greater weight on its industrial component. In formative ways, Dallas has been an industrial center, though not a factory town. Dallas's image has no place for the gritty concreteness and working-class identity that manufacturing brings to a city, consigning its working people to vast neglected corners of the urban landscape.

Fears of the downfall of the "can-do city" are a familiar Dallas refrain, the ever-present but often obscured underside of the city boosters' myth of continuous, limitless growth. During the 1990s, this chronic sense of insecurity combined with structural economic readjustments and significant political changes to raise unsettling doubts about the city's future. Reforms of the city council made elections more representative of Dallas's geographic and class diversity and allowed racial, ethnic, and economic politics to boil over. Long-standing, intractable problems in the Dallas public school system plunged the district into crisis. The population seemed to be increasingly polarized, with newly ascendant suburbs squaring off against areas that had less access to resources. Various factions of the old elite asked urgently whether Dallas was becoming a scandal-ridden, "can't-do city."[60] City myth became a site of struggle for power in a new form as African American, Hispanic, and other recently enfranchised political groups organized, lobbied, and campaigned for their share of the long-touted prizes of Dallas development. City myths tend to heighten conflict as they nostalgically romanticize a past in which consensus and prosperity reigned; measured against an imagined past, the present and likely future appear bleak and contentious. In one of the historical ironies that marks urban development in the United States, previously marginalized and disenfranchised groups gained access to power just when the available resources contracted sharply. The demands of newly entitled groups become especially threatening under circumstances that remind citizens that their city's future is not assured.

The myth of the great city, Dallasites must realize, has limits, just as the city itself does. Dangers lurk amid those limits, especially when unrecognized or ignored. The myth of a "city with no limits" creates its own countermyth of shameless individualism, lawless disorder, and violence, which threatens to become self-destructive. It appears especially during downturns and hard times—amid the economic and political instability of the 1920s and 1930s—and at fearful moments: amid the anticommunism and anxiety about racial integration that marked the 1950s. When myth is shattered, as it was by the Kennedy assassination and, more farcically than tragically, by the loss of "America's team" with its winning reputation, gnawing self-doubt comes into public view. The countermyth increases the risks that Dallasites will take themselves and their constructed city too seriously, heightening fears of falling short or failing. Fleeing the city's nightmare doppelgänger, Dallas boosters promote pale imitations of safer places.

Dallas boosterism and its urban rivalries combine in mutually reinforcing, yet paradoxical ways. Promotional claims about a "historic" district, an arts district, or a sports and entertainment district are expected to create in their wake the realities they pitch; nothing that already exists is quite good enough, so a new and improved version must be built. Dallas's assertions of distinctiveness all too often point to a lack that must be filled, typically by models borrowed from other cities. More theme park than historical site, "historic" Dallas has a habit of presenting buildings and geographic places as something different—more important, more interconnected, or more integral—than they really were or are. Projects aimed at enhancing the assets Dallas actually has tend to empty out their local content and significance, turning them into poor imitations of somewhere else.

Dallas's Deep Ellum, an inner-city transitional area that during the early twentieth century served as a center for urban blues and cross-class and race mixing, was proclaimed in the 1970s and 1980s to be Dallas's version of New York City's Soho. Ironically and amusingly, city planners and promoters worried that the historical name—Deep Ellum, as in elm trees—was insufficiently grand for Dallas's imitative effort to turn "history" into entertainment and tourism dollars and drape the city in historic garb.[61] Reconstruction of other areas along the lines of historical motifs followed, no more accurately or persuasively, in the "historic" (merely older, not historical) West End. "Uptown" was constructed from whole cloth as a yuppie apartment and townhouse residential area just north of downtown. Denying its own history instead of recognizing a need to preserve it, sometimes in a rush to imitate other cities, Dallas is pressed to invent a new past.

INVENTING A PAST FOR DALLAS

While forgetting, neglecting, denying, or abusing its own history, Dallas invented the exciting, even "exuberant" past that seemed necessary to rank it among "great" American cities.[62] A variety of Dallasites contributed to this creative act: civic leaders, city planners, and politicians; entrepreneurs and developers; builders and custodians of institutions that purport to collect, preserve, exhibit, and interpret history's remains; neighborhood groups, property owners, and the newly arrived seeking to set their lives in historical scenery; and racial, ethnic, gender, and other identity groups in search of "roots."[63]

Historically, the act of defining and composing "history" is inseparable from city founding and city building, part of the transition of culture and society from settlers' and migrants' points of origin. At the center of this process is the interweaving of the remembered "old" with the immediately "new," the simultaneous experiences of transplantation, adaptation, and transformation, continuity and change, and the invention of "tradition" and "uniqueness." During Dallas's first half-century, this common experience of commemorating origins occasionally may have been attended by conflict, especially over Texas's allegiance to the Confederacy and its participation in the Civil War. Dallas and its environs have long hosted local historical societies and genealogy groups, as well as chapters of the Daughters of 1812 and Daughters of the Confederacy. In most respects, though, seasonal family and community celebrations were so ordinary that they seldom warranted the label or guise of "historical." State and county fairs provided the major occasions for commemoration.

The 1936 Texas Centennial Exhibition, located in Dallas on the grounds where the state fair had been held for the previous half-century, had next to nothing to do with Dallas and little to do with history. Replicas of the Alamo (in San Antonio) and the Spanish mission in Socorro (in East Texas) and a log cabin exhibit on the Texas Rangers (not the baseball team, but frontier fighters who operated mostly along the Mexican border) were complemented by the soaring Art Deco Hall of State, with exhibition rooms for the four quadrants of Texas and a separate "Hall of Negro Life." Presenting history allegorically, the Centennial treated the past as prologue in a grand celebration of the march of progress, filling the main buildings with exhibitions by 135 business enterprises. In typical Dallas style, the Art Deco buildings in Fair Park, complete with murals and sculptures presenting epic and symbolic figures from the imagined past and envisioned future, were allowed to decay for the next half-century while "progress" continued elsewhere—mostly in downtown Dallas nearby. When the time capsule was opened in 1986, the newspapers that were so carefully deposited there had turned to dust and blew away.

Little organized effort at active collecting or display, let alone serious research or interpretation of Dallas's history, took place before the 1970s. As in many other places, the United States' Bicentennial was one stimulus. "Old City Park" on the edge of downtown was Dallas's first bicentennial project: The city's first urban park dating from 1876–88 was transformed into an outdoor museum of relocated buildings, many far removed from the city's or county's history. A city that neglects its own past filled the park with artifacts rescued from other places. The Dallas Historical Society, ensconced in the Hall of State, collected fashions, sponsored lectures, offered tours, and hosted visiting exhibitions, often far removed from Dallas or historical themes, for its donor-members. Although it recently advertised that "the Society is committed to letting people relive all periods of Dallas history," that is not part of its conventionally stated mission. Renting out its fabulous building for private parties became its major revenue source. No Dallas-area institution took responsibility for initiating and supporting programs to collect or preserve, study, interpret, and present Dallas past or present. Ironically, Dallas distinguished itself from other cities precisely in its lack of interest in its own history and institutional efforts to preserve and promote it. By the 1970s and 1980s, much of Dallas's material, documentary, and remembered past was gone or left to deteriorate. My students and I found government documents stacked unprotected in basements, attics, closets, or damp corridors of old buildings. There was little sense of what was important to preserve or mourn.

Developers brought down buildings proposed for preservation in the middle of the night and at the eleventh hour. Economic and real estate interests normally outweigh popular sentiment, even for such long-recognized landmarks as the Dr. Pepper Plant or the H. L. Green Building. Recently, the Historic Preservation League, trendily renamed Preservation Dallas, has acted more like a realty firm, especially when old warehouses, department stores, and office buildings were slated for transformation into lofts or apartments. Dallas has an active band of old tree preservationists, the Dallas Historic Tree Coalition; as far as I can tell, their success rate in saving objects exceeds the achievements of the landmark and preservation organizations.[64] Historic preservation in Dallas is marked by the expected biases of class, race, and ethnicity, a cultural process in which the objects of preservation share a great deal with the social characteristics of preservationists, with only the occasional nod toward buildings associated with Hispanic or African Americans. Black Dallasites have had to fight to save old cemeteries from freeway planners and developers.[65]

The lack of physical remains of Dallas history both constrains and expands the possibilities for promoters and serious commemorators. As in other American cities, Dallas newspapers and magazines publish photos of disappearing traces of the urban past, nostalgically relishing a "lost" Dallas. Preservationists campaign with mixed results to save structures less noteworthy historically or aesthetically than we sometimes wish or claim, simply because these are the only buildings left to preserve. In the mid-1980s, a group at the Dallas Institute of Humanities and Culture led by art historian Mary Vernon proposed to preserve the "half-rubbled, burn-blackened, crumbling, toothless, still-somehow-standing" shell of the arsonist-torched Trinity United Methodist Church near downtown. These remains would serve as a memorial to fallen policemen and "a ruin to remind Dallas of its past." According to Vernon, "The thing that ruins do in great cities is that they prevent the complete domination of your mind by the idea of total scrubbing. . . . So you remember that old and battered things are alive, weeds that are pretty are alive, even rock-hauling trucks on the freeway are alive." *Dallas Times Herald* columnist Jim Schutze embraced the notion that Dallas "needs a ruin": "Trinity Methodist, in particular, should stand because it bears the eloquent scars that our time has inflicted on it: almost reduced to sand by the war we have waged on our own past but still standing, resolute, refusing to fall. . . . a historic site that has been raped and torched and bashed and entombed alive by the racing wall of glitter going up all around it, should be turned into downtown Dallas's first and only official ruin."[66] Despite these flights of rhetoric, this perversely creative idea led nowhere.[67] Downtown Dallas has been scrubbed clean, clearing the field for invented rather than rescued pasts.

Some historic preservation efforts saved structures by moving them out of the path of development to less hotly coveted real estate. The Wilson Block on Swiss Avenue, one face of a city block north and east of downtown, comprises a set of exceptionally attractive buildings from the late nineteenth and early twentieth centuries with a parking lot behind them. The oil revenue–funded Meadows Foundation paid for these fine buildings to be relocated from other places in the city. Formerly domestic structures, they serve as offices for nonprofit organizations, including Preservation Dallas and the Meadows Foundation itself. Historically, these buildings never occupied this space, yet this collection of old houses, newly assembled in this location, is presented as if it had always occupied the spot and belongs there.

Dallas still engages in the curious practice of celebrating history without history. Two recent sesquicentennials, Texas in 1986 and Dallas in 1991, were announced as yearlong celebrations of the past, present, and future but proved disappointing. Narrowly conceived and poorly funded, they failed to take seriously the history avowedly commemorated.[68] Like the Centennial, the State Sesquicentennial had little place for Dallas history, because Dallas did not exist in 1836. But the 1986 events brought much-needed attention to the Centennial's site, newly recognized as "the largest collection of Art Deco buildings in the United States." In dire need of preservation and careful renovation, the complex had spent many years on the National Trust's list of most endangered historic structures. The deterioration of the neighborhoods around Fair Park, home to the Cotton Bowl, discouraged both private developers and public agencies from investing in its restoration and creative reuse.[69] Since 1986, emerging cultural and educational institutions—the African American Museum and the Women's Museum, in particular—have moved into renovated and new buildings in Fair Park, while well-established museums and performing arts venues have departed for a downtown arts district.[70] As this historic site was rescued from decay, it was revitalized by historically marginalized groups. While African Americans and women gained visibility, the mainstream of "progress" continues to flow toward downtown.

The Sesquicentennial of Dallas County in 1996 brought a past of dubious provenance into the center of the city, including longhorns "stroll[ing] down Main Street" in downtown Dallas and "musicians and historical characters . . . entertain[ing] near the John Neely Bryan cabin."[71] This blend of appropriation and fabrication distorted Dallas history. The "Bryan" cabin takes historic invention to extremes. A pastiche from multiple relocations and reconstructions, the small log structure located in the shadow of skyscrapers on Founders Plaza has no known or documented association with Bryan. A historical marker admits this fact, yet the building is still widely identified with town founder Bryan and early Dallas. As Dana Rubin put it in "Little House on the Plaza" for the *Texas Monthly,* "John Neely Bryan's cabin may be a fake, but as Dallas' only claim to its past, it's a beloved fake. . . . Civic leaders desperately wish it were for real. . . . In a city practically devoid of special places, John Neely Bryan's cabin is an endearing exception." The author makes a virtue of invention as the offspring of necessity:

Despite its murky provenance, the very fakeness of the cabin constitutes its charm. For those who love the city, even for those who come to hate it, the cabin has become a kind of anti-icon, cherished because of what it isn't. For all its pretensions, or maybe because of them, there is something particularly Dallas-ish about it. In a place that's forever looking forward and striving for world-class distinction, this absurd little relic somehow speaks to the city's civic character—to its sense of self, or rather its need to constantly remake itself. Perhaps it's because Dallas, throughout most of its history, has so relentlessly wiped out any trace of its origins that it now so vigorously makes an effort to shore up this scrap from the past. What the cabin lacks in historical veracity, we Dallasites make up for in imagination.[72]

"Fakeness," "anti-iconic," "absurd little relic"—that imagination is not historical imagination.

The "parade along a cattle drive route" featured twenty-five longhorns herded by ten cowboys; the lead longhorn was ridden by a cowboy, resembling a rodeo trick more than a historical reenactment. The *Dallas Morning*

FIGURE 14. Cattle drive with skyline, 1984. Photographer: Paula Nelson; courtesy of the *Dallas Morning News*.

News acerbically remarked, "You're more likely to see a herd of Chevys than a herd of cattle among the glass skyscrapers of downtown Dallas." Longhorns and cattle drives never played an important part in Dallas history, economic development, or culture. A section of the Shawnee Trail passed through the area, but was not used after 1872. The history appropriated for the sesquicentennial was not that of Dallas but of the western frontier and, ironically, longtime rival Fort Worth along the Chisholm Trail.[73] Fort Worth's important role in the cattle industry continued into the twentieth century, commemorated in its renovated Stockyards and annual Fat Stock Show. Westerners and frontier buffs see these differences immediately, but they are invisible to city dwellers. When history is prized and celebrated in Dallas, it is often not Dallas's past but the "Wild West," presumed to be more exciting, glamorous, and marketable. With no sense of contradiction, newspaper coverage of the parade declared, "Parents, children and others cheered the Wild West scene, which never dominated Dallas history. In a country where the term 'branding' evokes images of fashion designers, not livestock, the cows were a hit."[74]

More outrageous, provocative, and comical is the permanent installation in 1994 of a herd of forty larger-than-life bronze steers, with three vaqueros rounding up strays, along a trail descending a cliff to a gurgling steam in Pioneer Plaza, an open space located between City Hall and the Dallas Convention Center. Sponsored by the Texas Trees Foundation, the project was condemned by critics, artists, and the city's Public Art Committee and mocked by national media. The *Dallas Morning News* summarized the issues: "The project has spurred criticism from some city public art officials who said a cattle drive would more accurately depict Fort Worth's history than Dallas'—something *The New York Times,* among others, poked fun at. Still other critics said the steers didn't represent art."[75] Some dubbed the sculptures "frankensteer." The private interests that raised almost four of the nine million dollars required to build the park disagreed. By paying the piper, they called the tune. Pioneer Plaza cochair Jack Beckman predicted the park would become a landmark, and that "the sculpture will become a part of the city's identity and could result in hallmark souvenirs. 'It will be on postcards, T-shirts, ashtrays, and there will be plastic models,'" he said.[76] The "bronze steers pastured on urban range" have been a hit among tourists, taxi and airport shuttle drivers, local promoters and developers, and writers of letters to the editor.[77]

FIGURE 15. Pioneer Plaza, bronze steers and real cowboy, 1996. Photographer: Richard Michael Pruitt; courtesy of *Dallas Morning News*.

There is a refreshing, if superficial and distressing, honesty in the recognition that civic identity and landmarks are so easily invented and constructed. Marketing is the name of the game for theme-park history. According to the vice president for sales and marketing of Gray Line bus company of Dallas/Fort Worth, "Pioneer Place has been a boon for the image of our city. When you go to Washington, you see great monuments; when you go to Miami, you see art-deco stuff. There wasn't a signature piece to say, 'This is Dallas.' It's really nice to show visitors we've taken care of our heritage."[78] The *New York Times* observed, "Dallas's prosperity grew out of things that are much more difficult to romanticize than cowboys, like financial services," and could not refrain from pointing out that Pioneer Plaza "comes against the perennial backdrop of civic angst that the chief tourist attraction in Dallas is the . . . site of President John F. Kennedy's assassination."[79]

Pioneer Plaza is the epitome of Dallas's use and abuse of its own and others' history and its material and rhetorical reconstruction of itself, past and present. This site embodies the complex interplay of public and private interests and policy issues shaping the urban environment. Several critical elements underlay the conception, development, and reception of the sculptures. First is the appropriation of history and its transformation into a prominent, public statement of identity, however accurate or appropriate. Second, the Public Art Committee's vote against the proposal was ignored by the Cultural Affairs Committee and the City Council. The construction of Pioneer Plaza involved private donations, public approval, public donation of the land and funding for upkeep, loss of revenue from a parking lot formerly on the site, and the revenues foregone by building a cattle park instead of a hotel. Each point proved controversial, and the muddy clash between public and private interests was never clearly articulated.[80] Third, large public and private economic interests were part of the park proposal's provenance from its conception. Trammel Crow, the wealthy developer, Dallas promoter, and chair of the Dallas Parks Foundation, owned a nearby hotel that would have suffered major competition if a rival hotel had been constructed on the site bordering the Convention Center. In a sort of real-estate checkmate, history and art are no more separable from economics than they are from politics. The pretense of this separation stands boldly as an error made by spokespersons on all sides of the bronze steers question.[81] Confusion of private and public interests blurs uninformed discussions of art and history. *Texas Monthly's* report concluded, "Pioneer Plaza may ultimately be a success, but it will not be a monument that defines the city."[82] Although no single landmark, brand, or image can define any city, the process through which Pioneer Park was planned and the ersatz history it presents serve as a definitive model of how Dallas incorporates an invented past into its built environment.

Dallas Heritage Village, in Old City Park on the southern edge of downtown, is the hallmark of Dallas's renewed interest in its history and the showpiece of the publicly and privately supported Dallas County Heritage Society. Old City Park represents the transformation of the city's first urban park into a "living history museum" of rural life.[83] A grouping of buildings that hosts reenactments of frontier life, Heritage Village is "'an outdoor museum of architectural and cultural history between 1840 and 1910, whose focus is North Central Texas, not Dallas alone,' according to former director

Tom Smith. The buildings represent eight counties in the area and serve as a vehicle to interpret the collective lifestyles of the people who used the structures and the items they contain."[84] Visitors can view a blacksmithing demonstration, watch a bank robbery, visit a small farmstead, and witness a land speculator attempting to swindle potential immigrants. The park's connection with the city of Dallas has been obliterated, so that here, as at other Dallas "historic" sites, "Old" seems the most accurate part of the appellation. The reconstructed, collected, and synthetic nature of the enterprise, including its regional scope, has been unnecessarily and misleadingly obscured.[85]

Smith's careful description of the site came in response to criticism penned in 1988 by *Dallas Times Herald* columnist Jim Schutze: "The problem is that Old City Park presents too pretty and far too narrow a window on the city's past. What you see at Old City Park, in the charming old cabins and churches and schoolhouses that have been moved here and restored is an almost totally European-American and heavily sentimental vision of the past. In particular, the issues of race and slavery are treated with a kind of sugar-coated disdain, as if not really that important." Other journalists, critics, and academics also charged that this presentation of history was "too clean" or "pretty."[86] Behind the conflict stood the museum's refusal to include the house of a major mid-twentieth-century African American civil rights activist and Dallas city council member, Juanita Craft, on the grounds that it did not fit within the park's established chronology. The issue opened the way for a wider-ranging critique of the underrepresentation of black and brown as well as white, slave as well as free, poor as well as rich residents of the area. To accuse Dallas Heritage Village of "segregation" only begins to explore the meanings of public representations of the past and the control of public historical representation itself in Dallas.[87]

The very successful Black Dallas Remembered (BDR) project, formed in 1983, has stimulated African Americans to seek out their families' histories and documents. The nonprofit organization conducted tours, compiled research, and led the way in establishing the Juanita Craft Civil Rights House under the auspices of the City of Dallas Cultural Center. The enormous voluntary contribution and most of the appreciation of this historical recovery comes principally from within the African American community. Lines between racial groups, along with institutional and funding boundaries, limit the visibility of such projects, although BDR has steadily raised its profile with the expansion of the Craft House and gardens through private and foundation support.[88] African American historical concerns entered the public domain more directly when highway or real estate development collided with historically black cemeteries and threatened to remove the remains. Along with other community groups, BDR mobilized African Americans to bring the issue to public attention and modify development plans and schedules, for example, of Freedom's Cemetery north of downtown along the Central Expressway (U.S. 75).[89]

Dallas Heritage Village, the struggles of Black Dallas Remembered, and other questionable historic sites demonstrate the continuing inability of Dallasites to open the conversation and confront the more troubling aspects of its past and present. *Dallas Times Herald* columnist Anita Creamer, showing an out-of–town visitor the sights in 1985, did not find any place that "captured the essence of Dallas' illustrious past." She supports historic preservation and condemns the extent of demolition: "Dallas seems always to have been a city anxiously shaking off its past and desperately grabbing hold of its future. Small wonder historic buildings (and local history) are so little valued." While applauding efforts like Old City Park, she finds no satisfaction in the results: "they're about as real as a Hollywood facade. There's no spirit here, no life, little character. These houses and buildings are shells of their former incarnations."[90] Summing up preservation in Dallas, she sarcastically hyperbolizes: "The result is too cute, too clean, too sterile—and too planned, as if the idea were perfecting the past instead of preserving it. One suspects that if the Acropolis were somehow miraculously transported into Dallas County, our response would be to raise funds to get it reroofed, only to have it torn down to make room for a parking lot. What amazes me even more is that we're constantly creating the necessity of amassing more Old City Park collections of buildings in the future [by continuing] one of Dallas's most cherished traditions: tearing down the past."[91]

Creamer and others observe the consequences of Dallas's distinctive relationship to its past and note some of the important factors contributing to that peculiar fusion of denial and invention. Their observations also register, though less fully and clearly, the ways in which Dallas's mythohistory influences constructions of the city past, present, and future. Less often noted, rarely questioned or subjected to critical review, these constructions are powerful forces in the continuing process of making and remaking Dallas, ranging from the mundane to the sublime and the downright ridiculous, as the figure of a flying horse—erected as oil company logo, metamorphosed into a beacon for the city, lost, reproduced, and promoted as a direction-less sign—attests.[92]

IDEOLOGY

The power of myths to shape a city is intensified when they are substituted for history. Myths that reduce the past to caricature limit and distort the city materially and ideologically. In Dallas, the reigning conceptions of the "city as enterprise" and the "city as growth machine" narrow the terms of success for individuals and groups. The image of "America's city," like "America's team," homogenizes the players and reduces the field rather than ex-pands it. Acceptance of unequal opportunities, the unequal distribution of benefits, and a stratified and fragmented social geography follow from the notions of "destiny" and "man's conquest of nature." In civic culture, Dal-las's myths reinforce the emphasis on conspicuous display and the limited and insecure identity given by manufactured images. Myth underlies the use and abuse of history in Dallas, just as history—especially appropriated, reconstructed, and fabricated history—underlies myth.

Much of what passes for "historic" Dallas could be anywhere, eliding the city's own past. The silvery, sleek, and shining glass and steel ultramodern-istic image of Dallas cast by space-age Reunion Tower with its nighttime light shows and adjacent Reunion Hyatt Hotel plays primarily in promo-tional photos. These towers memorialize the name, yet invert the meaning of La Réunion, a short-lived, mid-nineteenth-century utopian socialist com-munity settled by French, Swiss, and Belgian Fourierists just west of Dallas that failed because they were unfamiliar with farming the prairie. Those artisans and artists who remained in Dallas, including bakers, craftspeople, painters, musicians, and teachers, gave the town a veneer of European cul-ture. The mythical version of La Réunion's radicals as Dallas's first "vision-aries" enhances the city's prestige while forgetting their work and politics.

Dallas's dominant ideology combines the myth of the city as destiny with the myth of the city as a product of innovation to proclaim, produce, and rationalize "progress" under the auspices of its entrepreneurial elite.[93] Through a complex social process, myth is translated into ideology, and ideology underlies promotion, action, and justification. Economic growth and geographic expansion came to be defined as Dallas's manifest destiny, the reason to exist in a city that otherwise had none. Public politics is devoted to the advance of private interests; businessmen constitute the "natural elite" of civic leaders; and fears of failing individually and collectively form an anxious undercurrent to the dominant upbeat tempo.

Raymond Williams usefully describes ideology as "the set of ideas which arise from a given set of material interests or, more broadly, from a definite class or group. . . . Ideology in each case is the system of ideas appropriate to that class. One ideology can be claimed as correct and progressive as against another ideology."[94] Ideology is neither true nor false, neither right nor wrong. It can, however, be asserted to be so, in order to advance the interests of a class or group. This perspective facilitates a dynamic approach that encourages the identification and appreciation of ideas, their framers and adherents, and their expression in social, political, economic, and cultural contexts. These ideas compete for acceptance against other understandings of social relationships. Ideology provides connections between expectations and experiences, actions and their justifications; it links attitudes and desires to material and political interests. We need not view ideology as narrow, reductionist, or deterministic. For Dallas, this critical approach cautions us against too-easy acceptance of notions of destiny or inevitability, unequivocal success, disinterested players, or long-standing consensus across a diverse population. All those notions are themselves ideological.

Understood in this way, ideology obscures the distinctions between history and myth, contributing to shaping generalized beliefs about Dallas and stimulating characteristic patterns of action. On the eve of the 1984 Republican National Convention, Griffin Smith Jr. praised Dallas as a place whose "people know their city's catechism by heart."[95] Two decades earlier, Warren Leslie enunciated a longer-standing truism about the workings of ideology in Dallas. The city, he writes, "has been shaped as few cities have ever been by *men,* and much of the psychology of Dallas traces back to this. Its existence is an invention of the human mind and a tribute to human energy."[96] "Shaping" the "psychology" of a city's residents through energetic "invention" is a receipt for the ideological construction of this place called Dallas. Here, as elsewhere, the local press, especially the *Dallas Morning News,* has been a major circulating agent.

Ideology functions by emphasizing one way of seeing, while distracting from and discrediting another. Former Dallas mayor R. L. Thornton elaborated on the association of Dallas with progress in his inimitable way: "The Dallas spirit is probably better defined as . . . a snappy, forward, progressive citizenship interest," and Dallas is "a city where men and women move along on the streets and where push and energy vibrate the very atmosphere."[97] Progress becomes the essence of the "can-do city," not simply its achievement. While the "Dallas Spirit" is primarily ideational, based in character, attitude, faith, conviction, and industriousness, the Dallas Way is more the "how to"—strategies, tactics, mechanics—of the "can do."

John Bainbridge's observations in his 1961 minor classic, *The Super-Americans,* neatly capture this phenomenon. Bainbridge commences with the catechism, using a mixture of transportation metaphors that Thornton would appreciate: "Dallas citizens are convinced that by putting their shoulders to the wheel, to borrow a popular localism, they can put their city so far over the top that it need take a back seat to no other, New York included." Putting faith into action means shifting from catechetical to axiomatic: "If anything about Dallas doesn't look rosy, . . . Dallas citizens pitch in and make it so." Bainbridge tells one story that is emblematic of the many Dallas success stories: "A while back, for example, they realized that their zoo was not up to snuff. Instantly, the Dallas Zoological Society summoned its members to a 'kickoff meeting,' listened to Mayor Thornton explain how a bigger and better zoo would 'benefit the city economically by bringing customers into Dallas stores,' and pledged support." This mode of marshalling support, which was inaugurated officially with the city's bid for the Texas Centennial, includes enticements, strong-arming, and other, more covert methods of persuasion and coercion.[98]

Dallas's ideology unmistakably marks the city. Bainbridge's observation, made well before the Kennedy assassination, holds uncannily true even today: "Everything is on the surface: youthfulness, pride, desperate ambition—a combination that naturally wells up from a community on the make. One trait above all dominates the Dallas personality—reverence for business. If, as Calvin Coolidge so trenchantly observed, the business of America is business, Dallas may well be *the* All-American city, for it is a city of the businessmen, by the businessmen, and for the businessmen."[99]

Dallas's ideology has an underside, a striking element of anxiety and fear of failing that is also associated with Dallas's major myths, images, and identity. Noting this characteristic, Bainbridge asks: "To what extent, one might wonder, does the almost hectic activity that characterizes the present behavior of the people of Dallas result from a haunting uneasiness, going way back, that comes from being committed to a never-ending struggle that calls for a bold and constant mockery of both logic and nature?"[100] While Bainbridge's final phrasing reflects his inability to escape Dallas's second origin myth, he was right about "a haunting uneasiness." On the one hand, there is the refrain bespeaking the active worry that Dallas has lost its magic and is no longer the "can-do" "city that works" and that all the world will see this shame.[101] On the other hand, city promoters, leaders, and observers like the *Dallas Morning News* vigilantly watch for signs that Dallas has faced another "turning point" or "crossroads" in its progress, or at least its growth. In the immediate aftermath of the narrow electoral victory in support of public underwriting for a new downtown arena early in 1998, the *News* editorialized, "voting results will help restore the city's 'can do' image."[102] In 1991, the newspaper declaimed, "City, State Lose Can-Do Illusions." The quest for the illusory "Dallas Spirit" and the "Dallas Way" has never ceased— nor has the fear of losing them.

Revising Dallas's Histories

It seemed strange when *Dallas Morning News* editor Henry Tatum announced in February 2003, "Dallasites Would Benefit by Knowing Local History."[1] "There is a lot to be said for knowing the community where you live. It helps make sense of things," he counseled. Tatum recognized some of the difficulties Dallasites have in discovering the city's past: "How do you teach the history of a city that isn't even sure about the origin of its name? How do you tell the true story of a town so driven by a need to succeed that it has changed its public image about as many times as a snake sheds its skin?" Yet the history he requests is composed primarily of stories of the "hidden" underside of the past that add up to little more than another change in the city's image.

This city spent so many years polishing its image that a lot of really good stories got swept under the rug. To the outsider, Dallas can appear to be a very uptight town. But the colorful and sometimes hilarious history of this city says that just isn't so.

Did you know that Dallas had an authorized red-light district downtown in the early 1900s? Many buildings where those "bawdy houses" operated were owned by prominent Dallas citizens. Have you heard the story about the "hot-dog mayor"? . . . How about the first real-estate huckster in Dallas? . . . How about the mayor whose Volkswagen was seized? . . .

Why does anyone need to know this stuff? There are a couple of good reasons.

Understanding how Dallas overcame its own shortcomings in the 1900s
lets us know that doing the same thing in the 21st century might not be as
impossible as it seems right now.

And knowing some of the wild and crazy things this town was capable
of doing during its growing years might persuade us to be little less uptight
these days. I certainly hope so.[2]

Tatum unself-consciously delights in the trivialization of history; he solic-
its a version of the past that can be marketed and consumed for fun and
profit. But it is as unnecessarily limited, replaceable, replicable, context-free,
and two-dimensional as a neon Pegasus logo, without the depth and accuracy to guide a major city into the twenty-first century.

This shift in the *Morning News*'s position accords with a recent trend in
Dallas histories and mythologies that flows against the current of "a city with
no history" to rediscover "Dallas's destiny" and display a highly selective but
consumable view of its past.[3] Reconstructing a comprehensive history of a
place that long claimed it has none and did little to preserve whatever remained of its past is a difficult, if not quixotic, undertaking. But, as Dallas's
leaders and promoters have recognized, a "great city" needs a great history.
The realization that Dallas has multiple histories and needs many historians
to tell the divergent stories of its various citizens and communities has yet to
take hold. Dallas's history, including its myths, helps to explain the city's
long-term and more recent development far better than any of the alternative notions of its growth encountered so far. Pursuing that history also illuminates the roots of Dallas's problems with its image and identity. In ways
that Henry Tatum and the *Dallas Morning News* only began to see in 2003,
establishing the terms and currents of its history is vital to the city's search for
definition and future direction. Although Tatum's goals for a history of Dallas differ profoundly from mine, I agree that "understanding how Dallas
overcame its own shortcomings in the 1900s lets us know that doing the same
thing in the 21st century might not be as impossible as it seems right now."
For Tatum, that acknowledgement is a place to end; for me, it serves as a
place to begin. History matters: for understanding the city's socioeconomic
context and securing its identity; for developing a more flexible discourse
and more fitting narratives; for confronting demons past and future and
imagining alternatives in the present. This chapter suggests several different
ways of approaching Dallas's past that offer us new historical perspectives.

PLACING DALLAS IN HISTORICAL CONTEXT

Prevailing popular and academic notions of the process of urban growth incorporate a sense of historical change, marked by qualitative transformation as well as quantitative expansion. Narratives of most North American cities include at least three historical stages. Depending on what relationship is posited between economic structures and urban forms, typical triads include (1) preindustrial, industrial, and deindustrial or postindustrial eras; (2) founding and settlement, growth of commerce or industry, and then either decline or revitalization; (3) walking city, streetcar or mass transit metropole, and automobile megalopolis. Historian Eric H. Monkkonen states: "The basic chronology of U.S. cities has three parts": (1) the premodern era to about 1830, when cities functioned commercially and politically; (2) a century-long period of unprecedented economic and population growth to 1930, when cities worked out new modes of providing services; and (3) post-Depression cities in which innovations of the previous century became permanent and less visible, as bureaucracies developed to supervise public services.[4]

Examining Dallas along with Houston and San Antonio, Miller and Johnson demarcate three stages of Texas urbanization. A "critical first stage" appeared between 1836 and the late 1880s. "It was then that the three emerging urban communities to a large extent operated independently of one

Census Year	Population
1880	10,358
1890	38,067
1900	42,638
1910	92,104
1920	158,976
1930	260,475
1940	294,734
1950	434,462
1960	679,684
1970	844,000
1980	904,078
1990	1,006,877
2000	1,188,580

FIGURE 16. Dallas's population.

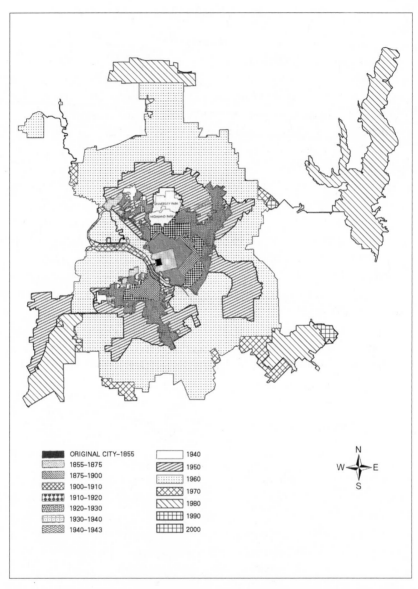

MAP 2. Dallas expands, 1841–2000. According to Stuart Murchison, director of GIS, City of Dallas, there were no significant changes between 1990 and 2000, so these two periods are labeled identically. Portions of boundary data compiled by Ronald Drake and Alex Michael Wolde. Drawn by Paul Hoeffler from Harland Bartholomew and Associates, "A Master Plan for Dallas, Texas," 1943.

City	Area (square miles)	Population
Dallas	26	158,976
Houston	40	138,076
San Antonio	36	161,379

FIGURE 17. Population and size of Dallas,
Houston, and San Antonio, 1920.

Year	Area (square miles)
1920	22.8
1940	40.6
1960	279.9
1970	265.8
1980	332.9
1990	342.4

FIGURE 18. Dallas area expansion.

Year	Percentage of Population
1900	21.3
1910	19.6
1920	15.2
1930	14.9
1940	17.1
1950	13.2
1960	19.3
1970	24.9
1980	29.4
1990	29.5

FIGURE 19. Dallas's African American
population.

another, an independence that would diminish with the laying down of a statewide railroad network during the late nineteenth century." A second stage began "when each of these cities began to compete directly with the others for regional supremacy. This competition fundamentally reshuffled the state's urban hierarchy by the 1920s." A third stage emerged during the 1930s and especially during World War II, "when Dallas, Houston, and San Antonio in different ways sought to capitalize on (and extend) their resource bases, which were critical for the accelerated growth and development of Sunbelt Texas."[5] (See the appendixes.)

Dallas myths imagine the city outside the normal bounds of time and space, exempt from history itself. Simplistic notions divide its development in two: then and now, prehistory and posthistory, local insignificance and cosmopolitan stature. The second term in each pair dominates the first; sometimes it appears that only the present counts. Prevailing narratives of

Dallas's rise to greatness exhibit striking consensus on the key historical actors and agents. About the dating of the two stages and the nature of the transition, unanswered questions and differences of opinion abound.[6] When was the foundation for urban progress firmly laid? Was Dallas's transformation surprising or predictable, difficult or easy, accompanied by consensus or conflict and resistance, marked by rhetorical persuasion or physical force, accomplished at great or small cost, and with shared or unequal sacrifices and benefits? Do different factors and chronologies define the city's history for Anglos, women, African Americans, and Mexican or Hispanic Americans? Did change come through long-term processes of evolution and/or at "revolutionary" moments? Instead of pursuing these questions, Dallas's history is foreshortened, reduced to a relatively brief preface in the ideal coffee-table book illustrating Dallas's present greatness. (Compare to the appendixes.)

In the usual images of Dallas history, Monkkonen's first stage is absent, the second stage barely exists, and the modern city originates during the 1930s or even World War II. The first two stages in Miller and Johnson's model of Texas cities are also missing: growth in connection with its rich agricultural hinterland and the formation of regional networks (the rise of urban competition being the third). A comprehensive history cannot be composed of a handful of odd, colorful, or enterprising characters: town founder John Neely Bryan, early entrepreneur Sarah Horton Cockrell, the failed European utopians of La Réunion colony, and bold entrepreneurs and promoters. At least implicitly, their colorfulness contrasts with the greater seriousness and duller substance of Dallas's movers and shakers from the 1920s forward.[7] Nineteenth- and early twentieth-century Dallas is sorely neglected.[8] Truncating Dallas's history makes the city appear to be "born modern," with the aura of progress and the jazzy art deco aesthetic of the Centennial State Fair. City leaders such as Mayor Thornton are painted with a down-home folksiness that belies their economic and institutional power. Dallas's history is generally told outside of the terms and frames of American and international urban development as well. Civic boosters take enormous pride in their city's prominence, but resist the risks inherent in comparing Dallas systematically with other regional, national, and international centers. Entirely absent is any serious historical context for Dallas's development, whether for comparison, explanation, or interpretation.

The alternative urban historical approach proposed here presents those prior periods, and the people and activities that constitute them, as fundamental, foundational, and inextricably connected to the major metropolis that Dallas became. The revisioning of Dallas's history is only beginning, as historical researchers discover the city as an open and interesting topic for study.[9] This chapter offers several different but interrelated approaches: first, a précis of a transformed Dallas history that situates its similarities to and differences from other cities in political-economic and social-historical context; second, a set of principles for reconstructing historical studies of Dallas; and, third, a chronology of Dallas history accompanied by a summary of stages in the city's historical development.

Dallas's principal ahistorical or antihistorical narratives slight the significance of the city's commercial, transportation, and industrial foundations, which here as elsewhere were accompanied by class differences, cultural diversity, labor organizing, and political conflicts. From the 1880s through 1919 and beyond, labor unions and radical movements challenged major corporate employers and the municipality itself, as they did in other urban centers across the nation. The city's central labor council, the Dallas Trades

FIGURE 20. Main Street looking east, ca. 1887. Shortly after the railroad came to Dallas, the central business district had low wooden and brick buildings, unpaved roads, and electric wires strung on poles. From the collections of the Texas/Dallas History and Archives Division, Dallas Public Library.

Figure 21. Main Street, ca. 1899. The city center was rising, solid, stylish, and in motion. From the collections of the Texas/Dallas History and Archives Division, Dallas Public Library.

Assembly, allied with socialists, feminists, and civil rights advocates to challenge business elites for control of local government. Conservative reformers responded by modernizing urban governance, extending public services, and undertaking massive infrastructure projects to stabilize society as well as accelerate economic growth, exercising a substantial degree of power well before the Depression and World War II. (See the appendixes.)

From the start, Dallas business leaders secured major assets for the city by appropriating public funds and land to lure private enterprises and federal institutions, using bribery and theft when persuasion and outright purchase did not suffice. Dallas won the designation as county seat by building and rebuilding courthouses. The two railroads that made Dallas a crossroads were induced not to bypass the city with gifts of public funds, land,

and rights-of-way, as well as state legislation, between 1870 and 1872. In 1914, Dallas secured the 11th District Federal Reserve Bank, reinforcing its position as a regional financial center. The Ford Motor Company was lured to a large factory site near downtown in 1914. Municipal and state power, from the police to the courts, was frequently deployed to prevent labor organizing. Contrary to the myth of Dallas's self-creation, its political-economic history from 1932 onward is marked by the active solicitation of federal funding and the creative utilization of public support for private enterprises, a pattern that undergirds the growth of cities in the West as well.

On the other hand, Dallas really is different. Some differences undergird popular images of Dallas as positively distinguished, but others qualify

FIGURE 22. Commerce Street, looking west, ca. 1906. The third city hall is visible on the far right, with the ornately detailed police station and firehouse next door. Along with the adjacent offices of *Dallas Dispatch,* these stately public buildings were constructed in 1888 and demolished in 1911. From William L. McDonald, *Dallas Rediscovered: A Photographic Chronicle of Urban Expansion, 1870–1925* (Dallas: Dallas Historical Society, 1978); courtesy of Charles Coldwell Private Collection.

or contradict the central images conveyed by customary tellings of the Dallas tale. Key examples include the remarkably long and resilient tradition of elite organization, control of formal politics, and undemocratic exercise of power. The racial segregation of residential neighborhoods was sanctified by municipal ordinances and by restrictive covenants on deeds. White Dallas was notable for its intolerance of diversity, acceptance of political extremism, and frequent recourse to violence. Long a stronghold of the Ku Klux Klan, the city became as famous for its public lynchings as for its state fair. The impressive resistance and historical agency of racial, ethnic, and working-class communities in the face of such repression demands recognition. Equally significant, and equally unremarked, is the underdevelopment of the city's cultural and educational institutions and the public sphere. Only the Civic Federation's Dallas Open Forum provided a venue for public debate during the interwar period.

Although the "Dallas Way" is usually identified with the Dallas Citizens Council from the mid-1930s forward, its ideology, provenance, and power predate that period. Truly exceptional for any large American city, I argue, is Dallas's distinctive political economy and political culture: the creation and reproduction of self-perpetuating elites over long periods; public and private maintenance of their hegemonic power with scant criticism or challenge until the Kennedy assassination and beyond; and the extent of private domination of the public sphere. The myth of a selfless leadership class concerned only with the public interest was crucial in establishing and maintaining elite political hegemony; so were proclamations of growth and prosperity despite persistent and increasing economic and geographic disparities.

This book explicates the intricate interrelationships between the mythology and ideology of Dallas's rise and achievement, expressed in its symbols and identity, on the one hand, and the creation, operation, and maintenance of an elite-dominated growth machine and its centers of power, on the other. Here the neglect and fear of history and its replacement in mythology and the ideology built upon it are especially telling. The *new* Dallas tales that this book begins to tell pivot to an unprecedented extent on factors of race, class, ethnicity, gender, geography, power, and democracy. Dallas's achievements have come at great human, environmental, cultural, and political costs. (See the appendixes.)

PRINCIPLES FOR RECONSTRUCTING
DALLAS HISTORY

My approach to reconstructing Dallas's history begins with a critique of existing Dallas histories, moves to approaches that assist in recasting Dallas studies, and identifies key elements and emphases in a revised historiography. Taken together, these principles chart an agenda for the future of Dallas's past. This project presumes that history undergirds both Dallas's famous and infamous differences from other places and its resemblances to other urban centers. This perspective relocates Dallas's place within the spectrum of American urban experiences, tracing common patterns of growth and characteristic processes of change. These principles blend observations with cautions, corrections, and an epistemology of ways of thinking about the city's history. Readers should keep in mind the important distinction between history—"the past"—and historiography: the serious study of the past and presentation of the results of historical research. At present, we can only imagine how new histories of Dallas might be constructed and presented. In the act of imagination lie alternative paths to different histories for Dallas, and with them different views of its present and future.

The mythologies of Dallas have taken the place of its history. Not only have the major myths substituted for historical research and understanding, but Dallas's principal myths have become inordinately powerful historical forces in themselves. More than a century's proudly avowed and publicly announced expectations for a great, "can-do" city "with no limits" stand as an undeniable force in the physical as well as political construction of Dallas. On occasion, fears of loss or decline, often equally exaggerated, were more powerful impulses for action than were stated goals and actual achievements.

There is no single history of Dallas. There are multiple histories of many Dallases, most as yet unwritten. These alternative histories, constructed around distinct subjects and from different points of view, cannot be fitted together neatly like pieces of a jigsaw puzzle. Like Dallas itself, they embody conflicts as well as distinctions and differences. University of Texas at Arlington historian Robert Fairbanks's notion of "the city as a whole" evades the fundamental question of whose "city" this is and whether it ever formed a social "whole." The prevailing version of Dallas's written history is that of a minority among its population, though the most powerful, prominent, well-to-do, and visible minority: the overwhelmingly Anglo and male entrepreneurial and leadership class. Even that historical account is as yet incomplete. An inclusive history that embraces racial, ethnic, gender, class, and geographic differences kaleidoscopically transforms the city's historical landscape. The histories of Dallas's racial and ethnic minorities, with their essential chapters of migration and settlement, segregation and inequality, conflict, resistance, dissent, and struggles for rights and a place for themselves, community development and advancement, are just beginning to be researched and written. Here, too, stories of relationships across as well as along lines of social division are central. The shape of Dallas geographically and metaphorically embodies and can be "read" for its histories and its mythologies. One powerful narrative of Dallas past and Dallas present takes the form of a "tale of two cities": rich and poor, North versus South and West Dallas, and Anglo versus African American and Hispanic communities. Another narrative traces the city's "monumental" and mimetic urban development.

To acknowledge that there is no *one* Dallas and no *one* history of Dallas is to recognize a powerful and long-neglected truth: views of history shift depending on who is included and excluded and where the viewer stands. In conceptualizing history for a city that lacks even a standard urban biography, let alone a comprehensive historical account of its making and remaking, the temptation to present *the* history rather than *a* history must be resisted. Just as we reject genres of history structured around narratives of "before and after" and "rise and decline" and sometimes "rebirth," among other fallacies, we must reject the lure of a conventional urban biography. That history would be anachronistic and, because of its exclusion of non-Anglos and the working class and its assignment of historical agency only to Anglo elites, likely to offend substantial numbers of Dallas residents today. Subordinated racial and ethnic groups—those who literally built the city and contributed strikingly to its distinctiveness—would at best be only partially visible, appearing primarily as victims, resisters, and otherwise outliers, often late in the day. In relation to women and the working class, too, a single history limits their active historical presence and promotes their segregation across racial and ethnic lines. (Compare to the appendixes.)

Spatially, there are many Dallases. Social and geographic space play upon each other in shaping the physical, economic, social, and cultural city.

Geography appears to underlie certain forms of destiny: for example, North Dallas's advantages and visibility, as opposed to South and West Dallas's neglect. Embracing many Dallases means embracing many Dallasites: in their different circumstances, experiences, and spaces, and in their representations as images both active and acted upon. It means seeking out their intersections and relationships as well as their separateness to construct a history of social, cultural, economic, and political relations. A serious search for African American Dallas has started, with stimulus and major support from the community, but there are fewer signs of historical research on Native American or Hispanic Dallas, or on other immigrant groups whose imprints on the city's fabric are fading. Research into the histories of women and the working class in Dallas has begun.[10]

The Dallas story, both material and discursive, presents itself as a "tale of two cities," written or etched in geography, race, ethnicity, class, development, resource distribution, standards of living, health status, life chances, and access to opportunities. While simplistic dichotomies can be dangerously misleading, sharply contrasting patterns and images across virtually all dimensions mark Dallas throughout its history and remain visible today. Emphasizing the need to compare Dallas and its peoples over time, this perspective raises key questions about social and economic policies, theories of urban development and historical change, and pathways toward equity and equality.

An inclusive history of Dallas needs to be imagined, perhaps first as a new mythology. Active research could then follow.[11] Is Dallas a house with many rooms across time and space, or is it best envisioned in other ways, for example, as separate structures of radically different shapes and sizes, with or without communications, fences, or other boundaries between them? Critical here are relationships, connections, the play of power and agency, and the quality of life. Maintaining the city itself in its multiple dimensions as the principal goal of research and writing aids in the tricky navigation between peoples and places and tracking their interactions. Only when the cast is broadly inclusive will we grasp how Dallas was built, materially and discursively, upon those social relationships. Different Dallases and different Dallasites hold different ways of telling their histories, sometimes with dramatically divergent genres and judgments. They disagree about how Dallas's growth is best evaluated, about its successes and persisting problems, about winners and losers, benefits and costs. A history of Dallas demands many voices and more than a few ragged edges.

A more inclusive and longer-term perspective highlights the shifting balances and relations of change and continuity in the making and remaking of Dallas. Most writing about Dallas tends to stress change. Yet, at least as myth, Dallas history describes the city as changing mainly to grow into its predetermined shape or destiny, becoming more itself. Change is quantitative rather than qualitative, rarely conceived as fundamental or transformative. Questions about the extent of continuity, even with respect to elite power or goals, and the extent of conflict among different groups in the city remain unasked and unanswered. At least until recently, insecurity and fear pivot around the uncertainty about reaching or failing to reach destined greatness, not about what goals Dallas should seek.

Dallas's historical development is inseparable from the larger patterns of urban, American, and global history and must be understood in that context. Conversely, Dallas's historical experience is valuable for its contributions to historical knowledge and social theory. Dallas's history is a major chapter in the creation story of the differential, unequal shares in opportunities and benefits within the American urban polity. Those inequalities shape the place spatially, socially, economically, and culturally. Dallas's history is marked prominently and powerfully by long-standing traditions of prejudice, intolerance, racism, violence, extremism, segregation, and other efforts aimed at control. Struggles of race, ethnicity, gender, and social class have deeply scarred and sometimes rent the urban fabric, even if the traces of these ruptures have been mended and ironed out in retrospect. While not unique, Dallas is disturbingly exceptional, especially with respect to African Americans and Mexican Americans. Race is a central element in Dallas's past, present, and future. Throughout Dallas's history, gender has cut across the lines of discrimination, desegregation, and the quest for civil rights; variations in the means and modes of hegemony; and the construction of public and private domains. Collectively and individually, different women stood and contributed to each of the different sides or divisions along those lines. In some circumstances, at some moments, gender mediated and lessened the power of class, race, ethnicity, and geography; at other times, it did not.

Chronology constitutes another form of inclusiveness in a history of the social relations and social processes that built cities and continue to remake them. Chronology and conceptualization work together. Defining chronological periods requires us to place myriad discrete events in broader context, attending to processes of change, and enables useful comparisons over time and with other places. Dallas looks different from the perspective of 160 years than one of eighty years or less. Neither changes nor continuities, the sweep of the local, regional, or global, come into clear focus when the lens is too narrow and the frame too close. (See the appendixes.)

From the time of its permanent settlement, Dallas always has been an urban place, a metropole at a crossroads located within an expanding regional, national, and international network. A great deal of Dallas's history is encapsulated by a series of stages of urban development: from crossroads settlement to county town and service center for a prosperous agricultural region; chartered city, administrative, financial, industrial, and at times, labor center; and metropolitan center, gaining in size, influence, complexity, and diversity. Especially important and glaringly absent from existing accounts are the relationships of those stages or periods to each other, the interplay and influence of successive presents and futures on how we construct their pasts.

Dallas's history highlights the transformation of the market from a place to an all-pervasive form of political and cultural as well as economic power.[12] Urban from its conception, the city is a fascinating example of self-promotion. Exaggerated presumptions of Dallas's autonomy and misconceptions of history as destiny have long blocked observers from placing the city in appropriate historical context, illuminating such themes as colonization, territorial expansion, slavery, agricultural development, commercialization, migration, and innovations in transportation. Dallas was born on the cusp of world-making phenomena. Along with other U.S. cities, Dallas was a "gateway to the West," a site on the "urban frontier."[13]

Historian Stuart Blumin explains two paths of city development. "In some countries, most notably the United States, much town formation must be attributed to territorial expansion"; the other scenario for city development, often erroneously assumed to be universal, is "the continuing development of long-settled regions." Many towns, including Dallas, "sprang not from farming communities but from forts, trading posts, and even the wilderness itself—at fords, at railway junctions, at sites arbitrarily selected as the seats for county government, and at seemingly random points on the faceless prairie, purchased, platted and promoted by the luckier or more skillful of the thousands of speculators who hoped to make their fortunes out of frontier urban development." Dallas began as a crossroads, a promising site for trading and building a city, not as a village in a settled agricultural area that grew into urbanity. Dallas facilitated the capitalist development of the exceptionally rich agricultural region of North Texas, and the city prospered in inseparable and reciprocal connection with the region it served.[14]

Places on the urban frontier formed an ethos out of their origins, rapid growth, and dynamic connections. "Growth itself was embraced as the source and symbol of community vitality," Blumin explains. For emerging towns in urbanizing societies, "the increasing communal identity and pride

FIGURE 23. Wilson Building, architects Sauguinett and Staats, built 1902–3, ca. 1915. Another jewel in the crown of the rising city and a prime example of mimetic urban development. From the collections of the Texas/Dallas History and Archives Division, Dallas Public Library.

FIGURE 24. Main and Ervay streets, 1920s. This intersection was "the heart of things": Neiman Marcus's new building to the left, the Federal Building across the street, the Wilson Building on the right. From A. C. Greene, *Dallas: The Deciding Years—A Historical Portrait* (Austin: Encino Press, 1973).

of the middle and upper classes derived not only from local growth but also from the intensification of regular contact with the outside world."[15] These towns, including Dallas, became cities by imitating established cities: "by copying the ordinance books, street names, institutions and manners of existing cities, a process repeated over and over again, with neither hesitation nor apology, as the population advanced into new territories and thickened in old ones. It could be accomplished in months." This process helps to explain Dallas's propensity for development through the tools of mimesis or imitation, monumental development, and appropriation by stealth or purchase of objects of desire. The nature and relative speed of Dallas's rise depended on its place within what Blumin identifies as "the urban network as a spatial and functional system. Towns that emerge during the later stages of any society's urban development are profoundly affected by the existing network of cities."[16] Blumin's model outlines an agenda for the historical economic geography of developing Dallas and its expanding region.

Within the bounds of elements that Dallas shares with other urban places, including boosterism, the city is distinguished by particular and persistent, though not unique, patterns and relationships of power. The hegemonic domination of civic leadership by the business class has been unusually long-term, continuous, and self-reproducing, despite some differences over time in political regimes, alliances, public proclamations, and, on occasion, programs and outcomes. The political power behind Dallas's urban development has often been cast in terms of "reform," with leaders portrayed as disinterested and selfless, serving the "public good" rather than

FIGURE 25. Main Street east at Akard, 1935. With tall commercial blocks lining the streets, Dallas looked toward the future as an automobile metropolis. From Holmes and Saxon, *WPA Dallas Guide and History.*

FIGURE 26. Southwestern Life Building, ca. 1920. "Begun in 1911 and finished in 1913, the Southwestern Life Building was a Sullivanesque masterpiece of the art of skyscraper construction. Located at the southwest corner of Main and Akard streets, the crisp lines and classic beauty of the magnificent structure were destroyed in 1972 when it was leveled for a parking lot." McDonald, *Dallas Rediscovered*. Reprinted with permission of Southwestern Life Insurance Company.

catering to "special interests." Yet, as the local version of the apocryphal but proverbial saying, "What's good for General Motors is good for the country,"[17] puts it, "the business of Dallas is business."[18] Despite the purported "democratization" of the city and proclamations of the decline of the business leadership's power, the entrepreneurial elite remains a potent force both publicly and privately.

Equally distinctive has been the nearly uncontested domination of private interests over the public domain, a profound confusion between public and private, the recurrent use of public influence and expenditures for private gain, and strict limitations on the development of a public sphere. Dallas's long-term dependence on infusions of funds from federal, state, and local governments contradicts the dominant ideology of leadership acting to stimulate and secure growth independently of public monies and outside control. Although city leaders did their best to avoid the "compromise" and "contamination" involved in taking federal monies earmarked for public housing and integrated public schools, a great deal of government funding helped Dallas economically—or at least those in a position to profit from its growth. At the same time, city leaders have routinely used public resources for private purposes, from subsidizing the relocation of railway lines in 1870–72 to extending the airport runway at public expense to lure aircraft manufacturer Chance Vought to Dallas in 1948.

That business elites serving as civic leaders were able to appropriate public funds to subsidize private enterprises without imputations of conflict of interest is remarkable testament to their local hegemony. In most cities, political debate is highly sensitive to the intersection of public expense and private profit; because most urban projects are visible and costly, spatial configurations are expressions of power. In Dallas, as elsewhere, the media far more often lauded and drew attention to private spending and sponsorship that purportedly benefited the public than to the reverse. Obvious instances of massive public spending to benefit private developers, such as the American Airlines Center and the surrounding Victory area, were contested. But even in those cases the rhetorical division between public and private interests was blurred. When a hotel owner presented the city with a herd of sculpted bronze steers, he was praised publicly as a civic benefactor; if there was snickering about the fact that this gift, set up on an empty lot, blocked competing hotels from locating nearby, the laughter was kept out of media analysis. Other examples of confusing crossover in

Dallas include public responsibility for site and infrastructure work for privately owned structures, public construction and maintenance of convention center facilities whose benefits fall more quickly and directly into corporate hands than city coffers, and public guarantees to limit potential losses for developers who build upscale housing downtown but not for those who build public housing for low-income families.

Even more nebulous and challenging is the recent interest in public-private partnerships, tax waivers and incentives, and zoning and planning schemes that play in suburbs as well as city centers—all part of cities' attempts to make up for dwindling tax receipts and state and federal revenues. The illusion that Dallas was autonomous from federal subsidies and immune from national economic trends shattered as the contractions of the late twentieth century hit home.

At key moments in Dallas past and present, the leadership class has been divided among itself. Major, overlapping differences between old and new regimes often hinge on matters of social class, race, ethnicity, gender, geographic orientation, political ideology, visions for Dallas's development, and economic assumptions and strategies. Studies of urban politics warn us to be wary of actions or campaigns that boast and boost "reform."[19] Indeed, the concepts of "reform" and "reformers" are not much clearer conceptually or practically than "public" and "private." Those two sets of complications overlap each other historically. Reform has often been allied at least putatively or rhetorically with the "public," typically a progressive stand, but at other times with "private" interests, typically a more conservative or corporate agenda. Given Dallas's characteristic public-private entanglements, questions of reforming urban governance constitute a major and continuing concern.

Great debates and campaigns over restructuring the city council, with respect to its size, composition, representation, and authority, and the city's executive offices, defining the positions and prerogatives of mayor, commissioners, and/or city manager, took place in the early twentieth century, again in the 1920s and early 1930s, and from the 1970s well into the 1990s. They continue today. At the turn of the twentieth century, reform meant removing governance from politics by installing bureaucratic city commissions and a professional city manager; at the end of the twentieth century, when "democracy" belatedly came to Dallas, reform meant increasing the authority of locally elected officials accountable to voters. Currents proposing and opposing "reform" arose in close connection to pressing concerns about the most appropriate and effective uses of municipal power and the public purse, the city's economic prospects, and divisions within elites and among groups of citizens who defined themselves by geographic residence, race or ethnicity, and ideology. Recent debates have been marked by deep divisions over the need to make substantial amendments to the city charter, increase the power of the mayor, and either abolish or radically reduce the authority of the city manager.[20]

The usual telling of the Dallas story neglects the city's extraordinary long-term problems of urban governance, which are intimately tied to unresolved issues of social order, social justice, and social relations. Matters of race, ethnicity, and class mark law enforcement, authorized and extralegal violence, and inequality in access to and distribution of civic resources. The lack of democracy in Dallas became more difficult to ignore during the civil rights and postassassination eras. In his gloss on the myths of Dallas's history, Michael Hazel states complacently that these conflicts "inevitably arose in a fast-growing city with an increasingly diverse population" in which "more democratic methods have slowly become dominant."[21] This narrative of progress does not take into account Dallas's history and legacy of racial and ethnic violence and quick resort to force as a response to an enormous range of problems.[22] Hazel and other recent writers of Dallas history treat evidence of racism and violence with a new form of denial, recognizing these problems but relegating them to the past rather than acknowledging their persistence in the present.

Finally, placing Dallas in political-economic and social-historical context and recognizing both its shared and distinctive patterns of urban development enables us to realize that the very same factors which account for its growth are also the principal factors which contribute to the city's most pressing, long-term problems. Social order and disorder, exclusion and separation, discrimination and inequality, growth and its complications are seldom far from questions about governance, public and private, and image and identity over the course of Dallas's history.

DISCOVERING HISTORIC DALLAS

During the late twentieth century, Dallas began to discover and reinterpret its past.[23] The shift was positive, even if the hour was late and the patterns were copied from elsewhere. Some of the causal and contributing factors in Dallas's attention to the past had specific local roots as well as national models. Dallas's history seemed to accrue potential value, so it became the site of a struggle for control. Ironically, the dynamics shaping the presentation of this history exhibit many of the same patterns—preoccupation with image, denial of history, and substitution of myths—that are evident in the city's past. (See the appendixes.)

Throughout the United Sates, during the last quarter of the twentieth century, the marketing of history became a major economic and cultural engine, often with the help of tax exemptions and incentives at various levels of government: to attract residents, tourists, and conventioneers; for consumption materially, from buying an old house or a downtown loft for home or office, frequenting a hotel or restaurant in an old building, adopting retro styles in clothing or furnishings; vicariously, imbibing a "spirit" or sense of the past through film and other media, often as entertainment; and experientially, from visiting the remains and reconstructions of the past, including an unending variety of theme parks, to playacting in costume at historical reenactments.[24]

Internationally, the 1980s and 1990s were a great age of celebrating the past—or at least some people's notion of the past—and of reinventing history, for marketing, purchase, and consumption, often as a "theme park" playground. With help from professional and amateur historians, historical and preservation societies, architects, realtors, and entrepreneurs, municipalities eagerly jumped on the bandwagon in the history parade, promoting this postmodern version of the past to sell everything from coffee-table books to entire neighborhoods. History added a veneer of sentimental nostalgia to the urban landscape and mixed, often comfortably but sometimes contradictorily, with gentrification, redevelopment, and renewal. There is nothing in such a history to study and learn from, nothing even to spark curiosity or engagement, let alone to illuminate vital connections between past and present or offer alternative perspectives on the future. As a revisionist reconstruction of the past aimed explicitly at display and consumption, it manifests a cleanliness, orderliness, friendliness, homogeneity, and equanimity that the real past never had. This portrayal of the past resists the recognition and representation of working-class immigrants, Hispanics, and African Americans, especially those who were enslaved.[25] Nationally and internationally, the movement proliferates city museums, historic districts, and sites for sightseers that increasingly resemble one another just as airports do. For example, New York City's South Street Seaport has spawned copies everywhere from Baltimore to Boston and San Francisco to Seattle. In typically facile fashion, the new urban historicism shares important ground with the so-called New Urbanism, especially a fear of the disorder inherent in urban life when not tightly contained, carefully monitored, and commercially packaged.[26]

In Dallas, the new interest in the city's past arose from a gnawing awareness of its problems of identity and image and a dawning perception that there was money to be made from what was old as well as new. As the headline for a 1999 article by *Dallas Morning News* urban affairs writer Chris Kelley put it, "Past Provides a View of Dallas' Future: City Looks to Its Roots to Develop a More Authentic Sense of Place." Discovering this past included reclaiming nature, recycling downtown buildings, and constructing new center-city neighborhoods. Taken together, the authenticity that the past contributes to a sense of place is supposed to make the cityscape more "people-centered," with a scale suited to consumers and pedestrians.[27] In 2001, Ron Kirk contributed to the National Trust for Historical Preservation's *Forum Journal* under the title "Dallas: A New City Discovers Its Past." The mayor explained, "Dallas is the new American city. . . . Over the last several years, we've also realized that the places of our past add to the fabric of our community. Historic preservation has become a tool for increased economic activity. . . . Dallas may not have the lengthy history of other great American cities. However, as a 'new' city, we're laying claim to our history—and ensuring that those who would preserve it, can."[28] Making historic preservation and adaptive reuse by private interests possible is not the same as embracing it as a matter of public policy, but for Dallas, it represented a real shift—and one that, characteristically, was spurred by the recognition that revitalizing the city's historic fabric could make a substantial contribution to its economy.

Dallas creatively devises new "historic districts," most of which are simply old and rundown, and offers redevelopers incentives and exemptions to recycle the usable structures and combine these remnants with new construction. Vacant space in downtown office buildings and old warehouses is turned into loft apartments with names meant to evoke the past and benefit from southwestern and even more remote associations, for example, Santa Fe Terminal Urban Lofts. The "Historic West End" lacks the architecturally distinguished buildings, socially significant associations, and intact urban fabric that would ordinarily qualify a district for preservation, but, happily, its lack of integrity allows infilling with new structures that mimic what developers and consumers imagine the past ought to have looked like, but never was there. Theme-park versions of Dallas's past bear an uncanny resemblance to its newly designed suburbs.

To the north, ultra-suburban Las Colinas has its own "Urban Center" replete with a monorail, parking garages fronted with facades meant to evoke Amsterdam town houses, and an array of rearing stallions, cast in bronze, symbolizing wildness in a controlled environment. The *AIA Guide to Dallas Architecture* enthused:

> The success of DFW Airport led directly to Ben Carpenter's dream of developing the family ranch into Las Colinas, a planned community of 12,000 acres to the east in an undeveloped part of Irving. By 1985, the mesquite-covered hill had become the premier corporate address in Texas, with much to offer the architectural tourist both in the way of elegant headquarters in verdant settings and an Urban Center built around a 125-acre man-made lake and canals. With the recent expansion of mid-density housing to go with bell towers, water taxis and a fixed guideway people-mover, this corporate Disneyland is starting to exude a real sense of place.[29]

Taken to its logical ends, imitation without local grounding leads to Las Vegas.[30] Borrowing of other places' pasts is closely tied to the market for recent urban visions, especially strategies to promote the economic revival of downtown through the return of residents, tourism by visitors from near and far, and conventioneers who can walk to historic sites from their hotels. The restaurants, clubs, and boutiques that fill the "new" downtown and "new" historic areas represent deals with the devils of the past, postmodern consumerism staged within the shells of older structures. The imitation and promotion of historic city centers is vital to urban competition. Flying in the face of their own claims about uniqueness, urban centers become more, not less, alike.[31]

As politics, ideology, and the market intersected in the discovery and invention of a profitable urban past, Dallas confronted challenging conflicts over whether and how to acknowledge aspects of its own history that were more disturbing than the historic values it borrowed from other places.

Figure 27. Las Colinas, 1978. Photographer: Doug Tomlinson. From *Dallas Architecture 1936–1986,* photographs by Doug Tomlinson, text by David Dillon (Austin: Texas Monthly Press, 1985).

Played out on a small stage, these issues involve many of the same factors that led to public "history wars" nationally: over the Smithsonian's proposed exhibit of the "Enola Gay" aircraft that dropped the first atomic bomb, which raised questions about U.S. responsibility for nuclear catastrophe; over museum interpretations placing artistic representations of the American West in relation to territorial expansion as an imperial enterprise; and over revisionist trends and countercurrents in U.S. history course content and textbooks.[32] Dallas, long known for its traditions of violence and, after 1963, dubbed "the city that hates" or "the city that kills," is unusually sensitive about giving offense or attracting criticism. That weighs upon its approach to admitting and presenting its history.

In 2003, a "history war" broke out in Dallas over the importance of identifying a formerly "Whites Only" water fountain at the Dallas County Courthouse. The *Dallas Morning News* asked, "How should relics of a racist past be handled? What should be done with relics that many deem offensive?"[33] The public issues are superficially simple: the need for each generation to remember and to learn from accurate commemorative markers of the past, despite its ugliness, on the one hand; and sullying the marketability of historic locations by marking the cruelty of past practices in that place, on the other. It does not take long for questions to arise, sometimes implicitly: *whose* past, *whose* offense, *whose* responsibility? These unanswered questions resonate in the present as well as the past.

The small and unobtrusive "Whites Only" sign was covered during the controversy. County commissioners voted by a margin of four to one to preserve the sign and add a historical plaque, with an explanation that politely ended, "The Dallas County Commissioners Court has chosen to leave the remnants of this sign in the original location to remind us of this unpleasant portion of our history—if we cannot remember it, we will not learn from it, and we will not appreciate or respect the rights and responsibilities we enjoy." Acknowledging but reducing Jim Crow to an "unpleasant portion of our history" did not resolve the controversy. To some, it seemed as inadequate as removing the sign would have been; to others, it seemed to compound the offense.

Although usually cast in terms of a debate between two sides, the conflict involved a wider range of viewpoints. In the *Dallas Morning News*'s account, the winning position articulated the hope that signage would serve as a reminder "that segregation is a shameful but unforgettable chapter in

American history." African American leader and county commissioner John Wiley Price explained, "Our only real option is to preserve it, review it, and use it as a barometer and a landmark for the future."[34] The main opposition, as summarized in the *Dallas Morning News,* believed that the presence of the sign "would embarrass the county and hurt people who, in years past, would have been targets of the sign's exclusionary edict." That statement blends and blurs two distinct and incompatible positions. Fear of embarrassing the county identifies a distinctly different target (the whites who imposed apartheid) and potential cost (fear of a public loss of face and economic value) than fear of hurting those who had been "targets of the sign." The first of those viewpoints questions the importance of being "reminded of that offensive activity in a public county-owned building"; the second view underscores the additional offense of patronizing African Americans.

Another proposal, which also garnered support across racial lines, was to preserve such "relics of the racist past" in museums rather than on site. As the *Morning News* observed, controversy over the water fountain increased awareness that "examples of Dallas' past can be found all over town." One example was the gray granite cornerstone of Hope Cottage, built in 1922–23 by one of the city's oldest adoption agencies, identifying the Ku Klux Klan as a major donor. When Hope Cottage relocated in 1978, the cornerstone was relegated to a closet. In 1995, the Hope Cottage board voted unanimously to destroy the stone. "'It was a real relief to get rid of it,' recalled Dr. Aileen Edgington, executive director of Hope Cottage in 1995. 'The KKK was like the Nazis. Maybe they did something good sometime. But who cares?'"[35] An important question, indeed. Eight years later, concerned persons made a strong case for the preservation of signs, markers, and other remains of the past, preferably in museums. Dr. Robert Edison, an African American historian and educator, advocated saving both signs and cornerstones and presenting them in museums because of their potential to stimulate "teaching moments." He explained to the *Dallas Morning News,* "If you destroy it, that doesn't mean it didn't exist." Edison, the reporter repeated with audible astonishment, "also defends the preservation of monuments such as the Confederate War Memorial in Pioneer Park, which includes a small historic cemetery next to the Dallas Convention Center. . . . 'They have as much right to honor their dead as we have to honor Martin Luther King.'"[36]

The form in which history is presented has significant consequences. Displaying remains of a scarred past can be used, implicitly or explicitly, to proclaim that the present is different and the problem of racial exclusion has been resolved. The history of racial discrimination and conflict is an especially touchy subject in Dallas, although no commentators broached the question of what legacy the city's violent white supremacist tradition bequeaths to the present. Two interrelated omissions deserve consideration: the geographic location of historic remains, and their public or private provenance. Concerns about giving offense, embarrassing residents or tourists, and casting shadows on the present bear heavily in center cities, downtowns, "historic" neighborhoods, and other places likely to be visited. These concerns weigh less on more out-of-the-way locations. Hardly a matter of historical accuracy or even value alone, serious concerns for the preservation and presence of the past can conflict directly with equally serious concerns about the state and fate of the present. It is much easier to insist on the preservation and display of historically significant objects in places owned or governed by public agencies than in privately owned spaces or structures. Opinions often differ sharply on whether the value of preserving a community's past should prevail over the rights of private property owners, but these issues become even more deeply fraught when the past in question is seen as shameful or insulting. While relocation carries costs, people can choose whether or not to visit these isolated remnants of the past. "Museumization" disconnects past from present, removing historic artifacts to a place where they are stripped of social context and reinterpreted, rather than preserving their problematic and provocative integration into the fabric of the city.

Dallas's historical establishment has benefited from, more than stimulated, the recent revival of popular interest in the past. The Dallas Historical Society now focuses on the city. Since the late 1980s, it has collaborated with Old City Park and the Sixth Floor Museum, and more recently the Old Red Foundation, in publishing *Legacies: A History Journal for Dallas and North Central Texas,* a twice-yearly magazine overseen by academics but intended for a broader audience. Since the early 2000s, *Legacies* has drawn on papers presented at annual one-day conferences devoted to Dallas-area history.[37] An annual Dallas history week was instituted in 2002. A series of receptions, open houses, tours, and presentations, many with food and drink, culminated in a Dallas Heart Ball benefiting Children's Medical Center and UT Southwestern Medical Center for Pediatric Heart Research. The sponsors of these events recognize that attention to history carries expectations of profit and represents a kind of investment. These ventures join many others in an effort to give Dallas a revised past that supports a proud present and bright future.[38]

Giving Dallas a more prominent past goes hand-in-hand with making Dallas a livelier, more interesting city.[39] The Dallas Historical Society's most visibly successful activity is its tours of Historic Dallas. Among those promoted in 2006 were "East and South Dallas Historic Discovery Journey," "Discover the Heart of Historic Centennial Fair Park," "Historic Cemeteries," "Legend of Bonnie and Clyde," a JFK tour called "Following the Steps of Lee Harvey Oswald," and "Amid the Skyscrapers of Downtown Dallas."[40] Descriptions feature the contemporary "relevance" of these urban adventures. For example, the "Blues and Heritage Tour of Deep Ellum" "explores the mythology, folklore, and cultural origins of Deep Ellum from the early days through its creation as a bohemian village to its future as an urban oasis for creative community living."[41] The historical society's Web site is touted as a haven for history buffs of all kinds.

The recent discovery of Dallas history will be crowned with a new institution, the Museum of Dallas History and Culture in the Old Red County Courthouse downtown, finally opened in May 2007.[42] Announcing plans for the museum, the *Dallas Morning News* proclaimed, "Dallas History: Old Red Will Reveal There Is Such a Thing."[43] David Schultz, the museum's first executive director, sought to "dispel the myth of a 'city without a history.' . . . Dallas didn't 'jes happen.' Its founding was steeped in a heady combination of Old World social experiment and New World ambitious independence." At the museum, as Schultz put it, "Dallas' past comes to life in stories of individuals." Tellingly, all the "people of vision" featured in the museum—with the notable exception of Leadbelly—come from the ranks of the entrepreneurial elite.[44]

The description of the building in *Dallas Rediscovered* articulates the recent, striking shift in the valuation of surviving structures from the past:

> The magnificent Victorian Romanesque structure built 1891–92 on John Neely Bryan's original courthouse square is the last survivor of a long series of ill-fated 19th-century buildings. . . . Fortunately, the only damage the surviving

"Old Red" has sustained in its near ninety years was the removal of its clock tower in 1919 along with one of its two griffins, christened "Hindsight" and "Foresight." In spite of being labeled in the 1940s as "unsafe, unsightly . . . a decayed monument to the grandiose and ornate taste of the 1890s . . . and an architectural monstrosity," Old Red has survived her critics and is now protected by a listing in the National Historic Register.[45]

A replica of the clock tower was a key feature of the recent restoration, but the griffins that signified historical perspective by looking toward past and future have not been replaced, a strange and perhaps significant absence from the history museum building.

FIGURE 28. Sixth Dallas County Courthouse ("Old Red"), built 1891–92, ca. 1895. The elaborate new courthouse was a crown for the commercial city and a herald of the imagined metropolis of the future. From the collections of the Texas/Dallas History and Archives Division, Dallas Public Library.

As Dallas not only discovers that it has a history but borrows historic elements that it lacks from other places and invents a history it never had, its particularities are blurred rather than magnified, contradicting its avowed quest but emanating from its strategic actions. In his introduction to *Variations on a Theme Park,* Michael Sorkin helps to explain this curious contradiction and its consequences:

> The new city likewise eradicates genuine particularity in favor of a continuous urban field, a conceptual grid of boundless reach. It's a process of erasure much noted. . . . The new city threatens an unimagined sameness even as it multiplies the illusory choices of the TV system.
>
> Three salient characteristics mark this city. The first is the dissipation of all stable relations to local physical and cultural geography, the loosening of ties to any specific place. . . . The new city replaces the anomaly and delight of such places with a universal particular, a generic urbanism inflected only by appliqué. . . .
>
> A second characteristic of the new city is its obsession with "security," with rising levels of manipulation and surveillance over its citizenry and with a proliferation of new modes of segregation. . . .
>
> Finally, this new realm is city of simulations, television city, the city as theme park.[46]

So goes the search for history, authenticity, and distinctive urban experience when it is guided and spurred by the desire for mimesis. The paths converge on the urban theme park.

REVISING DALLAS HISTORY

Beginning in the late 1980s and accelerating in the 1990s, Dallas witnessed a flurry of historical writings, both popular and academic. Most were revisionist in intent and spirit.[47] This surge of publications was part of the wider effort to discover and invent a history for Dallas that would be a positive force in shaping the city's future.[48] Purposefully written to dispel the image of Dallas as a "city with no history," an "accidental" city with "no reason to exist," revisionist histories tend to return to the first origin myth of Dallas as a city destined for greatness. The myth of visionary individuals, most of them Anglo entrepreneurs, creating the city through "faith and determination" mixes with the myth of Dallas as destined for greatness. Whichever myth prevails, this is a Dallas liberated from its traumas and contradictions. Violence, racism, disorder, and inequality are either excluded from these narratives or acknowledged only as problems in the past that progressively have been overcome; their legacies in the present are too uncomfortable to explore. Although some of these revisionist histories include women, racial and ethnic minorities, and workers and more ordinary folk, the actions and achievements of business elites and their partners in urban development form the dominant theme. For a "new" history of Dallas launched when American social and urban historians had initiated a plethora of "new histories," this body of work deals surprisingly little with systemic imbalances of power, inequalities of race and class, or dynamics of segregation and fragmentation. Nor is it conceptually or methodologically innovative; most of these books ignore the quantitative and graphic methods of analyzing demographic growth, social stratification and mobility, and geographic configurations that were being developed at this time. Classic motifs of rise and fall, decline and recovery shape these writings, often without reflection on the assumptions they entail and the implications they suggest.

Darwin Payne's *Big D: Triumphs and Troubles of an American Supercity in the 20th Century* (1994) epitomizes the genre; in five hundred pages, the journalist-historian traces the arc of Dallas's modern history from "Making the Future Happen" to "Boom and Bust." Michael Hazel's *Dallas: A History of "Big D"* (1997) covers 150 years in seventy-three pages for a popular audience, highlighting Dallas's geographic advantages and "how individuals capitalized on the city's natural assets." Elizabeth Enstam's *Women and the Creation of Urban Life: Dallas, Texas, 1843–1920* (1998), the only book to focus substantially on nineteenth-century Dallas, is joined in its attention to women as active advocates of social reform by Jacquelyn McElhaney's study, *Pauline Periwinkle and Progressive Reform in Dallas* (1998). The contrast between William H. Wilson's *Hamilton Park: A Planned Black Community in Dallas* (1998) and the chapters on Dallas in Wilson's *City Beautiful Movement* (1989) and Robert Fairbanks's *For the City as a Whole: Planning, Politics, and the Public Interest in Dallas, Texas, 1900–1965* (1998) illuminates the tensions between planners' comprehensive views of urban systems and the interactions of different social groups in specific neighborhoods.[49]

Another, less cohesive set of professional historians has been criticized by the first group as overly critical of the city, perhaps because their works probe the more offensive and conflict-filled aspects of the past and take a critical stance toward the business elite and the uses of reform. Patricia Hill's *Dallas: The Making of a Modern City* (1996) examines "the activities of organized labor, women's groups, racial minorities, Populist and social-ist radicals, and Progressive reformers—all of whom competed and compro-mised with business leaders" in the decades before World War II, showing "that Dallas can accommodate dissent and conflict as it moves toward a more inclusive public life."[50] My own work, including this book, places me in this group.[51] Marvin Dulaney's series of articles on African American activism in Dallas and Michael Phillips's *White Metropolis: Race, Ethnicity, and Religion in Dallas, 1841–2001* (2006) investigate racial inequality as a fundamental feature of the city's ongoing history rather than a problem Dallas has left behind. Royce Hanson's *Civic Culture and Urban Change: Governing Dallas* (2003) and Ruth Morgan's *Governance by Decree: The Impact of the Voting Rights Action in Dallas* (2004), two works of political science, use the city for case studies in public policy; Morgan emphasizes the unintended negative consequences of political reforms, while Hanson examines the city's inability to adapt to the economic and demographic shifts of the late twentieth century because of a civic culture dominated by entrenched elites.[52] Amy Bridges's *Morning Glories: Municipal Reform in the Southwest* (1997), which includes Dallas among the cities it studies, complements Hill and Hanson.[53] What was at stake in the differences be-tween these recent approaches to Dallas history was important enough to stimulate a debate in the media. In April 1999, the *Dallas Morning News* published "Two Views of Dallas: Scholars Differ on What the Vision of City Has Been and Should Be" in its Sunday features section. The *Dallas Morning News* reporter began by saying that Robert Fairbanks, University of Texas at Arlington historian, and Royce Hanson, University of Texas at Dallas former dean of social science and urban policy scholar, both claimed to take major lessons from Dallas's past but "their conclusions and advice could not be more different."[54]

The dispute deals with questions and issues absolutely central to Dallas's history and, more pragmatically, the city's present and future. In Fairbanks's view, Dallas "once distinguished itself by looking to the welfare of the whole, nearly always putting the common good over special interests. The loss of that overriding civic vision, Dr. Fairbanks says, has fed ethnic politics, neighborhood jealousies and school board chaos." Hanson argues that "the Dallas way of doing things—first crafted by a small group of business leaders in the 1920s—stunted the city's political growth by excluding minorities and stifling debate." Hanson's view, as summarized by the *Morning News,* is that local political clashes are "the inevitable result of nearly a century of paternalistic governance by a small elite." Where Hanson calls for seeing "diversity of opinion as a source of civic strength," Fairbanks calls for a rejection of "special interests."

The two scholars' dramatically divergent conclusions and prescriptions for change arise in part from their different disciplines and interests. Fairbanks concentrates on unfulfilled progressive urban planning traditions, and Hanson focuses on political culture in the period after 1960. They hold almost diametrically opposed assumptions about the nature of urban societies and polities, especially in their conceptions of conflict, and different perspectives on how history and its understanding shape the present. Where Fairbanks seeks a return to a "politics of consensus," Hanson advocates a political process that recognizes divergent interests and negotiates compromises for the "public good."

In my view, Fairbanks confuses Dallas's political history with a myth of the "city as a whole," a notion that certain members of the business and financial elite found in the perspectives of Dallas's city planners. When joined with an elite-driven politics of reform, the notion undergirded an ideology that proved very useful in shaping Dallas's polity and cityscape. Elites defined their interests as those of "the whole"; they represented their views as a "consensus" without allowing debate. Others' interests were branded as private, parochial, divisive, or selfish. Dominant interests, especially those centered on downtown's economic engines and their needs, became one with the "public." Fairbanks tolerates or makes apologies for the biases and inequalities that accompanied the triumph of that false or fabricated "whole."

Both Fairbanks's and Hanson's histories have limited evidentiary bases that cannot entirely bear the weight of their arguments. Hanson's notions of political culture and the "public good" are inadequate to bridge the divides and inequalities left by decades of elite domination of the political economy and to heal the collateral damage to culture and society. Most valuable, however, is his clear delineation of the consequences of this pattern for Dallas past, present, and future. In contrast to Fairbanks, who yearns for a revival of a consensus that never existed, Hanson's political actors are believable, and the alternative courses of action he proposes are realistic.

DEFINING THE STAGES OF URBAN DEVELOPMENT

Revisionist histories of Dallas should critique the city's myths and acknowledge the conflicts that mark its past and present. Ideally, they should enable Dallasites to see their city's similarities to and differences from other American cities and understand the dynamics of its growth. The charts that follow define the stages of Dallas's development by placing them in relation to broader patterns of American urban history and show how this conceptualization of urban development organizes Dallas's historical chronology. (See the appendixes.)

This approach is rooted in the full sweep of Dallas's past, recognizing its urban origins in the mid-nineteenth century rather than privileging the twentieth century or isolating the modern city from its precedents. By placing local developments within their historical contexts, we can comprehend their causes and consequences and consider their meanings today. In this view, Dallas's history appears, not as predestined or invented, but as a process of social action and interaction that shapes and is shaped by political economic structures, cultures, and ideologies. The city's achievements appear, not as inevitable or willful, but accompanied by their human complications, costs, and historical legacies of inequality and subordination.

This perspective encourages us to connect the history of Dallas's political economy with its urban historical geography, social structures and relationships, and cultural configurations, paying close attention to time, place, and persons. As history, not accident or destiny, the relationships between successive stages are contingent and variable, not linear or deterministic. Those who participate in the making of history are human, their agency limited by circumstances and connections; the cast of historical actors is inclusive, both individual and collective. These approaches and presumptions shape the multidimensional readings of Dallas past and present that constitute this experimental book.

The historicity of this conceptualization rests on historians' special ability to look backward and forward at almost the same moment. This version of Dallas's history is not the only possible revision; seeing the city from multiple perspectives is crucial to a comprehensive understanding of its growth and prospects. This revision of Dallas history aims explicitly at advancing our understanding of Dallas past and Dallas present, and in so doing, influences our ability to frame choices for Dallas's future. We search for the presence of the past in the present—earlier Dallas developments in the context of later and contemporary urban historical experiences—and, simultaneously, contingently, and reciprocally, we search for the origins, seeds, and beginnings of the present in the past.

PART II

UNDERSTANDING DALLAS

The Dallas Way

In 1987, a special edition of the *Dallas Times Herald* commemorating the fiftieth anniversary of the Dallas Citizens Council (DCC) began by asking, "Who runs Dallas?" The answer is:

They are all millionaires, some dozens of times over, and their influence reaches into nearly every corner of economic, political and cultural life in Dallas. The 10 most influential people in Dallas, as identified in a *Times Herald* survey of business leaders, primarily come from the ranks of the city's chief executive officers. Eight of the 10 are members of the Dallas Citizens Council. . . .

The city's chief "yes and no" men—the chieftains of Dallas' largest businesses, those who could unilaterally commit their companies' power and wealth to "what's good for Dallas"—would decide what needed to be done, raise the money to do it and see that it got done. If they needed City Council help, they could get it because council members owed their incumbency to the Citizens Council. If they needed electorate support for, say, a bond issue, they could get it because—well, because the voters wanted to do "what's good for Dallas," too.

That was "the Dallas way"—a philosophy very much alive today, in principle if not practical application.

Whatever Dallas needed in order to grow—freeways, sewers, reservoirs, airports—got financed and built with barely a whisper of opposition. Corporations like Chance-Vought were wooed fervently and ceaselessly. Developers and entrepreneurs were given financial and psychological encouragement to ply their schemes in Dallas.

In return for the help and favors that Dallas gave them, the companies and their bosses were expected to plow part of their winnings back into the civic weal to provide orchestras, operas, museums, libraries and charities. Those were good for the city, too, and it was what he contributed to "what's good for Dallas" that determined a businessman's status in the community. Only if he worked hard for Dallas' civic welfare and believed fervently in its glittering destiny—and, of course, succeeded at his business—might he hope to be invited to join the Citizen's Council and become one of the city's decision-makers.

That, too, was "the Dallas Way."

"Perhaps not since the great cities of Renaissance Italy has there been such a striking example of an oligarchy in action," wrote *Fortune* magazine in 1949. "Like them, it has been a mercantile oligarchy, for it is the bankers and the merchants who largely run Dallas. They run it well, with self-effacement, and not for private gain."[1]

Only in Dallas would being called an "oligarchy in action" count as praise. In other cities, power brokers conceal their sway under the cover of democracy, but in Dallas elite rule was open and unabashed. So, too, was the conception of the city as a growth machine. The businessmen who made fortunes from the city's "favors" were expected to return some portion of their profits to the city in the form of culture or charity. Banish the thought of self-interest: like the Medicis, the bankers and merchants who run the city are committed to "what's good for Dallas."

The *Dallas Times Herald* unself-consciously mixed ideology, mythology, and nostalgia and offered this litany of Dallas-speak as a substitute for a history and political economy of the city. The article does not ask what the Dallas Way did *not* do, nor does the article question the legitimacy of power, its social bases, and its uses. The proper relationship between private interests and the public domain, fair limits to the power of self-appointed "oligarchs," and careful consideration of who benefits from and who pays for Dallas developments are deliberately ignored. Power in its many dimensions configures urban space, race and ethnicity, social class, and gender, extending or denying fairness, opportunity, and equity. Those elements constitute the *civic hegemony* of the Dallas Way and have worked to sustain it over most of the city's history, although in forms and with authority and force that shifted over time. Ideology and discourse, while undergoing changes, have experienced less transformation than the material city and the circumstances of its citizens.[2] Increasing over time, those disparities carried complicated consequences.

Reflecting on a 1982 *Texas Monthly* article describing Dallas as a uniquely "plutocratic version of democracy," veteran *Times Herald* reporter Jim Henderson commented:

> For most of this century, that had been the popular perception of Dallas, a major city run by a tight circle of rich, white, elderly men—predominantly developers and land speculators—who, at regular intervals, chose a mayor and city council to be ratified by the electorate. If that version of Dallas was a cliché, it was one glutted with veracity.
>
> Dallas had always belonged to the men who built it, men who did not need zoning laws to tell them where to put skyscrapers or which pastures to subdivide. . . . They ran their government the way they ran their privately held businesses.
>
> At-large elections kept the process relatively simple. Members of the old Citizens Charter Association would gather in some male-only, high-rise enclave, pick a slate of candidates, pony up campaign funds and retire to the bar for a pre-victory celebration. From 1934 through 1985, the "establishment" candidate for mayor was defeated only once.[3]

In this version, the city was ruled by developers who put skyscrapers and subdivisions wherever they chose and ensured that elected officials validated their decisions. Henderson recognized that a city ruled by the elite in the same "way they ran their privately held businesses" was not a democracy, even though its decisions were ratified by a passive electorate.

Postmortems of the reign of the Dallas Citizens Council, as well as the unrepresentative at-large city council system, either raise the specter or wave the banner of democracy arriving in Dallas, at long last, for good or ill. Some residents express deeply felt angst over the decline of the Dallas Way, occasionally mixed with nostalgia for the good old days (and boys)[4] and often filled with anxiety about the divisiveness that attends contested elections and controversial issues. Others worry about the continued power of the business elite behind the scenes. Although the city's political system has changed in recent decades, reports of the Dallas Way's demise may be premature.[5]

Over the twentieth century, the city was defined more powerfully by the Dallas Way than by any other single image or ideology. Providing a legitimating discourse as well as a revealing description of the private conduct of public business, the Dallas Way is arguably the key to the city, a mode of accounting for its growth and for its characteristic responses to threats from without and within. The Dallas Way is built upon, embraces, and promotes the best and the worst in Dallas. Its partialities, exclusions, inequities, and contradictions have limited, distorted, and profoundly damaged the city. Like so much else, the Dallas Way is an exaggeration of general trends that many urban places share—but so huge an exaggeration as to mark Dallas as different in degree, if not in kind.

Ranking high among the long-standing defining powers of the Dallas Way has been the power to shape the discourse and consequently the perception of Dallas, at home and often beyond. Control of the major media, and especially the tireless work of the Dealey family's *Dallas Morning News,* greatly aided that process. Geographer David Wilson reminds us of "the power of locally grounded metaphors to fashion social reality and to legitimate a dominant growth discourse and uneven development in the city. . . . These metaphors contribute to an everyday consciousness—already steeped in decades of pernicious power relations, to be sure—that powerfully transforms, via a wealth of signifiers, a process that is negotiable, political, and contestable into an unproblematic neutral object."[6] The discourse of the Dallas Way and actions claiming to follow it shaped and reinforced one another in both everyday life and dominant narratives in Dallas. The Dallas Way simultaneously denies and invents histories for its city. It informs expectations, shapes the field of vision and possibility, and provides the basis for Dallas discourse.

One of the most remarkable, yet least remarked, features of the Dallas Way is its singularity.[7] The notion that there is *one* and *only* one Dallas Way is, at its core, ruling out consideration of alternatives. The way is both means and end. In many ways, it parallels the construction and usage of the American way.

FIVE TAKES ON THE DALLAS WAY

Five exemplary stories of the Dallas Way, starting with the most legendary, reveal the breadth, complexity, power, and contradictoriness of the Dallas Way as construct and as practice.

TAKE 1: AS PHILOSOPHY AND FAITH

The Dallas Way endorses the myth of a "can-do" city with "no limits." As a writer crowed in 1925, "The growth of the 'Metropolis of the Southwest' can only be attributed to the spirit and industry of its inhabitants and to their unbounded faith in the future of their city."[8] This Dallas Way provides the spiritual and moral underpinnings of the city itself.

TAKE 2: AS YOUTHFUL AMBITION AND INCESSANT ACTIVITY

A second take, replete with adjectives and adverbs, points toward a familiar narrative, rooted in a familiar trope. This "Dallas Way" admits to a certain immaturity and ambition, but never to understatement or doubts about Dallas's destiny. "These people," said John Bainbridge in 1961 of Dallas residents, both native and newly arrived, "had the energy of the Yankee and the thrift of the New Englander, and they took on the optimism of the Texan. But, most important, no matter where they came from, they right away picked up the great old Dallas tradition of go-go-go." All this rushing around, according to Bainbridge, resulted in a "sketchy" or vaguely defined "communal character" in which "everything is on the surface: youthfulness, pride, desperate ambition—a combination that naturally wells up from a community on the make." What is shared is primarily a "reverence for business." "If, as Calvin Coolidge so trenchantly observed, the business of America is business, Dallas may well be the *all* American city, for it is a city of the businessmen, by the businessmen, and for the businessmen."[9] There is no place, in this Dallas, for irony or other forms of qualification, self-examination, or reflection, for heterogeneity or difference. Commerce is king. The *Dallas Times Herald* explains the city's public face: "Dallas was proud of its prudence and self-possession."[10] Yet observers note more combustible and contradictory elements: "youthfulness, pride, desperate ambition" clash with respectability and unity; desire must be reined in with conformity.

TAKE 3: THE WAY IT'S SUPPOSED TO BE

A third take combines memory with ideology to create a haze over history, in the clichéd and classic version of the Dallas Way as dictated by former mayor Robert L. Thornton. These stories suggest that there was a definite period—the era of the Citizens Council—in which the Dallas Way reigned supremely, although they fail to describe its development and demise. A note of nostalgia accompanies its passing.[11] The descriptive vocabulary of the Dallas Way combines enthusiastic assertions with inconsistencies, ambiguities, and vagaries:

> It used to be so simple: Uncle Bob Thornton would make a few phone calls or Erik Jonsson would have half a dozen other members of the Dallas Citizens Council to lunch at the City Club, and the problem was solved—or answers were furnished, conclusions reached, action begun. That was community leadership, that was municipal power. Everybody knew who ran Dallas: the business establishment, the decision makers, the oligarchy—call it what you would. Once the pyramid of power (which numbered as few as three at the apex and as many as 250 at the base) was convinced, things moved quickly and (in most cases) smoothly to a foregone conclusion. Of course, there were crises when, pushed by the clock, the calendar, or circumstances, this process didn't allow the broad citizenry in on the action. Accomplishments were announced more often than they were debated. But the decision makers (as one writer named them) figured that was all right. They'd earned the right to trust from those who counted in the community. Scandal, machine politics in City Hall, personal jealousy were not a part of the leadership game. . . . Through the 1940s, the '50s, and most of the '60s it worked that way: a machine that wasn't a machine, an aristocracy that volunteered its services but was absolute in its control. Might was inherited along business lines instead of bloodlines, and all of it based on a sort of gentleman's agreement that no one would grab for private power or overreach for personal gain.[12]

One of the most fabled examples of the Dallas Way in action demonstrates that this "gentleman's agreement" was based on the notion that competition was acceptable only with other cities; within Dallas, creating a positive climate for business was the common goal. Note the proud gloss on "civic doing," along with the gendered gamesmanship:

> Beisel, head of Chance-Vought Aircraft, had been getting the company set to move from Bridgeport, Connecticut to Dallas. Then, one black Friday, he looked at the charts of Dallas' airport, checked again with his engineers, and put through a phone call to "Deck" Hulcy, one of the Dallas boosters who were helping to expedite the migration.

"About that move to Dallas—" he said. "It all hinges on whether those runways there can be extended. They're not big enough."

There was a pause on the other end. Runways? How big *should* they be? No—the exact measurements. Two thousand feet more? Hulcy and his friends would look into the matter.

Three hours and forty minutes later Beisel's phone rang. It was Hulcy. He just wanted to let Beisel know that the City Council had been persuaded to call an emergency meeting. Two hundred and fifty-six thousand dollars had been voted for the runways. Work would begin Monday morning. Any time they could be of service. . . . Beisel, like any normal person exposed to the men of Dallas, was thunderstruck, but to them the matter was so routine that they have scarcely given it a second thought—excepting possibly, a regret that they hadn't anticipated the runway idea so Beisel wouldn't have had to phone in the first place. Civic doing is their natural function, the great ideal of their lives and they give so prodigally of their time that it is a wonder they have any left for making all the money they do. "It's like a big game," explains Hulcy. It is also something more: it is about the only reason there is a Dallas at all.[13]

In this big game, the Dallas Way provided the playbook so that Dallas could receive the spoils of victory.

Take 4: The Limits of Business Methods in Making Civic Decisions

Competition with other Texas cities to secure the foundations for economic growth required resources and networks outside the bounds of traditional government. According to a 1940 survey of city governmental institutions, Dallas leaders "of 1871 nearly bankrupted the municipality, so generous was their subsidy to the Houston and Texas Central Railroad." "Voluntarily organized civic agencies" stepped in to make sure that Dallas succeeded. "These agencies were more quickly responsive to the demands of business leaders than were the traditional institutions of government. They used modern business methods earnestly and efficiently."[14] One consequence of bypassing public bodies and review boards, these analysts observed, is a "conspicuous lack of planning and zoning." In this take on the Dallas Way, the propensity to avoid making public decisions portends problems: "The withdrawal of the leading citizens to the suburbs has seriously weakened the civic structure of Dallas. The city has grown rapidly and haphazardly. Its ambition to become a metropolis of skyscrapers has led it to imitate the large eastern cities, particularly in its business district, and has produced a striking contrast between its big city aspects and the marks of the frontier, which are not easily erased."[15]

As the *WPA Guide to Dallas* admitted, the "bonds that created the city in the first place and which have kept it together since have been almost purely economic ones." Despite the "vision, civic pride, and public mindedness" shown by successive generations of business leaders,[16] blinders, omissions, and contradictions marked the Dallas Way. The business elite's interests did not include everyone in Dallas, extend to all parts of town, or elicit alternative visions of progress. City space was configured along lines of race, ethnicity, and class. Entire residential districts excluded African Americans, Hispanics, and working-class Anglos. Sometimes the elite divided among itself. Planning and zoning were used inconsistently and selectively to the advantage of certain places and groups.

Business-dominated competitive progress left gaps and scars in the urban fabric. Inequities abounded, not only in planning and zoning but also in investment and infrastructure, producing vast disparities in the quality of life. Persons of influence were not interested in the material "city as a whole," except as a rhetorical device.[17] The elite focused on their business districts, especially downtown, and modes of access to them, and their residential

FIGURE 29. Expansion unlimited: In the postwar period, freeways ran through the city center to the suburbs. Woodall Rodgers freeway and downtown Dallas, 1985. Photographer: Doug Tomlinson. From Dillon and Tomlinson, *Dallas Architecture*.

suburbs, especially the legally separate Park Cities and ever-expanding North Dallas. Expending public resources on certain aspects of the public city bene-fited commerce and enhanced the rewards for those principally involved. Little attention fell on the spaces and peoples in between—a legacy of the Dallas Way that persists into the twenty-first century. The Dallas Way has been selective, exclusionary, and inequitable. Like its successes, its silences and distortions are written into the landscape and social fabric of Dallas.

That the elite increasingly lived outside the legal boundaries of the city, or in its exclusive, even privileged subdivisions, exacerbated divisions. The ambition to become a "metropolis of skyscrapers" contributed to a pattern of urban development by imitation of other city centers. The "striking con-trast between its big city aspects and the marks of the frontier" became a subject of denial. "Frontier" conditions long persisted, especially in Dallas west and south, beyond the gaze of city builders. As D'Eramo observes, "The presence of the skyscraper serves merely to demonstrate the power of the host city . . . express the city's bourgeois values. . . . Counting a city's sky-scrapers is a way of establishing an urban league table"—listing each city's total and ranking the city accordingly—regardless of the structures' eco-nomic significance.[18]

Take 4 points to the paradoxical role of government in the development of Dallas. The 1940 study articulated the prevailing view: "Numerous vol-untarily organized civic agencies . . . dedicated to the rapid accomplish-ment of a bigger and better city," applying modern, efficient methods to advance the interests of business leaders, replaced "traditional institutions of government," which played a "small segment" in Dallas's development. That presumption, which is partially if not entirely mythical, forms a cen-tral tenet of the ideology and discourse of the Dallas Way. Dallas leaders pride themselves on adhering to the twin principles of limited government and civic leadership by entrepreneurial citizens who refuse government aid. This rhetorical stance has been attractive to conservatives, but it has often been contradicted by complaints that the city did not receive its fair share of revenue from the nation or the State of Texas. More importantly, the claim that local businessmen built Dallas without outside assistance or in-terference ignores the enormously important contributions of the state and federal governments, as well as the role of nonelites. Dallas took the pseudo-principled stand that it could ignore desegregation rulings because it did not accept federal urban renewal, social welfare, or education funds, but this disingenuous stance was calculated to mislead. Dallas's commercial, financial, industrial, transportation, defense, aerospace, and high-tech growth, as well as its demographic and geographic expansion, are unimaginable without the fundamental support of state and federal monies and policies.[19] Accounting for its development by denial, as well as by imitation and stealth, makes for poor history and dangerously distorted policies and civic understanding. Within its limits, but contrary to its own rhetoric, the Dallas Way often led to an activist governing polity. But Dallas's Way, ideologically and rhetorically, was to deny or contradict Dallas's actual course of action.

In a major untold story, Dallas's individual and collective leadership worked with the political state on a myriad of levels to secure local advantages and obtain key resources. "Public-private partnerships" have had a long reign in Dallas, in tandem with effective lobbying on the state and federal levels. But the connections between the state and leaders are obscured by what political scientist Stephen Elkin called a "'pure entrepreneurial' regime" and Amy Bridges termed a narrow "rhetorical monopoly, a monopoly of public discourse."[20]

From the beginning, the Dallas Way had a more sinister side, only occasionally exposed or probed, in part because of the elite's control over major media and law enforcement. Racial, ethnic, class, and political differences stood among its principal axes; racism scarred Dallas deeply. Acceptance or toleration of violence ranked high among Dallas's ways, including lynching, assault, and arson committed by agents ranging from the Ku Klux Klan to union busters. One especially critical moment came in the wake of the Kennedy assassination, an unprecedented public and publicized act of extremism. The assassination followed near-assaults on Lyndon Johnson and Adlai Stevenson, as well as numerous threats against Kennedy. Locally, the balance of racial politics almost certainly suffered the greatest burden of violence and control by force.[21]

TAKE 5: THE DALLAS WAY CONDEMNED

After the Kennedy assassination, Dallas was viewed as "a place so steeped in violence and political extremism that school children would cheer the President's death and citizens openly declare they were glad 'the son of a bitch is dead.'" But this portrayal painted all of Dallas with a broad brush, and reaction soon followed: "Then within Dallas itself an extraordinary thing occurred: the business leadership of the city began to be singled out for censure. . . . The attitude of the critics was simply that the business leadership was *responsible for the character of Dallas,* and if they had done a better job of leading, the city would not have earned its international reputation for violence and hatred and intolerance. . . . Their view was that . . . a self-perpetuating oligarchy of businessmen, unreachable by the hundreds and thousands of Dallasites, was sitting in a self-selected caucus making decisions."[22]

Stanley Marcus, president of Neiman Marcus and former head of the Dallas Citizens Council, pointed to the city's "sterility and a lack of progress." He explained, "This is the price you pay. Our leadership has been singularly lacking in men of wealth who have a genuine concern for intellectual freedom. . . . Now we have a large but homogeneous group of businessmen intent on unity and conformity."[23] Asserting at the same time that "there's a lot right with Dallas," Marcus's oblique criticism of local leadership was stunning, but only scratched the surface.

Although its oligarchic aspects are well known, the Dallas Way's connections with racial, ethnic, and class divisions, civil rights struggles, labor wars, and violent coercion are missing from almost all commentaries and histories. The elite lent "respectability to certain drives and causes" and pushes toward homogeneity and unanimity. The stamp of authority had different edges for different people in different locations across Dallas's history and geography, bearing down oppressively on some and striking others more violently.[24] Any sign of dissent or resistance was met by force. *That* legacy is not remembered and commemorated as part of the Dallas Way, although this denial is a central feature of its hegemonic power.

CIVIC HEGEMONY

The signal achievement of the Dallas Way lay in its success in persuading a significant proportion of the city's population, as well as those outside the city, to accept a narrative or story, broadcast in a readily understood form, of the triumphant rise of Dallas owing to the prowess of its business leaders. The message underlined the imperative that the authority of its leadership and the dominance of its way of doing civic business be accepted and maintained. Over time, the urban elite tended toward increasingly formal organization and a narrower, more exclusive membership. The pivotal point for the civic hegemony of the Dallas Way came with the equation of the business elite's interest with the public interest. Deliberately promoting this message, the elite gained sufficient consent to act without fear of interference. For some residents, acceptance may have reflected the realities of control and order. Citizens and newcomers were bound to the ideology and mythology of the Dallas Way with the acceptance of the pursuit of economic growth as an overarching good, along with a willingness to take certain risks and ignore certain obstacles, boundaries, and civilities in achieving that goal. Those outside the city became familiar with the Dallas Way, especially when trumpeted by national publications such as *Fortune, Life, Atlantic Monthly,* and *Colliers.* Corporations considered Dallas a major market and potential headquarters site, confirming its promise of prosperity.

Over the full span of Dallas's urban history, long before the era of the Dallas Citizens Council, the Dallas Way wove together a number of distinct elements, starting with development by stealth and purchase. The longevity and reach of the Dallas Way is best illustrated by the actions of the "best men" who mobilized to secure Dallas's status as county seat and then its town and city charters; the railroad and a chartered bank; urban governmental, commercial, service, social, and cultural institutions; elite subdivisions and steel-framed skyscrapers; a Federal Reserve Bank and a Ford auto plant; and a city plan—all prior to 1920. Much of what became the hallmarks of the Dallas Way under the leadership of Robert L. Thornton had historical precedents.

An exclusive focus on moments of formal political change, especially on the 1930s, obscures the longevity and malleability of the Dallas Way, hiding its long-standing presence, variable power and organizational forms, and indirect as well as direct modes of influence. Focusing exclusively on the DCC obscures differences, competition, and major conflicts within the elite.[25] Part of the Dallas Way's success over the decades lay in its being always "on call" for various purposes. The slipperiness of the Dallas Way is both a weakness and a strength. Its covert functioning and blurry parameters led supporters of the Dallas Way to exaggerate its power, or conversely to deny its responsibility for extremist expressions or actions by its adherents.[26] The Dallas Way proved more useful for taking advantage of opportunities than for responding to crises. In accord with its dismissal of Dallas history, it was seldom prepared for social change, including the imperative of a more democratically representative polity, the widening of civil rights, and claims for equal opportunity.

The Dallas Way was a mode of governance shaped specifically for creating and maintaining the civic hegemony of major entrepreneurs in the pursuit of economic development that advanced their own vision of Dallas. The public discourse and actions articulating the Dallas Way embraced and promoted the presumption of equivalence of public development and private gain, the dominance of commerce over polity and society, and the legitimacy of self-appointed private agents or authorities as civic leaders. Urban growth, defined and directed by the business elite, always supported private profit as a proper and expected product of public policy. Reopening the question of the Dallas Way alters how we look at the connections between private and public power.

When sheer repetition of the tenets of the Dallas Way failed to convince, especially in the face of its failure to deliver the goods, then "the powers that be" were quick to resort to force in order to maintain order and control. Discourse did not suffice when conflicts related to race, ethnicity, social class, and organized labor overstepped their usual boundaries.[27] Racism indelibly marked—and continues to mark—life in Dallas. Over the full span of the city's history, both implicitly and explicitly sanctioned violence sent clear messages about where power lay. Slaves were lynched for "insolence" and at the mere rumor of rebellion. In 1910, African American Allen Brooks was taken from the courthouse and hanged by a mob before he could be tried for the "unspeakable" crime of which he stood accused. Houses purchased by African Americans in Anglo neighborhoods were firebombed. Police harassed and assaulted African Americans and Mexican Americans, and both groups had their voting rights denied. The Ku Klux Klan was tolerated. Labor organizers were tarred, feathered, and beaten. The available but inconclusive evidence points to the possibility that this violence was officially sanctioned; at the very least, popular violence was tolerated by the powers that ruled the city. Politicians perceived to be communist, socialist, or dangerously liberal were physically threatened and harassed. A frequent refrain of the Dallas Way was a not-so-veiled threat to preserve order by any means necessary—persuasion if possible, but violence if not.[28]

Dallas could be embarrassed by its own extremism. Dallas was long known as a rough-and-tumble place, a wide-open city in which certain levels of personal violence were accepted. But when its reputation threatened to harm the city's image as a stable place to do business, civic leaders suppressed violent conflicts. Instances in which extremism overstepped this invisible line included the Klan; attacks on civil rights; police violence against minorities; illegal conduct by police, public officeholders, and professional athletes and their gun-toting coach; attacks on homosexuals; "riots" after public celebrations of the Cowboys' Super Bowl victories; and drunken crowds on downtown streets on the weekend of the annual University of Texas–Oklahoma University football game. Space and race, along with media coverage and widespread attention, were pivotal factors. Assertive, sometimes quasi-legal/quasi-illegal public displays of carefully orchestrated disorder, most strikingly choreographed by African American officeholder John Wiley Price, were especially challenging in a city where Anglos did not expect "misconduct" by minorities to be tolerated. That, of course, *had* been the Dallas Way. Over time, especially after the Kennedy assassination, managing extremist violence to secure social order and maintain control increasingly became the Dallas Way.[29]

Necessary changes, especially the decline in acceptance of public extremism and overt violence, were uneasily assimilated into promotions of city progress and individual interests, the two inseparably if sometimes contradictorily linked. Less frequently, but also prompted by external imposition, another mode of the Dallas Way was put into action: building public opinion in support of carefully planned and orchestrated change. The postassassination Goals for Dallas campaign, an attempt to employ citizen participation to rebuild Dallas's image and set an agenda for reform, is perhaps the best-known example.[30] Equally important, but much quieter, was the citywide campaign in support of limited school desegregation in the early 1960s. A carefully organized series of public information meetings was capped by the production and screening of a twenty-minute film to neighborhood, school, and religious groups throughout the city on the eve of court-ordered school desegregation in 1961. Narrated by Walter Cronkite, "Dallas at the Crossroads" did not so much promote integration as warn sternly against resisting it. A succession of local authorities, including a psychiatrist, a judge, and the police chief, advised white Dallasites to go along peacefully. Newsreel footage of public violence in Little Rock and New Orleans was held up as an example of actions that would harm Dallas's reputation and prosperity. The threat of immediate forceful response to any resistance could not be missed. As the press put it: "There was a quiet revolution orchestrated by a 14-member biracial (later triracial) committee created by the Dallas Citizens Council in 1961. . . . The all-white council handled the issue in a businesslike manner with a public-relations campaign. . . . Dallas residents were not asked to change their opinions, but to obey the law to avoid the violence that tore other cities."[31]

MUNICIPAL REFORM

The Dallas Way was constituted by the institutional reform of electoral politics. The pioneering research of Harold A. Stone, Don K. Price, and Kathryn H. Stone on city manager governance during the 1930s and the recent study of municipal reform in the early twentieth-century Southwest by Amy Bridges situate Dallas in comparative perspective. Efforts to institute a city commission system in the Progressive Era and the city manager-council system in the 1930s represent political reform, rather than simple opposition to more democratic modes of municipal governance. They were part of a search across America's cities in the first three decades of the twentieth century to balance democracy, power, order and efficiency, and progress in an apparently new era. Bridges observes: "Just as the big cities of the Northeast and Midwest were commonly governed by political machines, and the cities of the South by Bourbon coalitions, so the cities of the Southwest have in the twentieth century been governed by municipal reformers." They succeeded, Bridges contends, because "the growth of municipal reform in the southwest choked out its opponents, replacing parties with nonpartisanship, party politicians with a civic elite, mayors with commissioners and managers, competition with political monopoly." Within its regional context, Dallas was not unusual.[32] Partisan politics was cast as an alien and unwelcome intrusion.

In southwestern cities like Dallas, reform revolved around the Anglo middle class—"the core constituency of local politics"—and the exclusion of poor whites and persons of color. As Bridges recounts, "Without party organizations to defend them, the targets of political exclusion were more vulnerable in the Southwest than their counterparts . . . in the Northeast and Midwest."[33] Under the nonpartisan governance of the "best men" and "independent" professional managers, policies promoted the vision and interests of entrepreneurs and bankers, although at the turn of the twentieth century the elite was a more diffuse and fluid grouping than it later became. Class counted and Anglos were sometimes bitterly divided, but race made for significant difference, especially in Texas cities of the former

Confederacy. Racism and governance were inseparably entangled: "Racial considerations were also inscribed in local government's structure and activities. Every city policy—hiring of municipal employees, planning and annexation, housing, utilities, and education—reinforced racial divisions and hierarchy."[34] Physical force and violence directed toward racial minorities were everyday occurrences. For African Americans and Mexican Americans, resistance, self-assertion, and organization for civil rights were "continuous across this century," contradicting stereotypes of quiescence.[35]

Municipal reformers and their supporters "owned the mass media and, in the absence of well-organized opposition that could force public debate, the media excluded opposition voices." Minority newspapers had limited circulation and readership. Dallas's dailies, the *Times Herald* and the *Morning News,* kept the faith regardless of their ideological differences. A narrowed public discourse allowed little place for alternative proposals or dissent. According to Bridges, "the most energetic critics of local government—people of color"—were unable "to make claims that majority constituents recognized as legitimate," to seek allies, make coalitions, or participate in local politics.[36] Other Anglos were occasionally heard, defeating reformers in the mid-1930s, delaying the establishment of city manager-council governance, and electing as mayor a candidate running in opposition to the endorsed slate.

The form of the Dallas Way that triumphed in the mid-1930s is typically taken as quintessential, but the Dallas Citizens Council crystallized continuing political relationships. From roads to safety and services, public goods benefited middle-class Anglo neighborhoods. "Not the least of these public goods was the assistance to developers who designed communities for affluent and middle-class homeowners. There is no evidence of selflessness here. For example, there was opposition everywhere to providing low-income housing." Civic leaders and their corporations shared interests with developers.[37] Bridges explains, "The pursuit of growth as conducted by these governments . . . served their core constituents, as subsidies to developers in effect subsidized middle-class homeowners. The results were a small, contented political community that had good government and knew it was good, and political leaders well insulated from such popular discontent as might exist."[38] The constantly repeated discourse of growth was central to the reformers' maintenance of civic hegemony. Progress and profit were achieved without patronage or parties, but with professionalism and supposedly neutral scientific methods of planning and administration.

Residents of the "other" Dallas, particularly South and West Dallas, had little access to power and significantly fewer amenities; the neglect of these neighborhoods was sometimes catastrophic. That, too, is part of the Dallas Way. "Historian Arnold Hirsch commented that the self-proclaimed Good Government factions of southwestern cities might more credibly have been called Rapacious Land Developers on one hand and Businessmen United for Minority Repression on the other."[39] In Dallas, governmental activism was highly selective. The equation that what is good for business is good for the city was drawn unusually tightly in Dallas. Dominance by the business elite was clearer than in other cities in the region.

Civic leaders and their supporters were proud that they "planned and managed unprecedented growth," "recruited industry," and "coordinated . . . building and capital investment to provide homes, roads, water, and electricity for their rapidly growing populations. . . . They pointed to growth and improvements in public schooling, parks, pools and golf courses, libraries, airports, all with tax rates controlled, all without scandal at the top of the municipal hierarchy or patronage at the bottom."[40] What they failed to do was to promote equality in the conditions of urban life, to expand opportunities, and to extend the civic vision and services that fairness would require. Instead, they developed two cities, separate and unequal. The costs and the losses in the end were shared by all of Dallas, from environmental degradation to the lack of transit and infrastructure; the failures of public welfare, public schools, public order; and the denial of equal opportunities, democratic rights, and equality under the law. Calculating the bottom-line payoff from the "Dallas way of getting things done" as a path of development is difficult, since the benefits were as unevenly distributed as the burdens.

What, then, brought about the formalization of these long-standing patterns of power politics in the mid-1930s? Extraordinary levels of conflict within the elite arose over different views of governance, control, and reform, divergent visions of the city's development, and the avowed interests of opposing political parties during the 1920s. A decade of exhilarating and unsettling demographic and economic expansion was accompanied by widespread dissatisfaction with municipal government. The city commission system was beset by squabbling among the commissioners and questions about their budgets. That institutional structure was the product of the city's Progressive-Era quest, supported by Dealey's *Dallas Morning News,* for centralized authority and accountable government, a reform that had divided the elite. In 1931, there was no doubt that the city was in serious difficulties, with a multimillion-dollar deficit in the public works department, other departments in debt and disorder, and garbage collection and code enforcement in disarray.[41]

In their landmark study of city managers, Stone, Price, and Stone reported, "To the leaders of the civic organizations who considered themselves responsible for the commercial and civic progress of Dallas, 'politics' was a word with a completely objectionable meaning. They did not associate their own work in establishing commission government, promoting the Kessler Plan, and furthering municipal public works with 'politics.' This word meant to them the patronage and selfish intrigue of those who lived on the public payroll and were therefore considered hindrances to community development." The program of municipal reformers in Dallas began with the notion that politics could be abolished. Instead, the city's "affairs could be handled like those of a private corporation."[42] This notion linked Progressive-Era municipal reformers with those who instituted the city manager-council system in 1930.

The movement for institutional change began with the *Dallas Morning News's* sponsorship of a series of reports in 1927. The cause was taken up by a variety of civic groups including a Citizens Charter Association, which organized the ensuing political campaign. The new charter adopted in 1930 included a council of nine members, all elected at large, who then chose a mayor from among themselves; a city manager as the chief officer for the city; and a city planning commission. An extensive campaign aimed to reach voters at work, home, and elsewhere, with the strong endorsement of the media. Public campaigns, which often included implicit or thinly veiled threats of the disastrous consequences that would follow rejection, were a hallmark of the Dallas Way at such critical junctures. The charter was lauded as the foundation for a more progressive, businesslike Dallas: "For such community development and commercial purposes, Dallas should be run by its businessmen because 'the biggest business in Dallas is Dallas itself.'"[43]

It took a half-dozen years of rough city politics, including battles between city managers and various departments, and between the Charter

Association and their political opponents who organized themselves as the Catfish Club, before the "best men" found their way to office to stay, typified by the four-term mayoralty of R. L. Thornton. Big business did not completely defeat "politics"; the two more or less merged in the revised Dallas Way. As Stone and his colleagues saw it, "The Charter Association, in short, modified its theory of council-manager government, gave up its effort to put the municipality in the hands of businessmen who were by temperament unsuited for politics, enlisted some of its former enemies, and advocated a policy of strict law enforcement."[44] The goal of abolishing politics proved unattainable, but the formation of public policy and the conduct of municipal government were transformed. At issue was the power to redefine politics as part of business, and business as a product and beneficiary of politics.

Thornton's move to power followed directly from his success in winning the Texas Centennial Exposition for Dallas. Thornton later recalled his frustration in seeking corporate commitments to support the Centennial: "There was no organization. Sometimes you'd get a bunch of people together. They couldn't say yes or no. What we needed was men who could give you boss talk. Then I saw the idea. Why not organize the yes-and-no people?"[45] And so he did. But this solidification of power followed more than two decades of political and social conflict among the Dallas elite who fought over their degree of influence within the local polity and their assumptions about the optimal relationship of local government to commercial development. As Patricia Hill discovered, conflicts ranged widely among parties and persons over social issues; political organization, power, and leadership old and new; economic justice, rights of labor, women, and minorities; cosmopolitan and parochial orientations, aspirations, and fears; as well as visions of Dallas's future and the best way to achieve them. Players included liberal and radical political progressives, populists, and union organizers, as well as Ku Klux Klan members and other "extremists" of the right and the left. Depression-era fears about Dallas's prospects for continuing growth and prosperity and labor union struggles added to the dangerous mix, although the Great Depression's impact on Dallas was not as severe as on many other cities.[46]

The organized Dallas Way from the 1930s differed in important respects from its predecessors. The formal level of organization, size of membership, and public presence demarcated the Dallas Citizens Council from its precursors. In 1937, the Citizens Council included only the heads of the one hundred largest companies in Dallas. Each paid annual dues of $25. On the DCC's fiftieth anniversary, there were 268 members (several corporations had two) who paid $2,500 each. For much of its duration, the DCC included no professionals or women. In the early years, the DCC worked informally, almost personally, often over lunch in private clubs or at quickly called meetings of its executive. This practice was not new for the business elite. Under the DCC, it was regularized and, for many, sanctified. By 1987, the Council had a permanent office with a staff of four. Membership was always strictly by invitation, with the board of directors nominating new members who were then elected by the membership.

Changes in the organization and operations of these civic leaders paralleled, and resulted from, changes in the city. Dallas had grown tremendously in population, area, and complexity. A streamlined, nonpartisan council of the "best men" from business was touted as especially qualified to evaluate the advice of a professional city manager and other technical experts, planners, and engineers. New layers of specialization and expertise, new conceptions of cities planned, coordinated, and systematically integrated, made the tasks of governing for growth more difficult but also more imperative, it was claimed. Reformed municipal government fit Dallas's needs, as perceived by its business leaders by the third and fourth decades of the twentieth century. When push came to shove, business interests prevailed over the demands of modern urban planning and infrastructure.

Dallas's leaders were more homogeneous in social origins, attitudes, and aspirations. Many younger executives were from the Dallas area, a number of them "self-made." Researchers such as Hill find them lacking larger horizons and experience, more conformist, and likely to look to established cities for cultural trends and signs of urbanity to imitate—museums, galleries, symphony, theatre, architecture—but otherwise to look beyond Dallas only rarely. This provincialism fueled mimetic urban development.

The collective spirit of this new class of civic leaders stressed unity and harmony. An emphasis on collective action replaced patterns that were more individualistic, loosely organized, and competitive. The resulting orientation included a stake in certain aspects of Dallas, especially the central business district downtown, but rarely in "the city as a whole." The elite vision for Dallas stressed coordination, growth, and efficiency; fiscal restraint to keep taxes low, bond ratings high; a city attractive for new business. Hill summarizes: "A new generation of leaders matured by the end of the 1920s convinced that civic coherence depended on the business community's ability to speak with a single voice. This new elite sought to 'manage' the politics of competition and cooperation by ignoring those issues which fostered intraclass feuds and by promoting only those on which there was a general consensus among business leaders."[47]

In my view, the Dallas Way long preceded the 1930s. Its fullest and perhaps finest form, the era of the DCC, was but one of its incarnations. I take a longer, broader, and more complicated view of the Dallas Way. The practice and legacy of Dallas's domination by self-promoting, civic boosting, ambitious Anglo entrepreneurial leaders with expansive visions of their city's future dates from the early days of a settlement that was urban from its beginnings. When the Dallas Way is equated solely with the Citizens Council, its legacy is lost. Much of the city's rich history is lost with it—a history that saw important conflicts over opposing visions of the place called Dallas, as well as the city's ongoing shaping and reshaping. The reign of the DCC was no more than, perhaps, fifty years; the Dallas Way emerged and worked its ways for more than three times that duration.

DALLAS'S WAYS

Over the better part of a century and a half, recurring elements, strategies, and operations within a larger repertoire of city making marked the Dallas Way and its vision of the city as it was to be. Dallas's political and economic leaders worked unceasingly to establish and maintain civic hegemony through the rhetoric and promotion of urban growth. The Dallas Way as it developed from the nineteenth century on shaped a consistent, if flexible and wide-ranging, repertoire of orientations, approaches, and courses of action. Over time, the sense of both the possibilities and the limits shifted, as did Dallas's rhetoric of difference and destiny. Modes of governance and instruments of control were transformed. Yet, in historical perspective, it is the continuities that are most striking.

The supreme commander of the Dallas Way, longtime civic leader, banker, and mayor Robert L. Thornton, loved to brag about Dallas's successful bid to host the Texas Centennial Exposition by saying, "We didn't have any history in Dallas, we had all the other ingredients of 100 years of progress."[48] Broadly conceived, the Dallas Way strove for progress over the city's full history. But for history as a critical perspective rather than a paean to progress, we had to wait. I consider the Dallas Way not a self-evident truth but a historical and intellectual *problem* that needs to be explained, rather than praised or, conversely, condemned. As a set of responses to the challenging circumstances of a new and growing community, the Dallas Way constitutes a distinct mode of urban and historical development that pivots around power, politics, political economy, and civic cultures. The Dallas Way is also a conceptual and ethical problem that relates to political democracy, economic fairness, and social justice. Inseparable from the formation and intersections of social class, race, and politics and their spatial expression, it is central to Dallas's own urban process. It raises hard questions about ideology, discourse, authority, legitimacy, responsibility, and accountability. We must consider differences in opportunities and costs, the balance that lies beyond the arithmetic of profits and losses. We must attend to silences, absences, and unintended as well as anticipated results.[49]

The Dallas Way is hard to pin down, let alone to question and criticize. Its near-invisibility has been among its strengths.[50] It is hard to knock "progress" until access and accountability, long-term costs, and differential outcomes are assessed. Few discussions of the Dallas Way demonstrate an appreciation of the conceptual, political, and ethical dimensions of the problem or an awareness of the conflicts and contradictions that pervade its principles and practices. Concerns about democratic politics and civil rights accompanied the Dallas Way's public decline, but were only rarely heard or recorded during its reign. Alternative visions once expressed by African Americans, Mexican Americans, populists, progressives, socialists, liberals, left-labor supporters, and organized women's groups have long been lost and only recently regained audiences. Dallas's extremist and racist right wing was heard far more often. Criticisms of exclusion or claims for inclusion threatened discord. The Dallas Way responded to these threats with limited, sponsored mobility of individual members of minority communities through appointment and, more rarely, election to city positions, which sometimes failed to bind its chosen community representatives to the official cause.[51] As Amy Bridges aptly observes, "race both informed the design of reform politics and became the means of its undoing."[52]

The power of the Dallas Way is often exaggerated, a fallacy shared by both supporters and critics.[53] The Dallas Way is assigned agency and authority well beyond the possible, slighting inevitable conflicts and the counter-pressure of demands for rights and justice.[54] The pioneering research of Marvin Dulaney has begun to give the struggle for African American civil rights a deeply rooted local history. Patricia Hill accords workers, populists, socialists, and, along with Elizabeth Enstam, women to their important places in Dallas history. The local specificities of this mode of urban power cannot be understood without comparative studies, with Dallas's competitors in Texas and with the other cities it has compared itself to over the years: St Louis, Kansas City, Chicago, Atlanta, Miami, Charlotte, New Orleans, and Denver.[55]

The Dallas Way's success in promoting demographic, economic, and geographic growth laid the basis for its own undoing, propelling the creation of a more diverse city with different communities, conflicting interests, and more liberal social attitudes than those represented in the Dallas Way. Mounting inattentions, imbalances, and inequities generated "urban problems" from which white, middle-class Dallas long thought itself exempt. The days of the Dallas Way were numbered, its ultimate demise brought about by the contradictions it sowed within a divided city.

While it lasted, despite its limitations, exclusions, and distortions, the Dallas Way offered the city's power brokers a repertoire of strategies and tactics they deployed repeatedly in their pursuit of growth as an end in itself—or for themselves.

Stealth and Purchase

Stealth and purchase share a powerful though dubious and contested place on the proud roster of Dallas's ways. These constructions do not signify actions that are less than strictly legal. Dallas celebrates victories that come from the sorts of actions that blur lines of propriety and often involve secrecy. The rhetoric itself obstructs clarity: from "buying influence," "sweetening the deal," or "making an offer that can't be refused" to getting a great bargain or calling an easier-than-anticipated acquisition "a steal." Trading in and speculating over commodities, including real estate, cotton, and oil, owes much to stealth and purchase. Stealth denotes sneakiness, slyness, and covertness, but also hints at appropriation or theft.

Dallas progressed through stealth and purchase from its early days, as it secured the site of first the temporary and then the permanent county seat. In the early 1870s, stealth was critical to gaining access to the railroads. The

Houston & Texas Central Railroad's planned route bypassed Dallas by about nine miles, so the promoters of Dallas, a town of 3,800, seized an opportunity. They raised $5,000 and offered it to the H. & T. C., along with 115 acres of land and several miles of free right-of-way. The railroad changed its path. A year or so later, the Texas & Pacific announced that it had no intention of coming through Dallas. Apparently, no one noticed when a Dallas lawyer and a Fort Worth representative in the state legislature added a codicil to the T. & P.'s right-of-way bill specifying that the route should cross the Trinity River within a mile of Browder Springs in the southern part of Dallas. A bonus of $100,000 and twenty-five acres of land in East Dallas persuaded the railroad to extend its tracks into the city. By 1873, Dallas had situated itself as a city at the crossroads.

The creation of a new Federal Reserve Bank system in 1913 offered business leaders an opportunity to expand their standing and power in the

FIGURE 30. Esplanade of State, Texas Centennial Exhibition, Fair Park, 1936. From the collections of the Texas/Dallas History and Archives Division, Dallas Public Library.

FIGURE 31. Hall of State, Texas Centennial Exhibition, Fair Park, ca. 1936 (now Dallas Historical Society). From Holmes and Saxon, *WPA Dallas Guide and History.*

FIGURE 32. Maintenance Building, Texas Centennial Exhibition, Fair Park, built 1936. Photographer: Doug Tomlinson. From Dillon and Tomlinson, *Dallas Architecture.*

Southwest. "The city of the hour," as Dallas called itself, was one of the first to announce its intention to secure a branch of the bank. Representatives of the Chamber of Commerce, Dallas Cotton Exchange, local banks, and the *Dallas Morning News* dispatched telegrams to state and national leaders and rushed three bankers to Washington, D.C., to lobby members of the site selection committee. They acted too quickly. Texans in the federal government feared that premature or otherwise inappropriate meetings might be seen as compromising. When George Dealey learned through an inside source that A. S. Burleson, postmaster general and member of the site selection committee, was coming to Texas, he arranged for one of his top reporters to join a prominent Dallas banker in intercepting Burleson during a stop in St. Louis. Discreetly, Dallas won the location of the Federal Reserve Bank.[56]

One of the most notorious and celebrated examples of stealth and purchase was the Texas Centennial. In 1934, a state commission awarded the prize to Dallas, after business leaders, led by R. L. Thornton, campaigned under a clause in the state legislature's enabling bill that allowed the commission to award the exposition to the city offering the largest financial inducement and support. Urging that the exposition would put Dallas, as well as Texas, on the map and provide immediate relief from the Depression, Thornton presented the selection committee (chaired by a Dallas man) with an $8 million commitment, including the fairgrounds valued at $4 million, and a bond package if Dallas received the nod. Thornton promised that his city, unlike the other bidders, would put on an exposition even if no federal and state aid materialized. The *Dallas Morning News* trumpeted this triumph: "The [exposition's] lasting benefits will be in the intangibles—the spirit of unity, of hearty cooperation and of invincible confidence in the great future."[57] Thornton editorialized in the *News,* "The time has come when petty jealousies, sectional bickering, and personal differences must be cast aside by all Dallas citizens for the common good of the city."[58] He gave a public face to the Dallas Way, even if he did not follow these rules. The Exposition drew more than 6.4 million visitors. It lost money, but positive publicity flowed and little criticism was attached to Thornton or other business leaders. They got what they banked on. The Centennial's success in trying times led them to reincarnate the Dallas Way in the form of the Dallas Citizens Council.[59]

Another step toward paving the city's path to its future was the Chamber of Commerce's three-year "Industrial Dallas" campaign launched in 1928. Seven reports about the area and full-page ads in the *Saturday Evening Post, Nation's Business,* and *Literary Digest* stood at the center of a $500,000 publicity blitz. Despite the downward course of national economic conditions, Dallas attracted 126 new manufacturing plants. This campaign set a precedent for even larger corporate moves during and after World War II and again in the 1970s, when the prizes could be very substantial: American Airlines, JCPenney, Greyhound, and Blockbuster, among many others.

In an unusually transparent deal in the 1980s, the city guaranteed developer David Fox of Fox and Jacobs that if his cluster of townhouses near downtown did not prove to be profitable, the city would purchase them. This indemnity provoked outright condemnation. Referenda to commit the public purse to paying for nonprofit museums and performance halls or for-profit sports arenas are sometimes challenged, despite great swathes of rhetoric and promotion to the contrary. But using tax exemptions as incentives to lure corporations to Dallas is more confusing.[60] In the city's tradition of order and control, these promotions sometimes had a raw underbelly of implied coercion or intimidation, suggesting that "selfish" acts of disorder, protest, or criticism would harm the city's chances to gain materially and culturally. The reversal inherent in calling critiques of the use of public funds for private profit "selfish" goes unremarked.

The extent of publicity, the persons involved, and the amount of money expended in pursuit of far greater wealth as well as prominence varies enormously from one project to the next, as does the degree of stealth involved. Dallas won the Centennial "because it had the wit and daring and gumption to put up the biggest guarantee. The same tactics were used to bag the Metropolitan Opera, which in 1939, after a dozen years of persistent entreaty . . . finally offered to include Dallas in its spring tour if the city would furnish a guarantee of sixty-five thousand dollars."[61] ("Uncle Bob" Thornton promised to continue his support as long as he did not have to attend the opera.) Much, but not all, has changed in Dallas's ways since then. Dallas's renewed effort to house all its cultural institutions in palaces of culture downtown, designed by star architects and embracing public-private cooperation, clothed the Dallas Way in new garb.

Only partly in jest, *Dallas Magazine* publisher Wick Allison pronounced a paean to purchase as a strategy of development. He deemed this the "Deion Principle," after the football and baseball star Deion Sanders, who spent part of his playing career with the Dallas Cowboys. Allison explains, "Dallas and Fort Worth are marvelous places to live. . . . But when it comes to attracting talent—especially nonprofit talent—we face stiff competition. Dallas may be nice, but San Francisco may be nicer. Cleveland may seem more committed. New York and Boston may confer greater prestige. To attract the kind of talent it takes to build the great institutions that are the heart and soul of public life, we need to fight with the only weapon we have: money."[62] Allison revised his strategic formulae in 2002, still stinging from the Boeing Corporation's rejection of Dallas for its headquarters. In response to public debate over a major bond issue, he wrote:

> The lesson of social history is that wealth creates demand as much as commerce does. . . . Boeing didn't choose Chicago because it's a better business city than Dallas. It chose Chicago because it offers more as a place to live. . . . What do they want, these newly wealthy? Culture, style, fine dining, variety in entertainment, places to see and be seen. Most of all, they want an aesthetically gratifying environment: places to walk, greenery, shade, water, pleasing architecture, human scale. . . . We need a billion dollars on downtown alone, another half-billion on parks, and probably as much on our roadways. We need trees by the thousands, parks by the scores.[63]

Allison may well have been unaware of the long-standing historical foundation of development by stealth and purchase that his prescription echoed. But the "Deion Principle" is hallowed by Dallas's historical experience.[64]

DENIAL

Denial ranks at once among the crudest but also the most subtle of the planks in the platform on which the Dallas Way constructed the city. Denial mixes oddly with both imitation and claims of difference, and fits better with purchase and stealth, rhetoric and promotion. Specific denials provoke laughter: that a city of Dallas's size and prominence has "no reason to exist"; that some day, somehow, it will become a city by the water. Or that Dallas is a western city; no, a southern city; no, more southwestern. Its claims to be a "sophisticated," "cosmopolitan" place free from urban challenges are widely recognized as vacuous, although some cruelly point out that it faces big-city problems without offering the compensatory amenities of urbanity. Other denials stimulate near-reverence: "Dallas is primarily the result of the unstinting, unselfish labor of its business leaders." Still others stir anger, especially the city's legacies of racism, violence, and inequality.

Denying its history, Dallas deliberately forgets its heritage as a populist town and a center of organized labor; a wide open and freewheeling urban playground that crossed racial and class lines; and a highly segregated, violent, and racist city. A political economic oligarchy posits a different order. Disconnected elements of local history—warehouse and loft buildings, blues and jazz, proximity to downtown—are sanitized, recycled, and marketed for gentrified and tourist profits. No hint of Dallas's "two cities" is allowed to interfere with its promotion or to mark images of the city.[65] Along with the persistent denial of the role of almost all levels of government in contributing to Dallas's prosperity, from an active local state to massive infusions of federal defense, highway, aviation, and housing dollars, to both public and private enterprises, these denials prevent us from perceiving the power of the culture and politics of memory.[66] Finally, Dallas denies any suggestion that it imitates other cities, while continuing to do so.

IMITATION

When it comes to imitation as a strategy for developing a city with pretenses to uniqueness, Dallas has few rivals, other than the cliché capitals of Las Vegas and Orlando.[67] I take *mimesis* to be a central, common, and unexceptional mode of urban development. In itself, it is neither unusual nor especially problematic; indeed, it is not even particularly interesting. It is difficult to imagine city building without imitation: matters of language, culture, and technology, reference and comparison, precedent and priority, icons and images, identity and appropriation, competition and movement all serve to support it.

But Dallas, I am convinced, *is* different. Dallas seizes and depends upon imitation to an unusual and revealing degree. Despite decades of denial by city boosters, this is hardly news. Even early settlers remarked on the town's striving to be like more established places. The city's imitation of eastern centers with skyscrapers rising absurdly from the prairie attracted comment from Stone, Price, and Stone.[68] The *WPA Dallas Guide and History* made the critical connection: Dallas derives "a certain character peculiar to itself" from "its very lack of indigenous features."

Culture in Dallas tends to be imitative rather than dynamic and creative. The average Dallasite wants the latest fashions from Fifth Avenue, Bond Street, and the Rue de la Paix; the newest models in cars; and the best in functionally constructed, electrified, air-conditioned homes—but . . . the schools and universities, churches, and newspapers all lean strongly in the direction of conservatism. . . .

Though externally cosmopolitan, it retains many of the characteristics of Main Street. Nor is it altogether lacking in individuality. Its very lack of indigenous features gives it a certain character peculiar to itself. . . . It is a sort of archetypal American city, like Zenith, the home of Babbitt in Sinclair Lewis's novels—a city created by American business enterprise for its own special and individual purposes of pride and profit, according to the stereotypical pattern of the American city, relatively unmodified by geographical, racial, or other factors.[69]

Here is the Dallas Way, the spirit of promotion and denial, with its imitative modus operandi.

On its path from village to town to city to metropolis, Dallas mimetically, appropriately, and expectedly built an opera house, private social clubs, racially exclusive residential areas, amateur and then professional sports clubs and teams, and fraternal lodges. Like other cities, Dallas lured the railroads and later airplanes, formed its Cleaner Dallas League in 1899, adopted the commission form of municipal government in 1906, and shifted to the city manager-council form in 1930. Universities, museums, and other agents and badges of culture followed. Much else in the Dallas story, too, is from the realm of the expected. Imitation, the Dallas Way, combines a frankly stated acknowledgment of borrowing with an almost complete lack of self-consciousness about its meanings.

So devoted is Dallas to imitation that it sometimes seems curiously out of step with current developments nationally and internationally. Increasingly apparent over time, it often exaggerates prevailing patterns and continues to repeat them long after they have fallen out of fashion elsewhere: for example, maintaining half-empty office towers downtown, generating growth along loop roads, planting upscale shopping malls on the periphery, and creating edge-city simulacra. Dallas tries to conduct its business, public as well as private, as if it were immune to national and global economic trends. Imitation is a tricky business, sometimes leading Dallas to follow downward spirals started elsewhere.

The paradoxical presumption seemed to be that if Dallas imitated long, hard, and well enough, the results would be a Dallas that differed from other prominent cities. Objects of imitation shifted over time, as did Dallas's discursive, and sometimes developmental, dependence on them. A fascinating city map might be constructed from the pieces of other places that Dallas contemplated adding to its own space.[70] In the mid-nineteenth and early twentieth centuries, Dallas looked to midwestern metropolises for plans, designs, and stylistic elements deemed unmistakably urbanistic, however mis- or dislocated. Rooted in a limited conception of the "public" and a restricted notion of public space, this urban model anachronistically overemphasized center city and downtown and access routes from middle-class residential areas.[71] More recently, Atlanta, Miami, and Los Angeles serve as sites for mimesis and competition. Ironically, the freeway, with its synchronized but privatized mode of transport, seems the only real public space and prospect for urban vistas. Despite its touted self-creation, Dallas drew unmistakably, often admittedly, on other urban places, seeking confirmation as well as advantage. The mimetic act is meant to be transformative. Questions remain, however, about what Dallas wrought or bought and about the utility of this strategy over time.

MONUMENTALITY

Striving to be a great city, Dallas focused its mimetic energies on an urban developmental path I call monumental.[72] That designation refers to both the physical manifestations of monumentality in design and construction and to an underlying assumption that building on a grand scale signifies power and progress. Monumental development concentrates on highly visible major structures, with an emphasis on the sculptural, architectonic elements of individual buildings and on ensembles of cultural, governmental, and other public institutions—ideally, located in relation to one another within a comprehensive urban plan. In downtown Dallas, the predominance of private institutions and the absence of spatial integration among structures are striking.

In accord with the strategy of monumentalism, buildings are meant to attract widespread attention, but avoid controversy. Dallas's conservatism reinforces its imitative style. For its signature structures, Dallas typically turns to architectural innovators after their designs are already widely acclaimed elsewhere. The city's tradition of formal city plans reflects the monumental emphasis, from the plans of Kansas City's George Kessler in the 1910s and 1920s and St. Louis–based Harland Bartholomew in the 1940s to the Dallas Plan of the 1990s, all promoted by civic elites and the *Dallas Morning News*. Kessler's plans and the planning association his proposals spawned offered the grandest vision and most comprehensive approach. His legacy to Dallas includes portions of downtown, including Union Station, the landscaping of Turtle Creek in near North Dallas, and Kessler Park in Oak Cliff. Yet his plans, like those that followed, were only partly implemented.[73] The bits and fragments that exist in a state of disconnection testify to the gaps and rents in the city fabric that were among the real costs of monumental development.

Typically, this form of city construction substitutes monumental buildings, concentrated in its central district—from City Hall and Symphony Hall by I. M. Pei to the soaring, atrium-shaped Hyatt Hotels, and skyscrapers by Philip Johnson—for less grand but more pragmatic services, such as public health care or education, infrastructure for transportation, communications, and flood control, and environmental equity across neighborhoods. In its simultaneous neglect of spatial and structural order within downtown and the articulation of the central area within the larger urban space, monumentalism paradoxically limits and distorts center-city development. No less consequential is the question of what was not built because of the dominance of the monumental center. As usual, it is a matter of who pays and who benefits.

A strategy of monumentality based on imitation is rarely a successful path to urban distinction. Increasingly over time, it creates anachronisms, contradictions, and other complications, seldom adequately adapting forms or situating structures within a new aesthetic or physical setting and integrating them with other parts of the built environment. The relationship of the parts to the urban whole, including the center to the periphery, is especially challenging. In its almost total concentration on central areas without a consistent focus on linkages within that space, the dominance of the private supported by the public, and its inability to follow a coordinating plan to completion, Dallas's benefits from monumental development are circumscribed. As the city spread, it simply could not be sustained, either quantitatively or qualitatively. In its fusion with imitation, monumentality nevertheless has a powerful appeal that persists into the twenty-first century.

Making and Marking Difference

It is in the play of the rhetoric and images of difference, often in pursuit of similarity, that Dallas seems most distinctive when compared to other cities. The frequency and the intensity of Dallas's repeated claims to difference distinguish it more than its material achievements. Two recent historians, Amy Bridges and Robert Fairbanks, emphasize the ways in which Dallas's history resembles other cities regionally and nationally.[74] Yet assertions of Dallas's exceptionality continue, sometimes dangerously. In its most elemental form of difference, Dallas can be judged as constituting two cities, materially and metaphorically distinguished by race into distinct spaces with stark differentials in quality of life and opportunity for advancement, marked by inequality of rights, violence, and decades of bitterness. This division is a legacy of the city's history and a consequence of the Dallas Way. Dallas's differences neither sum nor cancel out; the human calculus allows no easy outs.

SIGNPOSTS TO THE DALLAS WAY

The Dallas Way has taken a variety of organizational forms and levels of visibility, but has always promoted growth as progress. By the twentieth century, this form of elite control was often presented in terms of reform, planning, and order. In the 1930s, it became more formal, institutionally organized, and visible. Its influence became more focused on and limited to "business, the business of Dallas," coordination, and the physical city.

Bold and brash boosterism, espousing an ideology of growth at almost any cost, occasionally clashed with a quest for sophistication or cosmopolitanism. Over time, leaders manifested a heightened concern with respectability, propriety, and appearances, especially in public, and demonstrated a clearer sense of appropriate roles for leading entrepreneurs and rewards for service, including election to mayor. Modes of urban development, governance, and leadership were shaped and directed by a largely self-appointed group of the "best men," primarily entrepreneurs. In earlier years this group was quite mixed, including former Confederate officers, ranchers and substantial farmers, merchants and storekeepers, who shared a more individualistic and competitive bent than their conformist successors. Both regimes tended to control local media and communications.

The predominantly white population, moved by racist fears, periodically perpetrated legal and extralegal violence against people of color. Continuous domination of the polity and society by the Anglo population worked to the disadvantage of racial and ethnic minorities, especially Native Americans, Mexican Americans, and African Americans. Racism influences social relationships and marks spatial development throughout Dallas's history. Social hierarchies rooted in race, ethnicity, class, and gender were expressed spatially in the city's physical development. On most measures, Dallas was—and is—one of the most racially segregated cities in the United States. Political extremism was a constant presence, using force and veiled force, and public and private violence, to enact white racist prejudice and enforce discrimination.

The politics and policies of exclusion included limitations on the voting rights of minorities and a host of city actions and inactions. Unhealthy and undeveloped areas where racial minorities congregated were not annexed by the city, while exclusively white areas where higher returns to developers were expected were. Discrimination pervaded city hiring policies, priorities in planning, and the provision of housing, utilities, education, and other services and collective goods. Dallasites have habitually used both legal and extralegal means to accomplish their goals. The operating assumption is that almost any commodity, institution, status, or person deemed useful or necessary in the pursuit of wealth and power can be acquired, by purchase, stealth, or theft.

The rhetoric of "reform" has been used repeatedly to place a more progressive, modern, efficient, and professional or businesslike spin on more conservative and less democratic actions. Reform is an ambiguous and contradictory element, with leadership and broad influence based not on business elite or growth coalitions alone but also on informal relationships between government authority (local and sometimes federal or state) and those in control of private resources.

Dallas's polity has been characterized by domination by the private sector over the public. Lines between public and private interests were often blurred, as the interests of the city were frequently equated with the interests of business. Private domination led to an increasingly narrow definition of the proper domain of public, governmental action. Although limited, local government was nonetheless active in guaranteeing conditions for the profitable conduct of business and used federal funds when deemed appropriate. Leaders used the state to promote popular endorsements and general acceptance of plans by distributing or promising discrete benefits to small businesses and community leaders and serving core constituents. A satisfied, predominantly middle-class political community recognized that the government served them well, and political leaders were relatively insulated from popular discontent.

The entrepreneurial elite and city government focused overwhelmingly on the physical city. City plans concentrated on downtown—the central city and central business district; transportation and communications, especially access between downtown and the suburbs—and on areas of the city slated for growth, especially suburban residential developments. Over time, focus on the physical city narrows in scope and in geographic reach. The limits of the strategy become more visible and more divisive among residents and the interests that claim to speak for them, as the following chapters explain.

Even in its own terms, the Dallas Way was incomplete and inconsistent, with high costs creating deep scars and bitterness. In broader, more inclusive terms, it was riddled with blinders, ambiguities, and contradictions that only intensified over time. Writing recently about Los Angeles, geographer Michael Dear's words apply as well to Dallas: "Los Angeles is a city without a past. It has constantly erased the physical traces of previous urbanisms and failed to produce a flow of historical studies that match and typify other national metropolises (e.g., Chicago and New York City). . . . In social terms, postmodern L.A. is a city split between extremes of wealth and poverty, in which a glittering First World city sits atop a polyglot Third World substructure. Economically, it is an emergent world city that is undergoing a simultaneous deindustrialization and reindustrialization. . . . One of the most characteristic themes of postmodern urbanism is fragmentation."[75] There is one inordinately important difference: in Dallas, the scars of its historical development, especially its two cities, are deeply etched into the city's spaces—if one knows where to look and how to read them.

chapter 5

Tales of Two Cities, North and South, in White, Black, and Brown

On January 2, 2000, the *Dallas Morning News* expressed its hopes and fears for the new millennium in a familiar discourse. Number one on its annual list of problems requiring rapid resolution was "Disparity between the Cans and Cannots":

> The persistent gap between the rich and poor, educated and uneducated. No longer is the great divide between the haves and the have-nots, but the cans and the cannots since education is the key to steady jobs. Dallas must press harder to spread economic development to the southern sector of the city, where the unemployment rate is five times higher than it is in North Dallas, where housing is scarcer and where life expectancy is shorter. . . . Education at all levels must improve. In some elementary schools in the southern sector, 75 percent of the students are not reading at grade level by the third grade. Only half of the students who enter high school in Dallas public schools graduate.[1]

Significantly, "race" is not mentioned explicitly. The city's population geography provides a code for designations by race or ethnicity. High levels of segregation underlie that sociospatial relationship. Despite the long-term residence of a substantial number of Hispanic Americans and a recent influx of Asian Americans, the language of race, ethnicity, residential location, and inequality is singular, not plural.[2] This language articulates the perceptions of dominant, primarily white Dallas, not of black or brown Dallas.

I underscore that this is the language of bias, prejudice, and distortion, not straightforward social description.

The *News*'s translation of inequality from "have" versus "have not" to "can" versus "cannot," from property and poverty to education and employment, is a contemporary but partial spin on the terms of class inequality. This conception also marks a shift from portraying the second Dallas as a threat capable of unleashing protests and riots, and, alternatively, from attempting to "sell" the second Dallas as a great investment opportunity, to a vision of a social chasm growing wider and more dangerous to the welfare of all.

This statement is framed by two powerful elements that define the city past, present, and future: the Dallas Way, and Dallas's tale of two cities. Knowing its intended readership, the *News* could presume those words' implicit racial resonance: black and brown versus white. Separate. Different. South and west versus north. Poor/rich. Can't do/can do. The first city is normative, the second "other." The contrasts are driven through the city like a stake through the heart, piercing language, geography, economic structures, modes of urban development and governance, images and ideologies. Most often viewed as the absence or antithesis of the Dallas Way, sometimes as an instance of its failure, the existence of the second city must be recognized as a fundamental part of the urban process in Dallas and evidence of the successes and limitations of the Dallas Way.[3] As the *Dallas Morning News* acknowledges, "Both these cities are Dallas. But the second city described is south Dallas, where a river, a freeway and invisible barriers keep the area in economic polarization."[4]

The identification of urban problems and uneven development with physical space is critical. Sharon Zukin explains, "The spatial consequences

Region of City	Labor Force Participation	Unemployment
South Dallas	46.0 percent	61.1 percent
Dallas (city)	65.9 percent	39.0 percent

FIGURE 33. Disparities within Dallas: employment and unemployment rates. Source: Marcus Martin, Tim Bray, Julie Kibler, Megan Thibos, Teri Wesson, and Justine Hines, *South Dallas Research Brief*, J. McDonald Williams Institute and the Foundation for Community Empowerment, June 16, 2006.

of combined social and economic power suggest that landscape is the major cultural product of our time. Our cognitive maps, aesthetic forms, and ideologies reflect the multiple shifts and contrasting patterns of growth and decline that shape the landscape."[5] The connections between Dallas's "two cities" are denser and more complicated than many recognize; the concentration of leadership, power, and control in one city has limited the development of the other. The striking degree of social separation between the two contributes to a quick and easy presumption that the second city falters because of its own failings or neglect, rather than as the result of practices and policies in the dominant Dallas. Blaming the victims for their lack of human capital and other economic resources does not explain conditions in the southern and western sectors. Stereotypes of minorities and the poor combine with a history of white racist violence and real disparities in life chances to magnify the perception of separateness and difference. Both natural and human-made physical barriers accentuate that sense of separation. The second city's disadvantages and difficulties seem to be timeless, rather than historically contingent. Race and space are equated and judged together, representing not simply a social mapping but a guide to

TABLE 1. Race, ethnicity, and poverty disparities within Dallas

Region of City	White	Hispanic	Black	Households earning less than $25,000 (2004)	Below 200% of federal poverty level (2000)
Northern Corridor	65.9%	20.0%	5.7%	9.5%	20.0%
Northwest Oak Cliff	25.0%	42.8%	29.6%	23.2%	35.3%
Dallas County	38.9%	35.1%	20.0%	23.3%	33.4%
East Dallas	41.8%	40.6%	13.0%	26.4%	38.5%
Southeast Dallas	33.1%	38.2%	25.5%	27.2%	40.0%
South Oak Cliff	8.4%	30.2%	60.1%	36.7%	48.1%
West Dallas	2.3%	66.6%	29.8%	51.1%	68.7%
South Dallas	4.6%	17.2%	76.9%	62.9%	71.1%

Source: Parkland Hospital, "Our Community Health Checkup, 2005, for Dallas County." Courtesy of Marcus Martin et al., *South Dallas Research Brief,* J. McDonald Williams Institute and the Foundation for Community Empowerment, June 2006.

County average	18.1
Northwest Oak Cliff	26
Southeast Dallas	33.3
South Dallas	50
West Dallas	55
South Oak Cliff	39.6
East Dallas	16.7

FIGURE 34. Education disparities within Dallas: percentage of population over twenty-five years of age in Dallas County with no high school degree. Sources: Parkland Hospital, "Our Community Health Checkup, 2005, for Dallas County"; Texas Health and Human Services Commission; U.S. Department of Health and Human Services. Courtesy of Martin et al., *South Dallas Research Brief.*

how the city is usually perceived and understood.[6] At the beginning of the twenty-first century, the Dallas Way continues to be called upon to raise the lower city, while its responsibilities for the plight of that area pass without notice. The discourse of the two cities is both a descriptive shorthand and a distancing device.[7]

In Dallas-speak, "southern sector" is pseudo-neutral code language for substantially African American South Dallas and significantly Mexican American but also partly African American West Dallas.[8] The language of two Dallases organizes and simplifies. It reduces many Dallases to two, conflating blacks and Hispanics. The conceptualization of two cities annuls the agency of minorities at the same time as it attempts to remove white racism from the story. In some versions, the tale of two cities narrates the second city as aberration, absent or deviant from the triumphant Dallas Way. In others, it is a latecomer to the Dallas edition of the American Dream. Dallas south and west awaits its turn, making do with what "trickles down" from the north. Lost is any conception of racial-ethnic minority communities as vocal, empowered, entitled, active in their own and the city's interests. Also lost are important and moving stories of long-term and continuing conflict and contention, the struggle for human rights and social welfare.

"The City"	The "Other" or "Second" City
"can do"	"can't do"
haves	have-nots
"city with no limits"	no city, walled city, divided city
ahistorical, antihistorical	contingent, reversible
"city of destiny"	going nowhere
the future	the past
"the Dallas Spirit"	stasis, doom, despair
progress	left behind
at the crossroads, on the verge	stuck, nowhere
"Millennial city"	obsolete, anachronistic
"a great city"	second rate
"America's city"	"the city that hates"
cosmopolitan, international	parochial
new	old
business enterprise	"politics"
suburban or "new urban"	urban
density moderate to low	density high
North	South and West
white/Anglo	black or African American, brown or Hispanic
majority	minority
well-to-do	poor
middle and upper middle class	working class
success	failure
privilege	limited prospects
opportunity	discrimination
promised land	land of unkept promises and last resorts
home ownership high	home ownership low
light	dark
hope	despair
remembered	forgotten
healthy physical environment	polluted physical environment
safe	dangerous
landscape attractive	ranges from neglected to well-cared-for
roads, utilities, amenities good	lack of infrastructure, poor quality, rundown
quality of life good	quality of life inferior
housing good	substandard housing
low rates of crime	high crime rates
safe from personal violence	vulnerable to personal violence

few gangs and group conflict	typical urban problems of drugs and conflict
police and fire fire protection good	underprotected by police and firefighters
job opportunities available	limited job opportunities available
public schools adequate	public schools failing
school attendance and retention rates high	high truancy and dropout rates
city and social services adequate to good	city and social services inadequate or poor
improvements in the works	promises unmet
prognosis good to fair	prognosis mixed to poor

FIGURE 35. Dallas's discourse of two cities.

SEGREGATION

Explicit racial and ethnic identification is conspicuously absent from public agendas, except when minorities' accomplishments are lauded. Often painting residents as "other"—alien, poor, uneducated, disorganized, or dangerous—recent Dallas diction translates them into the "forgotten," yet progressing, or at least hopeful, regardless of their own varied landscapes and hierarchies. The discourse of opposing qualities powerfully organizes and directs perceptions through its sets of dichotomies. The *Dallas Morning News* and other media outlets offer point-by-point contrasts of Dallas south and west with Dallas north in which the second city is dangerously lacking in everything except color. Discursively and often descriptively, the dominant city has wealth, education, jobs, housing, and health; the other city lacks all these assets. The blatant contrasts are consistent with the familiar language of the Dallas Way.

On the ground, the evidence of racial and ethnic segregation—increasingly overlain with social class and economic divisions within racial and ethnic groups—is stark and incontrovertible.[9] Both comparatively and absolutely, Dallas's scores on various indexes of racial concentration rank among the highest in the southern and southwestern regions and the nation. In their landmark study, *American Apartheid,* Massey and Denton find that in 1980 Dallas was one of only sixteen "hypersegregated" metropolitan areas in the United States. In these cities, one in every three black persons, not all of them poor, lived in hypersegregation. To achieve that status, a city had to display "high segregation" on at least four of the five dimensions measured: residential segregation; poor housing and physical environment; lack of services and stores; insufficient and low-paying jobs; and their social correlates and costs. Whether explanations emphasize race, place, or economic restructuring, the "ghetto" of concentration and isolation built on race and residence's iron grip persists.[10] As Katz contends, "segregation by itself can initiate a vicious process that concentrates poverty and intensifies its impact. . . . In addition to racial segregation, economic segregation, which exists independently of race, has also increased among African Americans—as well as among whites and Hispanics in cities of all sizes across the nation."[11]

In Dallas, residential segregation was visible by World War I and increased during the 1920s and 1930s, as African Americans fleeing the rural South and Mexicans escaping the revolution were drawn by the wartime and postwar demand for labor. People of color were excluded from new urban developments and from some older neighborhoods. African Americans moving into South Dallas encountered violent resistance. South Dallas, which stood adjacent to the central business district, had been home to many whites; members of the elite lived in Park Row, South Boulevard, and the Cedars before moving to North Dallas, the Park Cities, and the suburbs. West Dallas, which Dallas refused to annex and which bore the brunt of industrial environmental degradation, historically received the growing number of Mexican migrants as poor whites moved out. In the 1980s, gentrification north and east of the central area pushed African Americans into West and increasingly South Dallas. In the familiar scripts of urban change, slum clearance sometimes amounted to "Negro removal" and at other times resembled slum relocation.[12]

The construction of poor-quality public housing was an inadequate and politically controversial advance that actually increased levels of group concentration. Projects in West Dallas took space formerly occupied by black residents, another push toward a more African American South Dallas.[13] Public policy helped to cement the critical connections between race and place: substandard housing, unhealthy and dangerous environments, and conflict with whites. Here, too, Dallas exhibits patterns shared by most large American cities, but to an extreme degree.[14] The extent of the gap between its two cities contributes to a profound sense of difference, reflected in the social statistics and in the perceived disadvantages of racial-ethnic minority Dallasites and their neighborhoods.[15]

In the development of Dallas, key elements clashed and combined to stimulate rising levels of racism and segregation, with progress for some groups and exploitation for others. African American and Hispanic Dallasites offered cheap labor, concentrated in central locations, and required minimal public services. For decades, planners, developers, civic leaders, and many white citizens aimed for the outward and upward growth of the urban core; this task required low-wage, unskilled and skilled labor, conveniently located. Non-Anglo working people met much of that need.[16] According to Dallas author and historian H. Rhett James, African American workers "dug ditches and poured concrete for skyscrapers and highways. They laid the tracks for trains, worked as mechanics and in warehouses. They ran elevators, chauffeured executives, handled luggage, cared for children and worked the cotton fields and farms." Thousands of African Americans worked on the railroads, drawn "to Dallas from rural Texas and surrounding states."[17]

Areas of minority settlement had a central place in making and building Dallas. From the 1870s, railroads brought their loads of cattle to West Dallas, an unincorporated area that provided a convenient dumping ground. West Dallas was pockmarked by hazardous "cement plants, lead smelters, brick factories, rock quarries and gravel pits," according to "Forgotten Dallas," the *Dallas Morning News* series. Mexican workers were joined by "a dramatic migration of black workers from East Texas farms in the 1940s." Families lived in "shacks and 'shotgun houses' with no running water or indoor plumbing." The separation continued after annexation: "When West Dallas was incorporated into Dallas in 1952, Dallasites viewed the move as an unavoidable burden to stop the spread of disease to other areas." Federal money for public housing was required to make annexation a reality. In the 1950s and 1960s, 460 acres of West Dallas was converted to public housing, which "further concentrated people and locked them into a cycle of poverty." Racial tension and repression "exploded in 1973 with the police shooting of Jose Santos Rodriquez, a 12-year old boy. . . . Forty years after its annexation, West Dallas continues to be close but not fully a part of the city of Dallas."[18]

Segregation was politically as well as economically useful, especially when minorities lacked the vote. Many asserted that physical segregation reduced the likelihood of conflict and violence. Dallas leaders also attempted to maintain control through accommodation, sponsoring political careers of selected minority candidates and negotiating and managing change.[19] At the same time, local whites used violence to defend neighborhoods they thought belonged exclusively to them against the movement of African Americans into South Dallas and of Mexicans and Mexican Americans into West Dallas during the 1940s and 1950s. The police seldom interfered with such extralegal acts. Black potential homeowners were labeled "blockbusters" and targeted for abuse.[20] Working-class and lower-middle-class whites began to move to the burgeoning, stratified suburbs. At a time when there was a general lack of available housing in Dallas, but an especially acute housing shortage for racial-ethnic minorities, white families' movement northward opened older areas to black and brown families, increasing separation and inequality.

In Dallas, the divisions cut by race and racism were deeply rooted. Historian Marvin Dulaney notes, "African Americans in Texas confronted a racial environment as rigid as that in other parts of the Deep South—a system of racial violence and segregation. . . . a general pattern of apartheid that affected all aspects of African-American life in Dallas . . . developed almost immediately after the Civil War." Black citizens were stripped of the suffrage by a poll tax beginning in 1902 and a law that excluded African Americans from participating in primary elections for the Democratic Party from 1903. "Over the first three decades of this century, the city of Dallas systematically and deliberately circumscribed the social and political lives of the African-American population." In 1907, Dallas revised its city charter to allow racial segregation in public schools, housing, amusements, and churches. In 1916, the city amended its charter to legitimate residential segregation. In 1930, a charter amendment restricted African Americans' access to office by requiring all candidates to run at large and on a nonpartisan basis. Under the same charter amendment, the city council "also furthered apartheid" with an ordinance establishing segregation on public transportation. A second city was built in law as well as social practice.[21]

African Americans fought long and hard against great odds to secure their own unequal share of the Dallas Way. Violence from the Ku Klux Klan, the Klan-dominated police, and other whites did not stop the formation of what Dulaney calls "a viable and progressive community." The African American portion of Dallas's second city reconstructed itself spatially and socially, moving from a number of small settlements located around town (Hall Street–Thomas Avenue, Elm Thicket, Boggy Bayou, Wheatley Place, sections in Oak Cliff and East Dallas) toward South and West Dallas. Whites who sought to resist the black presence throughout the city and in their South Dallas neighborhoods pressed for more concentrated residential areas, and these efforts to limit African Americans' space also helped to consolidate the community's identity. Several decades later, Mexican Americans in Dallas embarked on community organizing. Both groups struggled for years to gain representation on the Dallas police force and other public bodies, including the city council.[22]

Organizing for protection, resisting discrimination, and fighting for a fairer share, African Americans attracted considerable attention, both positive and negative. Tactics ranged from courthouse and ballot box challenges through the sometimes barely civil disobedience of County Commissioner John Wiley Price to the armed self-defense of the New Black Panther Party.

Figure 36. Negro Achievement Day at State Fair of Texas, ca. 1950. From the collections of the Texas/Dallas History and Archives Division, Dallas Public Library.

FIGURE 37. Juanita Craft (third from right) and others picket Negro Achievement Day as "Negro Appeasement Day" at State Fair of Texas, 1955. From Payne, *Big D.*

Aided by spatial concentration and resisting the twin blows of racial discrimination and physical attacks, the community established businesses, the Dallas Negro Chamber of Commerce, churches, a newspaper, and a small middle class of teachers, physicians, lawyers, and other professionals. Already poor conditions worsened during the Depression and stimulated a long battle against inadequate housing, unpaved streets, lax law enforcement, neglect by city agencies, poor education, unequal share of federal relief, and limited access to consumer goods. As part of an effort to reactivate itself, the Negro Chamber of Commerce hired A. Maceo Smith as executive director in 1932. In 1936, at the same moment that R. L. Thornton organized the Dallas Citizens Council—in Dallas the citizens council did not need to put "white" in its name—black groups organized the Progressive Voters League, and Smith joined with civil rights organizer Juanita Craft and others to rejuvenate the Dallas NAACP and link it to the state and national civil rights movement.

According to the *Handbook of Texas Online:*

> In 1936 the Progressive Citizens League was renamed the Progressive Voters League to reflect the organization's emphasis on paying the poll tax and voting

as key objectives for achieving black citizenship rights in Dallas. In the same year the league coordinated the efforts of over 100 black organizations in Dallas in a massive poll tax–payment campaign. The league registered almost 7,000 voters and organized the black electorate into a voting bloc that carried the balance of power in the 1937 Dallas City Council elections. The league supported the Forward Dallas Association's slate of candidates over those of the Citizens Charter Association and assisted the former association in winning a majority of the seats on the Dallas City Council. . . . The 1937 election established the Progressive Voters League as a viable black political organization and set the tone for its activities for the next fifty years. The Forward Dallas Association rewarded the support provided by the league with a new black high school, more jobs for blacks in city government, and consideration of blacks for police jobs in the city. With this success, the league continued to register and organize black voters in the city, to endorse candidates in local elections, and to encourage black participation in the political process locally, statewide, and nationally.[23]

Crucial lessons were learned early. Their recognition marks a new chapter in histories of Dallas. Practicing those lessons regularly, and joining with other underrepresented ethnic and racial groups, remains difficult, especially in the face of white resistance and violence.

African Americans became a voice and force in Dallas politics, influencing city council elections and filing civil rights cases to gain employment for African Americans in the public sector and access to public facilities. Under Maceo Smith's leadership at the local and state levels, the Dallas NAACP served as the base for efforts to overturn the Democratic Party's white primary, equalize salaries for black teachers, and integrate the University of Texas. In 1941, black citizens regained the right to serve on juries. Five years later, they began to participate in the Dallas County Democratic Party conventions. In 1948, against loud protest and after a decade-long campaign, African American police were hired to patrol black neighborhoods. Slowly, public positions and defense industry jobs opened to African Americans, along with some public facilities. From the 1930s into the 1960s, the Dallas African American community advanced and gained a national reputation.[24]

Historian Robert Fairbanks sees Dallas's civic leaders and government officials as concerned about the plight of minorities but limited by their notions of acting for "the city as a whole." "For instance, civic leaders defined bad housing as a problem . . . because bad housing promoted sickness and criminality—forces that adversely affected urban stability. . . . Since the booster rhetoric of the city emphasized ordered growth above all else, government addressed urban social problems most expeditiously when they threatened to promote disorder. But when 'solutions' threatened to create turmoil and dissension among the white body politic, civic leaders withdrew or severely modified those solutions."[25] The racial terms of this formulation belie its supposed neutrality: elites moved to quell disorders among black citizens, but never at the expense of alienating white citizens. I view this dynamic as an implicit and explicit function of the Dallas Way. The discourse of "the city as a whole" could be considered as a construct, invention, or fiction, designed to promote social stability in the face of challenge. We must take care not to take the claims of the Dallas Way at face value. Leaders may have decided to leave social problems alone even without the negative pressure of conflicts that threatened their power, wealth, and control. The segregation and subordination of African Americans and Mexican Americans served many purposes. The concept of "for the city as a whole" was associated overwhelmingly with the development of the central area and its physical infrastructure, rather than for Dallas residents "as a whole." The city was active when and where it wanted, and needed, to be. That was the Dallas Way.[26]

Fairbanks argues, "The city's response to its black housing problem . . . reflected a concern with not antagonizing whites as well as a desire to improve the horrible housing conditions of blacks." But racial segregation trumped better housing. "Local officials appeared motivated by a wish to improve the city as a whole rather than to correct injustices suffered by blacks." In Dallas, as in other racially divided cities, the link between "a wish to improve the city as a whole" and "not antagonizing whites" was clearly stronger than concern to "correct injustices suffered by blacks." Until the 1930s, Dallas's main actions with respect to housing were passing racist zoning laws and promoting restrictive covenants. With conditions deteriorating in the 1930s, concern spread that guaranteeing the future of segregation required adequate housing for minority groups in "their own" areas. Building public housing with federal funds represented a possible solution to the problem. The Dallas Way dictated that if public housing projects were to be built at all, they must be built for whites as well as for African

Americans, "to avoid the appearance of giving special privilege to blacks."[27] Because of difficulty in finding a site in a black area, the only public housing built during the 1930s was a 181-unit, whites-only project. The effort to place minority public housing in white areas of Dallas continued without success throughout the century.

When a new federal Housing Act was passed in 1937, black leaders and their supporters pressed the city. Following the new Dallas Citizens Council's strong public stand in favor of slum elimination, the new Dallas Housing Authority proposed a black project, to be followed by white and Mexican developments. Slum clearance was intended to halt the spread of blight beyond minority areas, as well as to improve the housing in what "has definitely [become] established as a negro area"[28] and was expected to stay that way. Slum clearance drove African Americans out of their homes without providing for their relocation. In 1941, construction of the Roseland Homes destroyed 266 structures and replaced them with 188 units for black families. At the same time, more than six hundred whites gathered in a South Dallas school to protest the increasing presence of blacks in their area. Similar concerns were voiced in North Dallas. Fears of health hazards and unrest led to Little Mexico's reconstruction in 1941, with a 102-unit project and a community center for the larger Mexican American community. When push came to shove, the city did not speak for or listen to its black or Mexican American citizens and property owners. By the end of 1941, the Dallas Housing Authority started construction on three other housing projects: one for whites in East Dallas, an expansion of the white Cedar Springs project, and another two-hundred-unit development for blacks in East Dallas. Too few units were built, and displacement by clearance worsened the plight of the poor and increased racial concentration.

City policies and actions neither resolved the housing crisis nor addressed the problems of segregation and inequality for African Americans and Mexican Americans. All plans took the maintenance or advancement of segregated housing as a first milestone. Black leaders strongly rejected a proposal to build a complete "Negro city" on the Trinity River bottoms in northwest Dallas. Proposals for more public housing for minorities created major public backlashes in the 1950s and early 1960s for at least two Dallas mayors, Wallace Savage and Earle Cabell. With the support of the League of Women Voters and the *Dallas Morning News,* Cabell went so far as to suggest that private enterprise's failure to meet housing needs mandated public action. The mayor, this proposal, and its supporters were damned as "creeping socialism" by realtors and right-wing congressman Bruce Alger. Cabell was informed that his plan deviated from the Dallas Way of doing business.[29]

Dallas annexed West Dallas in 1952, considered by some a last-ditch act of self-defense against pollution and disease. The Dallas Housing Authority built 3,500 low-rent housing units there: 1,500 for whites, 1,500 for blacks, and 500 for Mexican Americans. Soon the projects' deterioration exceeded the limits of tolerance. No long-term plan set goals or standards for housing or considered it within the neighborhood setting. Acceptance of urban redevelopment and public housing grew, but solutions to racial inequality were not on the city's agenda.

Suburbanization or suburban-style dwellings for African Americans within the city limits were touted as solutions to urban problems. In 1941, as a growing black middle class began to buy homes in South Dallas, whites retaliated by bombing eighteen homes along Oakland Boulevard, "a transitional area" between a white and a growing black neighborhood, one of many stories of white violence and control. In the Dallas Way, "the city of Dallas tried to resolve the matter by buying out African-American homeowners or convincing them to return the homes to the original owners." More bombings of homes in the same area occurred in 1950 and 1951. Dallas police tried to protect blacks' homes, but no one was charged with the bombings until African Americans protested and the city began to receive national attention. Ten suspects were arrested, but none convicted. The grand jury claimed that the "plot reached into unbelievable places" and implicated two South Dallas neighborhood associations. The bombings stopped as Dallas leaders wished, but that hardly resolved the concerns of black homebuyers.[30]

The new master plan for Dallas developed in 1943 by Harlan Bartholomew's city planning firm allowed no room for the expansion of existing black neighborhoods or the establishment of new black residential areas. Proposals for nonprofit or philanthropic corporations to assist in the construction of single-family "low-cost housing . . . in and adjoining outlying non-white areas" followed.[31] Bartholomew identified an unacceptable site in West Dallas near Love Field. The search for an acceptable location, a contractor, and financial support took several years. Opposition from whites, near and far, followed the announcement of almost every proposed subdivision: "Whites based their resistance on the threat to land values and future white settlement, the doubtful suitability of the land for residences, and racial disharmony. The results were frustration for the contractors, black expansion into white neighborhoods and its attendant violence, an elaborate housing scheme rejected by blacks, and the intervention of elite whites. The latter factor ultimately quieted the violence and produced the north Dallas subdivision of Hamilton Park."[32] Dulaney concludes, "The city of Dallas finally acted to build several segregated, public-housing projects for African Americans and an all-black housing subdivision to resolve the crisis that African Americans faced because of the city's policy of residential segregation. Residential segregation thus continued in Dallas unresolved."[33]

Dallas leaders carefully planned and planted a small African American middle-class community in the shadows of a huge Texas Instruments complex on the Dallas-Richardson border: Hamilton Park. Within the boundaries of the Richardson Independent School District, a truly pioneering integrated elementary school was created. William Wilson and others have told the moving story of black-white interactions, African American community building, the triumph over racism, and the hard work of Dallas business leaders in launching this social experiment. We take nothing away from that great achievement when we recognize its very limited scale and numbers, no doubt part of its successes; its careful planning and vigilance; its relatively high cost; the race-based paternalism, almost tokenism, that underlay the experiment; and the fact that the community/school relationship and the fervent commitment that sustained it could not outlive the founding generation of participants.

The effort to build Hamilton Park revealed the outermost possibilities of the Dallas Way and the limits of private-dominated solutions. There was but one Hamilton Park, and its promise is now gone. Its contribution to the ongoing struggle for racial equality in Dallas was more symbolic than material. It could have been institutionalized or easily replicated. By itself, it had little impact on separation, social change, or the Dallas Independent School District. Measures of racial segregation continued to rise in Dallas. Exceptional developments like Hamilton Park functioned as a safety valve and a symbol, raising hopes for the integration but leading to frustrations when so little changed. Suburbanization reproduced much of the racial and class-based segregation of the city.[34]

Developments like Hamilton Park usefully countered at least some of the worst images and negative publicity that Dallas sparked, especially in the national media, as a right-wing "city that hates." These efforts fit neatly with media images of the lack of protest and violence during court-ordered desegregation of schools and public facilities. Following more than five years of judicial delay, perseverance by the NAACP led to a victory in the Fifth Circuit Court of Appeals in 1960 that forced the school board to develop a desegregation plan. In 1961, the Dallas school board initiated a "step-wise" plan in which schools desegregated one grade each year, beginning with first grade and continuing to twelfth.[35]

Desegregation was carefully controlled and orchestrated, led by the Dallas Citizens Council and Citizens Charter Association and backed up by threat of police or legal action. A biracial committee of fourteen negotiated the terms of desegregation, producing positive visual images of a peaceful process for broadcast at home and elsewhere. Citizens were coaxed with the lure of Dallas appearing better than other cities across the South and threatened with a strong public warning against any deviation from the script. In an eight-page booklet, Dallas Power and Light executive C. A. Tatum, stating that Dallas was once again "at a major crossroads," instructed ministers:

> Dallas leaders, assuming their responsibilities of civic leadership, have formulated and undertaken a program of public conditioning to create a peaceful climate in which the school changes can take place. . . .
>
> No minister, or any individual in the city, for that matter, is being asked to advocate either segregation or desegregation. We do ask [that you] stress the vital necessity of peaceful acceptance of the law in Dallas. . . .
>
> A number of instruments of communication have been designed to reach Dallasites on all levels with the message, "The courts have made desegregation law in Dallas. All responsible citizens will accept the law and the changes it brings with peace and good will. The alternative is violence, which will exact a price from Dallas and its citizens which they cannot afford to pay. And, if there is violence, those responsible can expect to be recognized as lawbreakers and punished as such."[36]

In August 1961, eighteen African American children enrolled without incident in previously all-white elementary schools. Dulaney comments, "This 'desegregation' occurred in Dallas without the massive demonstrations and confrontations that had characterized the process in Little Rock, Arkansas, and New Orleans, Louisiana. It also foreshadowed how African-American and white leadership would handle the process of desegregating public life in Dallas."[37]

The Dallas Way of desegregation worked for those whose primary concern was the maintenance of law and order. "On the surface, desegregation took place smoothly and with a minimum of racial strife," Dulaney concedes. "In reality, however, the city's desegregation actions were still tokenism." Despite progress in other respects, schools and housing long remained segregated. The slow pace of change frustrated African Americans and their supporters. It also took a toll on the civil rights movement in Dallas: "The continued existence of segregation and discrimination and the [committee of fourteen]'s policy of discouraging dissent and direct-action tactics eventually led some African Americans to challenge the city's established political culture of negotiating change. They would also legitimately charge that desegregation was taking place 'on white terms' with the city's power structure maintaining control of the situation." The emergence of direct action among some activists effectively divided the leadership and split the movement, hindering African American local politics for more than a decade.[38]

The history of Dallas indicates that racial change cannot be negotiated under the more or less private domination of one party seeking to limit change while preserving its public image. The much-revised and contested school desegregation order remained in effect for four decades. School boundaries were drawn and redrawn, and with them the extent of busing. Vanguard middle schools, magnet high schools, and academies were added. In recent years, a rapid succession of superintendents (including a spectrum of minorities), budget controversies, and squabbling among the elected board have exacerbated the usual problems of big-city schools and urban/suburban divides. Charges of racism from all sides punctuate the cacophony of criticism. Private, parochial, and charter schools and suburban school districts poached on the public system in well-to-do city neighborhoods. The Dallas schools are more segregated now than they were in 1960.[39]

The contrast between the two cities, separate and unequal, helped to underwrite elite and popular white support for the Dallas Way and its political officeholders.[40] The promotional images of Dallas were based on white elite culture, except when showcasing "local color" or "multicultural charm" was advantageous. The white population in rapidly expanding North Dallas and the suburbs was well served by the city's promises and privileges.[41] New high-tech manufacturing and white-collar jobs were located in North, East, and far west, but not South or West Dallas. Public transit opened bus routes (so-called maids' lines) to facilitate African and Mexican American domestic and unskilled laborers' journeys north to their employers' homes, offices, and hotels, but no mass transit connected their neighborhoods to better-paying, higher-status employment or to educational institutions. Richardson, well north of Dallas city lines and barely in Dallas County, was chosen in 1975 as the location for the University of Texas at Dallas, a center for scientific and technological research and development. Racial-ethnic diversity was not its hallmark, although its Web site touts the fact that many of its students are the first in their families to pursue higher education. Community colleges expanded and became more accessible, but El Centro, the downtown campus closest to students from West and South Dallas, struggled for a permanent home.

The underside of these spatial and racial relationships was pervasive racism rooted in separation and conflict, ignorance and fear. Dallas has a long history of unofficial violence and police brutality toward members of racial-ethnic minorities in the "cause" of social order and control. In these ways, Dallas conformed to patterns that pervade big cities in the North and Midwest, as well as the South. But Dallas differed from many other cities because of the relatively late date at which major changes in the political order arrived.

A 1975 federal court ruling shook the long-established Dallas Way by outlawing at-large election of all city council members as unconstitutional. The court mandated an 8–3 plan in which eight councilors were elected from fixed geographic districts and three at large. In a lengthy series of legal actions, that plan was also ruled unconstitutional. Then, in several bitterly fought elections, Dallas voters approved a 10–4–1 plan, which was opposed by 95 percent of African Americans and more than 70 percent of Hispanics. Finally, in 1990, the city council drafted a 14–1 plan, in which all councilors would be elected from and represent a specific district, with only the mayor elected at large. This plan was barely approved by voters.

Only in the early 1990s did "democracy come to Dallas," to qualify Jim Henderson's well-known August 23, 1987, *Dallas Times Herald* article.[42] He cited "a female mayor, a black city manager, a growth policy plan, a mass transit scheme, effective neighborhood activists, a Hispanic city councilman elected at large" as evidence. "The old oligarchy was all but vanquished and in its place was something less definite but infinitely more diverse— a loose coalition of neighborhoods, ethnic groups and economic interests." African American journalist Bob Ray Sanders and political scientist Royce Hanson, among others, argue that Henderson was overly optimistic.[43] The council's public divisiveness, loud clashes between the mayor and certain councilors, and the conflicts among clearly differing interests contrast markedly with images of the businesslike efficiency of government the Dallas Way. Conflicts stemming from physical location, race, class, and inequities of previous resource allocation generated a new kind of Dallas politics, too often mistakenly pegged as politics of "neighborhood."

The long years of elite domination exacted a high price. For many decades, the price was paid primarily by those excluded from the benefits of the Dallas Way; now the costs are paid by everyone. The demand for democratic civil and political rights can be delayed no longer, from equal opportunities for education, employment, and housing to repair of the city streets and restoration of a healthy environment. Partial and pseudo-changes have exhausted the private sector's credits with the population of Dallas. Race and space remain huge, unresolved problems. Ironically and contradictorily, the Dallas Way raised the price of development and the price of governance, exactly what it had claimed to reduce. The delays for the city and many of its residents increased the cost and the scale of the tasks facing the twenty-first century.[44]

FROM MANY DALLASES TO TWO DALLASES

Residents and observers have long seen Dallas not as a single city, but as a collection of different cities that happen to be contiguous physically. That recognition is often celebrated as a badge of multiculturalism and promoted as a spur to tourism. More rarely, the remark is meant critically, marking incoherence, fragmentation, opposition, or conflict. The crucial relationships that tie together the different Dallases and their joint historical development are rarely examined.[45]

Through much of the twentieth century, observers have come to a broad consensus when identifying different Dallases. In 1987, journalist Molly Ivins named six Dallases and implied the existence of still more: "There is a black Dallas, there is a Chicano Dallas, there is a Vietnamese Dallas, there is a gay Dallas, there is even a funky-Bohemian Dallas. But mostly there is North Dallas. A place so materialistic and Republican it makes your teeth hurt to contemplate it. . . . The disgrace of Dallas today is that it is probably the most segregated city this side of Johannesburg." Ivins's six Dallases group themselves into two cities whose degree of racial segregation she only slightly exaggerates.[46]

Twenty-five years earlier, Warren Leslie identified five Dallases that condensed into two. Oak Cliff, downtown, and "fashionable" North Dallas, which includes "two virtual islands near the center of the city"—Highland and University Parks—inhabited by "the people who built and manage downtown Dallas" form one city.[47] Leslie's "other" Dallas is west and south: "One general area is called West Dallas. Close to Oak Cliff, it was not even a part of the city until recently. It was not annexed because the city fathers simply did not wish to face the huge problem of cleaning it up." Writing in the aftermath of the Kennedy assassination, he saw that "South Dallas remains, as it has for years, slum and semi-slum area." His telling summation: "In the shadow of the downtown skyscrapers lie the slums, the second city of Dallas."[48]

Despite their apparent and fundamental separation and difference, the slums and the skyscrapers are inextricably interrelated. Each reflects and defines the other, each in its own ways depends on the other, from the need for cheap labor and low-quality housing in areas designated as "in transition" and lacking social services to the remaking of central city spaces under policies and in actions branded as slum clearance and urban redevelopment. Their relationships extend to new patterns of consumption and the symbolic cities of wealth and poverty that magnify each other's differences through comparison, especially in a virulently racist city undergoing the strains of major growth. Dallas's differential evaluation of and willingness to invest in each city ensured and solidified the differences. When Dallas had to turn its attention seriously toward improving its southern and western parts, the scale of the task and its costs escalated, as its effect on perceptions of difference and equality worsened.[49]

For Leslie, the two cities of Dallas extended beyond the distinct identities of Dallas's many cities. The two Dallases are places where space and race as well as past and future came together. Starkly separate and segregated in reverse image of each other, reflected in their own dialect of discourse represented by a lengthy roster of semantic opposites, they are also inextricably bound together. Dallas's two cities are parts and products of the urban historical process that built the city and its spaces, but the second city had no spirit or destiny seen as rooted in nineteenth-century Dallas. Earlier observers in the twentieth century acknowledged the existence of many Dallases but also recognized that at its core were two cities.[50] The notion, language, and fact of "two cities" were inscribed over the course of Dallas's development.

By 1937, political scientists Stone, Price, and Stone identified a familiar array of Dallas cities. Annexed to Dallas in 1904, middle-class white Oak Cliff joined North Dallas, "a large and homogeneous white-collar area," and the "wealthier leaders of the industrial and commercial life of Dallas [who] live outside the city in University Park and Highland Park." These observers, too, were struck by the city's physical boundaries: "The city is divided into a number of areas by the Trinity River and the railroad tracks. These barriers separate Mexicans and Negroes from the whites and from one another. There are, however, a number of Negro areas scattered about the city."[51] Over time, African Americans concentrated in South and West Dallas. Stone and his colleagues noticed the extent of class segregation at a time when twentieth-century Dallas was taking shape: "Laboring classes are quite definitely separated from white-collar residential areas, and the leading families live unto themselves in the suburbs." Many lines of separation divided Dallas on the eve of its suburban transformation. Less visible than race, class and ethnicity mattered; in their interstices grew the second city.[52]

In the second city, many people new to cities and/or the United States built homes and forged connections. They adapted to new environments, often using rural or "peasant" ways to get by, despite racist presumptions of their failure and anti-immigrant myths of "social breakdown." Historical and sociological researchers refute notions of individual, family, and community dysfunction in the confrontation with the new metropolis. Complex practices of urban adaptation built families and communities in Dallas's city south and west.[53]

In West Dallas, "Little Mexico" provided ground for homes and community in the clichéd shadows of the city center. It carried that label from the 1920s and perhaps earlier. At that time, only one in every forty-four persons in Dallas was Mexican American. Compared with African Americans—in 1930, one in seven residents of Dallas was black—the Hispanic community was very small indeed. Mexican Americans were probably more segregated than African Americans. Writing with ambivalence in 1937, Walter T. Watson observed, "So detached and segmented is the major Mexican colony, so unobtrusive and inconspicuous are the Mexicans themselves, that it is easily possible for the average citizen to live for many years in the city without any very vivid—and certainly without very accurate—impressions about local Mexican life."[54] His recognition, tolerance, and cautious stance on assimilation were rare. Forty years later, anthropologist Shirley Achor remarked on the simultaneous presence of "the towering downtown Dallas skyline across the river" and "a village-like quality about the neighborhood which belies its urban setting."[55]

FIGURE 38. "Shanty houses in Little Mexico with bank towers behind," ca. 1943–50. From the collections of the Texas/Dallas History and Archives Division, Dallas Public Library.

The *WPA Guide,* written at the same time as the report from Stone and associates, devoted special sections to the separate city of Mexican Americans and African Americans. Never quite voicing the notion of two Dallases, the *Guide* did not allocate comparable coverage to other areas or groups in the city, or present the second city explicitly in light of the first. The implicit identification and coupling of two groups and locales make the *Guide*'s designation and description more telling. Pointing to principal locations and offering contemporary racist explanations for groups' concentration, the writers highlight aspects of the urban historical process and the perceptions of contemporaries. The *Guide* occasionally found the exotic charm of the "other" appealing, but more often its reports expressed revulsion.

The *WPA Guide* begins by damning Little Mexico with faint praise as "one of the few slum areas in Dallas possessing individual character": "Surrounded by the huge warehouses and towering smokestacks of Dallas' wholesale district, Little Mexico is a close-packed mass of flimsy, tumbled-down frame shanties and 'shotgun' houses threaded by narrow, twisting unpaved streets, muddy or dusty according to the weather." The Mexican population was scattered across the city's poorer sections, with smaller colonies in West Dallas, Oak Cliff, and South Dallas. The great majority lived in "this congested wooden slum," two and three families to a house and others in sheds and outbuildings. Many lacked even primitive sanitary conveniences. Yet they found ways to survive and adapt. "The dominant notes are poverty and squalor with a relatively high ratio of malnutrition, tuberculosis, syphilis, and other diseases, but the inhabitants appear to endure their lot with the patient resignation of their race, and crime, drunkenness, and disorder are rare," the authors observe. Overwhelmingly working class, employed Mexicans worked as dishwashers, busboys, dining room foremen, gardeners and yardmen, tailors, ditch diggers, and common laborers in construction. Many also worked part of the year in agricultural tasks, including shelling pecans and picking cotton.[56]

The *WPA Guide* essentializes African Americans in their second city: "as in other large American cities the existing Negro sections grew up through the natural tendency of these people to live among their kind." The *Guide* combined economic and cultural determinism to claim, "While there is no formal segregation, economic conditions and environment combine with racial affinity to clearly mark the areas of Negro occupancy from those of the white race." Economics forced these residentially segregated groups

to overlap. Black Dallasites worked in industrial plants, as common laborers, chauffeurs, porters, janitors, household servants, waiters, and elevator
operators, most in some form of "serving" whites. African American professionals—physicians, dentists, lawyers, teachers, and merchants—were far
more likely to serve their own communities. An estimated impressive 25
percent owned or were buying homes, but "the racial group as a whole is
poorly housed." A 1938 municipal housing survey found that 3,270 African
American families lived in 2,037 houses, 86 percent of which were substandard. "Economic conditions were in some degree reflected by the fact that
of the group investigated only 187 Negro families were on direct relief, with
252 families dependent upon Federal or other relief employment." Federal
financing enabled slum clearance and new housing for 626 Negro families. A 1940 estimate that 25 percent of African Americans lived in servants'
houses on the premises of their white employers indicated that a substantial number lived with greater proximity to and oversight by whites.[57]

HOW MANY DALLASES DOES IT TAKE?

One Dallas's story is trumpeted, while the other is hardly mentioned, and
almost never recognized as a central part of the Dallas story. The public
face of Dallas offers the triumphant story of Dallas north, yet that success
is built upon both cities.[58] Admission or confession of the continuing existence of Dallas's two cities became a ritual that is repeated at irregular in-
tervals over the years. A sense of urgency but also self-congratulation and
promised uplift accompanies rediscovery, along with the assurance that
private enterprise will close the looming gap, with whatever help it can
command from the public sector. Particularly egregious examples include
the publicity accorded to a 1988 report published by the Dallas Alliance, a
civic organization, "Alliance Warns of Instability in Dallas." The report
"paints a disturbing portrait of racial separation in Dallas, a city divided
by social, educational and economic gaps between whites and minorities
that threaten the stability of the community."[59]

These rediscoveries often come at times of economic downturn and are
accompanied by criticism in the national or local press. The *Dallas Morning News* takes particular pride in this kind of fact-finding.[60] In 1997, for
example, the paper reported, "a million people with less than 4 percent
unemployment and a household income 16 percent higher than the national

average" live alongside a "city of 460,000 people with a ten percent unemployment rate and per capita incomes of only $11,350. Both these cities are
Dallas. But the second city described is southern Dallas."[61] These acknowledgments have multiple uses. The act of admission or confession serves
individuals and groups as a release and redirection. Rediscovery is coupled
with the repetition of a stated need for action or reminder of an unmet
social or political promise. For some, it is a renewal of a sincere moral or
even religious commitment to improved lives for the poor and people of
color. Moments of perceived crisis usually generate new activist groups,
cross-class and interracial coalitions of concerned professionals and volun-
teers, which often include present and future civic leaders and take names
like the Dallas Alliance or Dallas Together. This important work is limited
by its voluntary base and scant resources and confronts difficult problems
of legitimacy, authority, and accountability. The lines between public policy
and private initiative are often blurred or confused; voluntary work cannot
substitute for a comprehensive program of public welfare.[62]

The phenomenon and uses of the two cities are absolutely fundamental for understanding Dallas. As evident in the January 2000 *Dallas Morning News* editorial, the reification of the discourse of two cities can detract
attention from other kinds and levels of difference, which is especially dangerous with respect to differences among and between African Americans
and Mexican Americans, as well as other racial, ethnic, class, and geographic
distinctions. The path to the possible political union of these interests has
been hazardous, as real or implicit conflicts interfere with cooperation and
interest groups are played off against each other.[63] Piecemeal improvements
and broad pronouncements abound in the headlines: "West Dallas Isn't 'Forgotten' Anymore: Housing Construction Brings Hope to Once Neglected
Area"; "West Dallas Is Making Progress"; "A New Look, a New Way of
Life"; "Southern Dallas to Get Movie Complex: Mayor Hopes Cinemark
Theater Is Preview of Things to Come for Area"; "Hopes High for S. Dallas Businesses"; "South Dallas: Neighborhood Around Fair Park Is Improving"; "South Dallas: Legal Pressure Brings Improvement"; "Development
Helps Transform Area of South Dallas."[64]

This overblown discourse stimulates its own opposition and contradic-
tion. The headlines track a series of bitter disappointments: "Embattled S.
Dallas Apartment Complex Closing; Many See Nowhere to Go"; "Room for
Disagreement: Passions Collide on Developing Southern Dallas"; "Cadillac

Heights: City Must Address Chronic Neighborhood Problems"; "Cadillac Heights: Is It Livable?"; "Affordable Housing: It's Time to Get Results from Funds"; "Southern Half of Dallas Still Awaits Housing Boom"; "Toxic Housing: Low-Income Residents Shouldn't Be Placed in Jeopardy."[65] The most frequent hope for "improvement" turns on housing opportunities for middle-class minority families, but housing starts outpace the numbers of well-paying jobs. One seemingly trivial indicator of the limits to progress in Dallas's two cities is actually quite powerful and fundamental. Home delivery of prepared food is a bellwether for capitalist democracy, an early twenty-first-century updating of the uneven distribution of the fruits of modernity and progress. "Dallas officials said Monday they have found evidence that pizza shops 'redline' much of southern Dallas, but city leaders said they will not require them to deliver in areas the companies deem unsafe."[66] Hype does not sway the judgments of everyday capitalism. A fist-ful of presumptions about race, space, and safety keeps the second Dallas in a stranglehold.

The "economic development" that provides the first ingredient in the January 2000 *Dallas Morning News*'s formula for change in the city's south-ern sector is a refrain of a chorus of pleas and proposals advanced over many years. The fact that Dallas's characteristic patterns and processes of economic development have actually produced the underdevelopment of South and West Dallas escapes notice. It is no coincidence that these procla-mations accompany evidence of increasing segregation of African and Mexican Americans and growing concentrations of poverty and "social prob-lems" in Dallas south and west. The year 2000 brought mounting acknowl-edgment of the gravity of these circumstances and the threat they posed, including negative images of Dallas outside the city.[67]

Curiously, the characteristic response is to propose to turn economic liabilities into assets, or at least opportunities. Dallas Way discourse and presumptions ripple through these and many other reports: "Profitable Prospecting: Ignoring Southern Dallas Means Ignoring Opportunities"; "Economic Analysis Finds Area Poised for Investment."[68] South Dallas Development Corporation president Jim Reid laid it on the line in Dallas-speak, announcing the program in 1992: "Dallas at a Crossroads: To Be Reactive or Pro-Active." Linking the southern sector programs to efforts in Atlanta and Los Angeles, he urged Dallas leaders to act: "Dallas has the same urban conditions that provide a breeding ground for the kind of unrest that erupted in L.A. and seethed below the surface in Atlanta. Are we going to be 'pro-active' in rebuilding the inner city? . . . Or will we be seeking to frantically recover our equilibrium after a severe crisis?"[69]

Like Reid's opening, a great many of the past decades' initiatives, proposals, and plans for the southern sector evoke the Dallas Way, especially the domination of the private sector, including self-appointed committees or boards, over the public, and the expectation that public authority and funds, along with foundation grants, will promote, stimulate, and ease the way for corporate profitability. Thus the simultaneous stress on profits, "prospecting," investment, and business opportunities, and on loans, tax credits, and other incentives offered by local and federal governments.

The *Dallas Morning News* put it this way on December 28, 1995, in the editorial "Southern Dallas: This Is a Critical Time for Economic Strategies": "When established six years ago, the Southern Dallas Development Corporation received significant financial support from the municipal government. Now the agency must turn to the private sector for most of the money used to grant loans to businesses." That turn has been very slow in coming. Expectations of thousands of jobs and billions of dollars are a long way from realization. In commanding that the "city should end the economic polarization"—quite an order—the *News* gamely hits all the bases: "there is money to be made in southern Dallas. This is no charitable proposition. More than $1 billion in purchasing power annually flows out of southern Dallas to other parts of the city. Business needs to tap into that financial well. McKinsey & Co. also found the municipal government has not moved quickly enough on various initiatives to help southern Dallas. That's discouraging. . . . The city and business leadership must now put solid action behind the words." So far, the public-private partnership is unbalanced with respect to who contributes and who is meant to profit.[70]

One approach to solving the crisis has been the Southern Sector Initiative, portrayed as a humanitarian and social justice effort as well as an economic venture and involving veterans of the struggles for minority rights. J. McDonald Williams, former chairman of Trammell Crow Co. and the Dallas Citizens Council and head of the Dallas Together Forum, lauded "the most extraordinary, passionate and committed people, giving their daily lives and daily bread to help their fellow citizens" in Dallas's poorest areas. Corporations running welfare-to-work programs and garnering tax credits in return also received praise.[71] The Southern Sector Initiative promotes minority hiring and touts the economic advantages of South Dallas. In contrast with North Dallas and many suburbs, the southern sector has less traffic congestion, a shortage of entertainment and retail outlets, inexpensive utilities and solid waste disposal, lower blue-collar labor costs, a stable workforce nearby, and lots of vacant land. Therein lay the grounds for economic development, provided that expectations of payoffs for area residents were kept modest and that benefits for corporations include incentives like tax credits, infrastructure built at public expense, and loans. The community and the promoters learned that schools, housing, and community development require more patience than discount retail and grocery stores.

Leaders encourage business partnerships with schools, social programs, and volunteer opportunities. In Williams's view, "There is a crucial role for the public sector to play as well. The city and county must accelerate infrastructure support, permitting, code enforcement and funding for affordable housing. And targeted incentives from the city, county and school district must be competitive with the suburbs. . . . But I believe the engine for enduring change must be the private sector—with its profit motivation, its civic-mindedness, its entrepreneurialism and its financial and human resources. By teaming up with those in the south, we can have a city united by opportunities and services for all, instead of divided by inequities."[72] That is the Dallas Way, and the way in which returns are expected to flow. Questions might be raised, however, about the additions and divisions in Williams's social and economic arithmetic.

The entrepreneurial mentality that supports the initiative can be frightening when not amusing. Summarizing the various components of the Southern Sector Initiative, the *Dallas Morning News*'s editorial endorsement coolly calculated the gains open to those willing to "take the opportunity." "Retail is the opportunity that could be most quickly captured. Residents south of the Trinity and Interstate 30 have a combined retail demand of $3 billion. Yet many major intersections lack high-quality supermarkets, apparel and houseware stores and discount retailers." Longer-term plans list labor-intensive light industry, trucking and distribution, and business services. After hyping the "varied landscape" of southern Dallas, the *News* leaves reality far behind: "In other words, southern Dallas is pretty much like northern Dallas. The opportunities are there if businesses only look."[73]

This perspective runs the risk of crude caricature. The southern sector offers consumers, cheap land, and inexpensive labor. But without decent jobs, consumers purchase little. It offers attractive vistas, but also soil saturated with lead, marshes conducive to disease, and a levee system that does little to ease the severity of the Trinity River's flooding. Blighted areas outpace stately ones. The development vision is a plan for an economic colony, a sales and service periphery for downtown and North Dallas's moneymaking metropoles, not a developing Dallas south and west. Curiously, the high-tech manufacturing and production that is held up as one pillar in Dallas's economic future, developing in suburbs and towns west, north, and east, is not attached to Dallas south and west. Little is said about hopes for low-income housing, schools, and communities.

"Today, southern Dallas is, at least, on the map," declared the *Dallas Morning News* in March 2002. "A high-profile struggle" is taking place; another wave of revelation and discovery begins. The area whose "size compares to the city of Atlanta . . . doesn't have a movie complex, a major public university or easy access to an interstate highway." According to a group of experts brought together by the *News,* "Housing and business developments have sprouted there, many under the guidance of organized nonprofit groups. Banks have promised financing. With that, the experts say, an improved future now exists for a community where nine of every 10 residents is Latino or black. But progress, the group added, will not proceed in an orderly fashion, and it badly needs acceleration." Much has been accomplished, including $16.6 million from a city bond initiative for work on infrastructure and the start of three business parks. But so much more remains to be done, from affordable housing to capital investment.

A 2002 decision over two Wal-Mart stores sheds light on basic urban contradictions, when West Dallas said yes to a store while Park Cities opposed one proposed for the Love Field area. In rejecting the Wal-Mart, city plan commissioners called the proposed outlet "'an oversized gorilla' that would worsen traffic and crime in an urban area sandwiched between Love Field and the Park Cities." In contrast, "Oak Cliff and West Dallas rolled out the welcome mat for a new Wal-Mart Supercenter." In the same way, South Dallas longed for a movie theater complex; the single entertainment center in a massively underinvested area was viewed as a crown jewel.[74]

"You've got to put the money on the street where it can make an impact," said Jim Reid, who noted that bank pledges to lend $1.5 billion in the southern sector translated into only $200–300 million in new money available to projects. "What makes me mad is overselling what we're doing and creating expectations," he continued. "And then no delivery. And that's just another way to eliminate the heart of the community." Not surprisingly, the experts differed on the issue of visions for southern Dallas. "Whichever vision is embraced, it should focus on making southern Dallas residents partners in the development," one participant added.[75] That path would challenge Dallas's tradition of private-sector dominance.

Activists and promoters working to elevate the second city offer several explanations of the continuing chasm. Those explanations reveal much about the region, its possibilities and problems, and the Dallas Way. For some, the problem is *control:* who decides on what kinds of development and where. For others, defining the *nature* of the problem to be confronted is the primary task. Some say that the problem is *neglect.* According to Donald Williams, "It is an institutional failure. The city of Dallas is a catastrophe in terms of its policies and its practices in terms of southern Dallas. No one in this community is looking out for the whole." Southern Dallas is correlate and consequence of the city's course of development. The lack of infrastructure or "basic building blocks" on which to advance is an enormous and expensive liability.

In the eyes of some community leaders, the number one problem is *racism,* a preexisting condition and the fuel of much neglect. One position is stark: "Dallas has never embraced African-Americans and Hispanics as anything more than 'workers for the elite,'" and "serving people," not "directing our own destiny," was the expected outcome.[76] Dallas's history of virulent racism and both public and private violence aimed at controlling persons of color is part of the Dallas Way. The Dallas Way's modes of urban development and governance created bitter racial conflict and ensured that West Dallas became predominantly black and brown, and South Dallas substantially black.

For many seeking racial justice, Dallas's shift to a ward system of city council elections in the 1990s offered hope of representation and fairness. But this change in the electoral system was not enough to change people's perceptions about the balance of power. The *Dallas Morning News* reported in 1997: "Majority Sees No Change in Dallas Race Relations: Most in Poll Say 14–1 Council Hasn't Helped." Visibility didn't make for perceptions of progress: "Even with a black mayor at the helm and more minority members than ever before at City Hall, most Dallas residents think the city's race relations aren't any better than five years ago." "The mayor said the perception that city officials look out for some neighborhoods and not others is inaccurate but hard to turn around," and added, "'I think now we're paying for the sins of the past.' Most blacks and Hispanics surveyed said they were more likely than whites to be treated with disrespect or roughness by the Dallas police."[77]

In 1997, the *News* reported that, according to a White House official, Dallas was rejected as the site of a Clinton presidential town hall meeting because the city and its racial problems were "too big of a mess" and "they didn't see any leadership in the city actively and aggressively trying to do something about it."[78] Only two months earlier, at a meeting of Dallas Interfaith, a coalition of church groups, four attendees "scolded Dallas for bowing before the idol of the Golden Arena instead of working for better education and affordable housing."[79]

Other leaders emphasized the need to avoid the "controversy of racism" and playing the "race card." Here too Dallas history and the Dallas Way confront each other. "It's no longer a north-south issue. We can't change it, so why talk about it," asks a city economic development director. "I think what we have to look at is get beyond this southern sector and say this is a Dallas issue." The terms of the discussion then shift back to economics and politics, but defensively: "In recent years city leaders have come to see southern Dallas, which only provides a sixth of the municipal tax base, as a missed opportunity—especially as they have watched businesses and residents flock to the suburbs. Indeed, Dallas has virtually nowhere else to grow but south."

The "call for reinvigorated leadership" issued by the *News* in 2002 is a call for involvement of the traditional elites steering the city. The editorial notes that little work has been done in Dallas south and west, even to protect residents on the Trinity River floodplain, despite widespread recognition of the basic needs for schools, jobs, housing, and improved quality of life, and after more than a decade of work by the Southern Dallas Development Corporation and Dallas Together Forum. If economic development and education do not spread, dangers await not only the southern sector but also Dallas itself. Thus, "disparity" occupies first place on the annual agenda for 2000. According to the editors, however, the most pressing issue is not "disparity" or the very great needs of Dallas south and west. In the tradition of the Dallas Way, the problem is "Dallas's" and the danger is to "Dallas." It is therefore a question of "civic leadership." In other words, it is the question of the Dallas Way itself. In that mode, economic development and education will come when leaders agree on the benefits expected to accrue from investment.

In the end, the *Morning News* offers a general historical explanation, a generic rationalization that does not account persuasively for the "need for a new generation of leaders." The editorial acknowledges one important change: "The business leadership in the city has not completely recovered from the earthquake of the real estate and savings and loan crash of the 1980s, which led to management changes in all the major banking institutions in Dallas. Most of those banks and many other large corporations in the city are owned by out-of-state organizations without strong ties to the community. At the same time, many newer high-tech businesses have not embraced the civic culture. The leadership pool needs replenishing. . . . Who will step up for those jobs? Who will work to keep the city united and progressive?" Who indeed? With the city leadership pool scraping the bottom of the barrel, having to ask that question out loud and in public is not the Dallas Way. The eclipse of the Dallas Way may be signaled in this blatant plea. Race and space, taken together, reveal the failure of the tradition of the Dallas Way, and the shoals upon which private sector solutions to fundamental urban problems are torn to shreds, over and over again.[80]

Mimetic and Monumental Development: Memories Lost and Images Found

Dallas exhibits a deep identification with its skyscrapers. The 1894 *Souvenir Guide* marvels at the "tall spires" that mark Dallas as a city of "great enterprises and boundless public spirit."[1] The 1940 *WPA Guide* describes the "City of Towers" as a place where "recurrent waves of building have almost obliterated every vestige of the past. The use of natural gas as a fuel has made it a well-nigh smokeless city, and its pyramided downtown skyline, dominated by the twenty-nine story bulk of the Magnolia Building with its distinctive observation tower rises on the east bank of the Trinity like a segment of Lower Manhattan, sharp and clean-cut against the blue Texas sky."[2] The strangeness of mimicking New York City's dense verticality on the vast open prairie goes without comment. In the mid-1970s, the *Book of Dallas* affirmed, the city's "foremost symbol is the downtown skyline." "In spite of the sprawl away from downtown, the men behind the big banks and business institutions have committed themselves and their companies to remain at the core, at the heart of the city. . . . And developers have returned to the inner city with . . . provocative projects."[3]

Still, promoters speak with an edge of fear about the fate of downtown and its environs. Architect and planner Antonio Di Mambro, the *Dallas Morning News*'s and Dallas Institute of Humanities and Culture's guru of the moment, declares with great panache, "Dallas has 'no clue' how to develop a comprehensive city plan because 'market forces have taken over City Hall and brainwashed everybody. . . . we all know, deep down, as much as we love Dallas, that it is a second-tier city.' The heart of the problem, he said, is the heart of the city: downtown. 'This is where you have to meet the challenge. . . . You've put a noose around downtown,' he said, 'You've got to break it.'"[4]

In Di Mambro's view, Dallas lacked the characteristics of a "world-class" city, including a vibrant and memorable city center. Office towers by themselves do not suffice when downtown is encircled by freeways and acres of barren parking lots. Marco D'Eramo observes: "The presence of the skyscraper serves merely to demonstrate the power of the host city, just as elaborate medieval cathedrals were designed to show off the prosperity of the urban bourgeoisie. . . . From the freeway, even at a distance of several miles, you can size up a city's importance simply by measuring the height and number of skyscrapers rising over the flatlands."[5] The drive to display the city's power physically and rhetorically transcends functionality and spatial requirements. Central to that competition is monumental imitation, the fast track to legitimization and recognition, if not distinction.

Criticizing the skyline is a stunning act, because to many in Dallas, this criticism encompasses the soul of the city itself. I did not fully grasp this mentality, or realize the extent of my own faux pas, until I responded to a question about the Dallas skyline from *Dallas Morning News* columnist Steve Blow. He reported: "[Dr. Graff] stepped on my toes right off by referring to Dallas' 'absolutely horrendous skyline.' Horrendous? It's one of my favorite things about the city. I asked whether he stood by those words. 'Well,' he said, 'how about "less than dazzling" and "greatly overrated"?' Oh, much better. But the longer Dr. Graff talked, the more he began to make sense."[6] In addition to commenting about architectural and design aesthetics, I talked about the lack of attention to the physical location of the buildings with respect to each other and as an ensemble. That inattention produces air currents that literally blow pedestrians into traffic-filled streets. I talked about downtown's lack of connection to the larger city, the lack of open space, and the impact of both underground walkways and skyways.

Casting a critical eye to the skyline is addressing the heart of Dallas, as Sharon Zukin explains, outlining how the city's landscape and skyline are tied to its history, political economy, and dominant culture: "For a radical economic geographer, landscape is the *tabula rasa* of capital accumulation. It reflects the 'spatiality' of the capitalist mode of production in each of its historical phases. From this perspective, the underlying cause of repetition and singularity in the landscape is the profit motive, shifting capital between investment in industry and in property, cycling it into new construction or reconstruction, shuttling it between the downtown and the suburban periphery. This idea of landscape also suggests the opposition between market and place."[7] Zukin's formulation speaks clearly to Dallas; it captures and connects crucial elements of the capitalist development process and some of its central contradictions, including the opposition between market and place. The alternation between investment in production and investment in property suggests that at times real estate development may be less of a stimulus to growth than Dallas promoters thought, but that at other times real estate may be more profitable than industry. Zukin also proposes that the capitalist market tends to dissolve spatial particularity, making everything interchangeable and mobile and acting against distinction or inseparability for a given place and its landscape. Among the consequences for Dallas is the continuing thrust toward decentralization and sprawl despite plans, policies, and promises for the center. Dallas business and political leaders' continued commitment to downtown must be critically reassessed in view of the spatial economy's relentless push to the periphery. Finally, Zukin's conjoined terms, "repetition and singularity," serve as metonyms for my concepts of mimesis and monumentalism.

Zukin's conceptualization of landscape moves beyond the facades of individual buildings and points to recurring patterns in the built environment taken *ensemble.* The spatial dimensions of power and the rhythms of capital accumulation shape construction, destruction, and reconstruction.[8] Conflicts between social classes influence that process, but the constant circulation and transformation of commodities in the expanding market inexorably erode the particularities and solidarities of place. Economic power predominates over local autonomy and collective consciousness in the structuring and interweaving of people's lives and the landscape. Zukin indicates a key contradiction: "Yet in the quest for an image of distinction, local business and political leaders continue to build and rebuild as a sign of economic growth. Their blueprint for growth is often limited to constructing a microcosm of the past or a panorama of the future . . . that are completely detached from specific places. Without a specific social and material context, the organizing principle in these landscapes is simply a visual *theme.*"[9]

The Dallas Way of urban development, as it has accelerated over a century or more, is marked by mimesis and monumentalism. The constructions are multimedia: material, visual, rhetorical, ideological. Despite more than a century of effort, monumentality continues to prove insufficient to solve Dallas's problems of image and identity. In Dallas's tale of two cities, downtown and its northern periphery are the focus of investment, while Dallas's second city pays more than its share of the costs and reaps less than its share of the benefits. Not only do South and West Dallas suffer neglect, but the urban landscape is profoundly fragmented.

THE PRIVATE CITY

So striking is this feature of Dallas's development that the words "monumental," "monumentality," and "monumentalism" occurred to me as appropriate and useful, descriptively and categorically, even before I encountered these terms in the works of architectural historians and critics.[10] Semantically, metaphorically, and conceptually, monumentality facilitates our understanding of architecture and building, city planning, modes of urban development, and the crucial connections of all these in the making of Dallas.[11]

The propensity to conceive and construct buildings on a monumental scale is evident from the city's beginning. Prominent Dallas architect Walter Dahlberg breathlessly recites the "succession of superlatives," tellingly modeled on structures in other places and, equally tellingly, with only a few exceptions no longer standing in Dallas:

> the Adolphus Hotel, Beaux Arts design pushed to its limits; the Busch Building . . . a seminal example of the Gothic skyscraper; the Union Terminal, with its white glazed brick facade—fallout from the Chicago World's Fair— and the grandest space south of Kansas City; the Magnolia Building . . . with its revolving red horse, in 1921 [sic] the tallest building west of the Mississippi; the Medical Arts Building, in 1923 the world's tallest reinforced concrete structure; the Mercantile Bank Building, built just before World War II, another "tallest building west of the Mississippi"; the Republic National Bank with, in 1943, the fastest curtain wall in the West; the Southland Center, yet another tallest building this side of the Big River, and the first in Dallas to define its mass with nighttime lighting, a practice that has become something of a Dallas tradition.[12]

These structures are seen in relation to their counterparts in other places, rather than set in their local contexts and connections. The inclination to

FIGURE 39. Medical Arts Building, architect C. E. Barglebaugh, built 1923. Reported to be the first office building devoted specifically to the medical profession, it was razed in 1978. From Holmes and Saxon, *WPA Dallas Guide and History.*

mimesis dates back at least to the turn of the twentieth century, as this paean to urban development attests:

> The incomparably beautiful Wilson Building, a masterpiece of design by the Fort Worth architectural firm of Sanguinett and Staats, was a Second Empire elaboration of the Paris Grand Opera House designed by Charles Garnier in 1874. It also displayed striking similarities to two of the finest examples of American architectural artistry—Adler and Sullivan's Auditorium (Chicago, 1879) and H. H. Richardson's Marshall Field Store (Chicago, 1887). Built in 1902–03 at the northwest corner of Main and Ervay streets, the Wilson Building remains, without question, one of the most noble buildings ever constructed in Dallas.[13]

Tellingly, progress consisted of copying grand structures from other places in the past.

A monumental approach to envisioning, planning, and building major elements of central Dallas's cityscape had great appeal for civic leaders.[14] Monumentalism focused attention on individual structures—a railroad

FIGURE 40. Mercantile Bank and Magnolia Building with Pegasus, ca. 1950–55. After World War II, other towers and spires arose alongside the Magnolia Building. Photographer: Darwin Payne. From Payne, *Big D;* reprinted with permission of the photographer.

station, hotel, opera house, county courthouse, or city hall—while distracting it from real problems, including the city's lack of social and physical cohesion. Ideally and ideologically, monumentalism had no place for differences or conflicts of race, social class, gender, ethnicity, or generation. The exclusion of these contentious matters was part of its usefulness and contributed to its hegemony.[15] Completeness, integration, and social and spatial equality were not among monumentality's intentions or expectations, nor were they part of Dallas's piecemeal and fragmented implementation of supposedly comprehensive plans.

The ideas and practices that shaped Dallas's monumental approach to city building converged during the late nineteenth and early twentieth centuries and show distinctly midwestern influences in architecture, planning, and urban transformation.[16] Dallas's rapidly growing population exceeded the capacity of its infrastructure, and the physical condition of the city aroused concern. "The site . . . imposed severe practical as well as aesthetic limits."[17] "The muddy and foul-smelling Trinity River bottoms bordering the city's west end remained a sanctuary for wildlife, with vicious animals still appearing in the city at night."[18] Dusty streets, often unpaved or poorly paved, "ran in a crazy quilt over the city, with three independently oriented grids jamming together in and around the central business district. Downtown streets sometimes varied in width, jogged through offsets and angles, or halted abruptly, perhaps to begin a few blocks beyond, possibly under another name. The city's railroads daily flirted with chaos as they shunted freight and passengers this way and that over a mishmash of tracks."[19] Despite the city's expansion by annexation, housing was in short supply. These problems stimulated planning and political reform. William H. Wilson summarizes: "In 1910, some members of the Dallas elite began a sustained effort to beautify their city. Typically, the program rested upon a base of failed or partly successful ventures that provided the elite leadership with experience and the public with some awareness of problems."[20]

Monumental development had close connections with comprehensive approaches to city planning, despite the evident incompatibility between a focus on single structures and a concern for the urban fabric. Dallas was associated with and influenced by the City Beautiful Movement and its less aesthetically inclined relative, the city "practical," "efficient," or "functional." In his history of the City Beautiful Movement, William H. Wilson captures the moment, including the diffusion of urban planning ideals from place to place: "By 1910 a few prominent bankers, attorneys, merchants, and other businessmen had made fitful, piecemeal planning efforts. Organizationally and intellectually they moved from civic improvement plans to comprehensive City Beautiful planning and finally to the utilitarianism and specious inclusiveness of the city practical."[21]

George B. Dealey and his *Dallas Morning News*'s early leadership, strong endorsement, and promotion of city planning and the efforts of George Kessler, Dallas's first major planner, aroused intermittent public interest and spurred inconsistent implementation. Some saw planning as dangerously liberal, statist, or worse, not to mention expensive. But monumentalism's focus on downtown and self-serving promotion was fundamentally conservative. It was, after all, a movement by and for the city's elite, their professional experts, and their entrepreneurial supporters. Crucial declarations about Dallas's achievements and its future promise could be erected in concrete or finer materials without unnecessary excess and with reasonable public contribution.[22]

Alfred Koetter, writing in the *Harvard Architectural Review*, provides a helpful definition: "The term *monumentality* relates directly to the physical attributes of objects, including buildings or groups of buildings, and, unlike the act of monument making, may have little or nothing to do with a literal program of commemoration or enshrinement. At the same time, the monumental urban setting—square, street, groups of honorific buildings, and the like—may . . . transmit, in the implications of its appearance, an endorsement of social, cultural, and political values." Monumental settings endow urban spaces with meaning and uses across a spectrum of dimensions from the physical and political to the cultural and ideological.[23] In ideology and execution, monumentality suggests an almost intuitive simplicity in its transmittal and endorsement of values by surface appearances. Koetter wisely cautions, "As a public presence, the monumental setting . . . exists as a complex urban phenomenon." Monumentality meant substantial visible presence and careful location on the shifting continuum between public and private domains. Because of the workings of the private land market and the constraints of central Dallas's topography, however, monumentality did not necessarily mean careful geographic location within the city.

In Koetter's view, the relationships between the public domain and democracy, on the one hand, and the private domain and capitalism, on the other hand, are especially compelling and challenging. Koetter posits an American urban ideal rooted in a constructive balance between opposing elements, an archetypal Main Street:

> This combination of publicness and physical stability renders the monumental setting vital to the ongoing life of the city. Written into its disposition, impersonal, value-laden, long-lived, is an explicit distinction between public and private life—the proclamation that the public city and the value of publicness exist as a continuing and dependable counterbalance to the ever-present and necessary forces of transitory fashion, immediate effects, and private preoccupations. The public city, supported by its durable monumental settings, may (even in this era of supposed "constant change") continue to provide at least the illusion of permanent reference and stability.[24]

Mutually shaping and reinforcing in the making of many U.S. cities, these elements figure centrally in the construction of Dallas.

But in Dallas, the structures of political economic power differed, so the balance between these elements in the built environment shifted. As Zukin put it, "themes of power, coercion, and collective resistance shape landscape. . . . in the struggle for expansion in the built environment, and control over the uses of space, economic power predominates over both the state and vernacular culture."[25] In Dallas, private power exercised civic control almost unopposed, using public authority and purse to advance the development of the private city. To a startling degree, critical distinctions between public city and private enterprise blurred and faded. Public aid and cooperation replaced public/private conflict. Monumental Dallas was a white and masculine city, erasing differences related to class, race, and gender and suppressing conflicts based on geography.[26] The Dallas Way of interweaving public and private lent a peculiar character to the city's development. As Koetter explains, monumentality ordinarily served as a counterweight to the transitory character that came with the constant mobility of capital. Yet in early twentieth-century Dallas, funds were disproportionately invested in structures serving private corporations and cultural institutions. Commercial skyscrapers and palaces for performance, display, and consumption were unable to provide even "the illusion of permanent reference and stability."[27]

Koetter proclaims "the monumental gesture or setting is of great importance in the making of the urban public realm." But Dallas deviated from this normative version. The private domain was transcendent; but no less crucially, the Dallas Way succeeded in reducing the sense of opposition, even distinction between public and private. If the democratic ideal is manifested physically in the public city—in "the courthouse, the city hall, the meeting house, perhaps the public library—along with an array of establishments that embodied a commercial and capitalist ideal—the banking hall, the mercantile emporium, the grain exchange, the requisite drugstore, and an assortment of marginal ventures"—then in Dallas, it was the private city that was "materially embellished [as] an act of urban commemoration and an overt endorsement."[28] Public Dallas developed more slowly and to a lesser extent than private Dallas, with a few notable exceptions, including Dallas County's great "Old Red" courthouse of the 1890s and the art deco treasures of Fair Park. The public "domain"—if any property in Dallas could be said to belong to the public—was underdeveloped physically as well as figuratively. Downtown included relatively few substantial plazas and open lobbies until the 1970s, one sign of the domination of archetypically private values. Neither the federal buildings of the 1930s nor

FIGURE 41. Dallas Theatre Center, architect Frank Lloyd Wright, 1959. Photographer: Doug Tomlinson. From Dillon and Tomlinson, *Dallas Architecture*.

the civic center of the 1950s included spaces where people might gather outdoors.

Even today, a civic district constituted by city hall and central library fronting a wide boulevard, with the convention center down the road, remains aesthetically, structurally, and spatially incomplete. Private monumental spaces, especially plazas and enclosed gardens, do not function as public places. Consider Thanks-Giving Square, a spiral-shaped space designated for nondenominational meditation either inside the spiral-capped chapel or outside. A form of antiurban urbanism seemingly mimicking the medieval if not Mecca, it is surrounded by tall iron fencing, its entry locked at the end of each business day. The park-like space falls in the tradition

FIGURE 42. Thanks-Giving Square and Chapel, architects Philip Johnson and John Burgee, built 1976, 1977. Photographer: Doug Tomlinson. From Dillon and Tomlinson, *Dallas Architecture.*

of private gifts to the public, in this instance, the developers of Thanks-Giving Tower, whose site it shares. Designed by Philip Johnson, it is used mainly by office workers eating their lunch, not by urban pilgrims seeking spiritual rest. Pedestrian precincts, postage stamp squares, and promenades leading into concert halls and museums add little. Fountain Place, downtown Dallas's best open space with its fantastic computer-generated waterworks, is private property. Dallas works to blur distinctions between private and public domains, but private spaces with controlled access are no substitute for public gathering places.

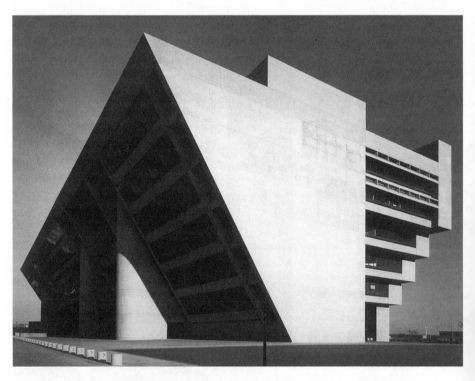

FIGURE 43. "I. M. Pei's heroic City Hall anchors Dallas' sprawling civic center complex on the southern edge of the central core. Its twelve-acre site was carved from a district of warehouse buildings, inaugurating downtown's first significant attempt at urban renewal." Larry Paul Fuller, ed., *The American Institute of Architects, Guide to Dallas Architecture with Regional Highlights* (Dallas: AIA Dallas Chapter, McGraw-Hill Information Group, 1999). Photographer: Doug Tomlinson. From Dillon and Tomlinson, *Dallas Architecture.*

FIGURE 44. City Hall, architect I. M. Pei, built 1978, photographed 1981. Photographer: Frank Branger; courtesy of the Library of Congress, Prints and Photographs Division, Historic American Buildings Survey or Historic American Engineering Record, reproduction number HABS TEX, 57-DAL, 1–4.

The amount of public space in downtown Dallas grew during the last quarter of the twentieth century. Nevertheless, major public spaces are limited in usefulness and in the power of their gestures. Dallas's 1978 City Hall, designed by I. M. Pei, is a superb example of monumentality. On its twentieth anniversary, *Dallas Morning News* architecture critic David Dillon wrote: "The building is a product of post-Kennedy assassination Dallas, when the city was struggling to change its image as a backwater of bigotry and violence. Mayor Erik Jonsson focused on rebuilding its civic institutions, starting with City Hall. . . . Jonsson made it clear that he was looking for 'a monument to the city's pride.' And Mr. Pei responded with a controversial design featuring a tilted facade that ran nearly 600 feet along a plaza that was twice the size of St. Mark's in Venice. . . . Pei's design reflected the sweep of the Texas landscape and also represented government with a capital G." Upon its completion, Mayor Jonsson proclaimed that the building represented "the strength and power that are symbolic of the fast-growing yet solid city that we are."[29]

Unfortunately, the size of its great plaza, bearing the full brunt of the Texas sun, and its location on an edge of the central area have undercut its usefulness as public space. City Hall's grand plaza was designed as an architectural statement, not as a people-friendly place. Consultant William H. Whyte recommended adding benches and trees to relieve the emptiness, light, and heat. Defying architectural ideals, the plaza occasionally turns rural for recreation, hosting mountains of dirt for weekend tractor and truck-pulling contests, or tons of sand and water for summer "beach parties" sponsored by popular radio stations.[30] The absence of benches is more than a matter of aesthetics; it is a dimension of *order and control*. In the spirit of Baron Haussmann's "improvement" of Paris in the 1870s, monumental urban planning emphasizes spatial order and control, grand boulevards and thoroughfares, central facilities or civic clusters, regulated land use, safety and surveillance, and surface notions of beautification.

Across the wide roadway from City Hall, the new central public library's open plaza had benches, which provoked the challenge of controlling their occupants. Unexamined notions of public access and openness were questioned when the poor and homeless—who were often persons of color, advanced age, or odd manners, deemed derelict and deviant—occupied the benches and appeared inside the library to use sanitary facilities and find comfortably cool resting places. Fear of the stranger, the unknown, the undesirable, especially in an environment with a clear racial, ethnic, and class hierarchy, is a powerful force. William Whyte observes: "For most businessmen, [the undesirables are] not muggers, dope dealers, or truly dangerous people. It is the winos, . . . the most harmless of the city's marginal peoples, but a symbol, perhaps of what one might become but for the grace of events. For retailers, the list of undesirables is considerably more inclusive: there are the bag women, people who act strangely in public, 'hippies,' teenagers, older people, street musicians, vendors of all kinds."

The private city creates its own demons: "The preoccupation with undesirables is a symptom of another problem. Many corporation executives who make key decisions about the city have surprisingly little acquaintance with the life of its streets and open spaces. . . . To them, the unknown city is a place of danger. If their building has a plaza, it is likely to be a defensive one that they will rarely use themselves. Few others will either. Places designed with distrust get what they were looking for. . . . Fear proves itself."[31] With its emphasis on privacy and control, Dallas exacerbates fears of difference. The central city epitomizes a social order designed, reinforced, and regulated by spatial segregation, stratified within its own boundaries.

A struggle over street vendors and street performers highlights the contradictions. In the 1980s, normative conceptions of safety and sanitation, replete with class, racial, ethnic, and gender prejudices, combined with pressures from sales and service establishments to legislate and enforce a ban on street vendors, especially food purveyors, and performers in the central business district. Neither group seemed appropriate to the city that many influential residents imagined.[32] Certainly, neither had a niche in monumental Dallas. Nevertheless, these judgments proved reversible. In the 1990s, Dallas decided that "great cities" have street life downtown. To compete with the vibrant, reborn downtowns of major cities, Dallas needed to imitate them. To acquire the appearance of public life, while remaining private and monumental, became its new challenge.[33] Touted by planning experts, the slow expansion of public, green, and open space has begun.[34] The often silly but revealing squabbles about street vendors erupted again in 2002, with fears that the homeless and panhandlers will offend visitors. The panhandler issue is framed in terms of the city's right to rid downtown streets of "undesirables," not the rights or needs of individuals.[35] These concerns occur simultaneously and contradictorily with the push for more "street life." A monumental city can act defensive and insecure.

The other recent turn in Dallas's urban planning and ideology of urban development is toward "districts." The development of functionally distinct precincts is controlled by the same predispositions toward mimesis and monumentalism that characterize the larger cityscape. Major institutions are relocated downtown, in new structures designed by architects who have already become famous elsewhere. Their work promotes recognition, confirming Dallas as a contemporary but conservative city averse to risk-taking and the avant-garde. Although privately sponsored and controlled, cultural institutions are viewed as if they were public or quasi-public. Through imitation and importation, as well as dominance of the private over the public, Dallas attempts to achieve urban distinction.

AN ARTS DISTRICT EMPTY OF ART

By necessity, if not by design, buildings do not stand alone. Whether as integrated ensembles or discombobulated fragments, clusters of buildings

Downtown

Arts District
Old City Park
West End
Victory/Palladium
"Civic" (City Hall, Public Library)
Main Street retail

Outside Downtown

Trinity River and environs
Uptown, Oak Lawn, Crescent, State–Thomas
Fair Park
City Place
South Boulevard–Park Row
Trade Center—InfoMart, other marts
The Cedars
Park Cities, Highland Park Village, NorthPark
Kessler Park
Southern Methodist University
Winnetka Heights
North Dallas, including Galleria
Deep Ellum
Park Central
Swiss Ave.–Munger Place
Lincoln Center
Wilson Block
Plano
Old East Dallas
Las Colinas
White Rock Lake
Dallas–Fort Worth International Airport

City-Designated Landmark Districts

Continental Gin
Swiss Avenue
Peak's Suburban Addition
Lake Cliff
Eastside Warehouse District
Tenth Street
Edison/La Vista Court
Magnolia Station
Sears Complex
West End
South Boulevard–Park Row
Munger Place
Fair Park

Wilson Block
State–Thomas
North Bishop Avenue
Harwood Street
Winnetka Heights

National Register of Historic Places, Dallas County Historic Districts

Alcalde Street—Crockett School
Munger Place
Bryan–Peak Commercial
Dealey Plaza
Cedar Springs Place
Peak's Suburban Addition
Colonial Hill
Queen City Heights
Dallas High School
Romine Avenue
North Bishop Avenue Commercial
Rosemont Crest
Kessler Park
South Boulevard–Park Row
King's Highway
Swiss Avenue
Texas Centennial Exposition Buildings
Tenth Street
Lancaster Avenue Commercial
Lake Cliff
Lawrence, Stephen Decatur, Farmstead
West End
Wheatley Place
Wilson Block
Winnetka Heights
Miller and Stemmons
Magnolia Petroleum Co. City Sales and Warehouse

Entertainment Districts (Convention Bureau)

Downtown
Greenville Avenue
West End
Uptown
Deep Ellum
Swiss Avenue
Fair Park
Highland Park

FIGURE 45. Dallas's districts.

contribute to a language and a logic that define distinct areas within the city. When sites are treated in a way that enhances their separate structures, districts take on greater monumentality.

Coherent districts generate a sense of spatial integration, offering rich and diverse opportunities that, even when sampled, seem satisfyingly complete. Their appeal is promoted widely, regardless of the accuracy of their frames. In some cities, such spatial configurations date back a century or more, either as part of the original city building process, as in New York or Boston, or in reconstruction after catastrophes, as in Chicago or San Francisco. In cities like Dallas, district development is recent, imposed upon more miscellaneous older areas whose derelict buildings are recycled and "historicized" into apartments or retail locations. Current efforts to transform inner-city neighborhoods into upscale districts owe more to ideology or imagination than to remnants left in bricks and mortar.[36] Whether by default or design, district development is often perceived as "adding value" to a declining downtown, advertising the city's attractiveness and helping to fill its coffers. Assembling districts by filling empty shells with new construction requires artful methods, including flexible zoning and creative financing. Cities offer incentives to developers, ranging from land and infrastructural support to tax benefits, and sometimes direct investment. Criticism abounds. Public interest groups see these districts as artificial centers promoting consumption and disrupting neighborhoods, and economists question the real value of these investments. But cities like Dallas continue to rush to private developers' aid and hasten to support semipublic monuments for arts, performances, conventions, and public open spaces. The public plays in and pays for the private.[37]

Referenda on public support for monumental new arts districts, like those for sports arenas, bring out the worst of contemporary urban boosterism. Veiled threats and gross exaggerations reign on all sides. Promoters and developers promise all things to almost all parties. Public-private relationships that seem clear at the start of campaigns get lost in the noise of claims and counterclaims. Critics in Dallas and elsewhere argue that the public makes a greater investment and takes a greater risk than private property owners and developers, especially when ratios of expenditures to likely returns and power over planning decisions are taken into account.

In Dallas, voters approved funds to purchase downtown sites for a new art museum and concert halls. The Arts District is anchored by the Dallas

Museum of Art. Designed by Edward Larrabee Barnes as an austere, limestone monument with a central vault, the $90 million building opened in 1984.[38] Seeking to broaden its public appeal, on the advice of a consultant, the institution changed its name from the Dallas Museum of Fine Arts when it relocated from the Fair Park historic area. The museum fought several skirmishes and a pitched battle in 1955, when it was attacked by patriotic groups for exhibiting works of art by known communists or fellow travelers. In the end, the museum stood against censorship, while bad press and embarrassment rained on Dallas.[39] According to the *New York Times* review, the new museum was promising, but its grandest interior and exterior spaces remained empty of artworks, and the undistinguished collection of nineteenth- and twentieth-century paintings was better suited to the modest spaces off the slanted corridor.[40] After it opened a second building only seven years after the first, art critic Janet Kutner concluded that the "Dallas Museum of Art Hasn't Met Expectations Raised by Its Expansion." The museum is rich in monies for bricks and mortar but not for strengthening its collections and mounting exhibitions: "Therein lies the Catch-22. To raise money a museum needs to generate excitement, and the best way to do that is through exhibitions. Yet it takes money to mount them."[41] Continuing financial support for the arts is more difficult to come by than public or private donations for major construction projects. Neither mimesis nor monumentalism solves that problem; indeed, both exacerbate it.

In seeking public commitment to build a symphony hall in the arts district, supporters appealed to every desire and fear they could imagine. An

FIGURE 46. West facade, Dallas Museum of Art, architect Edward Larrabee Barnes, 1984. This monumental structure by a signature architect was intended to be "the pivotal component of the Arts District." Photographer: Doug Tomlinson. From Dillon and Tomlinson, *Dallas Architecture.*

advertising flyer entitled "A Great Concert Hall for a Great City" listed "6 Reasons Why the Concert Hall Is Important for Dallas. And for You" and implied simple cause-and-effect relationships between monuments and success. "The very existence of an Arts District in downtown Dallas is dependent on a Concert Hall. . . . Designed by the renowned I. M. Pei, the Concert Hall would be a source of pride for all Dallasites and a magnet for tourists. It would be a landmark for Dallas just as are great concert halls in other major cities of the nation and world." And, of course, it was "Good for the Economy. An independent research study by the LWFW Group shows that the Concert Hall would generate a total economic impact from construction of $133 million, total ongoing economic activity of $26 million a year, and new tax revenue of $28 million. Construction of the hall also would create 400 to 600 new jobs in Dallas," or so its promoters forecast. The Dallas Concert Hall Committee reminded readers that the concert hall was emphatically a "Public/Private Partnership" and that the

Figure 47. Morton H. Myerson Symphony Center, architect I. M. Pei, 1989. This magnificent performance space "provided the Arts District with the critical mass and architectural distinction it needed to be recognized as a viable entity." Fuller, *American Institute of Architects, Guide to Dallas Architecture.*

hall would "serve every citizen now and for generations to come." Under the headline, "With a Texas-Size Ambition," the *New York Times* proclaimed that "with enough vision and money, you can indeed elevate your status."[42]

The impressive $85 million structure was completed in 1989 with the assistance of a $40 million contribution from Dallas billionaire H. Ross Perot, who named the building for his longtime business associate and friend Morton Myerson.[43] After the art museum and symphony center came other "great" arts venues, including a $250 million performance center for the Dallas Opera designed by Norman Foster and Rem Koolhaas. Even among the major donors, some skepticism greeted the building of monuments to the arts in Dallas. In announcing their $40 million gift for the opera hall, businessman Bill Winspear, whose wife, Margot, was the principal private donor, said, "I hope it gives it credibility. There are several major donors who are saying, 'Show us that you can do it' before they step in."[44] We have to ask here whether the problem of credibility rests in the arts themselves, the Arts District as concept or practice, or the price tag.

Monumental buildings create gaping holes to be filled by artworks and performers. After exhausting the usual clichés about the surprise of finding a century-old orchestra in a place like Dallas and praising the Myerson's design and acoustics, *New York Times* reporter Anne Midgette finds complications. She points to other great needs, including a substantial endowment to pay for electronics, recordings, and especially "to attract the top-flight players necessary to achieve its high-flown goals." Dallas's concertmaster and principal violinist was lured away to Philadelphia, closer to the nation's cultural hubs. The concertmaster admitted: "I want to have an impact on the history of music. I don't think I can do that in a Dallas or a Houston." Some symphony members suggested that they "see nothing wrong with embracing the status of an eminently respectable second-tier American orchestra and leaving it at that."[45] But Dallasites are reluctant to have a second-tier orchestra in a hall with a decidedly first-tier price tag.

Writer and critic Lee Cullem questions Dallas's ambitions: "Dallas cannot be Paris. . . . it's with the third tier of American cities that Dallas should concern itself."[46] In an article titled "Dreher and Hicks Read 'World Class' as 'a Tacit Sign of Galloping Insecurity,'" *Dallas Morning News* writers Rod Dreher and Victoria Loe Hicks groaned, less tactfully, "If we hear 'World Class' one more time."[47] Could Dallas embrace a strategy for "reduced" or "relative" greatness, or at least truth in advertising? Or is the Dallas Way too committed to grandiosity, even as it struggles to set the terms for comparison and competition?

Dallas won the Raymond and Patsy Nasher collection of Calder, de Kooning, Miro, Moore, and Picasso over the efforts of the Guggenheim in New York, the National Gallery in Washington, and the Tate in London, at least in part because the city is Raymond Nasher's home. The Nasher Foundation paid all costs for an indoor/outdoor sculpture center in the Arts District.[48] The Nasher Sculpture Garden, designed by Renzo Piano with landscape architect Peter Walker, opened to acclaim in 2003. Nasher said he hoped that the display of "the most important collection of modern sculpture in the world" would serve as a "catalyst for the future development of Dallas as one of the truly great international cities."[49] As he aims at elevating Dallas art, Nasher takes a direct and self-effacing approach: "At the moment, Dallas has nothing of real artistic significance, internationally. Perhaps this can be it. This is a nice city, but it's mostly about money. We're hoping to change that a little."[50]

IT COULD BE ANYWHERE

Planting new districts in an existing city center is at best a difficult undertaking. Architectural critic David Dillon relates the early history of Dallas's Arts District:

> The delays . . . have confused long-range planning in the district. Several developers who helped to create the district have since sold their property, and the commitment of the new owners to the original plan is unknown. So far, no developer has planned housing for the district, and local artists are not lining up to live and work in a planned cultural environment. With land prices in excess of $200 per square foot, their chances of doing so are zero anyway. This remains one of the cruelest ironies of the Arts District's evolution. The original Carr-Lynch report urged the city to bank land in the district in order to prevent small arts groups from being squeezed out. Loath to compete with private enterprise, even in the public interest, the city refused. Land that the museum bought in 1977–79 for $20 a square foot now costs more than $200 a square foot.[51]

Arts districts repeat familiar patterns of gentrification as developers see ground ripe for transformation.[52]

To balance the high-priced palaces of the elite art world, Dallas promised a complementary focus on the local and vernacular, but arts districts in Deep Ellum and Fair Park followed the common pattern. Architecture critic Dillon captured the contradictions in 1985:

> While the future of the official Dallas Arts District is being debated, an un-official one has emerged near Fair Park, where the cultural exodus began. Known as Deep Ellum, this area of warehouses and small commercial build-ings has already attracted a dozen galleries, several theaters, and several hun-dred artists in need of large spaces for little money. In March 1984 the Dallas City Council approved an ordinance designed to safeguard the funky, low-rise character of the area without discouraging new residential and commercial development. While the ordinance is a commendable example of grass-roots planning, its ultimate impact on Deep Ellum is hard to measure. Already, speculators have driven up the price of property to the point that some of the pioneering artists are being forced out.[53]

That trend continued, as Deep Ellum gained a reputation as an "in" place for entertainment, food and drink, and shops for locals and visitors. Prices continue to rise, contributing to high levels of turnover among businesses and residents. Crime and violence also plagued the area, threatening both in-town and out-of-town visitors on whose patronage the restaurants, bars and music spots, and galleries depend. Few observers continue to see Man-hattan's Soho or Chelsea in Deep Ellum.

At another end of the spectrum from inner-city Deep Ellum is City Place, conceived as a contemporary and trend-setting residential center on the urban periphery. Built in the 1980s by Southland Corporation, then own-ers of 7-Eleven convenience stores, a few miles north of downtown, this construction was planned as the catalyst for a mixed-use "neighborhood" close to center-city amenities but with lower density and higher security. The master plan called for massive twin towers on opposite sides of Cen-tral Expressway (U.S. 75), joined by an enclosed walkway high above the busy freeway, surrounded by mid-rise and low-rise structures for working, living, and playing. Only one tower has been built—fortunately, almost all say—and the area's western edge merges with Uptown's encroaching bor-ders. But far too many homes and other buildings were razed in early land acquisition and clearance for the monumental project. The underside of development or redevelopment is the wholesale destruction of countless older structures, often occupied by poorer and older persons. The tower of monumental Dallas leans to the north, the side of the private city, often with unacknowledged public subsidy. But for that difference, City Place could be Anytown or Notown.

Uptown, located between inner-city Deep Ellum and inner-suburb City Place, is booming now, unlike either of its neighbors. Its trendiness differs from both the arts in a milieu of seediness and danger in Deep Ellum and the failed, confused monumentalism in City Place. Chic restaurants, night-spots, boutiques, and gentrified older housing blend with higher-rising condos. Uptown's continued elevation depends strictly on the high income of its youthful residents combined with the continuing appeal of city living. Either can change. The fantasized and fictitious names of City Place and Uptown, unlike Deep Ellum, are inventions whose designation is meant to create the desired place. Neither name claims historical resonance in Dallas or in the locality where they are built. But, in part because they have meaning in other cities,[54] they sound legitimate.

Sometimes even residents have to stop and remind themselves that, yes, Dorothy, this is Dallas, despite all evidence to the contrary. Dallas promotes its difference from New York City, yet attempts with varying degrees of success and the occasional howler to mimic it: Deep Ellum is SoHo; the Victory-Palladium area around the new American Airlines arena is Times Square; the West End is the Lower East Side. White Rock Lake is Central Park—or is it San Francisco's Golden Gate Park? Older districts not redolent of Manhattan are "like" Chicago, Philadelphia, Boston; newer ones are "like" Los Angeles, Miami, Atlanta. If it were created, the festival harborfront would mimic Baltimore or Boston. Some hope Santiago Calatrava's signature bridges over the Trinity will call forth Sydney's Opera House and Paris's Eiffel Tower, St. Louis's Gateway Arch and San Francisco's Golden Gate Bridge.

Imitation combined with monumentality sometimes yields appalling buildings, as in the InfoMart computer industry trade center's outlandish mimicry of London's Crystal Palace of 1851 and its New York City replica of 1853. The inappropriateness of constructing a crystal palace to house secure information technology facilities would have been obvious had anyone examined the past: both "fireproof" structures burned to the ground, the New York City building in only thirty minutes. The building has suffered economic woes from the beginning, finding a niche in housing telecoms companies but changing hands via foreclosure in 2006. Other large-scale structures are impossibly eclectic. The developers of the Columbus Square apartment project in Uptown illustrate the vapid emptiness of so much imitative practice: "In creating Columbus Square, we looked at model urban communities in New York, Paris and London and fashioned a building with European esthetics and the practicality inherent in a New York or Boston neighborhood," they told the *New York Times.*[55]

The field for imitation is broad, and the allusions and illusions began early. Dallas *is* exceptional in the incessantly lengthening list of its similarities with other cities. Las Vegas does not take its representations of New

FIGURE 48. InfoMart, architect Martin Growald, 2006. "Legend has it that Martin Growald once described his eight-story InfoMart as the Information-age equivalent of Joseph Paxton's industrial revolution landmark, the Crystal Palace." Fuller, *American Institute of Architects, Guide to Dallas Architecture.* Photographer: Eric Anderson; printed with the permission of the photographer.

York or its virtual realities literally or very seriously.[56] Dallas copies with dead earnestness. It is tempting to argue that contemporary mimetic monumentalism is more blatant and unself-conscious, that the search for symbol and identity leading to a rediscovery of "history" is new, but finding newness in a mimetic city is difficult.

In each comparison with another "great" city lie a claim and an admission, sometimes implicit, sometimes explicit. That claim is about Dallas. It says: Dallas can be (or is) a great city *if* it has this element (building, district, institution, event, street life) because that's what great cities have, as exemplified by city X or Y. The admission is that without the element or need of the moment, Dallas is not a great city because "a great city needs a great _____." These comparisons are commonplace, trivial, and unremarkable, but the concentration and frequency of these concerns in Dallas is extraordinary.

Beyond the questions of accuracy or truth it raises, imitation stimulates more desires than it can possibly meet. As a counter to an insecure identity, imitation backfires because it interferes with the more difficult and fundamental task of setting priorities and making sustained efforts. The lure and trap of imitation helps to account for the fate of Dallas's successive city plans and for the curious ways in which both the mid-1990s Dallas Plan and the 2001 Di Mambro Global City plan evoke George Kessler's original plans of the 1910s. For years, the *Dallas Morning News* printed its wish lists for the city on the first of each new year under the heading "Dallas Tomorrow." Tomorrow, for Dallas, never seems to arrive.

POWER FAILURES

Certain patterns emerge when we examine the success of monumental development in blurring the distinctions between the public and the private. Public funding for basic infrastructure is usually uncontroversial and kept apart from "politics." For Dallas, like many cities, public investment in water, sewers, power, and streets began in the 1870s. Infrastructure spending came first and fullest to central city districts and prime locations within them, and then to the emerging residential districts of the entrepreneurial elite as they spread from downtown. Access to and benefits of this infrastructure went to the favored, who were well placed to influence decisions. Their property taxes contributed but were never expected to meet the costs of construction on the more difficult terrain along the Trinity to the south and west. Improvements incur major public responsibilities, including bonds and abatements, site preparation, and transit access, let alone amenities. The difficult balancing act involved in negotiating the shifting responsibilities along the public-private spectrum can lead to political and economic conflicts that the reformed, nonpartisan polity was meant to reduce or eliminate.[57]

A second pattern, related and at times inextricably interconnected to the first, is the use of public authority and funds to create a climate conducive to private economic development. Dallas has informally and even formally labeled itself a "growth machine," "selling place," "Downtown Inc."[58] The public realm offers direct and indirect inducements and incentives, including facilities, new industrial districts, and trade mart. Convention facilities mandate massive public expenditures in the cause of private and public benefits. Some assert that the interplay of land inducements, tax relief or abatements, and special tax increment districts unfairly burdens the public.[59]

A third pattern characteristic of Dallas's monumental development is the subtle but powerful erosion of public authority and accountability, as well as losses suffered by the public purse. Dallas's concentration on the private and its subordination—in legitimization, expenditure, and authorization—of the public underlies a set of costly and painful urban outcomes. Much of what is commonly deemed a public responsibility has been underdeveloped, underfunded, abdicated, or shifted to private hands. These political economic choices fell heavily on the areas that today we call human resources, and earlier were called public services or public welfare, including municipal government.

For Dallas, these choices constitute what urban policy scholar Royce Hanson aptly calls "power failures." Hanson tells a story of the "success of the growth machine" and "growth as a public good" in Dallas. Major elements in the plot are the "limits of the public city" with respect to vital services, education, and policing; the "private use of public powers" and the growth of privatization; and the "phantom publics of Dallas" that accompany these "power failures." This powerful and moving story of public city failure in the midst of private city success traces the propagation of inequality, discrimination, and irresponsibility in governance in the midst of wealth.[60]

Those "power failures" account for the present plight of policing, public housing, public schools, public libraries, public infrastructure such as roads, public space, and until recently public transit. Ironically, following its expert advisors, Dallas recently realized it was short on the green open spaces it needed to compete with other cities. This deficit results from the lack of short-term payoffs for aesthetics and beautification in a world where private economic calculations carry great weight. The subordination of the public to the private, the blurring of the lines of public responsibilities, and the narrowing of the definition of the public welfare all conspired to narrow the legitimate domain of politics. Equally, this failure is a consequence of Dallas's "two cities," a matter of race, class, gender, equality, justice, and geography. The south and west, black and brown city is viewed as belonging to the public because it is deemed less worthy of private investment, more open to inspection and intervention, but seldom the beneficiary of major improvements. Failure in the second city, however, does not indicate that the first city has succeeded by contrast. When push comes to shove, there is but one Dallas.[61]

Dallas developed through the interplay between private and public domains and the speculative land market, demonstrating the fragmentation of city building without integrative or cohesive planning.

PLANNING A SPRAWLING, FRAGMENTED CITY

Dallas's formal city plans exemplify the dominant emphasis on monumental, mimetic, and commercial development, while the partiality of their implementation evinces the power failures of a sprawling, fragmented city. From George Kessler's City Beautiful of the 1910s to Antonio Di Mambro's Global City of 2001, urban planning initiatives were promoted by civic elites and supported by the *Dallas Morning News,* whose publisher, George B. Dealey, had emerged as the chief proselytizer for planning by 1910.[62] Yet until the 1995 Dallas Plan, no plan was officially adopted; plans served more as ideological statements than as practical frameworks for development on the ground. The power of urban planners was always sharply constrained by the rights of private property and the prerogatives and mobility of capital. The limited scope of planning's authority is even clearer when we distinguish between what plans proposed and what was actually constructed.

Kessler Plan, 1911
Ulrickson Plan, 1927
Bartholomew Plan, 1946
Springer Plan, 1956
Goals for Dallas, 1966
Comprehensive Land Use Policy Plan, 1975
Dallas 2000, The Dallas Concept Plan, Planning for the Future, City of Dallas, 1980
Dallas Planning Policy Papers, Charles Anderson, City Manager, 1984
Dallas Visions for Community, A Process of Dreaming, James Pratt, Dallas Institute of
    Humanities and Culture, 1990–91
Dallas Crossroads, Peirce Report, *Dallas Morning News,* 1991
The Dallas Plan, 1995
Antonio Di Mambro, "The Global City: The Road Ahead for the Dallas–Fort Worth
    Metropolis in the 21st Century,". With David Rusk, "Dallas: Halfway Down the
    Road—to Decline," *Dallas Morning News,* 2001
Forward Dallas, 2005–6

FIGURE 49. Dallas's plans. Source: Chris Kelley, "Developing Dallas," *Dallas Morning News,* April 21, 1996.

George Kessler, the drafter of the first city plan, is the most famous of Dallas's major planners. Based in Kansas City and then St. Louis, he was renowned for his plans for those and other midwestern cities that Dallas held as models and rivals; Dallas's leaders selected him because of his successes elsewhere.[63] Although only fragments of his plan were enacted over the decades that followed, Kessler's original plan and the urban planning association his efforts spawned offered the most comprehensive vision in Dallas's history. Straddling the City Beautiful and City Practical Movements, his proposals featured a gateway civic center, parkway and greenbelt, and system of boulevards. But they were not "completely integrated on the program level" and were only partly implemented.[64] The "functional" took priority over the merely "beautiful." Construction of Union Station was completed in 1916. Over the years, the Kessler plan contributed to the ritualistic exorcism of such Dallas demons as flooding, obtrusive and dangerous railway tracks and crossings, inadequate roads and mass transit, unsafe conditions for families and children, and blight in or near downtown. The very successful landscaping of Turtle Creek parkway in near North Dallas was so belated that Mill Creek on the opposite side had already been obliterated. The Dallas Way concentrated on the central city to secure private power and benefit, and restricted planning's scope and power.

A broad, diffuse sentiment in support of planning constitutes Kessler's legacy to the city. The Kessler plan has been regularly rediscovered and integrated into successive plans, facilitating the repetition of his vision over many years. Part of its continuing appeal lies in its concern for strengthening the tenuous connections between the city and its natural environment. The 1927 plan put together by a committee led by businessman C. E. Ulrickson attended mainly to capital improvements in infrastructure. In 1946, Harland Bartholomew of St. Louis, "hired to develop a postwar master plan for Dallas," "recommended that City Hall establish 'effective controls over the character and direction of future growth,'" and a city planner was appointed. But, "in seven reports issued between 1956 and 1961," planner Marvin Springer only tried to keep up with the city's expansion, calling for ring roads and parking lots on the periphery of downtown.[65]

Planning was not alien or unpopular in Dallas, as many assume.[66] Rather, planning has been used selectively and flexibly, ideologically and symbolically, as well as actively, in accord with economic priorities and political possibilities. Mayor Erik Jonsson's participatory and seemingly transparent, yet privately controlled Goals for Dallas (1966) sought to revive the city in the wake of the Kennedy assassination. Within two decades, that planning enterprise had led to the new city hall and central library downtown, the community college system, and Dallas/Fort Worth International Airport. Other "Goals for Dallas" remain perennially on the *Dallas Morning News*'s annual wish list. City planners, by contrast, have been unable to wield much power. James Schroeder's Comprehensive Land Use Policy Plan, proposed in 1975, which would have focused on downtown redevelopment and limited expansion beyond areas served by mass transit, ran afoul of developer Robert Folsom. Jack Shoup's effort at developing a land-use plan in 1980 lacked business backing, so it met the same fate.[67]

Dallas's mimetic monumentalism leaned distinctly toward the private, not the public, domain. Here Dallas deviated from its midwestern urban mentors, which developed their civic centers somewhat earlier and more completely than Dallas. Dallas's eclipse of the public was visible early on. According to William H. Wilson, in 1911 master planner George Kessler

> recognized the desirability of grouping public buildings but was deliberately ambiguous about the composition or location of a civic center. Declaring it "essential that the approaches and first impressions of a city be as pleasing

as possible," he urged the city to purchase a "plaza" in front of the union station "regardless of expenditure." Surrounding "this park there should be grouped public or semi-public buildings, such as a post office" or "a traction terminal building." Other public buildings might be erected in the eastern sections of downtown. This curious recommendation stemmed from Kessler's own caution and from his careful consultation with Dealey and other Dallas business leaders. Dealey's *News* had received letters opposing the construction of a new courthouse or city hall near the "dirt, smoke, filth and noise" of a union station. Locating such public buildings there would block commercial expansion, serve only "to impress a traveler" and force their occupants to work behind closed windows, the writers claimed. Moreover, some businessmen were raising funds to build a civic center in the middle of downtown. The railroads, on the other hand, were considering station sites in the southwest corner of the commercial-retail district, too remote for a full-fledged civic center.[68]

The primacy accorded to business considerations in the location of civic space is characteristic of the Dallas Way; it was not until 1978, at the other end of downtown, that elements of a civic center finally emerged. At the century's end, certain basics had not changed. Despite the construction of a new skyline in the 1970s and 1980s, *Dallas Morning News* architecture critic Dillon observes, "The public realm is less clearly represented than the private. Dallas has not preserved views of its monuments and public buildings, as have Washington and Austin. Visitors cannot find City Hall without a map. It is barely visible even from freeways, perhaps our truest public spaces."[69]

RAISING THE SKYLINE

Dallas architect Walter Dahlberg observed in 1978, "On the whole, the character of Dallas design has been infused with a Middle-Western stolidity—conservative, somewhat lacking in excitement."[70] Dahlberg was right. But, more interested in contemporary aesthetic changes than in understanding Dallas's foundations, he misread the results of an early city-building strategy through his era's cultural bias. The city's stolid style embodied the influence of Kansas City, St. Louis, and Chicago.

In a refrain that became commonly accepted, Dahlberg posited change in Dallas with the 1970s: "Both architecture and planning here have begun to take a turn. There are among the city leaders, as well as the citizens as a whole, a growing appreciation of the arts, a more sophisticated sense of aesthetics, and an awareness that a cohesive plan is needed for dealing with urban concerns."[71] The change Dahlberg observed represented only a shift within an accepted frame, a new accent within a familiar idiom. The favored aesthetic was seldom challenging or risk-taking. The most prominent example is Philip Johnson's Fountain Place, arguably Dallas's best tower and without doubt its best outdoor plaza.[72] Dallas selects architects from the roster of those who have achieved recognition and stature and consciously seeks monumental or landmark buildings. But the results are not always stellar. R. W. Apple Jr. of the *New York Times* deplores what he calls "misfires" as well as "knockoffs." Apple explains: "Mr. Johnson, whose Houston buildings helped define that city's sleek skyline, has designed a number of duds in Dallas, including the Bank One tower, a weird neo-Palladian effort, and Crescent Court, which marries lacy New Orleans ironwork to a monstrosity of a mansard roof. Mr. Johnson once said (jokingly?) that he saved all of his best ideas for Houston."[73]

With respect to the "new skyline" of the 1980s, Dallas critic Dillon declared, "Once it looked like Everytown USA. Now Dallas has grown up." "Dallas finally has a compelling skyline, far more compelling than the familiar opening shot from *Dallas*. . . . That was a skyline of money and raw power expressed in slick reflective glass. The new skyline has architectural conviction as well, conveyed through a green glass prism and a rolltop tower with a gigantic skywindow punched through the middle (formerly Texas Commerce Bank Tower). It is far more up-to-date than Kansas City's, and is closing fast on Houston's. At night, it surpasses both. It has taken Dallas 50 years to reach these giddy heights. . . . We have cathedrals of commerce. . . . Dallas is a business and banking city, and its skyline says that. It is a city of competing entrepreneurs, and its skyline says that as well. The image is not egalitarian, with each segment of the community clearly represented, it is hierarchic, with capital at the top."[74] The metaphor is deadly accurate.

Mimetic monumentalism dominated by private capital creates problems at the same time that it attracts attention. Aesthetically and urbanistically, prominent constructions are a mixed bag, running the risk of misjudgments in scale, adaptation, placement, and usage. Dillon observes: "Downtown Dallas . . . has numerous 'knockoffs,' buildings derived with varying degrees of fidelity from more famous originals. Thanks-Giving Tower is an extremely literal rendition of Philip Johnson's IDS Center in Minneapolis, while San Jacinto Tower is the offspring of both Peachtree Center in Atlanta and Embarcadero Center in San Francisco. Lincoln Plaza refers explicitly back to the Bank of America in San Francisco." He scolds, "It is one thing, obviously, for an architect to work in the prevailing style of his time and quite another to work in the shadow of a particular builder or designer. . . . But the knockoff, the cold copy, usually speaks the cynical language of the marketplace. It says, 'If it worked in such and such a place, it's bound to work here.'" "Such buildings don't advance the art of architecture, which lies beyond mimicry, or enhance the reputation of the cities in which they are located," Dillon concludes.[75]

Reflecting on the city's construction, Dillon muses,

> the price of Dallas' relentlessly expansionist thinking is obvious, and not just to the form of sprawl and congestion but in the absence of more subtle and elusive qualities such as local identity and a sense of place. . . . it has become a city of discrete architectural monuments scattered along freeways and across old cotton fields in defiance of traditional notions of collective urban identity. . . . finding a way to humanize these vast development islands has become a major design and planning challenge. . . .
>
> Equally critical is the need for additional grace notes—for parks, plazas, trees, water, and public art. . . .
>
> Historically, Dallas has been a city of the grand plan and the big fix, in which the small and fragile parts of the community have been overlooked in the crush of doing business.[76]

The big fix and the grand plan are Dallas's Way, but despite its prominence and scale, Dallas has not been fixed or planned in the usual sense of these words. The Dallas Way reveals its material and ideological limits. The constant repetition of criticisms and proposals eventually becomes numbing.[77]

In 2001, introducing an in-depth study of the city commissioned by the *Dallas Morning News,* urban affairs consultant David Rusk declared, "Dallas is no longer an expanding Sun Belt city. Virtually trapped within its now 'inelastic' city limits, Dallas is becoming a slow-growth, poverty stricken, Northern-style central city. . . . My analysis shows the Dallas region is headed more toward fulfilling The Peirce Report's gloomy Vision I: opportunity lost."[78] Rusk, a former mayor of Albuquerque, uttered these grim words to preface planner Antonio Di Mambro's "Global City" report, commissioned by the *Dallas Morning News*. Di Mambro, an MIT professor, recommended that Dallas "abandon its 'Big D' mentality" and focus on resolving its image, economic, and cultural problems, if it wants to compete nationally and internationally. "Without urgent care, the Dallas-Fort Worth metropolis may well reach a point where well-established trends cannot be reversed—where these compounding problems cannot be resolved," warns Di Mambro. "If the Dallas region does not revise its 'old ways,' it could see serious degradation of the quality of life for its inhabitants across the economic spectrum. Dallas-Fort Worth cannot afford this scenario of a sprawling but fragmented metropolis."

Instead of "looking alive," as the *News* puts it, to Di Mambro "the center of Dallas suffers from arrested development, empty streets, an overwhelming number of parking lots, and blight and poverty in many of its surrounding neighborhoods to the east and south." Dallas "can wait no longer for market forces to make things happen downtown." Recent revitalization efforts have "yielded mixed results." To Di Mambro, downtown Dallas needs a new, nonmimetic vision: "Dallas should not mimic what Paris or other cities have done in their downtowns. The new vision must capture the imagination of its people, inspire them and embody their cultural and economic aspirations. Dallas has to rediscover its uniqueness and rekindle the collective civic pride of the region."[79]

Di Mambro's vision flies in the face of more than a century of mimetic monumentalism and a succession of city plans pursuing that goal. Speaking at a forum entitled "Imagining Dallas—What does the city want to be?" sponsored by the Dallas Institute, he boldly declared, "Dallas is the most American city you can imagine." For all its energy and promise, "it is a second-tier city."[80]

THE PROBLEMS WITH MONUMENTALITY AND MIMESIS

As modes of city building, monumentality and mimesis hold a great appeal to Dallas's promoters and developers. Fitting neatly with the Dallas Way, they contributed enormously to Dallas's growth and development, especially but not only in the center. Physically and rhetorically, structures, spaces, and plans constituted expressions of the city's advance and advantages, monuments of and to itself. At the same time, their impact is more complicated, even contradictory. Like much of the Dallas Way, the pursuit of monumental urban development simultaneously supported some of the city's greatest achievements and accompanied some of its largest liabilities. No strategy based on selectively following other cities can constitute a successful path to distinction. It leads instead to anachronisms and failures to adapt appropriate styles or forms, situate structures within the new physical or aesthetic setting, and meet the needs of other parts of the built environment.

The monumental path is littered with limits and conflicts. In its concentration on central areas, privileging the physical city, emphasis on large structures or projects without regard for nearby buildings and topography, and domination by the private domain, monumental development's benefits are circumscribed and its landscape limited. More than in many other cities, monumentality in Dallas explicitly favors the private domain and authorizes its active support with approval and funds from the public. In the process, the public sphere is restricted and the lines between public and private are blurred, often intentionally. Monumentalism itself becomes an agent and aspect of order and control over the public as well as the private domains.

In Dallas, themes of monumentalism, imitation, elite domination, and political reform were all of a piece. Together they worked for and benefited from the power of the entrepreneurial elite over the populace. As it evolved organizationally and institutionally, the Dallas Way was an effort to minimize conflict while securing and maintaining private dominance. Dallas's ongoing political challenge was to fashion the public sector to advance the city. A city council elected at large focused on the visible and prominent central city, including downtown, infrastructure, and means of access and movement. The city manager ran an efficient, cost-effective administration along the lines of the best of private business practices. Together their mission was to keep taxes low while promoting and supporting growth.

Well before the organized Dallas Citizens Council, like-minded Dallasites invested public monies in railroads, land deals, and other construction projects. Dallas's major political reforms contributed to a quick and easy use of public authority and funds to build a growing city. In pursuit of those ends, the operators and enactors of the Dallas Way rarely paused to inquire into the divisions or distinctions between private and public investments or outcomes. Persons who asked such questions and, worse, who voiced opposition to certain actions or expenditures were branded as "political," selfish, and anti-Dallas. They were denounced as self-interested, partisan, liberal, or extremist on either left or right. Adherents of the Dallas Way and their supporters avowed that the best government advanced public and private interests simultaneously and that selfishness never exceeded a fair, proper, and profitable disinterestedness. Although monumentality's origins may lie in the public domain, public monumentality developed relatively late and in a limited form in Dallas.

Dallas's "two cities" and their interrelationships are powerfully shaped by the logic and practice of monumentalism. These modes of urban development seldom acknowledge their strict topographic and socioeconomic limits, including segregation and the inequalities of race, ethnicity, gender, social class, and geography itself. Monumentality tends to reinforce those divisions just as it supports social and spatial fragmentation and segregation and restricts coherence, completeness, and integration, inside and outside the central area. Monumentality's direct benefits are concentrated on the center, the civic and business elite, and those associated with them. This indicator is important because the promoters of monumental development sing a different song, one that Robert Fairbanks recently paraphrased as "for the city as a whole." Only an uncritical reading of rhetoric and contradictory arguments, neglecting social context and social structure while accepting Dallas's credo, can sustain that view. The inclusions and exclusions of Dallas's major plans and the elements actually implemented, from Kessler's in the 1910s to Di Mambro's in 2001 and from Turtle Creek to the still-flooding Trinity River, tell a different tale and underlay a different narrative. Dallas plans and Dallas dreams are highly selective; they are stratified both spatially and socially. As developmental strategy, monumentality has major flaws. Its execution in Dallas remains incomplete and scored by key omissions and failings. "Comprehensive" city plans were never socially or spatially inclusive. If not by design, then in their limited scope they contributed to social segregation and spatial fragmentation inside and beyond the urban core.[81]

Crucially, monumentalism favors grand structures over more pragmatic and necessary public services (public health and education), infrastructure (transportation, communications, flood control), and environmental quality and equity among neighborhoods and social groups. It substitutes inadequately for the kinds of networks, connections, institutions, and services that might bring Dallas's different populations and areas into closer relationships or greater equality. Private-dominated and profit-driven development supports separation and fragmentation and undercuts integration, coherence, and inclusion. Joined with its emphasis on the physical city and the private city, monumentalism concentrates more resources on the relatively few than the many.

Mimetic monumentality contrasts instructively with other modes of development that take different paths, present different experiences, and often lead to different ends. Two compelling alternatives help to make this point. One emphasizes urban development as a complex political process of give-and-take, conflict and compromise, with opportunities for debate, review, and revision of proposals and plans and openings for more popular, democratic participation. Stopping short of romantic populism, the keystones here are *politics* and *process* with opportunities to express differences and sometimes to act on these differences. A related but not synonymous course of development, also different from Dallas's path, would include a broader understanding and construction of politics and political economics as rooted in a city's history, local identity, pluralism, and diversity. Here too we guard against romanticism and nostalgia while we strive to comprehend Dallas by appreciating what Dallas is not.

These perspectives and possibilities promote different views and alternative interpretations of Dallas's past, present, and future, its weaknesses and failures—in public and higher education, police and public protection, public health, community relations, distribution of resources, affordable housing, historical experience and identity, local cultures, political process and reform, equality and equity—as well as its accomplishments. By placing and examining these visions critically in specific contexts, especially Dallas's history, Dallas's ways, and comparative urban experiences, we see and remember how much of a city's history and its peoples' experience are simply not apprehended within the terms of monumentality.

Dallas, we can imagine, might have been different. After its Great Fire, Chicago also developed as a monumental midwestern American city. In *Constructing Chicago,* Daniel Bluestone argues, "The combination of a *tabula rasa* for a townsite, extraordinary growth, and massive economic resources concentrated greater city building energy in Chicago than in nearly any other American city." Chicagoans confronted their city's choices and its future differently than their peers in Dallas. "The question of what the city would become, aside from a commercial entrepôt, persisted because few people could ignore that a great city was indeed rising on a site that some city residents still recalled as an open prairie. . . . The city poured more resources into its own construction than other new cities" and supported a "thriving artistic culture. . . . Chicago, then, helped to define the terms of cosmopolitanism emulated by other cities."[82] As it pursued its commercial future principally through mimetic monumentalism, Dallas was among those looking to Chicago for examples. Dallas chose a significantly different foundation, especially with respect to civic culture and cosmopolitanism.

Despite its complications, monumentality retains a powerful attraction, as current downtown plans and dreams clearly illustrate. These plans and dreams offer salutary lessons and crucial choices for the future of Dallas.

chapter 7

A City at the Crossroads:
Dallas at the Tipping Point

Contemporary Dallas is riven by conflicts and contradictions. Developing over a number of years, they became more visible politically during the 1990s and the early years of the new millennium. Democracy finally came to Dallas with court-ordered city council redistricting, the election of the first African American mayor, and a growing demographic and electoral presence of Mexican Americans and African Americans. The Dallas Way was formally abandoned and faltered in practice, with the barely successful campaign for public support of a new downtown arena, failed efforts to lure the Boeing Corporation and the 2012 Olympics, and continuing confusion over the future of the Trinity River corridor. But severe budget deficits looming at city hall and the difficulty of forming a consensus on priorities prevented newly empowered public officials from addressing long-neglected necessities, let alone much-desired improvements. Inadequate and decaying infrastructure and poorly performing public schools competed with signature bridges and waterfront fantasies for vanishing public and private funds. At the turn of this century, Dallas was forced to confront both its divisions and its limits. The contraction of the local economy in the context of globalization intensified the pressure. The "city at the crossroads" was now more than ever "at the tipping point." When the precarious present is detached from the past and projected into the future, crisis turns into imagined catastrophe.

Italian-born and MIT-educated urban planner Antonio Di Mambro took Dallas by storm early in 2001, following the *Dallas Morning News*'s publication of the report it had commissioned, "The Global City: The Road Ahead for the Dallas-Fort Worth Metropolis in the 21st Century."[1] Di Mambro's report begins, "In the next decades, American cities will show, among other features, evidence of growing disparities in wealth; political landscapes ruled by suburban majorities; central cities and inner-ring suburbs inhabited by a perpetual underclass; and expanded superhighways to serve newly formed edge cities." Di Mambro boldly declares, "Dallas will not escape these trends."

This assessment was shocking news in Dallas, though hardly surprising to most observers of contemporary trends in urban development. Dallas was supposed to be the great exception, immune to economic recession and, like the United States when seen from an exceptionalist perspective, exempt from the costs and free from class disparities that accompany capitalist urban growth elsewhere. Di Mambro pressed on, pinching a sensitive nerve in his critique of Dallas's habitual solutions: "This is not a period to retire to the comfort of gated communities and security alarms. This is the time to rekindle—as a city, as a region—the collective civic pride of the Dallas-Fort Worth region, to forge a new spirit. Cooperation must replace rivalry."[2] Heretical words, given Dallas's longstanding competition with its nearest neighbor. Following Di Mambro, the *Dallas Morning News* endorsed regional planning and cooperation, mass transit, pollution control, airport improvements, bidding on large events and corporate relocations, and sharing costs.[3]

Despite Dallas's assets as a high-tech and business center, Di Mambro continued, "its ranking is hindered by an image problem that stems from below-average performance in the areas of social equity, cultural excellence, intellectual assets and tourism. . . . the character and quality of the place leaves much to be desired, especially in the center city." Both individual and corporate relocations will decline unless there is substantial improvement in education, community, housing, and "other elements of the American dream." Looking at Dallas at the millennium, Di Mambro points to social inequities and economic polarities, ecological and environmental problems, unhealed physical scars from inadequate infrastructure, and stark contrasts of poverty and opulence, obsolescence and expansion, individualism and community, isolation and "connectivity."

"DALLAS CALLS ITSELF 'THE CITY THAT WORKS.' DALLAS IS WRONG."

In 2004, the *Dallas Morning News* commissioned a study of the problems and prospects of the city by Booz Allen Hamilton, a strategic management and information technology consulting firm. The consultants' "Megacommunity Manifesto" declares:

> Public, private, and civil leaders should confront together the problems that none can solve alone. The challenges corporate leaders face—such as global competitiveness, health and environmental risks, or inadequate infrastructure—can no longer be solved by their organizations alone. Today, executives need to align the interests of the outside world with their own agendas and work to develop multi-organizational partnerships with public and civil leaders in a larger system that they do not control. Assembling multilateral groups to deal with key issues together presents the clearest path toward community growth and sustainable globalization.[4]

The notion that corporate leaders should "align the interests of the outside world with their own agendas" in order to deal with global forces they cannot control reveals the presumption that private business interests can control the polity. In less oligarchic cities, this assumption would smack of hubris; here it seems consonant with the Dallas Way.

The April 2004 report, "Dallas at the Tipping Point: A Road Map for Renewal," has the scope of Di Mambro's Global City report but little of its recognition of Dallas's inherent vulnerabilities. Instead, in the *Dallas Morning News*'s characteristically hyperbolic style, it juxtaposes prophecies of doom with paeans to the prospect of greatness. The headlines on the newspaper's twenty-page color special supplement warned: "Dallas calls itself 'the city that works.' DALLAS IS WRONG. By almost any measure that counts—crime, school quality, economic growth—DALLAS LOOKS BAD. It's not that City Hall is lying. CITY HALL SEEMS NOT TO KNOW."[5] Comparing Dallas with fourteen cities ranging from Austin and San Antonio to Baltimore, Columbus, Indianapolis, Memphis, San Diego, and San Jose, Booz Allen Hamilton found that North Texas's tremendous economic strength had masked important warning signs about the state of the city. The report listed "10 Reasons Why Dallas is At Risk—and Doesn't Know It":

1. Job growth and economic growth inside the city are occurring much more slowly than in the region as a whole.
2. Dallas' unemployment rate has run about 25 percent higher than that of the surrounding metro area.
3. The city fares poorly vs. its urban peers on the quality-of-life indicators that matter most to Dallas residents—crime, education and economic development.
4. Weak performance by the Dallas Independent School District holds down the growth of the well-educated workforce needed to keep an economy humming.
5. Most of Dallas' housing inventory is low-value homes and small apartments, despite the positive image that surrounds the $138,000 median price for home sales.
6. An antiquated City Charter leaves Dallas ill-equipped to respond to its challenges. Alone among its peer cities, Dallas lacks a long-term strategic plan that would help drive progress.
7. A dysfunctional government—and an "anti-business aura"—drive businesses to avoid the city and discourage business leaders from civic involvement.
8. Residential property now accounts for more of Dallas' tax base than commercial property—an imbalance typical of bedroom suburbs, not major cities.
9. Years of under-investment and lack of vision have saddled the city with pending bills for massive long-term liabilities.
10. Other cities have been more purposeful and successful in meeting quality-of-life challenges, putting Dallas at a competitive disadvantage.

None of this information was news, but its compilation into one list was devastating.

Senior *Dallas Morning News* reporter Victoria Loe Hicks summarized the report's dire predictions: "The numbers suggest that Dallas—lulled by past successes, cushioned by North Texas' robust growth, blinded by a lack of self-examination and hobbled by the legacy of racism and neglect—is at a tipping point, where wrong moves could precipitate a protracted slide. Crime and troubled schools send families scurrying for the suburbs; employers follow; the tax base and the city budget shrink; city services decline; the drift to the 'burbs accelerates." "Faced with Booz Allen's diagnosis,"

Hicks reported, "city leaders fell back on their habitual remedies." Most defensively denied the magnitude of the problem and reiterated their commitment to business as usual.

Revealingly, when they themselves stared down the steep slide of Dallas in decline, the *Dallas Morning News* team stepped back from the edge. "It doesn't have to be this way. . . ." Dallas has "tremendous natural advantages. . . . Within its borders are thousands of undeveloped acres—room for its population and its economy to grow. . . . The city boasts a strong transportation network of highways, rail lines and one of the world's great airports. . . . It doesn't cost a lot to live here. The city's economy is diverse. . . . The people of Dallas are ambitious and entrepreneurial. . . . The city's population is growing." All these were the raw materials of wealth and growth.

What was lacking to mobilize these resources, the *Dallas Morning News* concluded, was strategic planning.

In many ways Dallas comes up short. . . . Dallas is shortsighted, devoting little thought and fewer resources to planning for its future.

It is short with a dollar. . . .

It is short on trust: People don't trust City Hall, and City Hall doesn't trust people.

It is short on "civic capital." . . .

It is short on leaders who seem able to grasp and tackle these fundamental shortcomings. . . .

One thing it's long on is confusion. Booz Allen found that, under the city charter, almost no one has a well-defined job, authority to do that job and accountability for getting the job done. Even naturally strong leaders must operate within a culture that values making nice over making progress.

What was called for, then, was a shift in civic culture to fashion a new growth coalition.

The "Lessons: What Dallas Must Do to Move beyond Denial" were deceptively simple.

Develop a Strategic Plan
Update the City Charter
Invest in the Future

Model Best Practices
Trust the Public

The prescribed remedies seemed slight in comparison with the diagnosed problems.

The editorial ends with astonishingly reassuring words under the headline "Make a Great City Greater":

> Dallas is a wonderful place to live and work. Some of us are here by birth; others by choice. We all want to see the city and its residents prosper.
>
> We are by turns enchanted and excited by visions of a Trinity River extraordinaire, a robust Arts District, a bustling Fair Park and a bright economic future for all Dallasites from Oak Cliff to Old East Dallas, from Far North Dallas to the southern sector.
>
> This newspaper's love for the city is what drives it to outline so starkly in this special section the challenges the city faces, challenges that have long been camouflaged by the region's relative strength overall. We're optimistic that Dallas can dig itself out of these problems; we point them out because we're worried the city hasn't to date appreciated their gravity.
>
> Dallas: destiny or disaster? The answer is in your hands.

As the editorial admonishes citizens and civic leaders that the realization of Dallas's destiny lies in an act of will, the city's origin myths resurface.

Within the pages of "Dallas at the Tipping Point," the *Dallas Morning News*'s David Dillon quoted leaders of racial-ethnic minority groups voicing viewpoints not usually represented in civic discourse.

> There is no question that Dallas is a more diverse, demanding and dissenting place than it was 40 years ago . . . with new constituencies and new priorities.
>
> So the key question may not be "Who will lead Dallas?" but "Who is Dallas?"
>
> "We lack a sense of identity, of who we are as a city," said Andres Ruzo, former chairman of the Greater Dallas Hispanic Chamber of Commerce. "Dallas is a multicultural city, but we haven't embraced that richness."

With unusual emphasis, Dillon foregrounds race:

RACE IS THE UNACKNOWLEDGED driver of Dallas' civic agenda, the not-so-secret ingredient in how the city works and looks.

"It is a factor in every decision that is made in the city of Dallas," said Ben Click, who was police chief from 1993 to 1999. "I don't know if there is another city in the country with racial divisions as pronounced. That makes it very difficult day in and day out to make decisions. . . ."

In the last 10 years, Dallas has had a black mayor, a black police chief, and black and Hispanic school superintendents. Yet these breakthroughs, significant as they were, came later than in other big cities.

And some of Dallas' most important political and legal victories—single-member council districts, an end to court supervision of schools and public housing—were won only after bruising legal battles. Bitter memories from those past struggles shadow and shape today's Dallas. . . .

A Dallas discussion about racial divides is not just a black-white issue. The city is 36 percent Hispanic, and the Dallas Independent School District is nearly 60 percent Hispanic, with many new immigrants arriving unprepared for school.

Geography and history inextricably join race and inequality in constituting Dallas.

A demographic and economic barrier splits the northern and southern halves of the city like a geological fault line.

The southern sector accounts for roughly half of Dallas' land area, but development there lags so badly "that it would take over 30 years at aggressive growth rates for the south to catch up with the north," Booz Allen said.

Projects such as Pinnacle Park, much touted by the city's economic development department, have barely made a dent.

"South Dallas is your curse and your great opportunity," said Antonio Di Mambro . . . , a Boston planner and urban designer who is working on community-redevelopment projects in southern Dallas.

"A curse because the extraordinary level of decay and degeneration contributes to the negative image that people have of the city. It's your ugly racial divide, though you don't talk about it quite that way.

"Yet if you are going to have any additional growth in the city, you have no choice but to put it there."[6]

Di Mambro sought to turn the curse of southern sector underdevelopment into an opportunity. In that effort, at least, he enjoyed the rhetorical support of civic leaders.

The city's acknowledged "legacy of racism and neglect" was addressed primarily by plans to promote economic development that failed to confront its serious problems of infrastructure, impoverishment, crime, and, too often, public education. In December 2004 the *Dallas Morning News* published "Looking South," a follow-up to "Dallas at the Tipping Point" focused specifically on the African American and Hispanic sector of the city. Revealingly self-contradictory daily features appeared under familiar headlines: "Failure or a New Foundation? City's Fortune and Future Reside in the Sector It's Long Neglected"; "'Great Mysteries' and Broken Promises: 10 Years of Talk at City Hall Haven't Helped Sector's Economy"; "Area's Crime Problem Scaring Off Developers: Many Believe Southern Sector Isn't a Safe Bet; Police Plan to Increase Their Visibility"; "Can Other Cities' Solutions Work Here? Public-Private Initiatives Often Effective Tool for Development"; "Planting Hope for Tomorrow: Southern Dallas Can Flourish with Investment and Nurturing." The hope for quick profits in the southern sector proved empty. Dallas's two cities remain divided, and the gap between them widens as the city leaders apply more of the same.

"Forward Dallas," a comprehensive plan drafted by Fregonese Clathorpe Associates of Portland, Oregon, and formally adopted in 2005–6, was a pale shadow of even these recommendations. With no strategic perspective, it articulated "goals and ground rules for development" that remained flexible enough to respond to economic and cultural change. As the *Dallas Morning News* put it,

> It is hard to argue with the basic premises of Forward Dallas. . . . It calls for a denser community built around mass transit, mixed-use development, housing close to jobs and significant investment in new infrastructure, particularly in the disenfranchised southern sector. It talks about protecting stable neighborhoods and stabilizing fragile ones, streamlining Dallas' Byzantine development code and persuading pubic officials to stop dithering and take charge of the city's future before it is too late.[7]

Applying the "new urbanism" to Dallas was designed to ensure that the city did not "become a shell of its former self, a Sun Belt version of Detroit."

But the plan utterly disregarded the city's automobile-oriented culture and its private-homeowner and corporate-dominated political economy. No plan—especially a toothless, unfunded land-use plan—can reverse the sprawl, neglect of infrastructure, and racial segregation that mark the physical city. Citizen involvement promoted by the planning commission and city council and intended to secure broad democratic participation and support ensured that Forward Dallas did not shift the balance of power. The preeminent goal of "protecting stable neighborhoods" and "stabilizing fragile ones" meant that development and its disruptions were to be imposed on the less powerful second city to the south, at least when economic conditions promised sufficient returns to justify private investment in risky undertakings.

"DEMOCRACY COMES TO DALLAS"

Ron Kirk, Dallas's first African American mayor, elected in 1995, governed in a manner that synthesized the discourse and authority of the Dallas Way with a bid for more equal opportunities. Most of his goals fit within established paths. His agenda featured the monumental American Airlines Center arena on the edge of downtown, along with rhetoric in support of transforming the Trinity River with signature bridges, melding downtown into a version of Manhattan, and developing Dallas's neglected "southern sector." Failed efforts included Dallas's bids to become the new site of the Boeing Airlines headquarters and host the 2012 Olympics. Other goals remained mostly on paper, ritually reiterated in the newspaper's annual wish list.

At the millennium, Kirk spoke publicly as if Dallas ways and destinies were unaltered. As an African American member of a major law firm, Kirk belonged to both the dominant and minority communities. He garnered support from the Dallas Way's traditional base and from racial-ethnic groups newly empowered by city council reforms. Royce Hanson relates:

> As a symbol of black ascendancy in Dallas politics, and as a skilled mediator, he generally succeeded in lowering the decibel level of council meetings. He championed projects favored by business groups, tying them to values of the civic culture—economic growth, and the city's world-class destiny— but, critically for their success, he also linked them to new values of racial

equity, promising jobs and business for southern Dallas. If Kirk did not wander far beyond the boundaries of the traditional civic culture, he was more visible and willing to take limited political risks than most recent mayors were. But he was not running the city—a fact of which he was acutely aware.[8]

Often presented publicly as a populist and progressive candidate, Kirk was in fact the establishment candidate who found support for election and reelection among both minorities and Anglos.

Kirk was a popular mayor, yet debate over the style, quality, and results of his leadership erupted almost from the moment he resigned in 2001, after winning a second term, to run for the U.S. Senate. He failed in his 2002 race to become the first African American to represent Texas in the Senate, losing by a considerable margin to Houston-born, San Antonio–raised John Cornyn (R).[9] Kirk was criticized for concentrating on "big ticket" items like the Trinity River project and 2012 Olympics bid while acknowledging the chronic problems of crumbling streets, southern Dallas, blighted neighborhoods, and failing public schools.[10]

"A GREAT CITY NEEDS A GREAT SPORTS ARENA"

Sport teams serve as a key site of urban competition. In Dallas, winning professional teams provided reassurance when the economy was faltering. In fall 2003, enraptured by the Mavericks' winning streak, the *News* commented: "The Dallas economy hasn't exactly been moving this year. . . . Dallas City Council members aren't certain where they will come up with the money for next year's budget. . . . Oh, to heck with all that. How 'bout those Mavericks?"[11] Amusing, perhaps, but also a sad statement of Dallas's misplaced dreams.[12] Dallasites were bitterly disappointed by the defeat and departure of the Cowboys, the decline of the New Year's Day Cotton Bowl Classic football game, the suspension of Southern Methodist University's football team for rules violations, and the weak records of the basketball Mavericks and baseball Rangers. Losses on the field and ethical lapses off the field tarnished the reputation of a city that makes sports part of its core identity.[13]

Dallas continues—some would say beyond reason—to invest its hopes in sports franchises. In 1997–98, a city bond election to fund more than half the cost of a new downtown arena passed by the narrowest of margins.

Two professional teams, the hockey Stars and basketball Mavericks, agreed to pay the balance of the $250 million cost but take all the profits. Mavericks' co-owner Ross Perot Jr. expressed interest in a $1 billion economic development project to create a Manhattan-like entertainment district, called Victory, surrounding the arena. Enough voters were apparently persuaded by the promise of jobs and economic development, as well as the need to retain the prestige these teams brought to the city.[14] Many researchers consider these claims unrealistic at best, and at worst fraudulent.[15]

The *Dallas Morning News* responded to the threats, explicit and implicit, coming from the teams: "Let there be no mistake, Dallas is at extreme risk of losing its claim as a major league basketball and hockey city, as well as its claim to the annual New Year's Day Mobil Cotton Bowl classic. . . . Dallas needs to save its status as a major sports city. Or it will lose its reputation for being a 'can do' city as well."[16] For all their influence, Dallas business leaders had little experience in facing down threats at this level. Many Dallasites, including public officials, believed that a "great city" had to have professional sports teams and a great arena. In the ensuing battle, the public debate over priorities, costs, and public subsidies for private development was unusually shrill and divisive, full of heated charges and countercharges. Those opposed stated repeatedly, "It's a Bad Deal," citing arguments that an expensive arena would mean investing city funds in the form of tax breaks and public infrastructure in a private enterprise when money was sorely needed for other projects, such as streets and schools. Mayor Ron Kirk touted the arena's promise for economic development, especially new jobs for minorities. Support in South Dallas was not unanimous, however. At a meeting of Dallas Interfaith, a coalition of church groups, four attendees "scolded Dallas for bowing before the idol of the Golden Arena instead of working for better education and affordable housing."[17]

In 1998, the city-wide referendum passed by only 1,400 votes.[18] Not a disinterested party, the *Morning News* editorialized, "Despite the narrow margin, Saturday's voting results will help restore the city's 'can do' image." The *News* also drew attention to the "emergence of southern Dallas voters" as a voice and force.[19] The newspaper reminded readers of their own stake in the city center, implying an element of parochial selfishness among the opponents: "Cities that neglect their cores suffer perilous fates. . . . a decline in the central city also forces citizens in other areas of the city to assume even greater tax burdens for municipal services. . . . Most voters understood those points. They envisioned the arena, and the development that follows, as a new northern entranceway to downtown Dallas."[20]

Local political pundits drew opposing conclusions. The *News*'s Henry Tatum was surprised and pleased; he saw the vote as ending North Dallas's reign as "final arbiter in determining whether something is going to happen in this city."[21] Dallas political analyst and journalist Phil Seib, on the other hand, believed voters were swayed by "saturation advertising" and the mayor's endorsement of the plan. Seib was struck by the narrow margin of victory: "Here was a venture that would cost most Dallas residents nothing, would spur much-needed downtown development and would keep two sports franchises. . . . This was 'good for Dallas.'"

More than sixty thousand voters did not agree. "Part of the Dallas ethos has been that when rich people say 'Jump,' city officials ask, 'How high?' Then voters are expected to approve whatever the city's establishment endorses. The anti-arena campaign was, in part, a populist response to such condescension. The 49 percent who voted 'no' sent a message that they don't like being taken for granted." What stood out unusually clearly for Seib is a question about the role of government in the promotion of private enterprises, a feature of the Dallas Way:

> A dominant issue concerned whether the government should subsidize private enterprise. As with most such questions, the answer begins, "It depends. . . ." If the business in question is a small start-up effort in an economically high-risk area where government wants to spur development, then tax abatements or other such incentives make sense. But some projects, such as the arena, are likely to yield enormous profits to investors who could afford to fund the venture on their own. . . . Nevertheless, a majority of voters apparently said, "So what?". . . The trade-off—a nice new arena and strengthened downtown tax base—made the subsidy tolerable. Remaining unanswered was the fundamental question about why Mr. Perot and Mr. Hicks couldn't proceed on their own. . . . Presumably, Dallas' charitable inclinations were rooted in fears that unsubsidized team owners would decamp to a suburb. How explicit that extortion was probably never will be known, but clearly the owners cut an exceptional deal for themselves.

Seib stops just short of making the point that voters challenged but did not reject the Dallas Way. Dallas remains a city divided, erecting monuments in selected locations: "Soon, dirt will fly and profits will roll in. Perhaps some day, the same kind of energy that went into devising this scheme and selling it to voters will be directed at less glamorous ventures, such as bringing desperately needed economic life to southern Dallas. That would be truly amazing."[22]

The new downtown arena opened with great fanfare in July 2001. "American Airlines Arena will be the snazziest—and the costliest—sports arena in the nation," the *Dallas Morning News* trumpeted. The direct cost of $420 million overran budgets, but the project was proclaimed a great success. However, responsibility for the old Reunion Arena has threatened to become a political football (or, perhaps, basketball or hockey puck). Victory and Palladium, the in-town areas slated to be developed around the new center to resemble "great downtowns" in other cities, have been slow to take off, leading to complaints about the public underwriting of lures and financing to capture needed investment.[23]

The arena is home to the Mavericks, the next team expected to elevate Dallas to its desired heights. They came tantalizingly close in 2006. Dallas needs the team to fly high, especially in the wake of the arena's sponsor threatening to nose-dive. American Airlines almost failed in 2003, amid great embarrassment to Dallas, as senior executives gave themselves sweetheart deals while squeezing every dollar they could from their workers. What corporate logo will take its place over the arena's doors if American cannot meet its obligations?[24] In an unstable economic climate, Dallas's form of private-public partnership carries great risks as well as costs.

FAILING TO LAND BOEING

In 2001, Dallas launched a major effort to lure the new Boeing Corporation headquarters, engaging in a fierce battle with Chicago and Denver. The *Dallas Morning News* listed "20 good reasons to come to the Big D," mixing humorous remarks about the weather, food, and sports with serious claims about its special attractiveness to business. An overly aggressive posture combined with an avowed sense of superiority rings as loudly as the misplaced jibes at Seattle, the aerospace giant's current headquarters. The final reason proved fatally optimistic: "We've got plenty of Class A office space downtown to accommodate your corporate team. You can walk to work and have a brown bag lunch in the Nasher sculpture garden. And we guarantee Dallas Mayor Ron Kirk will be your friend for life."[25]

In announcing the decision to locate in Chicago rather than Dallas, Boeing chair Phil Condit declared, "No single factor made the difference. Each community we talked to had very positive attributes. Each would be great. It was a difficult decision."[26] But downtown office space that fit Boeing's needs was a critical factor: "According to John Warner, the building in Chicago was really well suited to Boeing's immediate occupancy and their long-term occupancy," Reid Record, executive vice president of economic development for the Fort Worth Chamber of Commerce, related. "In contrast, the real estate options that were available in downtown Dallas did not provide a contiguous large block of space that would allow them to have all their operations in one space."[27] This outcome was a far cry from the city's capture of Chance Vought, when the ruling elite extended the runway to meet the company's specifications.

Ignoring the company's own statement, Dallas leaders and boosters predictably focused their attention on differences between the downtowns of Dallas and Chicago to explain Boeing's selection. "Once Boeing Co. decided to locate its new headquarters in a downtown setting, Dallas didn't stand a chance. . . . Dallas didn't have the energetic street life that permeates downtown Chicago. 'I think they just saw downtown Chicago as having a little bit more vibrancy,' said Reid Record, executive vice president of economic development for the Fort Worth Chamber of Commerce. 'It's older and a more mature downtown. You have the river; you've got a multitude of residential opportunities. You've got the Magnificent Mile with all the major retailers, and I think that's a pretty strong attraction.'"[28]

Dallas's leaders were unable to take a more comprehensive urban perspective. To anyone familiar with both cities, it makes little sense to reduce the many differences to the "vibrancy" of "street life." Chicago's many amenities—including world-class museums, universities, arts, and performance groups; historical architecture and plan; lakefront setting; physical dimensions; and, not least of all, its metropolitan area—place it in another echelon of cities entirely. What remains striking is how easily, for Dallas, attention falls on the condition of the center city taken by itself. The political-economic uses of that judgment neglect the place of downtown in relationship to the shape and texture of the encompassing Metroplex. Boeing chose a city, not only a downtown. That Dallas could not fathom the distinction continues to limit the city on the Trinity.

The Boeing deal offered many lessons, but Dallas heard or responded to them selectively. Without reflecting on their city's past actions, Dallas boosters hinted that Chicago competed unfairly. The *Dallas Morning News* offered Chicago faint congratulations and sour grapes, claiming that Chicago "put on a spectacular show and promised the moon. Reportedly, the incentives package put together by the city and state could top $35 million. Michael Jordan couldn't have put a better full court press when he was playing for the Bulls." Chicago's superiority in the arts was acknowledged, and another lesson drawn was that the arts pay: "The arts generate more than $700 million each year in this area. They also define a community for corporations such as Boeing."[29]

For Dallas, all routes lead to downtown, and Dallas must hasten to build it "so they will come." Rena Pederson expounded with brio if not realism: "Takeaway for Dallas: We'll never have a Lake Michigan for regattas, but we should press full steam ahead with improvements to the Trinity River, where we could at least have pocket lakes surrounded by jogging trails and baseball diamonds and picnic grounds. The city desperately needs more scenic appeal. It's a sterile place." Pederson's other solutions were familiar, including an international airport terminal, expansion of the Arts District, the "intellectual heft" of a "world-class museum," high-profile architects to "add some dramatic splash to the skyline."[30] Where is Dallas, in this call to imitate New York City and Chicago?

LOSING THE OLYMPICS

Less than six months after the Boeing loss, Dallas's attempt to secure the U.S. site for the 2012 Olympics followed the same pattern of stated intention, quieting opposition, delusions of greatness and overconfidence, and disappointment. It stimulated less heat, but replayed the scenario. Despite public differences over costs to Dallas residents, the city submitted a bid in December 2000 that was "touted as a winner." The games were oversold locally with the promise of monumental payoffs, including a $265 million Olympic stadium in Fair Park, a new Fair Park Coliseum, a $125 million Olympic Village at the site proposed for a South Dallas campus of the University of North Texas or a "link village" at Fair Park, and a projected budget surplus of up to $357 million to benefit sports programs in the region.[31]

The Dallas Olympic Committee was so sure of the strength of its bid that it downplayed the competition with seven other U.S. sites, including New York City.[32] While awaiting the selection, attention focused on whether to hold a citywide referendum to support the bid in the form of an Olympic tax to meet the United States Olympic Committee's requirement for a guarantee.[33] A proposal to divert sales tax revenue of up to $100 million to an Olympic trust fund against possible shortfalls sparked disagreement and furious debate. Opponents claimed that Dallas 2012 organizers had promised to fund the games with private money and that there were far more pressing local needs for the use of tax revenues, especially with a budget deficit looming.[34] In a public forum, county judge Lee Jackson spoke of the millions of dollars in private investments and economic benefits likely to accrue to Dallas. City council member Laura Miller argued, "The Olympics are only the latest in a long line of private projects subsidized by public dollars." Opponents of the trust fund proclaimed, "'Put us first,' arguing that Dallas should focus on delivering basic services. . . . 'Why the Olympics?' one resident asked. 'Why can't we just try to make this a decent place to live for everybody, instead of trying to pursue some crazy dream?'"[35]

The *Morning News*'s Henry Tatum stumped for the old ways: "And yet the continuing debate about holding the Olympic Games in Dallas really isn't about such things as the financial guarantees. . . . It is about whether this city truly has the will and capability to pull off an event of such magnitude. A few decades ago, a local bank had a long-running TV ad that described Dallas as 'the city without limits.' Unfortunately, the economic free fall of the 1980s brought an end to that bank. Did it also bring an end to the philosophy espoused in that ad?" Tatum called on the public to speak: "The people of Dallas need to say who they are and what they believe this city can be. And there is nothing like an Olympic Games referendum to answer both those questions."[36] The *News* proclaimed that the "Olympics Would Revive Our 'Can Do' Spirit": "This is a city that staged the Texas Centennial in the midst of the Great Depression. It is time to rekindle that spirit. It is time for Dallas to move forward."[37]

In the end, that question did not have to be settled. In late October, the United States Olympic Committee announced that four cities' bids remained in contention; Dallas was not one of them.[38] Ironically, given

Dallas's overtly mimetic approach to development, Dallas 2012 president Richard Greene said that Dallas "suffered because of the perception that it resembled Atlanta. International Olympic Committee officials criticized Atlanta's 1996 Games for their commercialization."[39] The president of Dallas 2012 blamed the United States Olympic Committee's "mindset": "The USOC had already determined we didn't have the international character they were looking for."[40] The *Morning News* countered that Dallas's elimination "should not signal that the Southwest's financial capital couldn't play ball in the competitive world of international athletics."

The push and pull of competing needs within Dallas pervaded the debate. The unresolved tension is evident in Tatum's editorial. Echoing the resident who cried, "Why can't we just try to make this a decent place to live for everybody," he began: "The city must start with a stronger focus on basic services, such as improving its roads and strengthening its neighborhoods. That effort will help the city shine. More important, it will better serve the needs of local residents. Then, bids for international events cannot boil down into the wearisome potholes vs. projects debate that dogs so many recent discussions about Dallas' future."

But attention shifts to center-city Dallas with the curious segue of "likewise." In a flow of wild metaphors, odd analogies, and dictums, the city at large and its people are pushed to the edges: "Focusing on basic services also means working to expand cultural attractions. . . . Likewise, making downtown a 24-hour city with coffee shops, attractive parks, and bustling stores will give our core the feel of a place where people from all walks of life gather. That, after all, is what attracts people to the Parises, the Rios and the Tokyos." Tellingly, the *News* pluralizes these singular cities, assuming their allure can be duplicated. "The city also needs to build inviting gateways into downtown. Whether a designer bridge or manicured park, attractive portals will lead people into the city's living room."[41] Provided, of course, they are neither homeless nor disorderly; not all are welcome downtown.[42] For many Dallas residents, the crux lies with making the city livable and sustainable, neither a dreamed-of Paris or Tokyo on the Trinity nor a fearful version of Detroit or Cleveland in the Sunbelt.

BUDGET WOES AND POWER FAILURES

A few months later, in August 2002, the *Dallas Morning News* headlines blared: "Budget Turns Dallas Dream into Nightmare: The City's Bubbling

Optimism Hits a Fiscal Brick Wall." Tatum painted an oversimplified and denial-ridden picture of a city on constant simmer that suddenly found itself in an inexplicable crisis. Ever the "Go Dallas" booster, he wrote with melodramatic angst:

> Wasn't it just a short while ago that Dallas was gearing up to make its big pitch to host the Summer Olympics in 2012? Didn't the Dallas public library recently celebrate its 100th anniversary by unveiling a new master plan that would cost $50 million? . . . How quickly things change. The Stephen King horror story known as the Dallas municipal budget circa 2002–2003 has arrived. And City Council members are ready to run screaming out of the room. I am a 30-year veteran of these annual budget deliberations, and there are proposals in this package that have sent chills up even my spine.

Possible solutions included closing the Aquarium; reducing hours for swimming pools, recreation centers, and branch libraries; and raising the city property tax.[43] Many cities and states across the country were facing severe budget shortfalls at that time, but Dallas failed to raise its head and look around to gain wisdom or solace from those circumstances. Tatum's fearmongering rhetoric plays on Dallas's fears of urban decline and doom.[44] Nonetheless, the issues beneath the fears are real, and the responses elicited can be powerful.

Dallas's present and future prominence and power was at stake, exposing the city's greatest fears, perhaps the city's largest liability and weakness. Beneath the bravado, Tatum reveals a city where neither monuments to greatness nor lessons from its own history have provided an anchor to help weather crises:

> More power to the council members as they begin this painful process. But they must not lose sight of Dallas' fragile image. . . . It takes very little to change national perceptions of a city. Not long ago, Cleveland was the butt of comedians' jokes. Today, the city's heavy investment in infrastructure and new cultural facilities has made it a favorite example of how to turn around struggling urban centers. . . .
>
> Dallas still enjoys a certain mystique. But failed attempts to attract large corporations or major events in recent years have removed some of the glimmer. . . .

If municipal officials make cuts that portray Dallas as a city in decline, the free-fall will come quickly. This city's success has come largely through its ability to out hustle the competition. But it is going to be much harder to close the sale in shopworn clothing. . . . The adage that you have to spend money to make money may be hard to swallow in such difficult financial circumstances. But it is still true.[45]

This outburst is revealing. What city would envy Cleveland? The 2001 Di Mambro report might have sparked fears that, rather than a Paris on the rise, the city was closer to Cleveland's orbit: "Once believed to be immune from Rust Belt-style decay, Dallas at the start of the 21st century clearly is not."[46]

Equally significant is the overarching concern with images, surface appearances, and outsiders' perceptions. The fundamental issue is not the quality of city services, but preservation of a Dallas "mystique" to shield the city from being seen as "in decline," which would usher in a "free-fall" toward failure. Tatum's adage about needing to spend money to preserve this mystique continues the Dallas Way of public investment for private gain. Such financial counsel entails real costs and risks. A city that needs to invest significantly in basic services evokes an image and a presumption of an unusually active and wide-ranging public sphere. That seeming contradiction of Dallas's usual story is part of the Dallas Way's selective manipulation of public policy and the public purse.[47]

With the alarm bells of danger ringing in the background, Laura Miller, Oak Cliff resident, Democrat, and Kirk opponent on the city council, ran as the nonestablishment, post–Dallas Way candidate. Dallas political consultant Rob Allyn declared, "Ron Kirk was the perfect mayor for boom times. Laura Miller is the perfect mayor for tough times."[48] Miller's electoral strength came from "conservative" North Dallas; she attracted little support from African American areas in southern Dallas. Given the polling on the arena and her theme of "back to basics," Miller's victory was not surprising.[49]

Miller confronted—and, more unusually, admitted that she faced—a city beset by change: budget deficits had altered the city's priorities, and a new electoral council system had altered the face and composition of the city's leadership.[50] After Miller's first year in office, the *Morning News* begrudgingly acknowledged, "Mayor has done better than we expected" and saluted her focus, dedication, and competence, if not her ability to compromise and her style.[51] For her part, Miller "pledges 'no slowing up.' Homeless, jobless, Trinity on her agenda; she envisions city makeover." The budget, taxation, and basic services, not building monuments, claimed Miller's attention. In order to support any major public-private project, she vowed, "it would have to be a deal that's unprecedented in the history of Dallas. The city would have to be true economic partner." A democratic discussion of economic priorities and the principle of the public good prevailing over private interests would signal a new tune in city hall.[52]

Dallas's civic culture, once a source of pride, has become dysfunctional, in disrepair and disarray. Royce Hanson underscores the consequences with respect to such vital domains as public education, policing, race and representation, growth and development, and governance.[53] New political arrangements, the result of judicial decisions, are still adjusting to fundamental urban transformations, including spatial reordering, demographic shifts, and economic change. The fourteen-member city council, each elected from a single district with only the mayor elected at large, is the most obvious. The ethnic and racial remaking of the electorate is a key element in larger power shifts.[54] These changes continue to push the city to revise its charter and remember its peripheries and diverse constituents as well as its core.

One of the barometers of Dallas's difficulty is its inability to agree on the terms of a new city charter, despite widespread agreement that it needs major revisions, including some alteration in the power of key offices.[55] The long and bitter fight over the size and apportionment of the city council left deep scars and distrust in the city. Reminding readers of its leadership in instituting the city manager system in the 1920s, the *Dallas Morning News* trumpeted its belief that "it is time for a mayor with broad powers who is clearly accountable for the municipal government. The council-manager system installed here more than seven decades ago served Dallas well during earlier times. But the government does not function as effectively in a city of more than a million people with complex issues that did not exist here in the 1920s." Many, including members of racial-ethnic minority groups, resist ceding power to a central authority, while others fear the professionalization and politicization of the polity.[56] Unfortunately, the charter controversy became caught up in a bitter collateral contention over a "strong" versus a weaker mayor. On May 7, 2005, the *Dallas Morning*

News reported, "Strong Mayor Trounced: Turnout Unexpectedly High as Proposal Unites South Side, Splits North."[57]

Confounding this lack of consensus is the fact that Dallas lacks the human and social infrastructure required to serve its citizens' basic needs. The development of the city center through the use of public authority and funds, powerful means of promotion and control, and imitation and purchase constitutes a very different approach to city growth than more pluralistic, locally grounded developmental processes that help to advance the causes of inclusion, opportunity, and representation; public and higher education; welfare and well-being; and civic culture and the public sphere. An alternative approach would produce a more integrated city.[58]

MISSED OPPORTUNITIES

Prominent among the challenges the city faces are its failing public schools, controlled by the Dallas Independent School District (DISD). As the charter for Millennium Dallas declared: "Dallas cannot expect to be a city where people want to work and live if public education here remains rooted in mediocrity."[59] "Dallas at the Tipping Point" ranked the public schools number 4 among the "10 Reasons Why Dallas is At Risk," responsible for the lack of a skilled workforce. The report found that DISD schools performed poorly in comparison with the urban districts in Dallas's peer cities, and much worse in comparison with suburban schools in the Dallas area.

With its history of de jure and de facto segregation, chronic corruption, and endemic instructional failure, the state of public education is scandalous. Its defining racial and class dynamics are consonant with violent interactions between police and minority youth, residential segregation, resistance to public housing in white neighborhoods, and unequal facilities and opportunities.[60] Neither funding levels nor programs and leadership reflect serious efforts to reach a school population in which most students "come from homes classified as economically disadvantaged" and fewer than half of the 78 percent who graduate plan to attend a four-year college.[61] The national norm of "no child left behind" and the focus on schooling to develop human capital for economic productivity drastically narrow the vision of education.

In 2003, after three decades, court-mandated and supervised school desegregation ended.[62] Voters approved a record $1.37 billion bond issue in

January 2002, and the *Dallas Morning News* led the campaign with the fighting words, "It's time to free Dallas from federal control."[63] But not all agreed. The court's monitor called for more desegregation data and pointed to compliance problems. Others argued that sufficient progress had not been demonstrated.[64] Parents of children of color remained suspicious of the school district. Sam Tasby, the African American parent who sued the DISD in 1970, did not accept the judgment that segregation was a thing of the past.[65] In the eyes of many whites, regaining independence and escaping decades of shame was more important than the state of the schools. The *Morning News* declared in 2003 "A New Beginning": "We're confident the Dallas school board and Superintendent Mike Moses will capitalize on the increased flexibility and focus. . . . No challenge before Dallas today is of greater significance. Dallas' economic vitality is dependent on the district's ability to better educate children and instill public confidence in its commitment to high quality education for children of all ethnic backgrounds. . . . Judge Sanders' declaration also should help remove a stigma from Dallas public education."[66]

Yet the children of Dallas do not attend racially and ethnically integrated schools. When the desegregation order was first issued, the school population was 59 percent Anglo; in 2003, Anglo students comprised only 7 percent. One of the stranger manifestations of Dallas's extreme racial politics is the fact that suburban school district boundaries extend into the city proper to include substantial portions of Anglo and middle-class neighborhoods. Residents of these neighborhoods can ensure that their children attend predominantly white schools without moving to more expensive suburbs. Other Anglo parents send their children to private and parochial schools, which proliferated during the city's prolonged resistance to court-ordered desegregation. "White flight" ensured the resegregation of the city's schools. "Will Whites Come Back to Dallas Independent School District? District Hopes End to Desegregation Order Will Reverse Trend" warily repeats the *News*.[67] "Dallas Schools Need to Lure Anglos Back: White Students Have Become an Endangered Species in City."[68] The odds are not encouraging, especially as the school district leads the state in the number and proportion of its schools performing so badly that students are permitted to transfer out of them.[69] Deeply embedded racial conflicts, fiscal inequities, spatial segregation, and urban decline are unlikely to be remedied in the near future.

Faced with competition from private, church, and suburban schools, the DISD plods along, sometimes with test scores and public relations improving, sometimes not, trying unsuccessfully to meet great demands with inadequate resources. The *Morning News* joins superintendents in asking business leaders to "get involved." Mike Moses pleaded, the public schools "will take 'help in just about any way.'"[70] City-DISD partnerships develop very slowly. As in other domains, significant change is not indicated by regular calls for major assistance and repeated cries of crisis. During the nine-year period ending in 2001, the DISD suffered an unusual number of obstacles to effective management, including unstable leadership and corruption scandals. The revolving door on the superintendent's office saw the city's first African American and Hispanic superintendents come and go. From 1995 to 2005, the DISD had four permanent and three interim superintendents.[71] In July 2006, the FBI was investigating misuse of credit cards, among other suspicions of corruption.[72]

Postsecondary educational opportunities in the Dallas area are more available to the already privileged than to those who might become the skilled workers of the future. Tellingly, the public institutions of higher education that serve Dallas are located primarily in its suburbs: the Universities of Texas at Dallas (UTD) in Richardson and Arlington, University of North Texas (UNT) in Denton. UNT, with an outpost in South Dallas, dreams of becoming the first public university to open a campus within the city's boundaries. Among private universities, Southern Methodist is in Highland Park/University Park and the University of Dallas is in Irving. The location of campuses follows the segregated and fragmented social geography of the city and region, posing major problems of access and equity. Neither developing "human capital" nor offering economic stimulus has provided a strong enough incentive to extend badly needed educational opportunities to the city's racial-ethnic minority and working-class residents, or even to its working adults.[73]

Like Dallas's public schools, its institutions of higher education are not central to its proud self-image or its comparative standing among other cities. Few cities of Dallas's size, stature, and wealth lack even one distinguished institution; many regard a great university nearby as a sine qua non for a great city. As former UTD president Franklin Jenifer proclaimed, "Everyone agrees that Dallas, in order to prosper and eventually emerge as the world-class city that it is capable of becoming and that many of us believe is its destiny, needs a first-tier research institution." All that was needed to advance, he argued, was political will.[74] But that political will has long been lacking. The lack of a major institution of higher education arises from patterns of land ownership and valuation, as well as to the pro-business ideology and undervaluation of the liberal arts that has dominated Dallas's development. Wealthy Dallasites have contributed large sums to institutions outside the area. Now, belatedly, Dallas struggles against the underdevelopment of its research and development capacities. Plans for Dallas's advance accord a major place for a first-class research university, usually as a base for applied research that can be spun off and developed for high returns in the marketplace.

UT Southwestern Medical Center's recent rise is built on aggressive hiring of major medical researchers (including four Nobel laureates), successful fundraising, and emphasis on high-tech medicine. It aims to bring many millions to the institution and the city through biomedical and biotechnological research and development.[75] Expectations of economic payoff bolster anticipated health benefits in garnering support for growth. The main medical center complex is itself a public institution whose success depends at least as much on private contributions.[76] The danger, which is rarely acknowledged, is that the glory days of such linkages as San Diego's biotechnology takeoff with the University of California–San Diego campus in the 1960s and 1970s and Silicon Valley's with Stanford in the 1970s may well be over.[77] Innovation cannot depend on imitation. Monumentalism and purchase carry extremely high price tags, although UT Southwestern has purchased valuable talent.

Higher education's rung on the *Dallas Morning News*'s millennium city roster reads, "The impact of strong universities on the local economy cannot be overemphasized. Area institutions should work together to build the quality of higher education in this region."[78] Both items rose in importance with recognition of the almost monumental costs and competition for research in biotechnology, electronics, aerospace, and geosciences. The release of the Metroplex Higher Education Benchmarking Study and Enhancement Strategy in September 2002 seriously ratcheted up the heat and the stakes. Sponsored by the Dallas Citizens Council, it was conducted by the consulting firm SRI. The report offered several conclusions aimed to jar Dallas-area complacency and stimulate action, noting the low ranking of research and development in Dallas institutions on a national scale and overall lack of "a distinguished national profile." "The consensus amongst Dallas-Fort Worth Metroplex civic and business leaders is that the North Texas region is the only major national economic power without a major research university." The report concludes: "The universities and the economy in the Metroplex could be enhanced by a strong tradition of university and industry collaboration" in such areas as life sciences; electrical engineering; pharmaceuticals and biotechnology; business start-ups, entrepreneurial culture, and research parks; and industry funding of research.

The report stimulated a range of local responses. While the universities were not surprised, corporations expressed their shock in their own terms. The study "gave us a wake-up call that we don't have as much in research as we thought," said Mike Boone, Dallas Citizens Council chair, in contemporary business-speak. "We're behind the curve in getting our universities where they need to be. The business community has to step up and get involved in this." Through cooperation, he continued, "We're going to get a bigger bang for our dollars. We avoid duplication, and we don't end up with a bunch of mediocre schools. We end up with excellence."[79]

By 2005, however, the state budget shortfall had prevented Dallas-area campuses from undertaking ambitious projects, and little private investment was forthcoming.[80] An agreement with Texas Instruments and the State of Texas enhanced the status of UTD's engineering programs. The *Dallas Morning News* announced the plan with cautious optimism: "Texas and Dallas-area government officials think they've concocted the perfect recipe for the region's technology industry. Mix together a new chip factory and a research university growing in prominence, and the jobs, tax dollars and scientific breakthroughs will multiply. But there's one catch: The formula those officials announced this week will take years—even decades—to start cooking."[81]

Typically, the *Dallas Morning News* called for a mix of private and state subsidies to enhance the area's research and development capacity. "The short-term answer is for North Texas academic, business and political leaders to create a nonprofit organization that could serve as a catalyst for regional research dollars" through fund-raising and lobbying.[82] Ultimately, though, the state must provide substantial funding for the Dallas research initiative.[83] The assumption that "the more money private industry puts into North Texas' range of campuses, the more Austin will look favorably upon matching those investments" may well be fallacious when states' shares of public university budgets are declining. Setting priorities and promoting public-private collaboration are touted as key. "North Texans themselves must take the lead in building centers of excellence. Or else watch other metropolises outpace our region."[84]

The absence of research-oriented institutions to promote innovation results not from a lack of imagination but from a failure of political will. In 1961, Dr. Lloyd V. Berkner announced a pioneering project in the *Saturday Review:* "Renaissance in the Southwest: Science Brews New Respect for the Intellect on a By-passed Frontier."[85] A distinguished physicist, presidential science advisor, and chair of the National Academy of Sciences' Space Science Board, Berkner proposed a Research Center for the Southwest in Dallas. He aimed at nothing less than "restoring the pride of an intellectually backward region. Through that restoration certainly will come a new dignity and responsibility for the working of democracy": the advancement of both regional interests and of American education, science, technology, and economic growth. For Berkner, among the greatest needs was the training of PhDs in a Graduate Research Center closely linked to other colleges and universities.

Seriously pursuing this dream meant elevating and enlarging the Dallas Way to stratospheric levels, as well as adapting Stanford provost Frederick Terman's regional model. Growing with federal defense spending during and after World War II, Dallas-area technology leaders such as General Dynamics, Lockheed, Ling-Temco-Vought, and especially Texas Instruments required many more highly trained engineers and researchers than they could find locally or regionally. TI's electronics production took off with Jack Kilby's invention of the silicon-based "integrated circuit," or chip. TI chair Erik Jonsson turned to Berkner, who proposed the Graduate Research Center of the Southwest to serve regional development more generally.

But the grand plan could not be sustained. "After a fast start, including pledges of $16 million in TI stock and close cooperation with NASA administrator James Webb, the Graduate Research Center hit some snags," report Leslie and Kargon.[86] TI stock's value fell, and federal contracts failed to materialize. "Berkner's vision lived on, though on a more modest scale, through the Southern Methodist University Foundation for Science and Engineering," with Terman as president. In his narrower vision, a "form of partnership between the educational institution and the industrial community" with "close rapport, a high level of interaction, and mutual support" was needed. In partnership with high-tech industry, SMU engineering could "stand out as a great steeple of excellence in the Southwest . . . high enough to be clearly visible from the North." Berkner's dream exceeded the reach and the capacity of the Dallas Way. Local public funding and sponsorship were not feasible; expected federal millions never arrived to stimulate the endeavor. A local recession and loss of Dean Thomas Martin ended another promising start, and the Graduate Research Center of the Southwest was blended with the state institution to form the University of Texas at Dallas.[87] UTD was built in suburban Richardson, north of Dallas, on land donated by its "founders," TI's Erik Jonsson, Cecil McDermott, and Eugene Green. Its suburban location, long lacking ready access by public transit, reflected its corporate connections and auspices, not a popular vision as an accessible public university for the Dallas area.

Stuart Leslie and Robert Kargon conclude that here, as elsewhere, "the leaders of high technology industry in Texas discovered that educational institutions could not, by themselves, integrate a regional economy. With little direct interaction between its members as suppliers or competitors, the high technology community of Dallas could not move beyond a common interest in promoting research and education in selected specialties to true collective learning."[88] In the Dallas Way, the current dream hews to the narrower of these two paths.

BOND ISSUES

Monumental developments created in isolation generate underdevelopment both within and around them. Consider the paucity of great collections and performances within the shining palaces of culture designed by world-class architects and the vast vacancy outside the designated Arts District. If the Calatrava bridges over the Trinity River are ever built, where will they lead?

The Trinity is Dallas's impossible dream, the icon for the Dallas that has never been. The vision of a port threads its way through the city's history. More often a threat to poorer Dallasites located in the flood plain, the Trinity has been held out as the city's savior. "Trinity Gives Dallas another Chance to Think Big," reiterates the *Dallas Morning News*.[89] Touting the potential for the Trinity to become the largest city park in the United States, consultant and Harvard urban planning professor Alex Krieger knew his audience at a Central Dallas Association luncheon. Rhetorically turning continuity into change, he declared, "Few cities have an opportunity to redefine themselves these days. With the sluggish economy and the migration of residents to the suburbs, most urban centers simply try to hold on to what they have. It can be different for Dallas. The Trinity River drew settlers here in the early 1800s. Now, nearly two centuries later, it can be the catalyst to bring people here again." Aside from matters of historical accuracy and urban economics, major development would have negative environmental impacts on the health of the Great Trinity Forest.[90]

In June 2003, Santiago Calatrava came to town with a model for the first of a series of signature bridges over the river. Announcing that the Woodall Rodgers bridge "will not be a monument to itself," he insisted on the presence and power of bridges to "mark cities, define them and fix them in the collective memory," citing the Golden Gate and Brooklyn bridges. Architectural writer David Dillon declares, "Dallas has never seen anything like it," in response to the design for a 1,280-foot steel and concrete span with cables strung from a single 300-foot parabolic arch: "from the sides

FIGURE 50. Proposed Margaret Hunt Hill Bridge, designer Santiago Calatrava, 2006, Trinity River Corridor Project.

FIGURE 51. Proposed I-30/Woodall Rodgers Bridge, designer Santiago Calatrava, 2006, Trinity River Corridor Project.

it will be a spidery lattice, from the ends a series of mysteriously dissolving cones." The *Morning News* headlined his commentary "Simple, Elegant Design Could Help Define Dallas." Dillon urged the inclusion of sidewalks and bicycle lanes: "If Woodall Rodgers is to be Dallas' Golden Gate or Brooklyn Bridge, then people must be able to walk, jog, push and pedal across it. That's what public design means—something for everyone." He also expressed skepticism about a series of bridges: "The city's long-term interests might not be served by creating a Calatrava museum. One function of a masterpiece is to inspire others to surpass it."[91]

Antonio Di Mambro's 2001 Global City report proposed a remaking of the center city as well as critical rethinking of Trinity River development. His plan is distinguished by its observations on inequality and Dallas's relative disadvantages comparatively and competitively. Unlike other plans, it does not assign to aesthetic and landscape improvements far more weight than they can carry.[92] The *Dallas Morning News* managed without irony to turn Di Mambro's critique into praise for Dallas: "Dallas Is Just Beginning to Evolve into a Great City."[93] Hearing only part of the message, Dallas leaders launched a downtown improvement program that the *Morning News* dubbed "Go Dallas." Before long, a relabeled "Build a Better Dallas" pragmatically narrowed that vision to the passage of a set of bond proposals.

"What does Dallas want?" asked Henry Tatum at the end of 2001. "We have spent the past few years hearing a lot of talk about what some people don't want." He lists the detractors who oppose what they regard as wasteful spending. Then he evokes history:

> There seldom has been a time in this city's history when it didn't know exactly what it wanted. In the late 1800s, it wanted to be the biggest city in Texas and persuaded two major railroad companies to build their lines through downtown. In the 1930s, it decided not to be deterred by the Depression and staged the Texas Centennial celebration. In the 1960s, it was determined to overcome its "city of hate" image created by the assassination of John F. Kennedy and adopted a Goals for Dallas plan that proposed, among other things, building a regional airport. But as we head into the new year, the wants aren't as clearly defined.

Significantly, a "want" signifies both a lack and a desire. Each want, from better schools to cultural facilities, requires spending, euphemized as investment. Tatum's exposition blurs the fact that Dallas not only can but also must make choices.[94]

From "A Road Map to Renewal" and "Go Dallas" to "Build a Better Dallas," the *Dallas Morning News* was intransigent on city budget and bond issue questions in 2002–3 and after. The bottom line, repeated endlessly in various forms, was "City Can't Afford to Be Timid."[95] As the paper saw it, the value of major public investment in the city's future far outweighed the costs in dollars and negative public response. The *News* took this position after Mayor Miller and city councilors expressed concern about raising taxes or selling a high-priced bond issue to their constituents: "Miller says time not right to raise taxes. As bond plan splits council, mayor seeks restoration of trust."[96] Estimates for the bond package ranged from $255 million to $603 million. The *News* accused the mayor and councilors of neglecting the city "as a whole" and shortchanging the future. "Holding the line on taxes and protecting the city's triple-A bond rating might have seemed like smart stewardship in the late 1990s, but it has left Dallas facing an expanding list of critical needs. . . . Many Dallas business executives . . . worry that the city is falling behind its rival big cities. . . . Cities like Houston and Los Angeles have committed to larger bond programs during these tough economic times. Elected officials in both cities recognize that economic development and business competitiveness depend on safe roads, prosperous downtowns and neighborhoods, and a healthy tax base."

For the *News,* image is always a concern: "A city branded as unwilling to maintain streets or to invest in visionary projects to improve the quality of life citywide will lose business and residents to the suburbs or to other states. . . . A larger bond package, however, would make an enormous difference in the quality of city life. . . . And just as important, an aggressive bond program would signal that the city is committed to righting past mistakes and charting a better course for all of Dallas." Yet another key element in this rhetoric is the city-as-a-business model: "Dallas no longer can be averse to risk. . . . Dallas can't afford timidity."[97]

Alternatively threatening and reassuring, lecturing and pressing city councilors, businesses, and residents, the *News* leaves no room for dissent or debate. Invoking history, it speaks simultaneously to Dallas past, present, and future. The newspaper sees itself taking the reins of leadership and education as it had in the making of the Dallas Way.[98] Under the guise of promoting "nostalgia"—"leaders should remember how the city got that way"—Henry Tatum and the *Dallas Morning News* urge the city to spend: "Bubble gum and baling wire will not get Dallas where it has to go."[99]

"Build a Better Dallas," the slogan adopted in 2003, served as an effective banner for a discourse of Dallas that extends beyond downtown without ever posing potentially conflicting goals. The discourse effectively blended the need to threaten and evoke fear with the imperative to be constructive. It influenced voters, councilors, and leaders at home in part by pointing out the impact of the decision on others' images of Dallas. "Build a Better Dallas" provided a useful cudgel with which to beat recalcitrant elected officials by juxtaposing their parochial concerns with the future of the city "as a whole." Leaders with different viewpoints were cast as gutless, selfish, and backward-looking; the paper undercut city council members who spoke in terms of "representing their constituents."[100] The campaign avoided equating the city with downtown, addressing each region in an effort to create a sense of equity, fairness, and sharing among geographic sections.

In this formulation, only a bigger bond package could begin to meet the many needs without discriminating against some areas.[101]

Mayor Laura Miller promoted an alternative program aimed at meeting the city's most critical needs for less cost, saying "potholes, pools, police are priorities," but the effort was too little and too late.[102] The 3 Ps did not stand up well against the visionary, vague rhetoric of "Build a Better Dallas." By February, after "enough horseflesh was traded to supply several cavalry units," the city council endorsed a $555 million bond package, but organized the seventeen propositions in two tiers. "The process—as well as the product—had veterans of past bond campaigns reeling."[103] North Dallas councilor Lois Finkelman commented, "This has not been a pretty process." According to press reports, "The day, which opened on a testy note, soon threatened to devolve into anarchy. Council members took turns interrupting one another and shouting one another down."[104] The *Dallas Morning News* applauded the eleven of fifteen councilors who supported the entire program and called on them to "grab a megaphone and make clear to residents why each of the 17 propositions is critical to the economic vitality of our fair city. To make clear to residents how small is the individual cost and how great is the community good. To make clear to residents how they as city leaders will assure that taxpayer money is spent wisely and effectively."[105]

The campaign moved to voter meetings and the media, as politicians' personalities came into play. The "Build with Bonds" campaign, along with the *News,* presented the entire package as "no-frills," "meat and potatoes" that offered "immediate results," unlike other recent bond elections in support of the arena and Trinity River improvements.[106] Tatum announced, "If all 17 propositions pass, Dallas has a chance to get a grip on a downward slide that has been under way for the last few years. The plummeting sales tax revenue, pockmarked roads and missed opportunities on recruiting businesses have taken their toll. Dallas needs a home run. And the May 3 bond election is delivering the pitch."[107]

The "plight" of downtown did receive notice. Strategically, downtown's centrality was moderated, but not overlooked. With a spin that was surprisingly rare in the "Build a Better Dallas" campaign, the *News*'s downtown reporter, Victoria Loe Hicks, complained: "Talk is cheap. Resuscitating downtown is not. So perhaps it's a big *duh!* that downtown got stiffed in the $555 million May bond package." The rejected items included funds for building renovations, parkland, a homeless center, Performing Arts Center construction, Dallas Public Library, Arts District, and Dealey Plaza. "All 15 council members have been known to wax eloquent about how special, how vital, how indispensable downtown is to the health of the city. But when money is on the table, 14 of them are besieged by voices crying loudly—and often justifiably—that every penny is needed for streets, parks and libraries closer to home."[108] That those voices from different parts of the city were heard at all constitutes a historic reversal.

"Exhorted to 'Build with Bonds,' Dallas voters declared their willingness Saturday to do just that, granting easy passage to all 17 propositions in the city's $555 million bond package," trumpeted the *Dallas Morning News* on May 4, 2003. "In return they are to get hundreds of miles of improved roads, scores of spruced up parks, a top-notch animal shelter, new libraries and fire and police stations, better arts facilities and projects designed to spur economic development in the southern sector."[109]

"Build a Better Dallas" was a more modest slogan than a "city with no limits" or a "city reaching for greatness," and less melodramatic than "Dallas at the Tipping Point." It served implicitly as an alternative and counter to the more grandiose imperative: "do it!" Does "Build a Better Dallas" begin to serve the city and guide it more appropriately, effectively, and fairly than "reaching for greatness"? Can "Build a Better Dallas" begin to counter the city's growing "big divide" of social inequality and its articulation in the urban landscape?[110] Does "Build a Better Dallas" respond to "Dallas at the Tipping Point" and "two cities"? Does it offer an alternative perspective that promotes a more integrated and inclusive vision and set of goals for a new and different Dallas Way for the twenty-first century? Can it eclipse and in time replace the Dallas Ways of the nineteenth and the twentieth centuries? Has Dallas begun a fundamental process of redefinition and transformation as the twentieth century turned into the twenty-first century?

The resounding defeat of the "strong mayor" option for charter revision in May 2005[111] suggests that it has not. In the wake of successful efforts to frighten Dallasites with worst-case scenarios of undemocratic mayors without checks or balances, the electorate rejected a controversial plan to increase the power of the mayor. Mayor Miller's limited popularity combined with higher than expected turnout in predominantly African American South Dallas to confuse any simple sense of causation. But the Dallas Way withstood the perceived threat of a powerful political figure in control of the city. There are good reasons for limited expectations of major changes that promise to take the city in new directions. The *Dallas Morning News* reflected the uncertainties and ambiguities of the present moment and the precariousness of Dallas and the Dallas Way in the title of its editorial marking Dallas's 150th birthday: "The New Can-Do City: At 150, Dallas Is Rebounding, but It Needs Help."[112]

These recent developments raise basic questions about the status and future of the Dallas Way, and, equally if not quite synonymously, the state and future of Dallas. They offer an opportunity for taking stock and resetting agendas and priorities. The bond election, mayoral races, and earlier bond elections for schools, the arena, and Trinity River improvements may be the result of unusually adroit political manipulations. Alternatively, these elections may be early signs of a new and shifting politics of geographic self-interest as it plays across the entire city, north and south, east and west; Anglo, African American, and Hispanic. Miller's losing notion of a "return to basics" may yet gain support from a general consensus over minimally necessary actions. However, these basics could fall into new fissures of a fragmented city. By themselves, any of these viewpoints may be construed on balance as relatively constructive or destructive to the well-being of differently situated residents of Dallas.

THE PRESENCE OF THE PAST

Dallas contends with two great complications. First, the city has long struggled unsuccessfully against its weak identity, image, and perception of itself as urban place and space. Dallas's denial of its own history as well as its recent gestures at a revisionist history contribute to this dilemma, combined with mimetic practice that fails to examine those cities taken as models. Second, Dallas lacks a foundation in metropolitan integration. Indeed, it remains one of the most spatially segregated cities in the United States, whether measured along lines of race and ethnicity or of class. Metropolitan integration means not only social integration but also integration with respect to economic and social development, communications, transportation, and services, creating a general sense of connectedness throughout the city and its environs. Some observers term this "community" or "identity," but I hesitate to reduce it to such hackneyed terms. Persistent fragmentation has been exacerbated by the political self-assertion of more autonomous suburbs and limited moves toward regionalism. The *Dallas Morning News* acknowledges the need to "forge ties" across the city in order to "define Dallas."[113] Dallas's fragmentation obstructs regional planning and cooperation as well as urban consensus. Both complications reflect a great gap between the city as conceived and lived in pieces and the city as a whole. Some districts are dominant both practically and rhetorically, while the center and periphery diverge. The ideology and methods of the Dallas Way were so deeply flawed that they contributed to their own demise. Dallas's urban (or antiurban) visions must be reimagined, broadly and popularly.

"What does Dallas want?" ask the *Dallas Morning News,* the Dallas Institute for Humanities and Culture, and other commentators. They remove the question from the contexts of time and place that are needed to make it answerable, and to make its answers reasonable and responsible. This book replaces that question with a prior one: What has Dallas wrought? What are the consequences of its past for the present and the alternative choices it must face today? These questions are answered best in historical context, not in the abstract, ad hoc, or mythic modes often essayed.[114] These issues are not limited to Dallas. Yet, for better and for worse, Dallas has its differences, or at least its excessive sameness, which make these issues especially salient and visible.[115]

For me, history is more complicated, less linear, and less certain than it is for Tatum and others whose view of the past is tinted by nostalgia and partiality. In my view, Dallas history is a testament to the struggles of all peoples in a myriad of places. The trick, if there is one, lies in appreciating that these qualities enhance the value of history rather than limiting it. History is a mode of understanding ourselves and others in the special provenance of time, space, and human agency. History is particularly useful for criticizing arguments that lack grounding and for penetrating through myths that aim to replace history. History can help us explore the complicated but rich interweaving of myth and history that underlie Dallas's stories. While Tatum and other revisionists resurrect and refurbish the major myths of Dallas, I probe their uses and their limits. Dallasites would benefit from knowing a local history that is more closely aligned to the circumstances of their lives.

In "Deep in the Myths of Texas," an op-ed in the *New York Times* in 2003, journalist Mimi Swartz reminds us of the imperative to reexamine and relinquish myths, including those that we live by. Swartz examines the Texan (and American) emphasis on "moving on," a common phrase and approach that assumes an immediate "bouncing back" from the past, whether or not true change has taken place. Texas has changed, she says, "yet the stories we tell ourselves about ourselves, particularly in times of crisis, have hardly changed at all." Swartz provides a useful Dallas example: "The Kennedy assassination, too, was pressed into the same mythological mold: the shame of a president's murder committed in full view of the world, transformed Dallas from a mean, redneck city into a more circumspect and worldly place." She is right to conclude, "It's a rare Texan who can move on from the myth, even when, maybe, he should."[116] We might ask, too, whether Dallas is able to move beyond its myths.

The themes and forces of Dallas history come together in turn-of-the-century Dallas. Key pieces of a Dallas puzzle include its lack of historical sense, of identity, symbol, or icon, as well as its fears of failing and falling. The Dallas Way of monumental, mimetic development by purchase, stealth, and theft, with its great concentrations of wealth and power and center city focus, provides no substitute or replacement.[117] Today, the Dallas Way still sits precariously close to the precipice of a slippery slope, even as it seems reinvigorated by new uses and adaptations. Far from dead and gone, it has powerful supporters as well as a lengthy and mostly proud lineage in the city. The Dallas Way rests upon a foundation in myth, which for many has become its history. Even when Dallas's new historical revisionists move to "correct" or "refute" these myths, they fail to understand their power and importance and the ways in which myths are inextricably intertwined with their "revised" history.[118] The problem with myth is not that it is wrong. Persistent myths prove useful in explaining what and why things happened, at the same time that they distort visions, introducing and perpetuating biases and blind spots. As Mimi Swartz relates, myth blurs alternate ways of seeing and understanding, and therefore reduces our choices, sometimes drastically and dangerously.

We close with timely words for Dallas from policy scholar Royce Hanson, former dean of the School of Social Science at UTD: "Dallas is less in control of its own destiny than ever before. Reinventing its governance and adapting democratic institutions and processes to cope better with complexity is not surrender to chaos. It represents instead coming to grips with reality, shedding the old civic myths and the affinity for social control for a new vision of the city as a diverse seedbed of democracy, civic virtue, and entrepreneurial energy. What is not practical, in the truest construction of that term, is to continue a system that neither works nor advances the practice of urban democracy."[119] Hanson joins Di Mambro in situating Dallas firmly in the context of globalization, which subjects it to forces that local leaders cannot possibly control. The question is whether this loss of control will reveal, finally, the necessity of abandoning the Dallas Way, or whether city leaders will cling to its fragments and fictions, once again using it to steer a disintegrating city in the direction they feel is best for all, continuing to make and unmake the city. As it has been throughout its history, Dallas is at a crossroads. The stakes were never higher, the costs of failure to act never greater.

APPENDIX A.

DALLAS'S HISTORICAL DEVELOPMENT

BEFORE 1840: NATIVE PEOPLES; INTERNATIONAL
CONTACTS, TRADE, AND WARFARE

FOUNDING THE TOWN, 1840S–1870S

1840S–1850S CROSSROADS, SETTLEMENT, TOWN FOUNDING

- Settlement founded at intersection of east–west and north–south routes; Peters Colony and La Réunion agricultural settlements nearby
- Trading post, ferry, gristmill, hotel, newspaper; county seat

1850S–1870S MARKET TOWN

- Agricultural service center, including entrepôt, exchange, market, processing, and manufacturing; transportation hub, including railroad, communications, and distribution
- Town chartered
- Civil War and Emancipation, followed by failed Reconstruction; race relations marked by restoration of white supremacy, rapid resort to violence
- Urban entrepreneurial visions and developments

FROM TOWN TO CITY, 1870S–1910S

1870S–1890S REGIONAL COMMERCIAL SERVICE CENTER

- City charter replaces town charter
- Railway termini, manufactories, and mercantile establishments; institutional growth and diversification, including banks, Board of Trade,

insurance companies, commercial hotels, office buildings, post office building

- Urban amenities: gas lighting, waterworks, telephones, electric lights, street paving
- Residential development on the fringes of city center
- Public and private schools; *Dallas Morning News* and *Times Herald;* formation of labor organizations and other voluntary societies; opera house, baseball

1890S–1910S DEVELOPING CITY

- Urban maturation: mass transit with electric street cars; central business district grows "tall" buildings; commercial and industrial growth and diversification
- Geographic expansion with functional and residential distinctions and annexation of developing areas on the city's margins
- Institutions form: Carnegie Library, new opera house, symphony, motion picture shows, schools and colleges; hospitals; football, golf

FROM CITY TO METROPOLIS, 1900S–1940S

1900S–1930S MODERN CITY:
ECONOMIC GROWTH AND POLITICAL CONFLICTS

- Industry, including major Ford auto plant, insurance, oil
- Downtown development: rise of skyline; Federal Reserve Bank; new Cotton Exchange; Neiman Marcus department store; entertainment district
- Physical improvement: infrastructure and utilities, including water reservoirs; interurban railroads, airport
- Geographic expansion: close-in suburbs and autonomous Park cities, racially segregated residential developments
- Social conflicts: major strikes in building trades, utilities, garment industry; public lynching of African American taken by mob from courthouse; Ku Klux Klan
- Proposals for progressive reforms by various interests, including women's groups, labor, socialists, elites; adoption of commission form of government; first formal city plan
- Southern Methodist University; radio stations
- Beginnings of national recognition and identity

1930S–1940S MODERN CITY: "THE DALLAS WAY"

- Restructuring the social order, economy, polity, and space: R. L. Thornton, the Dallas Citizens Council, and the Citizens Charter Association; probusiness urban political machine, including use of state and federal funds; city council/city manager form of municipal government; antilabor activism; development of industrial districts
- 1936 Texas State Centennial
- World War II, with federal defense spending, aerospace and high-tech industries, in-migration, population growth; laying foundation for postwar growth, e.g., by using public funds to lure new industries; replacing mass transit and interurban trains with highways
- Civil rights movement
- Growing national and international attention

POSTWAR PROSPERITY UNEVENLY SHARED, 1940S–1960S

1940S–1950S EXPANSION UNLIMITED

- Growth on the periphery and at the center: central business district, rise of skyline, new facilities downtown; suburban residential sprawl; commercial and industrial decentralization and deconcentration; relocation and local expansion of high-tech, financial, and service sector, manufacturing industries; population growth, in-migration, and leapfrog suburbanization
- Expansion beyond the geographic bounds of the city, eroding tax base, decline of public services; metropolitanism, with regional planning but separate suburban and city polities and policies; uses and abuses of governmental relations, state and federal monies

1950S–1960S BUT PROSPERITY UNEVENLY SHARED

- Deepening racial-ethnic and socioeconomic divisions between downtown and the suburban north and the south and west sides of the city; deteriorating race relations, growing tensions, racial violence; legal struggles over African American and Hispanic representation on city council, voting rights, school integration, access to and quality of facilities, integration of businesses, housing, and jobs; politics of right-wing ideological extremism

- Major-league football and baseball
- Kennedy assassination and the "shame" of Dallas

METROPOLITAN CRISIS AND UNCERTAINTY,
1960s–2000s

1960s–1980s Metropolitan Crisis

- Economic booms and busts, with declines in energy (oil) price and supply sectors and real estate, threatening well-being and future prospects of city; selective and incomplete pursuit of the late twentieth-century millennium, with growing disparities along lines of class, race and ethnicity, and center city/suburbs; problems of municipal finance
- Responses to the Kennedy assassination: Goals for Dallas, symbolic and substantial redevelopment with city hall, art museum, concert hall, and regional international airport; massive image reconstruction and renewed but uneven, unequal growth
- Contradictory politics of center city remolding with growth on and beyond the edges; poverty, lack of jobs, few public services in the inner city, especially south and west; desegregation and resegregation; violence and crime, real and perceived; urban problems spread to the suburbs with spatial growth, migration, aging, and increasing heterogeneity; pursuing consumption and computers at home and at work; internationalization of economy and population
- A "new" Dallas, as a "city with no limits" confronts socioeconomic realities; the partial end of the "Dallas Way" as "democracy" comes to Dallas; protests and reform efforts directed at Dallas Independent School District and Dallas City Council continue; housing, equal opportunity, and affirmative action join political and educational rights; Hispanics actively seek change; struggles marked by violence as whites forcefully resist desegregation
- New levels of civic insecurity and fear of national and international embarrassment
- Dallas Cowboys; *Dallas* the TV series

1990s–2000s Uncertainty in a "Postmodern" Metroplex

- Political representation of African and Hispanic Americans and of inner-city neighborhoods achieved just when financial resources required for urban reconstruction disappear; controversies over investments in downtown vs. infrastructure; unresolved debate over restructuring city government

- In measurable demographic, economic, and political terms and in the presumed, often-repeated social and cultural dimensions, "quality of life" in the city proper declines in face of suburban ascendancy. Overall, metropolitan Dallas and the Dallas–Fort Worth "Metroplex" are seen as gaining in most dimensions. But the spread of prosperity—geographically, racially and ethnically, socially—is very uneven, and inequality may be deepening.
- Dallas "at the tipping point" and "at the crossroads"; costs of a "city without history" and "with no limits"; unresolved issues of race, ethnicity, gender, environment, education, and equality

APPENDIX B. CHRONOLOGY OF

DALLAS HISTORY

1542   In June–July, Luis Moscoso and survivors of DeSoto's Spanish exploring expedition cross northeastern part of present Dallas County, seeking route to Mexico City.

1712   Antoine Crozat and Bernard de La Harpe, French traders from Louisiana, visit Anadarko, native people living near Trinity River.

1760   Friar Calahorra y Saenz, Roman Catholic missionary from Nacogdoches, visits area, renaming river (previously called Arkikosa) Trinity, because of its three forks.

1818   Caddo native people drive Cherokees eastward after battle near three forks of the Trinity River,

FOUNDING THE TOWN

1840   Col. William Cooke surveys National Road from the Brazos to the Red rivers and names it Preston Road.

1841   John Neely Bryan, a trader, founds white settlement on his land claim and recruits families to join him.

       Although the origin of the town's name is not certain, most likely the town is named for U.S. naval hero Commodore Alexander James Dallas, and the county is named for his brother George Mifflin Dallas, vice president under James K. Polk.

1842   Peters' Colony Company emigrants settle near Dallas. With emigrants primarily from Kentucky and England, this immigration was organized and promoted by British and American investors who were granted land by the then-independent Republic of Texas.

1843   Republic of Texas signs peace treaty with Native chiefs to make the area safe for white settlers.

1844   Bryan appointed postmaster; his cabin serves as post office.

      J. P. Dumas surveys and plats Bryan's town site and sets the center block aside for a courthouse square.

1845   Trading post established at Cedar Springs, three miles from Dallas.

      Judge Hord settles Hord's Ridge, later known as Oak Cliff.

      Dallas votes twenty-nine to three for annexation of the Republic of Texas to the United States.

1846   Dallas County organized with Dallas as temporary county seat. Bryan's cabin serves as courthouse.

      Bryan begins ferry service across the Trinity River.

      Church organized by Orin Hatch, Methodist minister.

      Horse-powered gristmill erected on west side of river.

1847   Henry Harter builds hotel, the Dallas Tavern.

1848   Newspaper, *Cedar Snag* (later renamed *Dallas Herald*), founded by James Wellington "Weck" Latimer, who brings a printing press and piano to Dallas.

1850   Dallas wins run-off election with Hord's Ridge to become county seat.

      Census: town population 430, county 1,743.

1851   Cotton gin begins operations.

1852   Commercial cotton, twenty-two bales, shipped by barge from Dallas down the Trinity River to Galveston.

      M. Guillot sets up carriage factory.

      Crutchfield House, a leading hotel, opens.

1853   Alexander Cockrell purchases John Neely Bryan's property in Dallas for $7,000.

Brick plant opens.

"Legal" hanging takes place in Dallas for the first time—of Jane Elkins, a slave, convicted of murdering her master. Whites' fears of slave rebellion contributed to their action.

1854   La Réunion, French Fourierist utopian community led by Victor Considerant, formed west of Dallas, with French, Swiss, and Belgian members.

1855   Alexander Cockrell opens sawmill; lumber for frame construction available locally.

Cockrell builds bridge over the Trinity, located at the foot of Commerce Street.

Dallas builds new two-story brick courthouse.

John M. Crockett builds first two-story residence in town.

1856   Town charter granted; Dr. Samuel B. Pryor elected mayor.

Stagecoach line serves Dallas.

1857   La Réunion disbands after repeated crop failures. Most of its leaders return to Europe, but many colonists move to Dallas. The Swiss form a colony outside of town; the connecting road is later named Swiss Avenue.

Brewery established by a La Réunion emigrant.

Subscription library formed.

1858   Alexander Cockrell shot to death on the street by the town marshal, who owed him money.

Trinity River floods and washes out wooden bridge.

1859   Sarah Horton Cockrell, Alexander's widow, who became a real estate developer, opens Dallas's finest hotel, the St. Nicholas.

Dallas County Agricultural and Mechanical Association holds first fair in county.

1860   Fire destroys town. Two buildings survive—the brick courthouse and a brick hotel. In rebuilding, brick and stone replace frame construction. White Dallasites suspected the fire had been set by slaves at the instigation of abolitionists, and three black men were hanged by a lynch mob along the banks of the Trinity River.

1861   Dallas voters choose secession from the Union, 741 to 237. Four
        companies form to fight for Confederacy.

        Dallas serves as supply center for the Confederate army west of
        the Mississippi River.

1864   Ladies Welfare Association establishes soldiers' home.

1865   At end of war, 1,250 Dallas residents take oath of amnesty. John
        Crockett appointed mayor by Reconstruction government.

        Dallas ex-slaves form several Freedman's towns. "Deep Ellum" and
        "Little Egypt" later became known for African American blues
        singers and guitarists, Blind Lemon Jefferson and Huddie "Lead-
        belly" Ledbetter.

1866   Trinity floods, isolating town for a week.

1867   Gaston and Campbell form Dallas's first bank.

        J. R. Tennyson opens saddle shop.

1868   *Job Boat No. 1* travels from Galveston to Dallas; passage takes
        more than half a year. Steamboat *Sallie Hayes* built and launched
        in Dallas for Trinity River commerce, loaded with cotton and
        sent off for Galveston, but the water was too low. After a few trips
        to Magnolia, just southwest of Palestine, the boat hit a snag and
        sank.

        In first Reconstruction election, African American voters outnum-
        ber Anglos.

        Ku Klux Klan, violent white supremacist group, formed.

1869   Dallas Jockey Club forms; tent road show performs.

        Systematic extermination of great buffalo herds makes Dallas boom
        as hide market.

1870   Houston & Texas Central Railroad reaches Corsicana and plans
        a line to McKinney that would bypass Dallas. Dallas businessmen
        pay $5,000 in cash and deed 115 acres of land and three miles of
        right-of-way north and south of Main Street to get line rerouted
        into city.

        Census population 3,000.

FROM TOWN TO CITY

1871   City charter replaces town charter.

Dallas County Medical Society formed.

Dallas County Bank receives state charter.

1872   Texas state legislature amends Texas & Pacific Railroad charter, approving a line from Memphis to El Paso. Dallas lawyer adds clause requiring that the line, originally routed far to the south, cross the Trinity River within one mile of Browder Springs in the southern part of Dallas. Bonus of $100,000 and twenty-five acres of land in East Dallas persuades company to extend tracks into Dallas.

Sarah Horton Cockrell finances iron toll bridge across the Trinity.

Terminus merchants, such as E. M. Kahn and the Sanger Brothers, move to Dallas and establish mercantile businesses.

East Dallas begins as Houston & Texas Central Railroad community outside city's legal boundary.

On July 16, locomotive pulls into East Dallas's new wood-frame Union Depot.

Dallas County builds its fourth courthouse.

Dr. Matthew Cornelius appointed "city health doctor."

1873   Texas & Pacific locomotive arrives February 22, making Dallas the terminus for two major railroads.

Mule-drawn streetcars begin service.

Field Opera House opens.

National financial crisis stops construction of the Texas & Pacific route to Fort Worth; Dallas becomes the collection center for hides and leather.

1874   Gaston Building erected to house influx of cotton traders.

Artificial gas lighting installed.

National Bank chartered; Board of Trade established.

1875   New Commercial Hotel built; elaborate LeGrand hotel opens.

1876   Southwestern Life Insurance Company establishes home office in Dallas.

Dallas Musical Society organized.

1877   Dallas voters approve public school system; first school opens in 1883.

1878   Sam Bass and his gang rob trains on all sides of Dallas.

1879   Private company builds Browder Springs waterworks and pumps water to standpipe at Main and Harwood, in center of town. City purchases waterworks in 1881.

Telephone installed, connecting waterworks and fire department.

Buckner Orphans Home founded.

1880   Courthouse burns; granite structure with a square clock tower replaces it.

Census population 10,358.

1881   Telephone service begins. First line in the state links Philip Sanger's Cedars mansion with Sanger Brothers department store.

Electric lights installed; plant installed in 1882.

Town of East Dallas incorporated.

Knights of Labor, national labor union and reform group, organizes locally.

1882   Main and Elm Streets paved with wood blocks.

1883   Dallas Opera House, seating 1,200, opens, featuring popular concerts.

New, permanent site for post office purchased.

Manufacturing of cotton gins begins.

Railway workers walk out, in the city's first strike.

Dallas Amateur Baseball Association forms.

1884   Cedar Springs Road macadamized by county.

Idlewild Club, exclusive social club, organized.

1885   A. H. Belo of *Galveston News* founds *Dallas Morning News* and names G. B. Dealey editor.

Typographical Union No. 173 chartered on October 6, six days after *Morning News* begins publication. Carpenters local union forms in 1886. By 1892, Dallas has at least fifteen labor organizations and a Trades Assembly (later renamed Central Labor Council). A major goal at this time was an eight-hour workday.

1886   Dallas State Fair and Exposition receives charter and secures eighty acres of swampland, site of present Fair Park; first State Fair of Texas held.

1887   J. S. Armstrong and T. L. Marsalis end long partnership in a dispute about selling their land on Hord's Ridge. Armstrong moves to Dallas and later develops Highland Park as an elite, legally independent residential area within the boundaries of Dallas. Marsalis opens Oak Cliff residential district just south and west of Dallas, connected by steam railway.

Fair and Exposition consolidates with rival fair that had taken place concurrently on a different site; East Dallas site becomes Fairlands residential addition.

Dallas joins new Texas Baseball League.

John Henry Brown writes history of Dallas County.

1888   North Texas Building, at six stories Dallas's first skyscraper, built.

Cotton mill established.

Famous actor Thomas W. Keene visits Dallas and organizes Elks Lodge.

Times Herald forms by consolidation of *Evening Times* and *Dallas (Evening) Herald.*

1889   Electric streetcars put into service.

1890   Census population 36,067, making Dallas the largest city in Texas.

Courthouse burns and is replaced with a red sandstone and granite Romanesque structure, still standing, fondly called "Old Red."

Trinity River floods a two-mile-wide area.

Dallas annexes East Dallas and buys East Dallas waterworks.

Town of Oak Cliff incorporates.

1891   First major football game played; teams represent Dallas and Fort Worth.

1893   Dallas Commercial Club, predecessor of Chamber of Commerce, forms.

Steamboat *H. A. Harvey* reaches Dallas from Galveston after sixty-seven days, raising hopes of commercial navigation on Trinity River.

Oriental Hotel opens, famed throughout region.

North Texas National Bank, Central National Bank, and Bankers & Merchants fail in national economic panic; State National and Ninth National Banks fail in 1894.

1894   Army engineers begin to survey Trinity River from Dallas.

1895   State legislature bans world's heavyweight fight in Dallas.

1896   Dallas Commercial Club sponsors Record Crossing dam to establish a water route to Galveston.

Golf first played in Dallas.

1897   Moving picture shown in Dallas.

Modern hospital, St. Paul's Sanitarium, built.

1898   Linz Building, tallest fireproof building in the South, built.

Terpsichorean Club, sponsor of annual society balls, formed.

Street railway workers go on strike with substantial public support.

1899   "Horseless carriage" arrives. Dallasite Ned Green is first in Texas to own an automobile.

Andrew Carnegie donates $50,000 for Dallas public library.

Cleaner Dallas league organized to improve urban environment by promoting sanitation and end the use of small streams as sewers.

American Federation of Labor grants charter to Dallas Trades Assembly. Assembly existed until 1910 when the Central Labor Council was chartered.

1900   Elm Street paved with asphalt, a material used previously only in the East.

College of Medicine, University of Dallas established.

Dallas Golf Club, predecessor of Dallas Country Club, organized.

Dallas Symphony plays first concert.

Census population 42,638.

FROM CITY TO METROPOLIS

1901   Cement plant built.

Dallas Public Library opens; art exhibit held there.

New Dallas Opera House opens at Main and St. Paul streets.

1902   Art school established.

Dallas ranks first in world in output of saddles.

Electric Interurban Railroad begins service to Fort Worth. By 1923, service includes Sherman, Waco, Corsicana, and Terrell.

Confederate Reunion brings three thousand veterans and one hundred thousand visitors to Dallas.

1903   Oak Cliff residents vote for annexation to Dallas in 1904 on condition that sale of liquor is prohibited and artesian water system is retained.

1904   Wireless messages transmitted between Fort Worth and Dallas.

George Clifton Edwards begins publishing *Laborer,* with radical, prolabor views sympathetic to socialism and advocating equal rights for African Americans. Radicals and socialists, especially in Socialist Coalition of 1904–17, worked for education, improved working conditions, and restrictions on child labor, and were active voices in municipal politics.

1905   Munger Place opens as Dallas's first residential neighborhood with deeds restricting home ownership to whites.

Majestic Theatre built; Metropolitan Opera of New York comes to Dallas on tour.

President Theodore Roosevelt visits Dallas.

1906   Dallas adopts commission form of municipal government.

1907   Dallas Cotton Exchange chartered.

Herbert Marcus and Carrie Neiman open dress shop, starting Neiman Marcus department store.

Praetorian Building, Dallas's first steel-framed skyscraper, built with fourteen stories.

Highland Park opens as a legally independent residential area restricted to whites.

1908   The most devastating flood in Dallas's history; the Trinity crests at 51'3".

1909   *Dallas News* starts campaign in support of a formal city plan.

1910   Airplane lands in Dallas.

Dallas City Plan and Improvement League organized. Dallas Park Board hires George Kessler, Kansas City landscape architect, to develop city plan.

City purchases land for White Rock Lake to provide a reserve water supply.

Lynching of Allen Brooks, an African American accused of raping a three-year-old Anglo girl. An organized white mob took him from the courthouse at the time of his trial and hanged him before thousands of onlookers. Postcards showing his mutilated body hanging from the Elks Arch circulated nationally.

Census population 92,104.

1911   One hundred ten street lamps installed on Elm Street.

Socialist Party has about four hundred members eligible to vote in municipal elections.

1912   Oak Cliff (later called Houston Street) viaduct to Oak Cliff opens, acclaimed as the longest concrete structure in the world.

Adolphus Hotel built.

1913   City Criminal Courts Building erected.

1914   Dallas chosen as site for Eleventh District Federal Reserve Bank under the Federal Reserve Act of 1913.

Ford Motor Company plant, producing up to five thousand cars per year, opens near downtown.

1915   Southern Methodist University dedicated. J. J. Armstrong donated 133 acres for its Parks Cities' campus.

City Welfare Department established.

1916   Union Terminal, built at a cost of $6 million, opens.

Labor Temple dedicated by Governor James E. ("Pa") Ferguson.

City ordinance allowing residential racial segregation on a block-by-block basis adopted; it was reaffirmed in the early 1930s despite civil rights protests. Although found to be unconstitutional in court rulings from the 1930s and after, the practice continues extra-legally on a de facto basis and by banks' and mortgage lenders' redlining areas to prevent financing home ownership by blacks.

1917   Dallas businessmen purchase land for private airport. On U.S. entry into World War I, Love Field becomes an Army Air Corps Training base.

Dallas votes for prohibition, 10,625 to 8,551; saloons close October 20.

Civic Federation, with Elmer Scott as director, formed; it holds Dallas Open Forum in City Hall Auditorium from 1919 to 1937.

1918   Camp Dick established at Fair Park.

Great Influenza pandemic taxes medical facilities.

1919   Auto sales in Dallas exceed other cities in region.

Greatest strike in Dallas history takes place when building trades throughout North Texas go out in sympathy with striking linemen of Dallas Power & Light Company. Dallas's major labor unions decline in the 1920s. Labor organization splits over organizing by workers' skill level and race.

1920   George Kessler revises his first city plan to meet the needs of rapidly growing city.

City-county levee improvement district formed to channel the Trinity River.

Dallas Little Theatre begins.

Census population 158,976.

1921   New Ku Klux Klan appears, with white supremacist and anti-immigrant program.

Majestic Theatre, palatial movie and vaudeville house, opens on Elm Street.

• WRR, first municipal radio station in the United States, established.

1922   The twenty-nine-story Magnolia (Mobil) Petroleum Company Building completed, with lighted Pegasus revolving on its roof. For more than twenty years, it stands as the tallest building west of the Mississippi River.

WFAA radio station established.

Ku Klux Klan candidates carry election in Dallas County. The *Dallas Morning News* under Dealey campaigned against the KKK and its influence in local government. Its public opposition, and perhaps its exposure of Klan violence, help turn the tide of opinion in the business community against the Klan in 1924.

1923   Dallas removes Pacific Avenue railroad tracks, which limited growth of central business district to three streets; work completed in 1926.

Texas Scottish Rite Hospital for crippled children opens.

Dallas dentist Hiram Wesley Evans, Imperial Wizard of the Ku Klux Klan, greeted by 75,000 citizens on "Klan Day" at the State Fair.

1924   Lake Dallas water reservoir construction begins.

1925   Dealey Plaza built on the site of Bryan's first cabin.

New Cotton Exchange Building constructed.

Half-Century Club formed by fifty-year residents.

1926   Dallas begins bus service to outlying areas as an auxiliary to streetcar lines. City limits now include more than forty-two square miles, one hundred times larger than Bryan's original plat.

Work begins on Garza Dam in Denton County to create Lake Dallas and solve Dallas's water problem.

1927   Southern Methodist University completes McFarland Auditorium, Dallas's largest assembly hall.

C. E. Ulrickson proposes a city plan to develop a water and park system and improve streets, including Triple Underpass near Dealey Plaza. $24 million city bond issue approved.

Santa Fe Building erected, claimed to be largest single office and railroad terminal building in region.

1928   Dallas purchases Love Field for municipal airport. By 1930, Dallas is air transportation hub with overnight service to New York and Los Angeles. Hensley Field purchased by Dallas and leased to U.S. government for $1.00 per year.

Ground broken for Trinity River levee and reclamation project.

1929   Dallas's first zoning ordinance adopted.

Dallas Community Trust formed.

Trinity River floods in May, causing extensive damage.

1930   "Dad" Joiner strikes oil in East Texas oil fields, one hundred miles from Dallas.

Dallas voters adopt council-manager form of municipal government.

New Federal Building and Post Office opens.

Cotton Bowl, seating 46,400, built.

Great Depression felt in Dallas. Compared to other U.S. cities, however, Dallas's experience was not severe.

Census population 260,475.

1931   Private enterprise encouraged to undertake new construction in order to alleviate unemployment. Lone Star Gas, Dallas Power & Light, and Tower Petroleum build new offices.

Public works programs also create jobs. Dallas officially submits Trinity River channelization project for federal financing; WPA funds pay for Triple Underpass construction.

1932   City and county jointly apply to Reconstruction Finance Corporation for $450,000 loan for relief work programs.

Trinity Channel and levees work completed. Levee District, created from reclaimed land, extends from Bachman Lake to the Santa Fe Railroad.

Highland Park Shopping Center, one of the first in the United States with all stores facing away from the streets, opens.

Bonnie Parker and Clyde Barrow meet in Dallas and begin a two-year crime spree that attracts national attention.

1933   Only one Dallas bank, State Trust and Savings Bank, fails to reopen after bank holiday.

Heavy majority in Dallas votes for repeal of Prohibition.

1934   Dallas's bid for the site of the Texas Centennial Exhibition successful. Civic promoter and banker Robert L. "Bob" Thornton organizes high bid of $7.8 million and a promise that the Centennial would take place regardless of level of government expenditures.

Dallas chosen over Houston and San Antonio despite the fact that Dallas did not exist at the time of the founding of the Republic of Texas. City receives $6 million in state and federal funds. The project is instrumental in bringing the city out of the Depression and into national attention.

1935   Strike-related violence results in jailing of eighteen striking women garment workers. International Ladies Garment Workers Union attempts to organize garment workers in Dallas; it is forcefully opposed by an Open Shop Association, business interests, and major newspapers.

1936   President Franklin Delano Roosevelt attends opening ceremonies of the Texas Centennial. Attendance estimated at ten million. Centennial included a Hall of Negro Life and segregated restrooms. The tradition of "Negro Day," instituted to maintain segregation at Fair, long stood as a target for civil rights activists.

African American leaders form Progressive Voters League to organize the vote in support of change. Along with the *Dallas Express*, the NAACP, African American ministers, other activists, and supporting Anglos, the long and difficult movement for equal rights and opportunities begins. Key early leaders included A. Maceo Smith, Rev. Maynard Jackson, Juanita Craft.

Museum of Fine Arts opens in Fair Park.

Triple Underpass completed, linking Main, Commerce, and Elm streets with Oak Cliff.

1937   The Dallas Citizens Council, an elite group of business leaders, organized to reform city government. Along with its political wing, the Dallas Citizens Charter Association, it exerts major influence on city's political, economic, social, cultural life for at least a half century.

Pan-American Exposition and Pan-American Olympic Games take place on Centennial grounds.

First federally funded low-income housing built.

Strike of millinery workers and Congress of Industrial Organizations campaign to organize Ford Automobile assembly plant encounter concerted opposition, leading to numerous acts of violence. Governor sends a detail of Texas Rangers to restore order. Local business and political resources deployed to resist unionization of work force, as documented in report of National Labor Relations Bureau.

1938   Dallas cited as an economic bright spot in midst of continuing national depression.

1939   Dallas Grand Opera Association brings the Metropolitan Opera Company annually until 1986.

1940   Estimated population 294,734.

POSTWAR PROSPERITY UNEVENLY SHARED

1941   North American Aviation and the Naval Air Station build assembly plants in Grand Prairie, west of Dallas.

As United States enters World War II, Dallas-based petroleum and aviation industries become major parts of war effort and recipients of federal contracts.

1942   Dallas enters era of expansion. During this year, 41,000 residential units are built to house employees of war-related industries.

1943   Mercantile Bank Building, with thirty-one stories, eclipses Magnolia Building as Dallas's tallest.

Harland Bartholomew, city planner from St. Louis, prepares a new master plan proposing neighborhood concepts for subdivision developments, community responsibility for housing, and coordinated programs for parks and schools, as well as centrally located civic center.

On December 8, incendiary bomb factory burns. Fueled by seventeen carloads of magnesium, the devastating fire is visible from a one-hundred-mile radius.

1945   Voters approve bond issue to finance construction of civic center, but project is shelved and its funds diverted to build roads and extend city services to growing suburban areas.

1946   Trinity Industrial District opens on reclaimed land in the Levee District. Brookhollow and Empire Central Districts follow. Within a decade, the expansion encompasses ten thousand acres.

Dallas Citizens Council prompts founding of Greater Dallas Planning Council to promote "continuous progress and improvement of the city and its environs."

1947   Construction of estimated $10 million Central Expressway begins.

Margo Jones opens theatre in Fair Park.

1948   Chance Vought moves from Connecticut to Grand Prairie, described as biggest industrial relocation in U.S. history. Citizens Council action ensures the move by arranging for lengthening of runways at the World War II airfield.

KRLD granted television broadcast license; live telecast from WBAP radio studio.

Last interurban rail line suspends service.

1949   Dallas begins to construct series of reservoirs to provide sufficient water for suburbs.

Voters amend city charter so city council candidate with largest number of voters becomes mayor.

1950   Census population 434,462.

1951   "Big Tex" statue designed and installed for the opening of the State Fair of Texas: 52 feet tall, waist 23 feet, boot size 70, 90 gallon hat. "He" has greeted visitors with "How-dy Folks!" ever since.

3,500-unit West Dallas low-income public housing project completed, largest in the United States until 1961.

1953   Dallas enters another phase of rapid expansion after Korean War's end.

Robert L. "Bob" Thornton, founder of the Citizens Council and long-time civic leader, elected to first of four terms as mayor.

New Republic Bank building completed.

1955   Dallas NAACP chapter files suit in federal court to force the public schools to desegregate in compliance with the 1954 Supreme Court ruling in *Brown v. Board of Education*. The court rules against the suit, stating that equal opportunity for white and black children exists.

Dallas Public Library building replaces Carnegie Library.

New City Hall nears completion.

Great Southwest Corporation prepares a comprehensive master plan and begins to develop a 5,500-acre site between Dallas and Fort Worth. Six Flags Over Texas completed in 1961.

Development of trade center complex on Stemmons Freeway begins.

1956   Dallas discontinues streetcar service.

Following Citizens Council promotion of downtown convention facilities, 1,001-room Statler Hilton hotel opens.

Construction of Dallas–Fort Worth Turnpike begins; it opens in 1957.

1957   Dallas Memorial Auditorium opens on site intended for the Dallas Civic Center complex.

3525 Turtle Creek becomes one of Dallas's few luxury high-rise apartment developments.

Dallas city planner Marvin Springer proposes a ring of freeways around the central city to alleviate traffic flow downtown and encourage businesses to move to the ring.

The Fifth Circuit Court of Appeals reverses the 1955 judgment on school desegregation, leading to a ruling that Dallas public schools must desegregate in January 1958.

Tornado strikes city, killing ten persons and leaving five hundred homeless.

1958   Southland Center opens as the "tallest building west of the Mississippi." Later, First International Building takes this title.

Texas Instruments, Inc. completes its Richardson complex. Dallas adds electronics to its growing list of "clean" industries. TI engineer Jack Kilby makes the discoveries that led to the integrated circuit computer chip and the personal computer revolution.

1959   Dallas Theatre Center opens with fanfare owing mainly to its architect, Frank Lloyd Wright.

1960   Major league football comes to Dallas: Dallas Cowboys (originally called Rangers, but never played under that name) of the National Football League and Dallas Texans of the American Football League.

Census population 679,684.

1961   After years of civil rights movement protests, court cases, and racist violence over the denial of voting rights, discrimination in employment and housing, Jim Crow in public accommodations, and school segregation, Dallas's public schools and some downtown businesses are nominally desegregated. Dallas Independent School District remains under a series of court orders for three decades.

1962   H. Ross Perot starts Electronic Data Systems, commonly known as EDS.

METROPOLITAN CRISIS AND UNCERTAINTY

1963   President John F. Kennedy assassinated and Governor John B. Connally seriously wounded by gunshots near the Triple Underpass while riding in an open car in a motorcade. The assassination followed years of increasingly public and vicious displays of right-wing ideologies in Dallas. Congressman Bruce Alger and retired General Edwin Walker are among the major instigators; many influential supporters remain behind the scenes. Prior to the shooting of Kennedy, organized attacks on Vice President Lyndon Johnson and Senator Adlai Stevenson had taken place. Dallas had already acquired a national reputation for its strong support for right-wing, antiliberal politics and for tolerating actions outside the political and judicial system. The assassination immediately leads to a public shaming of the city and its residents that lasts for decades.

Dallas Texans football team moves to Kansas City.

1964   Erik Jonsson, Texas Instruments' cofounder, elected mayor with an agenda of promoting harmonious growth to rehabilitate Dallas and its reputation. Goals for Dallas programs feature new City Hall and regional airport.

Dallas has more headquarters for million-dollar oil companies than any other city.

1965   Dallas and Fort Worth agree to build a new regional airport to serve both cities.

NorthPark enclosed regional shopping mall opens.

1966   El Centro College, first of the Dallas Community College District campuses, opens in old Sanger Brothers department store building downtown.

Dallas County Heritage Society formed to save Millermore, largest surviving antebellum mansion in Dallas; first restored structure to open in City Park (1969).

Joseph Lockridge becomes the first African American elected to Texas legislature from Dallas.

1967   Texas Instruments invents electronic handheld calculator using integrated circuits.

Dr. Emmett Conrad is the first African American elected to Dallas School Board.

1969   Union Terminal closed to passenger traffic; reopened in 1974 for Amtrak and Surtran service.

Warren Travers and Vincent Ponti present "futuristic" Central Business District Plan, proposing pedestrian network below and above street level and opposing new downtown stadium.

Texas Instruments' founders, Erik Jonsson, Eugene McDermott, and Cecil Green, establish Southwest Center for Advanced Studies in science, which opens as the public University of Texas at Dallas in Richardson in 1975 with strong emphasis on science and technology.

Anita N. Martinez is the first Hispanic elected to Dallas City Council.

1970   Ford Motor Company closes its large assembly plant on East Grand Avenue.

Eastfield and Mountain View Colleges open as first suburban facilities in the Dallas County Community College District system.

Census population 844,000.

1971   Dallas commercial construction tops $366 million; fifty-two office complexes built.

Cowboys move from Cotton Bowl beside downtown to new stadium in suburban Irving.

1972   Texas Rangers baseball team comes to suburban Arlington.

Dallas Cowboys win Super Bowl VI.

Eddie Bernice Johnson elected to Texas House of Representatives, the first African American woman elected to public office in Dallas County.

1973   Swiss Avenue designated the city's first historic district.

In a multicounty referendum, voters defeat proposal for a new Trinity River channelization project and lake development.

Dallas Convention Center completed.

Dallas/Fort Worth Regional Airport begins air service.

Lucy Patterson is the first African American woman elected to Dallas City Council.

1975   Federal judge rules Dallas's system of electing all City Council members at large unconstitutional. The order mandates an 8–3 plan, with eight councilors elected from defined geographic districts and three at large, but plan is ruled unconstitutional. Voters approve a 10–4-1 plan, although 95 percent of African Americans and more than 70 percent of Hispanics oppose. Suits, countersuits, court rulings, and public referenda continue until 1990 when a city council–drafted 14–1 plan, barely approved by voters, finally goes into place.

1976   Mayor Pro Tem Adlene Harrison succeeds Mayor Wes Wise to become first woman mayor.

City Park renamed Old City Park as Dallas's first bicentennial project.

1978   Dallas's new City Hall, designed by I. M. Pei, opens.

Reunion Arena sports, entertainment, and convention complex opens.

Dallas television show debuts.

Dallas Cowboys win Super Bowl XII.

1979   Voters pass referendum including $24.8 million for new art museum and $2.25 million for concert hall site in new Arts District on north side of downtown.

Bryan Place, downtown housing development, opens.

1980   A record-setting eighty million viewers watch to see "who shot J.R." on *Dallas*.

Dallas Mavericks basketball team begins play.

National and international corporations relocate from East Coast or midwestern cities, often to the suburbs (e.g., American Airlines to Irving, JCPenney to Plano), though some to Dallas itself (e.g., Blockbuster Video to downtown).

Census population 904,078, making Dallas the seventh largest city in United States.

1981   Dallas Arboretum opens on grounds of DeGolyer Estate on White Rock Lake.

1982   Erik Jonsson Public Library central reference building opens in downtown Dallas, facing I. M. Pei's City Hall.

Braniff International Airline files for bankruptcy.

1983   Dallas Area Regional Transit endorsed in pubic referendum. Mass transit develops haltingly owing to funding and management problems, design difficulties, and major suburban-city political conflicts; some suburbs leave the regional authority and others threaten to do so. First light-rail lines open in 1996; ridership and public interest in 1996–97 exceed predictions.

1984   New Dallas Museum of Arts building, costing more than $50 million in pubic and private monies, designed by Edward Larrabee Barnes, opens as first building in new downtown Arts District. Temporary Dallas Theatre Center building joins it.

Republican National Convention meets in Dallas.

1985   InterFirst Plaza opens at Main and Griffin Streets, tallest building in Dallas.

1986   State Fair of Texas celebrates one hundredth anniversary and State of Texas sesquicentennial.

1987   Annette Strauss elected Dallas's first woman mayor.

1989   Morton H. Myerson Symphony Center, completed with major donation from H. Ross Perot (who named the I. M. Pei–designed structure for his corporate lieutenant), opens in the Arts District at a cost of $81.5 million in public and private monies.

Sixth Floor Museum, in the Texas School Book Depository Building, opens, memorializing the 1963 assassination of President Kennedy more than a quarter century after the event.

McKinney Avenue Trolley begins service between downtown and Oak Lawn.

1990   Census population 1,006,877.

1991   Dallas celebrates 150 years.

Dallas Times Herald stops publishing, making Dallas the United States' largest city with only one major daily newspaper.

After series of referenda and court cases, Dallas City Council transformed into fourteen single-member district representatives with only mayor elected at large.

1993   Dallas Stars hockey team relocates from Minneapolis.

1994   Cowboy's post–Super Bowl parade "riot."

Dallas Plan announced in effort to gain popular and political favor and fund its projects of "core assets," neighborhoods, economic development, Center City, Southern Sector, Trinity River Corridor.

Explicit and formal political dominance of the Dallas Citizens Council and Citizens Charter Association ends, though patterns they set continue.

1995   Ron Kirk elected as Dallas's first African American mayor.

Dallas threatened by prospect of professional sports teams—Mavericks, Stars—moving to suburban locations with new arenas if city does not build a new facility.

1996   Demise of the Southwestern Athletic Conference; decline of the Cotton Bowl.

"Race wars": New Black Panther Party, other African Americans, Hispanics versus Dallas Independent School Board; increased contentiousness in city council. Record numbers of female and minority elected members. Renewed efforts to improve public schools; suburbs versus court-ordered decentralization and relocation of public housing.

Opening of Lone Star Park for horseracing and Texas Motor Speedway for automobile racing in northern suburbs.

1995–
2000
Dallas Independent School District goes through five permanent or interim superintendents, including minorities, amid allegations of corruption and scandal.

Downtown and adjoining inner-city shopping, dining, entertainment, and residential areas likened to SoHo, Chelsea, Victoria, Uptown districts.

Workforce cutbacks by electronics companies, decline of American Airlines, and related problems raise questions about the economy and its research and development base, including universities.

Renewed efforts to secure new investment, building, and conversion of space for residential and commercial/entertainment uses. Dallas continues to seek a "brand" to sell itself competitively against other cities.

2000 Census population 1,188,580.

2001 New downtown arena American Airlines Center opens, home of Mavericks NBA basketball team and NHL Stars hockey team.

Bids for Boeing Corporation new headquarters and 2012 Olympics fail.

Mayor Kirk resigns to run for U.S. Senate, wins Democratic Party primary, but loses general election to Republican John Cornyn. Newspaper columnist and city council member Laura Miller defeats businessman Tom Dunning to finish Kirk's term as mayor.

2001–4 Designer-architect Arts District buildings announced: Frank Gehry Natural History Museum; Rem Koolhaas and Norman Foster Performance Hall.

2002 Santiago Calatrava signature bridges over Trinity River announced; further plans, proposals, and studies for development of Trinity.

2003 Laura Miller defeats Mary Poss in election marked by debate over size of city bond issue and development strategy; fate of city manager position in question.

Judge Barefoot Sanders ends court-ordered and monitored desegregation of Dallas Independent School District.

2004   Cowboys propose new stadium.

        City searches for a city manager; Dallas Independent School District searches for a superintendent.

2005   Debate over revisions to City Charter to establish a "strong mayor" ends in defeat of the proposition, supported strongly by incumbent Laura Miller and *Dallas Morning News;* continued squabbling among city councilors and with Mayor Miller.

        Cowboys choose to move to Arlington on promise of a new stadium.

2007   Cotton Bowl Classic football game announces move to new stadium in Arlington

Sources: "Dallas from the Ground Up," exhibition sponsored by Dallas Museum of Fine Arts, Historic Preservation League, City of Dallas Department of Urban Planning, American Institute of Architects, and Dallas County Heritage Society; Texas Writers Project, *Dallas Guide and History* (Works Progress Administration, 1940; Denton: Dallas Public Library, Texas Center for the Book and University of North Texas Press, 1992); Darwin Payne, *Dallas: An Illustrated History* (Dallas: Windsor Publications, 1982); Payne, *Big D: Triumphs and Troubles of an American Supercity in the 20th Century* (Dallas: Three Forks Press, 1994); Larenda Lyles Roberts, *Dallas Uncovered* (Plano: Republic of Texas Press, 1995); Jim Schutze, *The Accommodation: The Politics of Race in an American City* (Secaucus, N.J.: Citadel Press, 1986); Patricia Hill, "Origins of Modern Dallas" (PhD Diss., University of Texas at Dallas, 1990).

NOTES

PREFACE

1. My essay, "The 'New' Social History and the Southwest: The Dallas Social History Project," published in the University of Texas at Dallas's Southwest Center for Economic and Community Development *Papers, 1976–1977*, and then in the *East Texas Historical Journal* 16 (1978): 52–62, outlines the project I planned but chose not to undertake.

2. This guide to sources was published in the University of Texas at Dallas's Southwest Center for Economic and Community Development *Papers, 1977*, and then by the University of Texas Press (Austin, 1979).

INTRODUCTION

1. James Howard, *Big D Is for Dallas: Chapters in the Twentieth-Century History of Dallas* (Austin: University Co-operative Society for James Howard, 1957), 1.

2. John Gunther, *Inside U.S.A.* (New York: Harper, 1947), 815.

3. Howard, *Big D Is for Dallas*, 1.

4. Gunther, *Inside U.S.A.*, 815.

5. Justin F. Kimball, *Our City—Dallas: Yesterday and Tomorrow* (Dallas: Dallas Independent School District, authorized by the Board, 1953).

6. The film prepared for and shown to an extraordinary number of Dallas audiences at the time of the first court-ordered school desegregation in 1961 was entitled "Dallas at the Crossroads."

7. "Dallas at the Tipping Point," special supplement, *Dallas Morning News*, April 18, 2004.

8. Holland McCombs and William H. Whyte, "The Dydamic Men of Dallas," *Fortune*, February 1949, 2.

1. LOCATING THE CITY

1. "Westward," *Dallas Morning News,* June 12, 1994.

2. Stanley Walker, *The Dallas Story* (Dallas: Dallas Times Herald, 1956), 2. On Dallas's rivalries, see Gunther, *Inside U.S.A.;* John Bainbridge, *The Super-Americans: A Picture of Life in the United States as Brought into Focus, Bigger than Life, In the Land of the Millionaires—Texas* (Garden City, N.Y.: Doubleday, 1961). On race, see W. Marvin Dulaney, "Whatever Happened to the Civil Rights Movement in Dallas, Texas?" in *Essays on the American Civil Rights Movement,* ed. Dulaney and Kathleen Underwood, Walter Prescott Webb Memorial Lecture 26 (College Station: Texas A&M University Press and University of Texas at Arlington, 1993), 66–95; Dulaney, "The Progressive Voters League: A Political Voice for African Americans in Dallas," *Legacies* 3 (1991): 27–35; Michael Phillips, *White Metropolis: Race, Ethnicity, and Religion in Dallas, 1841–2001* (Austin: University of Texas Press, 2006); Stephanie Cole, "Finding Race in Turn-of-the-Century Dallas," in *Beyond Black and White: Race, Ethnicity, and Gender in the U.S. South and Southwest,* ed. Stephanie Cole and Alison M. Parker, Walter Prescott Webb Memorial Lecture 35 (College Station: Texas A&M University Press and University of Texas at Arlington, 2004), 75–86.

3. Mark Stuertz, "A Guide to the Metroplex," advertising supplement, *Texas Monthly,* August 1997, 144.

4. Kevin Lynch, *The Image of the City* (Cambridge, Mass.: MIT Press, 1960). See also Edward Krupat, *People in Cities: The Urban Environment and Its Effects* (Cambridge: Cambridge University Press, 1985); Sharon Zukin, *Landscapes of Power: From Detroit to Disney World* (Berkeley and Los Angeles: University of California Press, 1991); Carl Abbott, *The New Urban America* (Chapel Hill: University of North Carolina Press, 1987); John M. Findlay, *Magic Lands: Western Cityscapes and American Culture After 1940* (Berkeley and Los Angeles: University of California Press, 1992); Mike Davis, *City of Quartz: Excavating the Future in Los Angeles* (London: Verso, 1990); Michael J. Dear, *The Postmodern Urban Condition* (Oxford: Blackwell, 2000); Dear, ed., *From Chicago to LA: Making Sense of Urban Theory* (Thousand Oaks, Calif.: Sage, 2002); Dear, H. Eric Shockman, and Greg Hise, eds., *Rethinking Los Angeles* (Thousand Oaks, Calif.: Sage, 1997); James Donald, *Imagining the Modern City* (Minneapolis: University of Minnesota Press, 1999); Charles Rutheiser, *Imagineering Atlanta* (New York: Verso, 1996); Amy Bridges, *Morning Glories: Municipal Reform in the Southwest* (Princeton, N.J.: Princeton University Press, 1997); Deborah Dash Moore, *To the Golden Cities* (New York: Free Press, 1994); Richard M. Bernard and Bradley R. Rice, eds., *Sunbelt Cities* (Austin: University of Texas Press, 1984); Raymond A. Mohl, ed., *Searching for the Sunbelt* (Knoxville: University of Tennessee Press, 1990); Randall Miller and George Pozzetta, eds., *Shades of the Sunbelt* (Westport, Conn.: Greenwood Press, 1988); Robert Fairbanks and Kathleen Underwood, eds., *Essays on Sunbelt Cities and Recent Urban America* (College Station: Texas A&M University Press, 1990); David C. Perry and Alfred J. Watkins, eds., *The Rise of the Sunbelt Cities* (Beverly Hills, Calif.: Sage, 1977).

5. Marco D'Eramo, *The Pig and the Skyscraper. Chicago: A History of the Future*, trans. Graeme Thomson (1999; London: Verso, 2002), 142.

6. "Dallas at the Tipping Point" series, *Dallas Morning News*, December 12–16, 2004. See also Arnold R. Hirsch, "With or Without Jim Crow: Black Residential Segregation in the United States," in *Urban Policy in Twentieth Century America*, ed. Hirsch and Raymond A. Mohl (New Brunswick, N.J.: Rutgers University Press, 1993), 65–99; Michael B. Katz, *The Price of Citizenship: Redefining the American Welfare State* (New York: Metropolitan Books, 2001); Douglas S. Massey and Nancy A. Denton, *American Apartheid: Segregation and the Making of the Underclass* (Cambridge, Mass.: Harvard University Press, 1993); Zukin, *Landscapes of Power;* Frank Levy, *The New Dollars and Dreams: American Incomes and Economic Change* (New York: Russell Sage Foundation, 1998); Alice O'Connor, Chris Tilly, and Lawrence D. Bobo, eds., *Urban Inequality: Evidence from Four Cities* (New York: Russell Sage Foundation, 2004); Paul Jargowsky, *Poverty and Place: Ghettos, Barrios, and the American City* (New York: Russell Sage Foundation, 1997).

7. Michael Sorkin, ed., *Variations on a Theme Park: The New American City and the End of Public Space* (New York: Hill & Wang, 1992); Zukin, *Landscapes of Power;* Umberto Eco, *Travels in Hyperreality,* trans. William Weaver (1973; New York: Harcourt Brace, 1986); Christine Boyer, *Dreaming the Rational City* (Cambridge, Mass.: MIT Press, 1983); Boyer, *City of Collective Memory* (Cambridge, Mass.: MIT Press, 1996). On "theme park cities," see Susan Davis, *Spectacular Nature: Corporate Culture and the Sea World Experience* (Berkeley and Los Angeles: University of California Press, 1997); Nan Ellin, *Postmodern Urbanism* (Oxford: Blackwell, 1996); Mark Gottdiener et al., *The Theming of America* (Boulder, Colo.: Westview Press, 1997); Claudia Collins, David Dickens, and Mark Gottdiener, *Las Vegas: The Social Production of an All-American City* (Oxford: Blackwell, 1999); John Hannigan, *Fantasy City: Pleasure and Profit in the Postmodern Metropolis* (London: Routledge, 1998); Dennis Judd and Susan Fainstain, eds., *The Tourist City* (New Haven, Conn.: Yale University Press, 1999); Chris Mele, *Selling the Lower East Side: Culture, Real Estate, and Residence in New York City* (Minneapolis: University of Minnesota Press, 2000); Celeste Olalquiaga, *Megalopolis: Contemporary Cultural Sensibilities* (Minneapolis: University of Minnesota Press, 1992); Hal Rothman, *Devil's Bargains: Tourism in the Twentieth-Century American West* (Lawrence: University of Kansas Press, 2000); Rothman, *Neon Metropolis: How Las Vegas Started the Twenty-first Century* (New York: Routledge, 2003); Rothman and Mike Davis, eds., *The Grit Between the Glitter: Tales from the Real Las Vegas* (Berkeley and Los Angeles: University of California Press, 2002); Edward Soja, *Postmodern Geographies* (New York: Verso, 1989); Gerry Kearns and Chris Philo, eds., *Selling Places: The City as Cultural Capital, Past and Present* (Oxford: Pergamon, 1993); Stephen V. Ward, *Selling Places: The Marketing and Promotion of Towns and Cities, 1850–2000* (London: E&F Spon, 1998). On city branding, see "Dallas, the Brand: City Casts About for an Image That's Not So, Well, J.R. Ewing," *Dallas Morning News*, January 31, 2004; Henry Tatum, "We Need to Put a Brand on Dallas to Be Competitive," *Dallas Morning News*, February 4, 2004; "Symposium on Branding, the Entertainment

Economy, and Urban Place Building," *International Journal of Urban and Regional Research* 27 (June 2003): 352–440.

8. Lynch, *Image of the City,* 2, 3; see also Kevin Lynch, "Reconsidering *The Image of the City,*" in *Images and Themes of the City in the Social Sciences,* ed. Lloyd Rodwin and Robert M. Hollister (New York: Plenum Press, 1984), 151–61.

9. On reading urban images, see Grady Clay, *Close Up: How to Read the American City* (Chicago: University of Chicago Press, 1980); Alexander Gelley, "City Texts: Representation, Semiology, Urbanism," in *Politics, Theory, and Contemporary Culture,* ed. Mark Poster (New York: Columbia University Press, 1993), 237–60; William Sharpe and Leonard Wallock, eds., *Visions of the Modern City* (Baltimore, Md.: Johns Hopkins University Press, 1987); Michel de Certeau, "Walking in the City," in *The Practice of Everyday Life* (Berkeley and Los Angeles: University of California Press, 1984), 91–110; James Duncan and David Ley, eds., *Place/Culture/Representation* (London: Routledge, 1994); Norman M. Klein, *The History of Forgetting: Los Angeles and the Erasure of History* (New York: Verso, 1997). For theory, see David Harvey, *Social Justice and the City* (Baltimore, Md.: Johns Hopkins University Press, 1973); Harvey, *The Urbanization of Capital* (Baltimore, Md.: Johns Hopkins University Press, 1985); Harvey, *Consciousness and the Urban Experience* (Baltimore, Md.: Johns Hopkins University Press, 1985); Harvey, *The Condition of Postmodernity* (Oxford: Blackwell, 1989); Harvey, *Spaces of Capital* (New York: Routledge, 2001). Also on theory, see Henri Lefebvre, *The Urban Revolution,* trans. Robert Bononno (1970; Minneapolis: University of Minnesota Press, 2003); and Lefebvre, *The Production of Space,* trans. Donald Nicholson-Smith (1984; Oxford: Blackwell, 1991). Among important historical examples, see Warren I. Susman, "The City in American Culture," in *Culture as History* (New York: Pantheon, 1984), 237–51; Sam Bass Warner Jr., "Slums and Skyscrapers: Urban Images, Symbols, and Ideology," in Rodwin and Hollister, *Images and Themes of the City in the Social Sciences,* 181–94; William R. Taylor, *In Pursuit of Gotham: Culture and Commerce in New York City* (New York: Oxford University Press, 1992); Carla Cappetti, *Writing Chicago: Modernism, Ethnography, and the Novel* (New York: Columbia University Press, 1993); Hana Wirth-Nesher, *City Codes: Reading the Modern Urban Novel* (Cambridge: Cambridge University Press, 1996); Kevin R. McNamara, *Urban Verbs: Arts and Discourses of American Cities* (Stanford, Calif.: Stanford University Press, 1996); David M. Henkin, *City Reading: Written Words and Public Spaces in Antebellum New York* (New York: Columbia University Press, 1998); Deborah Nord, *Walking the Victorian Streets: Women, Representation, and the City* (Ithaca, N.Y.: Cornell University Press, 1995); Peter Preston and Paul Simpson-Houseley, eds., *Writing the City: Eden, Babylon, and the New Jerusalem* (London: Routledge, 1994); Carl Smith, *Chicago and the American Literary Imagination* (Chicago: University of Chicago, 1984); Judith Walkowitz, *City of Dreadful Delight: Narratives of Sexual Danger in Late-Victorian London* (Chicago: University of Chicago Press, 1992). See also Italo Calvino, *Invisible Cities,* trans. William Weaver (1972; New York: Harcourt Brace, 1974).

10. Zukin, *Landscapes of Power,* 20.

11. Gelley, "City Texts," 245. On cityscapes, in addition to works already cited, see

Reyner Banham, *Los Angeles: The Architecture of Four Ecologies* (New York: Harper and Row, 1971); Richard Walker, "Landscape and City Life: Four Ecologies of Residence in the San Francisco Bay Area," *Ecumene* 2 (1995): 33–64.

12. See Molly Ivins, *Molly Ivins Can't Say That, Can She?* (New York: Random House, 1991); C. W. Smith, "Dallas: The Urge for Cosmetic Surgery," *Texas Humanist* 6 (January–February 1983): 14–16.

13. "Mayor Ron Kirk—History Maker," *Register of the Dallas Historical Society,* Spring 1997, 2 (emphasis in original).

14. "Census Estimates Make Big D Feel a Little Smaller," *Dallas Morning News,* June 24, 2004; "Little D? San Antonio Population Tops Dallas: So What," *Dallas Morning News,* June 24, 2004. There is a long, almost legendary history of rhetorical and material competition between Dallas and Houston, San Antonio, and Fort Worth.

15. "Mayor Ron Kirk," 2.

16. For debates about the economic value of sports teams to cities, see Michael N. Danielson, *Home Team: Professional Sports and the American Metropolis* (Princeton, N.J.: Princeton University Press, 1997); Roger G. Noll and Andrew Zimbalist, eds., *Sports, Jobs and Taxes: The Economic Impact of Sports Teams and Stadiums* (Washington, D.C.: Brookings Institution, 1997); Joanna Cagan and Neil deMause, *Field of Schemes: How the Great Stadium Swindle Turns Public Money into Private Profit* (Monroe, Maine: Common Cause Press, 1998).

17. Horace Newcomb, "Texas: A Giant State of Mind," *Channels of Communication* 1 (1981); Gillian Swanson, "Dallas," *Framework* 14 (1982): 32–35, and 15 (1982): 81–85; Herta Herzog Massing, "Decoding 'Dallas,'" *Society,* November 1985, 74–77; Mary S. Mander, "*Dallas:* The Mythology of Crime and the Moral Occult," *Journal of Popular Culture* 17 (1983): 44–50; Elihu Katz and Tamar Liebes, "Once Upon a Time, in Dallas," *Intermedia* 12 (1984): 28–32; Tamar Liebes and Elihu Katz, *The Export of Meaning: Cross-Cultural Readings of "Dallas"* (New York: Oxford University Press, 1990); Ien Ang, *Watching Dallas: Soap Opera and the Melodramatic Imagination,* trans. Della Couling (London: Methuen, 1985).

18. See Davis, *City of Quartz;* Klein, *History of Forgetting;* and Rutheiser, *Imagineering Atlanta.*

19. The top choices were followed by oil and petroleum (9 percent, 10 percent), "big city in Texas" (5 percent, 4 percent), "rich cultural city" (3 percent, 4 percent), "new modern city" (1 percent, 1 percent), and "beautiful city" (1 percent, 1 percent).

20. Steven Reddicliffe, "Is J.R. Shot?" *Texas Monthly,* April 1988, 94–95, 140.

21. Joseph Guinto, "Who Shot J.R.?" *The Met,* August 31, 1995, 10.

22. While traveling in Europe, I was surprised by the keen interest scholars there showed in the TV *Dallas.* The series was aired with a one-year time lag outside the United States, so I was met by whispered questions about plot developments.

23. Darwin Payne, quoted in Guinto, "Who Shot J.R.?" 10.

24. Jim Schutze, "It's Ironic What a TV Show Has Done for Dallas' Image," *Dallas Times Herald,* April 1, 1984.

25. Jim Schutze, "Is Dallas the 'Dallas' of TV Fame, or Is It Something Better?" *Dallas Times Herald,* November 4, 1987.

26. Editorials, *Dallas Morning News,* March 8, 2006, February 21, 2006.

27. Stanley Marcus, "What's Right with Dallas?" advertisement in *Dallas Morning News,* January 1, 1964.

28. Lawrence Wright, *In the New World: Growing Up with America from the Sixties to the Eighties* (New York: Knopf, 1987), 4, 5; see also A. C. Greene, *Dallas U.S.A.* (Austin: Texas Monthly Press, 1984), 59.

29. Wright, *In the New World,* 65, 74, 75. See also Robert Wallace, "What Kind of Place Is Dallas?" *Life,* January 31, 1964; Marcus, "What's Right with Dallas"; Warren Leslie, *Dallas Public and Private: Aspects of an American City* (New York: Grossman, 1964; repr. Dallas: Southern Methodist University Press, 1998).

30. Leslie, *Dallas Public and Private,* 8.

31. Henry Tatum, "Dallas' Destiny No Longer Tied to Cowboys," *Dallas Morning News,* January 15, 1997.

32. Peter Gent, *North Dallas Forty* (New York: William Morrow, 1973). Professional athletes' alcohol and drug problems were not as commonly known or publicly admitted as they later became.

33. See also Nancy Taylor Rosenberg, *Trial by Fire* (New York: Dutton, 1996).

34. Gent, *North Dallas Forty,* 79, 178.

35. Editorial, *Dallas Morning News,* December 16, 1993.

36. Tatum, "Dallas' Destiny No Longer Tied to Cowboys"; "Outlaw Cowboys," *New York Times,* August 6, 1997.

37. Ibid.

38. See Gent, *North Dallas Forty.*

39. Tatum, "Dallas' Destiny No Longer Tied to Cowboys."

40. Peter King, "If This Is America's Team, Woe Is America," *Sports Illustrated,* 1996; Kevin Sherrington, "Are the Cowboys Ruining Our Lives?" *Dallas Morning News,* January 21, 1996.

41. Conover Hunt, *JFK for a New Generation* (Dallas: Sixth Floor Museum and Southern Methodist University Press, 1996); see also introduction by Harvey J. Graff and Patricia E. Hill to 1998 reprint of Leslie, *Dallas Public and Private.*

42. Jim Schutze, "Dallas Giving in to Stone to Prove We're Past the Guilt Thing," *Dallas Times Herald,* April 11, 1991.

43. Review of *JFK, Time Magazine,* December 23, 1991. For the film's version of conspiracy theory, see Robert S. Robins and Jerrold M. Post, "Political Paranoia as Cinematic Motif: Stone's 'J.F.K.,'" paper presented to the American Political Science Association, August–September 1997, Washington, D.C.

44. See Stanley Marcus's famous advertisement relieving Dallas of guilt and responsibility for the Kennedy assassination, "What's Right with Dallas?"

45. See Hunt, *JFK for a New Generation.*

46. "Mixing Tragedy with Art in Dallas," *New York Times,* March 3, 2003.

47. "Sixth Floor Museum Planning New Exhibit on 5 Key U.S. Traumas," *Dallas Morning News,* September 28, 2001.

48. "Aging JFK Memorial Earns City's Attention: Design Still Debated but Cleanup Plan Isn't," *Dallas Morning News,* November 22, 1999.

49. "Dallas Gives a Face Lift to JFK Memorial," *San Antonio Express-News,* May 28, 2000.

50. Published reports of the cost of repairs ran from $125,000 to $200,000.

51. Henry Tatum, "How Does JFK Memorial Fit in Plaza? Downtown Plans Have Skipped Around a Sensitive Subject," *Dallas Morning News,* November 27, 2002.

52. "Kennedy Memorial Restored," *Dallas Morning News,* June 25, 2000; "Kennedy Memorial Rededicated," *San Antonio Express-News,* June 25, 2000.

53. "Dallas Finally Comes to Grips with Its Past," *Dallas Morning News,* June 28, 2000.

54. "Memorial to JFK Won't Be Relocated," *Dallas Morning News,* March 26, 2003.

55. "County Was Right to Leave JFK Memorial in Its Original Place," *Dallas Morning News,* March 29, 2003.

56. Ibid.

57. See also John Marks, "A Texas Exorcism: Dallas Finds New Ways to Confront the Demons of Dealey Plaza," *U.S. News & World Report,* November 30, 1998; "Restoration of Battered JFK Memorial Begins," *Dallas Morning News,* March 26, 2000; "Retaining History: Several Sites Were Significant in JFK Saga," *Dallas Morning News,* November 22, 2002; "Seizing JFK Memories Before They're Gone: Historian Speeds Up Attempt to Log Historic Event as Witnesses Age," *Dallas Morning News,* November 22, 2002.

58. David Goldfield, *Cotton Fields and Skyscrapers: Southern City and Region, 1607–1980* (Baton Rouge: Louisiana State University Press, 1982); Goldfield, *Region, Race, and Cities: Interpreting the Urban South* (Baton Rouge: Louisiana State University Press, 1997); Don H. Doyle, *New Men, New Cities, New South: Atlanta, Nashville, Charleston, Mobile, 1860–1910* (Chapel Hill: University of North Carolina Press, 1990).

59. Willie Morris, "What Makes Dallas Different," *The New Republic,* June 1964, 20–22. More recently, see Jacquelynn Floyd, "40 Years Later, We Still Ask 'Why Here?'" *Dallas Morning News,* November 19, 2003; Michael E. Young, "Will Dallas Ever Shake the Kennedy Stigma?" *Dallas Morning News,* November 19, 2003; Ruben Navarrette, "We Should Lay Dallas' Past to Rest," *Dallas Morning News,* November 21, 2003; Carolyn Barta, "Assassination Compelled City to Change for the Better," *Dallas Morning News,* November 22, 2003.

60. Wallace, "What Kind of a Place Is Dallas?"

61. Ibid.

62. See, for example, "City Tainted by Scandals, Some Worry," *Dallas Morning News,* October 19, 1997.

63. Herbert Gambrell, "Hurrah for Dallas!" *Southwest Review* 30 (1945): 225.

64. Ibid., 229–30.

65. Richard A. Smith, "How Business Failed Dallas," *Fortune,* July 1964, 160.

66. Editorial, *Dallas Morning News,* December 16, 1993.

67. Harry Hurt III, "Houston Is Better Than Dallas," *Texas Monthly,* February 1978, 79.

68. Lon Tinkle, *The Key to Dallas* (Philadelphia: J. B. Lippincott, 1965), 112–13. "Keys to the Cities" was a series of books for young readers.

69. Ibid., 113–16.

70. Gambrell, "Hurrah for Dallas!" See, for example, Bernard and Rice, *Sunbelt Cities;* Mohl, *Searching for the Sunbelt;* Miller and Pozzetta, *Shades of the Sunbelt;* Fairbanks and Underwood, *Essays on Sunbelt Cities;* Perry and Watkins, *Rise of the Sunbelt Cities;* Hirsch and Mohl, *Urban Policy in Twentieth Century America.*

71. *Texas Almanac,* 1945.

72. Lynn Ashby, "Dallas vs. Houston . . . They Are Like Brothers," *Dallas Morning News,* June 15, 1994. The purebred Charolais cattle that Ashby treats as a Texas trademark were imported from France. The city of Bowie is located in the exact geographic center of the state of Texas. It is named after Jim Bowie, who died at the Alamo. Bowie was born in Kentucky of Scots descent, grew up in Louisiana, became famous for wielding a knife in a fight in Natchez, Mississippi, and married the daughter of the Hispanic governor of Texas when it was still Mexican territory; he may or may not have found the silver mines near the town named after him.

73. Gunther, *Inside U.S.A.,* 815.

74. Mayor Ron Kirk, quoted in *Dallas Morning News,* June 5, 1995.

75. "Dallas, Texas, U.S.A.: An International City, Ready to Trade," editorial, *Dallas Morning News,* May 17, 1996.

76. Larry Powell, "'Happy' Is an Amusing Part of the Mayor's Vocabulary," *Dallas Morning News,* August 1, 1995.

77. See John Beldon Billingsley, "A Trip to Texas," ed. Robert L. Jones and Pauline Jones, *Texana,* 7 (1969): 201–19; Elizabeth York Enstam, ed., *When Dallas Became a City: Letters of John Milton McCoy, 1870–1881* (Dallas: Dallas Historical Society, 1982). On Western cities, see Richard C. Wade, *The Urban Frontier: Pioneer Life in Early Pittsburgh, Cincinnati, Lexington, Louisville, and St. Louis* (Chicago: University of Chicago Press, 1964); William Cronon, *Nature's Metropolis: Chicago and the Great West* (New York: Norton, 1992). On urban culture, see Susman, "City in American Culture"; Thomas Bender, *Toward an Urban Vision* (Lexington: University Press of Kentucky, 1975). On the racist "underside" of urban dreams, see Phillips, *White Metropolis,* and Michael Phillips, "The Fire This Time: The Battle over Racial, Regional, and Religious Identities in Dallas, Texas, 1860–1990" (PhD diss., University of Texas at Austin, 2002).

78. Haynes Johnson, *The Washington Post,* August 7, 1983. See also "Dallas in Wonderland," *Fortune,* November 1937, 112–20, 200–209; "Texas Tells 'Em: Neiman-Marcus Company," *Colliers,* September 16, 1939; David L. Corn, "Dallas," *Atlantic Monthly,* October 1940, 453–60; McCombs and Whyte, "Dydamic Men of Dallas," 2; James Street, "Dazzling Dallas," *Holiday,* March 1953. More recently, see "Dallas Takes Off (In the Backyard of Bush and Cheney, the Sky's the Limit)," special issue, *The American Enterprise,* October–November 2000.

79. Bender, *Toward an Urban Vision;* Susman, "City in American Culture"; Phillips, *White Metropolis.*

80. See Carl Abbott, "The International City Hypothesis: An Approach to the Recent History of U.S. Cities," *Journal of Urban History* 24 (1997): 28–52; Saskia Sassen, *The Global City: New York, London, Tokyo* (1991; repr., Princeton, N.J.: Princeton University Press, 2001); Sassen, *Globalization and Its Discontents* (New York: New Press, 1998); Janet Abu-Lughod, *New York, Chicago, Los Angeles: America's Global Cities* (Minneapolis: University of Minnesota Press, 1999).

81. My thanks to Michael Phillips for his perspective on Dallas in song.

82. Sam Howe Verhovek, "Looking at the Flippo Side of Dallas," *Dallas Morning News,* July 23, 1997.

83. As historian John William Rogers puts it, "Of history in the political sense that it is traditionally conceived—battles fought and spectacular moments in the destiny of a state—it is plain Dallas possesses not a trace. Its century of existence has been relatively so innocent of the play of dramatic forces which tear down and create governments that it could stand as an arch-type *[sic]* among cities of the world that have achieved color and individuality from these confusions." John William Rogers, *The Lusty Texans of Dallas* (1951; repr., New York: E. P. Dutton, 1965), 361.

84. Greene, *Dallas U.S.A.,* 236–39.

85. Bill Porterfield in *The Book of Dallas,* ed. Evelyn Oppenheimer and Porterfield (Garden City, N.Y.: Doubleday, 1976), 257.

86. See, for example, Griffin Smith Jr., "Dallas!" in *National Geographic,* September 1984, 272–304; Darwin Payne, *Big D: Triumphs and Troubles of an American Supercity in the 20th Century* (Dallas: Three Forks Press, 1994); Oppenheimer and Porterfield, *Book of Dallas.*

87. James Hillman, "City Limits," in *Imagining Dallas* (Dallas: Dallas Institute for History and Culture, 1982), 59. For wonderful demonstrations totally lacking in self-awareness, see Mark Seal, "Round the Clock in Dallas: A Day in the City of Infinite Possibility," *American Way* (American Airlines), April 1, 1997, 40–43, 119–22; and Stuertz, "Guide to the Metroplex," 144.

88. Larry Paul Fuller, ed., *The American Institute of Architects, Guide to Dallas Architecture with Regional Highlights* (Dallas: AIA Dallas Chapter, McGraw-Hill Information Group, 1999), 24. Designed by New York City architect Alfred Blossom, the Magnolia Building bears a close resemblance to Houston's Hilton Hotel, built during the same period, especially in its flying segmented arch linking the two towers at the seventeenth floor. With seven elevators, five hundred offices, and 1,700 telephones, it was Dallas's most modern office building.

89. "Chicago had its cows, New Orleans promoted its fish. And St. Paul featured Snoopy. Now Dallas officials, looking to get into the more creative aspects of public art, want to join the fray with Pegasus," wrote the *Dallas Morning News*'s Gromer Jeffers Jr. Unabashedly imitative, the goals were excitement, fun, and "free spirit." Veletta Forsythe Lill, chair of the city Arts, Education, and Libraries Committee, elaborated: "The Pegasus is an icon of Dallas and extremely unique. I think the project will

encourage imagination and participation. It's an exciting opportunity for a very small investment." For the campaign from start to finish see "Revelers Get Flying Start: Downtown Pegasus Party Leads Way for Celebration," *Dallas Morning News,* January 1, 2000; "Dallas Officials Hope Pegasus Takes Off as Public Art Display," *Dallas Morning News,* August 28, 2000; "Pegasus Gets Protection," *Dallas Morning News,* October 25, 2000; "Things Are Herd All Over: Program Plans Stampede of 2000 Pegasus Replicas," *Dallas Morning News,* April 14, 2001; "Wing & a Flair: Artist Peter Max Enjoys Pegasus Flight of Fantasy," *Dallas Morning News,* May 4, 2001; "Horsing Around: Pegasus Project Shows Fun Side of Dallas," *Dallas Morning News,* July 18, 2001; "A Wing and a Painter: Pegasus Statues Beginning to Brighten Downtown Dallas," *Dallas Morning News,* August 1, 2001; "Pegasus Stampeding through City: A Whole New Breed," *Dallas Morning News,* September 22, 2001; "As Dallas' New Pegasus Soars, Original Is Still Hanging Around," *Dallas Morning News,* November 3, 2001; "Hopes for Pegasus Project Clipped by Economy, War: Dallas Soars! Scales Back Decorative Fund-Raiser by Half," *Dallas Morning News,* November 6, 2001; "Motley Cavalcade: Pegasus Project Brightens City, but Is It All Just Horsefeathers?" *Dallas Morning News,* December 30, 2001; "Pegasus Gives Artist, Company Rough Ride: Sculptor, Firm Reach Settlement after Battle over City Project," *Dallas Morning News,* January 19, 2002; "Sisters on Prowl for Pegasus Statues," *Dallas Morning News,* February 12, 2002; "New Directions: Signs Could Lead Way Downtown: $4 Million Project Would Feature Pegasus on About 800 Markers," *Dallas Morning News,* May 17, 2002; "Pegasus Lifts Off from Closed Service Station," *Dallas Morning News,* June 28, 2002; "Caught! a Pegasus, in Fence, with Camera: Clues in Contest Send Sleuths on Sightseeing Hunt Around Dallas," *Dallas Morning News,* September 29, 2002; "Museum Lands Pegasus: Neon and Steel Steed to Be Housed at Old Red Courthouse," *Dallas Morning News,* October 18, 2002; "Peter Max Pegasus No Longer Soaring: The Star among the Winged Horses Designed to Symbolize the City Is Relegated to an Ebay Auction," *Dallas Morning News,* May 7, 2003.

90. "Things Are Herd All Over."

91. "Wing & a Flair"; "Hopes for Pegasus Project Clipped by Economy, War."

92. "Motley Cavalcade."

93. "New Directions."

94. "Peter Max Pegasus No Longer Soaring." See also A. C. Greene, "Myths Take Wing on Pegasus Plaza," *Dallas Morning News,* January 22, 1995.

95. David Dillon, "City Hall Turns 20, and You Can't Beat It," *Dallas Morning News,* March 9, 1998.

96. "Vandalism of Henry Moore Sculpture also Defaces Dallas," editorial, *Dallas Morning News,* November 1, 1996.

97. "City Tainted by Scandals, Some Worry," *Dallas Morning News,* October 19, 1997.

98. "Heady Days of J.R. and Landry Are History in Humbled Dallas," *Dallas Times Herald,* December 20, 2004. Locally, see "Panel Seeks into Future of Dallas: Trinity River Project Tops Discussion of City's Potential for Rebirth," *Dallas Morning News,* January 30, 2004; Henry Tatum, "Is This the Image Dallas Wants? Crime and Physical

Fitness Reports Show City in a Very Poor Light," *Dallas Morning News*, January 7, 2004; "Mayor: Trinity Work Key for City's Future," *Dallas Morning News*, June 24, 2004; "Charting a Future: Dallas' Businesses Must Become More Engaged in City," *Dallas Morning News*, November 26, 2004.

99. William Sharpe and Leonard Wallock, "From 'Great Town' to 'Nonplace Urban Realm': Reading the Modern City," in Sharpe and Wallock, *Visions of the Modern City*, 1–50.

100. Paul A. Bové, "Discourse," in *Critical Terms for Literary Study*, ed. Frank Lentriccia and Thomas McLaughlin, 2nd ed. (Chicago: University of Chicago Press, 1990), 54, 58–59.

101. "It is discussed by all sorts of commentators, particularly in the more applied sense of how the 'marketing' of places does and should occur, as well as in the context of debates over how North American cities seek to achieve 'growth' through self-promotion." Chris Philo and Jerry Kearns, "Culture, History, Capital: A Critical Introduction to the Selling of Places," in *Selling Places: The City as Cultural Capital, Past and Present* (Oxford: Pergamon, 1993), 18, 20–21.

102. David Wilson, "Metaphors, Growth Coalition Discourses and Black Poverty Neighborhoods in a U.S. City," *Antipode* 28 (1996): 91.

2. CONSTRUCTING A CITY WITH NO LIMITS

1. See Ivins, *Molly Ivins Can't Say That, Can She?;* Leslie, *Dallas Public and Private;* Gail Thomas, ed., *Imagining Dallas* (Dallas: Pegasus Foundation for the Dallas Institute for Humanities and Culture, 1982); Robert Sardello and Gail Thomas, eds., *Stirrings of Culture* (Dallas: Dallas Institute Publications, 1986).

2. A. C. Greene, "What Makes Dallas a Different City," in Thomas, *Imagining Dallas*, 51.

3. Greene, *Dallas U.S.A.,* 59.

4. Smith, "How Business Failed Dallas," 160. Not coincidentally, Smith used a metaphor of flight at the moment when Dallas leaders were deciding to build a major new airport jointly with Fort Worth.

5. James Donald, "Metropolis: The City as Text," in *Social and Cultural Forms of Modernity*, ed. Robert Bocock and Kenneth Thompson (Cambridge: Polity Press, 1992), 427. The term "imagined environment" refers to Benedict Anderson, *Imagined Communities: Reflections on the Origin and Spread of Nationalism*, rev. ed. (London: Verso, 1991). See also Rob Shields, "A Guide to Urban Representation and What to Do About It: Alternative Traditions of Urban Theory," in *Re-Presenting the City: Ethnicity, Capital and Culture in the Twenty-first-Century Metropolis*, ed. Anthony D. King (New York: New York University Press, 1996), 227–52.

6. Zukin, *Landscapes of Power*, 18. See also D'Eramo, *The Pig and the Skyscraper*, 142, 143, 144.

7. Wirth-Nesher, *City Codes*, 8–9. See also Taylor, *In Pursuit of Gotham*.

8. See Boyer, *City of Collective Memory;* Dolores Hayden, *The Power of Place: Urban Landscapes as Public History* (Cambridge, Mass.: MIT Press, 1995).

9. Findlay, *Magic Lands,* 282, 283. Findlay draws upon the work of Amos Rapoport, Kevin Lynch, Yi-Fu Tuan, Anselm Strauss, Grady Clay, Roger Downs and David Stea, and Peter Orleans.

10. Davis, *City of Quartz,* 23.

11. Gervase Rosser, "Myth, Image and Social Process in the English Medieval Town," *Urban History* 23 (1996): 25.

12. Noteworthy examples are the writings of Sam Acheson, John William Rogers, Lon Tinkle, and A. C. Greene.

13. Patricia Evridge Hill, *Dallas: The Making of a Modern City* (Austin: University of Texas Press, 1996). In his review of her book, historian William H. Wilson expresses the impossible hope that, through Hill's work, "the myth will now be laid to rest"; see *Legacies* 9 (1997): 60.

14. Michael V. Hazel, *Dallas: A History of "Big D,"* Fred Rider Cotten Popular History Series, No. 11 (Austin: Texas State Historical Association, 1997), 64–65.

15. Raymond Williams, *Keywords: A Vocabulary of Culture and Society,* rev. ed. (New York: Oxford University Press, 1983), 210–12.

16. William H. McNeill, "Mythistory, or Truth, Myth, History, and Historians," in *Mythistory and Other Essays* (Chicago: University of Chicago Press, 1986), 3, 7. I prefer "mythohistory" to McNeill's "mythistory."

17. *Memorial and Biographical History of Dallas County, Texas* (Chicago: Lewis Publishing, 1892), 272, 273.

18. Colonel John F. Elliott, "substantial and influential citizen" and writer, is quoted in *Memorial and Biographical History,* 275. This work exaggerated the city's population and rate of growth.

19. Billingsley, "Trip to Texas," 203–04.

20. *Memorial and Biographical History,* 275–76.

21. Enstam, *When Dallas Became a City,* 47, 61.

22. McCoy, quoted in ibid., 77.

23. *Souvenir Guide of Dallas . . . with a Directory of the Leading Business Firms and Professional Men,* compiled by the D. M. Anderson Directory Company (Dallas: J. M. Colville's Franklin Trust, 1894), 5, 7.

24. Ibid., 11, 19.

25. See J. McElhaney, "Navigating the Trinity," in *Dallas Reconsidered: Essays in Local History,* ed. Michael Hazel (Dallas: Three Forks Press, 1995), 45–69, reprinted from *Legacies.*

26. See architect James Pratt's "Dallas: Visions for Community: Toward a 21st-Century Urban Design," *Dallas Morning News,* November 19, 1990.

27. The best introduction to politics in Dallas history is Hill, *Dallas.* See also Elizabeth York Enstam, *Women and the Creation of Urban Life: Dallas, Texas, 1843–1920* (College Station: Texas A&M University Press, 1998); Jacquelyn Masur McElhaney, *Pauline Periwinkle and Progressive Reform in Dallas* (College Station: Texas A&M University Press, 1998); Alicia E. Rodriquez, "Disenfranchisement in Dallas: The Democratic Party and the Suppression of Independent Political Challenges in Dallas, Texas,

1891–1894," *Southwestern Historical Quarterly* 108 (2004): 43–64; Payne, *Big D;* Royce Hanson, *Civic Culture and Urban Change: Governing Dallas* (Detroit: Wayne State University Press, 2003); Ruth P. Morgan, *Governance by Decree: The Impact of the Voting Rights Action in Dallas* (Lawrence: University Press of Kansas, 2004); Bridges, *Morning Glories.* On race, see Phillips, *White Metropolis;* Phillips, "The Fire This Time"; Michael Phillips, "White Violence, Hegemony, and Slave Rebellion in Dallas, Texas, Before the Civil War," *East Texas Historical Journal* 37 (1999): 25–35; Dulaney, "Whatever Happened to the Civil Rights Movement?"; Dulaney, "Progressive Voters League"; William H. Wilson, *Hamilton Park: A Planned Black Community in Dallas* (Baltimore, Md.: Johns Hopkins University Press, 1998); Wilson, "Desegregation of the Hamilton Park School, 1955–1975," *Southwestern Historical Quarterly* 95 (1991): 42–63; Wilson, "Living in the Planned Community: Residents of Hamilton Park, Dallas, 1954–1990," *Proceedings of the Fourth National Conference on American Planning History & Fifth International Conference of Planning History Group* 4 (1993): 687–99; Wilson, "'This Negro Housing Matter': The Search for a Viable African-American Residential Subdivision in Dallas, 1945–1950," *Legacies* 6 (1994): 28–40; Wilson, "Private Planning for Black Housing in Dallas, Texas, 1945–1955," *Proceedings of the Second National Conference on Planning History* 2 (1988): 67–84; Glenn M. Linden, *Desegregating Schools in Dallas: Four Decades in the Federal Courts* (Dallas: Three Forks Press, 1995). On planning in Dallas, see Robert B. Fairbanks, *For the City as a Whole: Planning, Politics, and the Public Interest in Dallas, Texas, 1900–1965* (Columbus: Ohio State University Press, 1998); Fairbanks, "Rethinking Urban Problems: Planning, Zoning, and City Government in Dallas, 1900–1930," *Journal of Urban History* 25 (1999): 809–37; Fairbanks, "Making Better Citizens in Dallas: The Kessler Plan Association and Consensus Building in the 1920s," *Legacies* 11 (1999): 26–36; Fairbanks, "Public Housing for the City as a Whole: The Texas Experience, 1934–1955," *Southwestern Historical Quarterly* 103 (2000): 403–24.

28. On political elites, see Hill, *Dallas;* C. E. Thometz, *The Decision-Makers: The Power Structure of Dallas* (Dallas: Southern Methodist University Press, 1964); C. J. Barta, "The *Dallas News* and Council-Manager Government" (master's thesis, University of Texas, 1970).

29. Here I differ in emphasis from Patricia Hill's and Elizabeth Enstam's arguments about the importance of women in the making of Dallas.

30. Examples include "Dallas in Wonderland," *Fortune,* November 1937, 112–20, 200–209; "Texas Tells 'Em: Neiman-Marcus Company," *Colliers,* September 16, 1939; Corn, "Dallas"; George Sessions Perry, "Dallas and Fort Worth," *Saturday Evening Post,* March 30, 1946; McCombs and Whyte, "Dydamic Men of Dallas"; Street, "Dazzling Dallas"; "Dallas," *Nation's Business,* January 1975; Smith, "Dallas!"

31. McCombs and Whyte, "Dydamic Men of Dallas," 99, 101. The "Super-American" reference is Bainbridge's. In 1964, after the assassination, *Fortune* repudiated much of this image.

32. McCombs and Whyte, "Dydamic Men of Dallas," 99, 101.

33. "Dallas Texas USA: Love Where You're From," *Dallas Morning News,* August 8, 1993.

34. Ted Jones, *Dallas: Its History, Its Development, Its Beauty* (Dallas: Lamar & Barton, compliments of the Republic National Bank and Republic Trust and Savings Bank, 1925), 7. On urban boosterism, see Kathleen Conzen, "Community Studies, Urban History, and American Local History," in *The Past Before Us*, ed. Michael Kammen (Ithaca, N.Y.: Cornell University Press, 1980), 270–91; Wade, *Urban Frontier;* Goldfield, *Cotton Fields and Skyscrapers;* Cronon, *Nature's Metropolis;* Timothy Mahoney, *River Towns in the Great West: The Structure of Provincial Urbanization in the American Midwest, 1820–1870* (Cambridge: Cambridge University Press, 1990); Mahoney, *Provincial Lives: Middle-Class Experience in the Antebellum Middle West* (Cambridge: Cambridge University Press, 1999).

35. Hill, *Dallas,* xiv.

36. On politics, see Bradley Rice, *Progressive Cities: The Commission Government Movement in America, 1901–1920* (Austin: University of Texas Press, 1977). On race, see also Jim Schutze, *The Accommodation: The Politics of Race in an American City* (Secaucus, N.J.: Citadel Press, 1986). On planning, see also William Black, "Empire of Consensus: City Planning, Zoning, and Annexation in Dallas, Texas, 1900–1960" (PhD diss., Columbia University, 1982); A. B. Govenar and J. F. Brakefield, *Deep Ellum and Central Track: Where the Black and White Worlds of Dallas Converged* (Denton: University of North Texas Press, 1998). On reform, see Hanson, *Civic Culture and Urban Change;* Morgan, *Governance By Decree;* Patricia E. Gower, "Dallas in the Progressive Era" (PhD diss., Texas A&M University, 1996); Alicia Rodriquez, "Urban Populism: Challenges to Democratic Control in Dallas, Texas, 1887–1900" (PhD diss., University of California, Santa Barbara, 1998).

37. See Kenneth B. Ragsdale, *The Year America Discovered Texas: Centennial '36* (College Station: Texas A&M University Press, 1987). On politics, in addition to Hill's *Dallas* and Bridges's *Morning Glories,* see Robert Fairbanks, "The Good Government Machine: The Citizens Charter Association and Dallas Politics, 1930–1960," in Fairbanks and Underwood, *Essays on Sunbelt Cities,* 125–50; Fairbanks, "Metropolitan Planning and Downtown Redevelopment: The Cincinnati and Dallas Experiences, 1940–1960," *Planning Perspectives* 2 (1987): 237–53; Fairbanks, "From Consensus to Controversy: The Rise and Fall of Public Housing in Dallas," *Legacies* 1 (1989): 37–43; Fairbanks, "Planning, Public Works, and Politics: The Trinity River Reclamation Project in Dallas," in *Planning the Twentieth-Century American City,* ed. Mary Corbin Sies and Christopher Silver (Baltimore, Md.: Johns Hopkins University Press, 1996), 187–212; Fairbanks, "Responding to the Airplane: Urban Rivalry, Metropolitan Regionalism, and Airport Development in Dallas, 1927–1965," in *Technical Knowledge in American Culture: Science, Technology, and Medicine since the Early 1800s,* ed. Hamilton Cravens, Alan I. Marcus, and David M. Katzman (Tuscaloosa: University of Alabama Press, 1996), 171–88; Fairbanks, *For the City as a Whole.* But compare William H. Wilson, *The City Beautiful Movement* (Baltimore, Md.: Johns Hopkins University Press, 1989); Wilson, "Adapting to Growth: Dallas, Texas, and the Kessler Plan, 1908–1933," *Arizona and the West* 25 (1983): 245–60; Wilson, "'Merely Unpractical Dreams': Removing the Texas & Pacific

Tracks from Pacific Avenue," *Legacies* 2 (1990): 26–34; Roger Biles, "The New Deal in Dallas," *Southwestern Historical Quarterly* 95 (1991): 1–19.

38. Walker, *The Dallas Story,* 2–3.

39. Quoted in "The Dallas Way," special section commemorating the fiftieth anniversary of the Dallas Citizens Council, *Dallas Times Herald,* November 15, 1987. See also John Anders, *Dallas Morning News,* February 3, 1995; Charlotte James, letter to the editor, *Dallas Morning News,* November 15, 1989.

40. R. L. Thornton, *Dallas: The Southwest's Leading City* (from *Dallas Morning News,* n.d., but before 1936), 43, 45.

41. Dallas author and professor Marshall Terry captures this spirit in his story, "The Prince of Dallas," one of the few pieces of fiction sited in Dallas. Standing in an office and surveying the cityscape, a character reflects on the Dallas myth: "not the old Neely Bryan bit exactly, for he knew just how corny that was, but the idea of the lack of strong geographical or other reasons for a great city to have sprung up, to have been built here, by strong men, by pirates and pioneers. They were all proud of that, and it had, he thought, its degree of truth." Marshall Terry, "The Prince of Dallas," in *Dallas Stories* (Dallas: Southern Methodist University Press, 1987), 1.

42. Among many representations of Dallas, see for example, Leslie, *Dallas Public and Private;* meetings and publications of the Dallas Institute for Humanities and Culture; spreads in mass-market publications such as *National Geographic* on the 1984 Republican National Convention in Dallas; television commercials; tourist promotions; mentions in movies and fiction.

43. "Dallas Texas USA: Love Where You're From."

44. For example, see Harvey J. Graff, "Teaching Historical Understanding: Disciplining Historical Imagination with Historical Context," in *The Social Worlds of Higher Education: Handbook for Teaching in a New Century,* ed. Bernice A. Pescosolido and Ronald Aminzade (Thousand Oaks, Calif.: Pine Forge Press/Sage Publications for the American Sociological Association, 1999), 280–94.

45. One volume aimed at the popular market, Oppenheimer and Porterfield, *Book of Dallas,* begins with "Dallas Trademarks and Symbols." The chapter mentions automobiles, highways, and the skyline but fails to make Dallas-specific connections, such as cotton, Neiman Marcus, or the Cowboys. It has no historical chapter. Newspapers, magazines, and even books on Dallas delight in presenting pages of trivia. See, among many examples, "So You Think You Know Everything About Dallas," *D Magazine,* June 1982; "Dallas Firsts," *D Magazine,* August 1983; Chris Tucker, "A Muckraker's Tour of Dallas," *D Magazine,* June 1984; "Marking History," *Dallas Morning News* "Guide," November 20, 1992; Rose-Mary Rumbley, *The Unauthorized History of Dallas: The Scenic Route Through 150 Years in "Big D"* (Austin: Eakin Press, 1991); "Dallas Mileposts Abound," *Dallas Morning News,* January 1, 1994; Larenda Lyles Roberts, *Undiscovered Dallas* (Plano: Republic of Texas Press, Wordware, 1995).

46. Greene, "What Makes Dallas a Different City," 49, 51.

47. Wick Allison, "Revisioning the Past: Why Dallas Is Here," in Thomas, *Imagining Dallas,* 28.

48. A. C. Greene, *Dallas: The Deciding Years—A Historical Portrait,* Published for Sanger-Harris in Commemoration of its 100th Year in Dallas (Austin: Encino Press, 1973), v.

49. Ibid.

50. William L. McDonald, *Dallas Rediscovered: A Photographic Chronicle of Urban Expansion, 1870–1925* (Dallas: Dallas Historical Society, 1978), 7.

51. For an earlier version, see Maxine Holmes and Gerald D. Saxon, eds., *WPA Dallas Guide and History* (1936–42; Denton: Dallas Public Library, Texas Center for the Book, and University of North Texas Press, 1992).

52. A. C. Greene, "Myths Take Wing on Pegasus Plaza," *Dallas Morning News,* January 22, 1995. On the role of cities in stimulating development in Texas, see Char Miller and David Johnson, "The Rise of Urban Texas," in *Urban Texas: Politics and Development,* ed. Miller and Heywood T. Sanders (College Station: Texas A&M University Press, 1990), 3–29; Kenneth Wheeler, *To Wear a City's Crown: The Beginnings of Urban Growth in Texas, 1836–1865* (Cambridge, Mass.: Harvard University Press, 1968).

53. See Miller and Johnson, "Rise of Urban Texas"; Goldfield, *Cotton Fields and Skyscrapers;* Goldfield, *Region, Race, and Cities;* Harold Platt, *City Building in the New South: The Growth of Public Services in Houston, Texas, 1830–1920* (Philadelphia: Temple University Press, 1983); Wheeler, *To Wear a City's Crown.* For the role of cities in the settlement of the Midwest and West, see Wade, *Urban Frontier;* Cronon, *Nature's Metropolis;* Eric H. Monkkonen, *America Becomes Urban: The Development of U.S. Cities and Towns 1780–1980* (Berkeley and Los Angeles: University of California Press, 1988).

54. Frederick Wiseman's excellent film *The Store* (1983) portrays Neiman Marcus.

55. See, for example, Smith, "Dallas!" 278, especially the photographs.

56. That Jim Schutze is a journalist, not a historian, and that *The Accommodation* was underdocumented do not begin to explain why there was a concerted effort to suppress this work. Although the course of events remains murky, it was widely presumed that influential Dallasites pressured Dallas-based Taylor Publishing to cancel its contract to publish the book. The accusation circulated widely, including in national media such as *The New York Times,* and embarrassed the city. See Ruth Miller Fitzgibbons, "Editor's Page: Why Shoot the Messenger for Bearing the Bad News?" *D Magazine,* November 1986, 11–12; Gregory Curtis, "Behind the Lines: A Book's Improper Burial," *Texas Monthly,* November 1986, 5–6, 242. See also Darwin Payne, "Race and Dallas: A Flawed Indictment," *Dallas Times Herald,* April 26, 1987.

57. For comparisons, see Zukin, *Landscapes of Power;* Robert A. Beauregard, *Voices of Decline: The Postwar Fate of U.S. Cities,* 2nd ed. (New York: Routledge, 2003); Dear, *Postmodern Urban Condition;* Dear, *From Chicago to LA;* Dear, Shockman, and Hise, *Rethinking Los Angeles;* Soja, *Postmodern Geographies.*

58. Dallas investors suffered significant losses in real estate, gas, and oil in the 1970s and 1980s.

59. Contra historian Robert Fairbanks, Dallas never was "the city as a whole," nor did its elite act on behalf of the city as a whole.

60. "City Tainted by Scandals, Some Worry," *Dallas Morning News,* October 19,

1997. Other telling examples include "Arena Vote," *Dallas Morning News,* January 1, 1998; "Housing Summit: Attendees Try to Prod Dallas toward Greatness," *Dallas Morning News,* February 3, 1998.

61. On the eclipse of history by theme park, see Davis, *City of Quartz;* Klein, *History of Forgetting;* Rutheiser, *Imagineering Atlanta;* Thomas Frank, "A Machine for Forgetting: Kansas City and the Declining Significance of Place," *The Baffler* 7 (1995).

62. The major works on "inventing" history include Eric Hobsbawn and Terence Ranger, eds., *The Invention of Tradition* (Cambridge: Cambridge University Press, 1972); Raphael Samuel, *Theatres of Memory: Past and Present in Contemporary Culture* (London: Verso, 1994); David Lowenthal, *The Past is a Foreign Country* (Cambridge: Cambridge University Press, 1985); Lowenthal, *The Heritage Crusade and the Spoils of History* (Cambridge: Cambridge University Press, 1998); Roy Rosenzweig and David Thelen, *The Presence of the Past: Popular Uses of History in American Life* (New York: Columbia University Press, 1998); Susan Porter Benson, Stephen Brier, and Roy Rosenzweig, eds., *Presenting the Past: Essays on History and the Public* (Philadelphia: Temple University Press, 1986); Mike Wallace, *Mickey Mouse History and Other Essays on American Memory* (Philadelphia: Temple University Press, 1996).

63. For an effort at business appropriation of history, see Darwin Payne, *Dallas: An Illustrated History* (Dallas: Windsor Publications, 1982); for "neighborhood" appropriation, see McDonald, *Dallas Rediscovered.*

64. "Out with the Old, in with the New: Dallas Developers, Preservationists Often at Odds," *Dallas Morning News,* October 23, 1994; "Arbor Ways: Tree Preservationists, Developers Clash over Dallas' Urban Forest," *Dallas Morning News,* May 29, 1996. On adaptive reuse and invention, see Sharon Zukin, *Loft Living: Culture and Capital in Urban Change* (Baltimore, Md.: Johns Hopkins University Press, 1982); Mele, *Selling the Lower East Side.*

65. See Joe Holley, "Landmarks That Should Be Saved . . . But Can Anybody Afford To?" *D Magazine,* August 1997, 70–75; George Toomer, "Dallas Deco," *D Magazine,* February 1978, 89–91; Larry Herold, "Pillars of the Past," *D Magazine,* September 1983, 58–63; "Dallas Historic Preservation Plan," prepared by the Dallas Landmark Committee and the Department of Planning and Development, August 1983; David Dillon, "Council Has Plans—for a Vacant Lot," *Dallas Morning News,* January 24, 1993.

66. Jim Schutze, "Dallas Needs a Ruin to Remind It of Past," *Dallas Times Herald,* February 14, 1985.

67. For a serious discussion of this subject from the perspective of cultural geography and landscape history, see John Brinkerhoff Jackson, *The Necessity for Ruins, and other Topics* (Amherst: University of Massachusetts Press, 1980).

68. See John Gillis, *Commemorations* (Princeton, N.J.: Princeton University Press, 1996).

69. "Voters Reject Tax Hike Benefiting Fair Park," *Dallas Morning News,* August 9, 1992; Marina Isola, "Deep in the Heart of Dallas, Art Deco Deluxe," *New York Times,* November 12, 1995.

70. The African American Museum, opened in 1993, features African and African

American art. The Women's Museum, subtitled "An Institute for the Future," describes itself as "a national center for the celebration and study of the immeasurable contributions women have made to society." Exhibits commemorate the women's movement and women who have excelled in the arts, sports, politics, and science. It opened in 2000 in the former Coliseum building, part of the State Fair site since 1909. The Museum of Nature and Science was formed through the merger of the older Dallas Museum of Natural History and Science Place, a newer museum of science and technology. It plans to build a new facility downtown.

71. "Sesquicentennial: Dallas County Celebrates 150 Years of History," editorial, *Dallas Morning News,* March 31, 1996; "Dallas' Cattle Call to Celebration," *Dallas Morning News,* April 21, 1996. See also "Chisholm Trail Designated, But Purists Object," *New York Times,* November 29, 2001; "Cabin on the Move Again: Symbolic Home of Dallas' Founding Father Crossing the Street," *Dallas Morning News,* March 16, 2004; "Bryan Cabin Is Feeling Unsettled as Officials Vote to Move Landmark," *Dallas Morning News,* June 29, 2004; "Descendants of Dallas' Founder Turning Up Cabin Pressure: They Don't Want County to Remove Replica from Downtown," *Dallas Morning News,* July 11, 2004. In 2004, the cabin was slated to move across the street, closer to the Old Red site of the new museum, clearing space for excavation of a new underground parking garage. David Schultz of the Old Red Foundation stated, "The cabin is a significant replica. For the folks who go through this area, it creates a sense of understanding that we hold our past close and are proud of our origins" (ibid.).

72. Dana Rubin, "Little House on the Plaza," *Texas Monthly,* July 1990, 40, 46.

73. A. C. Greene, "History Shows That Big D Was a Cowtown," *Dallas Morning News,* July 24, 1994.

74. "Dallas' Cattle Call to Celebration"; "Chisholm Trail Designated."

75. "Dallas, Where West Ends, Casts Image as a Cowtown," *New York Times,* January 17, 1994. The *Dallas Morning News* responded to aesthetic criticism of the sculptures by calling the city's Public Art Committee misguided snobs who used the wrong definition of art; "Art Vote: City Should Hang onto Longhorns," *Dallas Morning News,* March 13, 1993.

76. "Landmark Event," *Dallas Morning News,* March 6, 1994.

77. "Steer Crazy," *Dallas Morning News,* May 27, 1996.

78. Dallas megadeveloper and self-proclaimed connoisseur Trammel Crow, who was instrumental in the land deals that made Pioneer Plaza possible, enthused, "I think the artistry of the sculptures is magnificent, the design of the area is spectacular. It's a real depiction of the way this country was 150 years ago": "Dallas, Where West Ends, Casts Image as a Cowtown."

79. Ibid.

80. See also Dana Rubin, "Hoof in Mouth," *Texas Monthly,* October 1995, 58–62.

81. Laura Miller, "A Vote Cast in Bronze," *Dallas Observer,* September 30–October 6, 1993; Miller, "Bad Taste on the Hoof," *Dallas Observer,* August 5–11, 1993; Ellise Pierce, "Bum Steers: Why Trammel Crow Wants to Turn a Downtown Parking Lot into

Cowboy," *Dallas Observer,* March 4–10, 1993; "Luna, Lipscomb Want to Halt Plan for Steer Sculpture," *Dallas Morning News,* April 22, 1993.

82. Rubin, "Hoof in Mouth."

83. Given to the city in 1876, the park had garden walkways, augmented by such recreational facilities as tennis courts and a swimming pool, but over the years it was allowed to decay, and some of its acreage was taken for the freeway.

84. Thomas H. Smith, "Old City Park Focus May Be Misunderstood," *Dallas Times Herald,* February 16, 1988.

85. Heritage Village has made an effort to be more inclusive, adding a Jewish household, telling the docents to discuss slavery more extensively, and sponsoring events such as a debate on Michael Phillips's book *White Metropolis.*

86. Jim Schutze, "Old City Park Presents Too Pretty a Picture of Dallas' Past," *Dallas Times Herald,* February 10, 1988; Anita Creamer, "Cleaning Up Dallas' Past for the Future," *Dallas Times Herald,* October 17, 1985; Molly Ivins, "Urban Cleansing: Dallas Polishes Its Reactionary, Heartless Image," *Dallas Observer,* May 20–26, 1993.

87. See Wallace, *Mickey Mouse History;* Richard Handler and Eric Gale, *The New History in an Old Museum: Creating the Past in Colonial Williamsburg* (Durham, N.C.: Duke University Press, 1997); Warren Leon and Roy Rosenzweig, eds., *History Museums in the United States: A Critical Assessment* (Urbana: University of Illinois Press, 1989); Patrick Wright, *On Living in an Old Country: The National Past in Contemporary Britain* (London: Verso, 1986).

88. See www.dallasculture.org/JuanitaCraftHouse.cfm.

89. I was privileged to speak at the first public event of Black Dallas Remembered.

90. Creamer, "Cleaning Up Dallas' Past for the Future."

91. Ibid. For Molly Ivins, this effort includes literally hiding the poor, for example, at the time of the 1984 Republican National Convention. See also Jim Schutze's column.

92. See also the works of Davis, Rutheiser, Klein, Samuels, and Wright.

93. Quoted in "The Dallas Way." See also John Anders, *Dallas Morning News,* February 3, 1995; Charlotte James, letter to the editor, *Dallas Morning News,* November 15, 1995. For a precedent, see *Dallas, the Convention City* (Dallas: Chamber of Commerce, 1912).

94. Williams, *Keywords,* 153–57. See also Lentriccia and McLaughlin, *Critical Terms for Literary Study;* Irena R. Makaryk, ed., *Encyclopedia of Contemporary Literary Theory: Approaches, Scholars, Terms* (Toronto: University of Toronto Press, 1993); Adam Kuper and Jessica Kuper, eds., *The Social Science Encyclopedia* (London: Routledge, 1985).

95. Smith, "Dallas!" 278.

96. Leslie, *Dallas Public and Private,* 21–23.

97. Thornton, *Dallas: The Southwest's Leading City,* 39.

98. Bainbridge, *Super-Americans,* 142.

99. Ibid., 145. On the youthfulness and homogeneity of the city, see Holmes and Saxon, *WPA Dallas Guide and History:* "Dallas has been repeatedly called cosmopolitan, and some have accused it of lacking soul and individual character. Neither is quite accurate. Though externally cosmopolitan, it retains many of the characteristics of Main Street. Nor is it altogether lacking in individuality. Its very lack of indigenous features

gives it a certain character peculiar to itself. It has been called a 'Northern city under a Southern sun and in a Southern setting.' Its setting and climate are Northern; its sophistication and modishness Eastern; and its civic pride and youthful, confident spirit, delighting in newness and bigness for their own sake, Western. It is a sort of archetypal American city, like Zenith, the home town of Babbitt in Sinclair Lewis's novels—a city created by American business enterprise for its own special and individual purposes of pride and profit, according to the stereotyped pattern of the American city, relatively unmodified by geographical, racial, or other factors" (10).

100. Bainbridge, *Super-Americans,* 144.

101. "City, State Lose Can-Do Illusions," *Dallas Morning News,* June 23, 1991; "City Tainted by Scandals, Some Worry"; "Will Town Lake Remain a Far-Off Dream?" *Dallas Morning News,* February 18, 1998.

102. "Arena Vote," *Dallas Morning News,* January 21, 1998; "Arena Victory," *Dallas Morning News,* January 19, 1998.

3. REVISING DALLAS'S HISTORIES

The appendixes to this volume supplement this chapter in particular.

1. "Dallasites Would Benefit by Knowing Local History," *Dallas Morning News,* February 19, 2003. See also "Students Can Learn about Texas, George Washington and Napoleon . . . but What about Dallas's Past? Budget and Time Constraints Block Efforts to Teach about Area's Roots," *Dallas Morning News,* February 16, 2003; "Net Offers Haven for History Buffs," *Dallas Morning News,* March 16, 2003.

2. "Dallasites Would Benefit by Knowing Local History."

3. See also David Schultz, "Dallas' Historical Myth," *Dallas Morning News,* September 29, 2002; "Dallas History: Old Red Will Reveal There Is Such a Thing," *Dallas Morning News,* December 5, 2001; "History Beyond the Obvious: Museum Seeks to Show Facets of Everyday Life in Dallas County," *Dallas Morning News,* January 10, 2004.

4. Monkkonen, *America Becomes Urban,* 5–6.

5. Miller and Johnson, "Rise of Urban Texas," 9. On "Sunbelt" cities, see Carl Abbott, *The Metropolitan Frontier: Cities in the Modern American West* (Tucson: University of Arizona Press, 1987); Goldfield, *Cotton Fields and Skyscrapers;* Goldfield, *Region, Race, and Cities;* Bernard and Rice, *Sunbelt Cities;* Mohl, *Searching for the Sunbelt;* Miller and Pozzetta, *Shades of the Sunbelt;* Fairbanks and Underwood, *Essays on Sunbelt Cities;* Perry and Watkins, *Rise of the Sunbelt Cities.*

6. For beginnings, see Enstam, *Women and the Creation of Urban Life;* Wilson, *Hamilton Park;* Dulaney, "Whatever Happened to the Civil Rights Movement?"; Dulaney, "Progressive Voters League"; Phillips, *White Metropolis;* Phillips, "The Fire This Time"; Cole, "Finding Race in Turn-of-the-Century Dallas."

7. Contrast this, for example, with Payne, *Big D, D Magazine*'s updated "mugbook" history, and *Legacies,* originally a joint publication of Dallas Historical Society and Old City Park, and joined by the Old Red Foundation and Sixth Floor Museum at Dealey Place as additional sponsors.

8. Some recent work includes earlier periods: Hill, *Dallas;* Enstam, *Women and the Creation of Urban Life;* Fairbanks, *For the City as a Whole;* McElhaney, *Pauline Periwinkle;* Phillips, *White Metropolis.*

9. My approach is certainly not the only one; it is neither a consensus nor a popular view. But it is one of several currents revising Dallas history and historiography. This growing body of work includes Philips, *White Metropolis;* Cole, "Finding Race in Turn-of-the-Century Dallas"; Rodriquez, "Urban Populism." See also Enstam, *Women and the Creation of Urban Life;* Fairbanks, *For the City as a Whole;* Hazel, *Dallas;* Payne, *Big D;* Black, "Empire of Consensus"; Gower, "Dallas in the Progressive Era."

10. See, on race, Dulaney, "Whatever Happened to the Civil Rights Movement?"; Phillips, *White Metropolis;* Cole "Finding Race in Turn-of-the-Century Dallas"; on the working class and organized labor, Hill, *Dallas;* on women, Enstam, *Women and the Creation of Urban Life;* McElhaney, *Pauline Periwinkle.*

11. See Michael Wallace and Edwin Burrows, *Gotham: A History of New York City to 1898* (New York: Oxford University Press, 1998).

12. See Jean-Christophe Agnew, "The Threshold of Exchange: Speculations on the Market," *Radical History Review* 21 (Fall 1979): 99–118.

13. See Wade, *Urban Frontier,* and the literature that followed, including Cronon, *Nature's Metropolis;* Mahoney, *River Towns in the Great West;* Mahoney, *Provincial Lives.*

14. Stuart M. Blumin, "When Villages Become Towns: The Historical Contexts of Town Formation," in *The Pursuit of Urban History,* ed. Derek Fraser and Anthony Sutcliffe (London: Edward Arnold, 1983), 55, 56, 57.

15. Ibid., 57.

16. Ibid., 59. Blumin's frequent example was Kingston, New York, but his generalizations hold for early Dallas. See also Allan R. Pred, *Urban Growth and the Circulation of Information: The United States System of Cities 1790–1840* (Cambridge, Mass.: Harvard University Press, 1973); Pred, *Urban Growth and City-Systems in the United States, 1840–1860* (Cambridge, Mass.: Harvard University Press, 1980); Cronon, *Nature's Metropolis.* Kerry A. Odell and David F. Weiman, "Metropolitan Development, Regional Financial Centers, and the Founding of the Fed in the Lower South," *Journal of Economic History* 58 (1998): 103–25, identifies the metropolitan network status of Atlanta and Dallas as centers for wholesale distribution, financial transaction, and banking after 1880.

17. This statement is erroneously attributed to General Motors President Charles Wilson in testimony before the U.S. Senate in 1955. Nonetheless, its persistence attests to its power to epitomize what some regard as the "American Way."

18. The city's entrepreneurs have seldom been as autonomous, omniscient, or successful as they are portrayed. Compare Hanson, *Civic Culture and Urban Change,* and Hill, *Dallas,* with Payne, *Big D,* Fairbanks, *For the City as a Whole,* and Hazel, *Dallas.* See also Morgan, *Governance by Decree.*

19. Especially important is Bridges, *Morning Glories.* See also John Logan and Harvey Molotch, *Urban Fortunes* (Berkeley and Los Angeles: University of California Press, 1987); John H. Mollenkopf, *The Contested City* (Princeton, N.J.: Princeton University

Press, 1983); Neil Smith, *The New Urban Frontier: Gentrification and the Revanchist City* (New York: Routledge, 1996); Zukin, *Landscapes of Power;* Clarence N. Stone, *Regime Politics: Governing Atlanta, 1946–1988* (Lawrence: University of Kansas Press, 1989); Stone and Heywood T. Sanders, eds., *The Politics of Urban Development* (Lawrence: University of Kansas Press, 1987); Hanson, *Civic Culture and Urban Change.*

20. The question of charter revision was raised periodically throughout the 1990s. In May 2005, the "strong mayor" proposal was roundly rejected.

21. Hazel, *Dallas,* 65. Compare Hazel, Payne's *Big D,* and Fairbanks's *For the City as a Whole* to Phillips's *White Metropolis,* Dulaney's "Whatever Happened to the Civil Rights Movement?" Hill's *Dallas,* Hanson's *Civic Culture and Urban Change,* and especially to the reception accorded Schutze, *The Accommodation.*

22. Compare Hazel, *Dallas,* to Phillips, *White Metropolis;* Hill, *Dallas;* Dulaney, "Whatever Happened to the Civil Rights Movement?"; Dulaney, "Progressive Voters League"; Wilson, *Hamilton Park;* Schutze, *The Accommodation.*

23. Local institutions include Dallas Historical Society, Preservation Dallas, Dallas County Historical Society, Old City Park, Old Red Courthouse Museum of Dallas. See Hazel, *Dallas;* Payne, *Big D;* Fairbanks, *For the City as a Whole;* Enstam, *Women and the Creation of Urban Life;* McElhaney, *Pauline Periwinkle;* Wilson, *Hamilton Park.*

24. This complex phenomenon is fraught with controversy, including questions about "authentic copies," "faithful" or "authentic" historical preservation by reproduction, reconstruction, renovation, or fabrication, and "restoration," all of which aim at reproducing an improved past. See Ada Louise Huxtable, "Inventing American Reality," *New York Review,* December 3, 1992; Lowenthal, *The Past Is a Foreign Country;* David Lowenthal, *Possessed by the Past: The Heritage Crusade and the Spoils of History* (New York: Free Press, 1996); Wright, *On Living in an Old Country;* Sorkin, *Variations on a Theme Park;* Boyer, *Dreaming the Rational City;* Hayden, *Power of Place;* Smith, *New Urban Frontier;* Mele, *Selling the Lower East Side;* Kearns and Philo, *Selling Places;* Ward, *Selling Places.*

25. See the critical literature on Colonial Williamsburg, Disneyland and Disney World, Greenfield Village, and other history theme parks: Wallace, *Mickey Mouse History;* Handler and Gale, *New History in an Old Museum;* Sorkin, *Variations on a Theme Park;* Zukin, *Landscapes of Power;* Findlay, *Magic Lands.* On theme park cities, see Davis, *City of Quartz;* Davis, *Spectacular Nature;* Soja, *Postmodern Geographies;* Dear, *Postmodern Urban Condition;* Gottdiener et al., *Theming of America;* Hannigan, *Fantasy City;* Judd and Fainstain, *Tourist City;* Mele, *Selling the Lower East Side.*

26. Although I cannot pursue the connections here, the new urban historicism shares a great deal with the "New Urbanism," including a thick coating of sentimentality and nostalgia; neglect of inequality, power, and social difference; and great exaggerations about both novelty and historical roots. Architects Andres Dunay and Elizabeth Plater-Zyberk are often regarded as its founders. For the "design movement," see Congress for the New Urbanism Web site (http://www.cnu.org/) or New Urbanism Web site (http://www.newurbanism.org/pages/416429/). For criticism, see Alex Marshall, *How Cities Work: Suburbs, Sprawl, and the Road Not Taken* (Austin: University of Texas Press, 2001).

27. Chris Kelley, "Past Provides a View of Dallas' Future: City Looks to Its Roots to Develop a More Authentic Sense of Place," *Dallas Morning News,* January 24, 1999. See also David Dillon, "Reaching for the Sky," *Dallas Morning News,* May 2, 1999; Dillon, "Where We Live," *Dallas Morning News,* May 5, 1999.

28. Ron Kirk, "Dallas: A New City Discovers Its Past," *Forum Journal,* Fall 2001, 40, 44. See also Kelley, "Past Provides a View of Dallas' Future"; Dillon, "Reaching for the Sky"; Dillon, "Where We Live."

29. Fuller, *American Institute of Architects, Guide to Dallas Architecture,* 165.

30. See, for example, Mark Gottdiener et al., *Las Vegas: The Social Production of an All-American City* (Oxford: Blackwell, 1999); Rothman, *Devil's Bargains;* Rothman, *Neon Metropolis;* Rothman and Davis, *Grit Between the Glitter.*

31. Compare Sorkin, *Variations on a Theme Park,* with Kelley, "Past Provides a View of Dallas' Future."

32. For discussion of the major issues in the relationship of history to its various publics, see Rosenzweig and Thelen, *Presence of the Past;* Benson, Brier, and Rosenzweig, *Presenting the Past;* Gary B. Nash, Charlotte Crabtree, and Ross E. Dunn, *History on Trial: Culture Wars and the Teaching of the Past* (New York: Knopf, 1997); Wallace, *Mickey Mouse History.*

33. Scott Parks, "How Should Relics of a Racist Past Be Handled?" *Dallas Morning News,* February 24, 2003. See also Steve Blow, "By Hiding Racial Scars, We Lose Sight of Fight," *Dallas Morning News,* February 21, 2003; Dave Michaels, "Dallas County Will Keep 'Whites Only' Sign," *Dallas Morning News,* March 12, 2003; Steve Blow, "Segregation History Lesson Becomes Difficult to Discern," *Dallas Morning News,* April 25, 2003. See also James Loewen, *Lies Across America: What Our Historic Sites Get Wrong* (New York: New Press, 1999).

34. Michaels, "Dallas County Will Keep 'Whites Only' Sign."

35. Parks, *Dallas Morning News,* February 24, 2003. The KKK donated an estimated $50,000–$80,000 for the building. The agency was founded in 1918 as a home for infants abandoned by unwed mothers. Its close association with the KKK seems to have been generally known at the time but forgotten when the Klan fell into disrepute.

36. Ibid.

37. "Conference to Look Back at City's Often-Ignored Past," *Dallas Morning News,* September 28, 1999.

38. "Great to Know You, Dallas," *Dallas Morning News,* November 22, 2002. See also "Stashed Away in Dallas' Attic: Historical Society Hangs on to Vast Collection of Artifacts Representing the City's Past," *Dallas Morning News,* October 6, 2002; "Underground Museum Proposed to Display Dallas Artifacts," *Dallas Morning News,* October 8, 2001. Before the 1990s, my Dallas history courses and Darwin Payne's Liberal Studies course at Southern Methodist University constituted the only formal teaching of Dallas history.

39. The July 2006 Web site of the Dallas Convention and Visitors Bureau lists historical "attractions" under all its headings: arts and culture (museums and architecture), family fun (Old City Park), romance (Uptown hotels, McKinney Avenue trolley, and

nearby Grapevine), nightlife (Deep Ellum), and, of course, sports. History seems to rank along with other newly discovered qualities that make Dallas cosmopolitan. "Diverse Dallas" boasts of early Tejanos and newly arrived Hispanics, Chinese railroad workers and recent Asian immigrants, African American entrepreneurs, and the sixth largest Gay, Lesbian, Bisexual, and Transsexual community in the United States.

40. In 2006, none of the tours listed were specifically about Latino Dallas, and only the Deep Ellum tour mentioned African Americans.

41. See Dallas Historical Society Web site: http://dallashistory.org/activities/tours .htm (accessed 4 July 2006).

42. The *Dallas Morning News* for June 29, 2006, headlined the news that a $1 million donation from Nancy and Ray Hunt would enable the museum to open in spring 2007. The scheduled opening had been deferred because of lack of funds for exhibit fabrication and delays in repairs to the clock tower. Of the $16 million projected cost, $12.9 million had been raised by the time of the museum's scheduled opening. The restoration of the building itself has cost $35.6 million from county, state, and federal funds. The exhibitions, installed in four renovated courtrooms, feature "The Early Years" until the coming of the railroads; "Trading Center," until World War I; "Big D," until World War II; and "World Crossroads," "chronicling the area's explosive postwar growth." All exhibits, even interactive computerized ones, will be tailored to visitors' two-minute attention span and designed to entertain in order to educate. The Web site touts the educational, cultural, and economic benefits the museum will bring to the region. Significantly, the museum will exhibit collections of other historical organizations without assuming any responsibility for acquiring, curating, conserving, or storing them. This policy makes contemporary collecting impossible and ensures that the history enshrined there does nothing to change reigning representations of Dallas's past. For more on the Old Red Museum of Dallas History and Culture, see its Web site: http://www.oldred.org.

43. "Dallas History: Old Red."

44. Schultz credits me and my sesquicentennial essay; Schultz, "Dallas' Historical Myth." See also "Old Red, Home to History: Courthouse to Be Revived as Museum about Dallas County," *Dallas Morning News,* December 5, 2001; and the Museum of Dallas History and Culture's Web site, http://www.oldred.org/oldredmuseum.html.

45. McDonald, *Dallas Rediscovered,* 65. The National Register of Historic Places lists structures worthy of protection, but does not absolutely forbid their destruction and carries no funding for preservation.

46. Sorkin, *Variations on a Theme Park,* xii, xiii, xiv.

47. For an odd case of the "Dallas as destiny" myth, see "Dallas Takes Off," *The American Enterprise,* October–November 2000. See also Holmes and Saxon, *WPA Dallas Guide and History;* Leslie, *Dallas Public and Private.*

48. The flourishing of research and writing on Dallas's history is more consequence than cause of popular interest in the past. None of the museums, historic districts, and preservation projects results directly from serious scholarly work, and none shows an overriding concern with accuracy. At the same time, it is easy to overdo public policing

and scholarly calls for authenticity, which are neither the only expectations nor always the most appropriate ones for public audiences.

49. Dallas is the subject or setting of a growing number of doctoral dissertations, and Southern Methodist University's new History PhD program in association with the Clements Center for Southwest Studies will add to their number.

50. Quoted from the blurb on the back cover of Hill's book. Disclosure: Hill is my former graduate student.

51. In addition to this book, I have prepared a bibliography, essays, and teaching materials. With Patricia Evridge Hill, I coedited Leslie's *Dallas Public and Private*.

52. The contrast between the views of Morgan and Hanson is fundamental. Hanson's vita says that he was a voting rights activist and "a leader of the fair representation movement that resulted in the Supreme Court decision that established the One Person-One Vote rule for apportionment of state legislatures." Morgan's book argues that minority representation from single electoral districts has resulted in cronyism, careerism, and corruption, serving neither minority communities nor the city as a whole.

53. Black's "Empire of Consensus" and Schutze's *Accommodation* also fit here. For recent reviews, see Alan Lessof, "America's City: Dallas and United States Urban History," *Journal of Urban History* 26 (2000): 530–44; Robert Hodder, "Twentieth Century Renewal in Dallas, Texas," H-Urban Electronic List, November 8, 1999, a review of Robert Fairbanks's and William Wilson's books at http://www.h-net.org/reviews/showrev.cgi?path=5743944066170.

54. Randy Lee Loftis, "Two Views of Dallas: Scholars Differ on What the Vision of City Has Been and Should Be," *Dallas Morning News,* April 25, 1999. Hanson subsequently relocated to University of Maryland Baltimore County and then to George Washington University.

4. THE DALLAS WAY

1. "The Dallas Way," special section commemorating the fiftieth anniversary of the Dallas Citizens Council, *Dallas Times Herald,* November 15, 1987.

2. Fairbanks, *For the City as a Whole;* Hazel, *Dallas;* Payne, *Big D;* John Fullinwider, "Dallas: The City with No Limits?" *In These Times* 5 (December 1980): 17–23; Hill, *Dallas*.

3. Jim Henderson, "Democracy in Dallas," *Dallas Times Herald,* August 23, 1987, reprinted in "The Dallas Way"; "Citizens Council Adapting to Its New Role in Dallas," *Dallas Morning News,* March 17, 1993; Jim Schutze, "Peep-Hole Power," *Dallas Observer,* November 5, 1998. Note that "democracy coming" means political reform, but outside elite control and beyond the terms of its civic hegemony. For a regional perspective, see Bridges, *Morning Glories;* Amy Bridges, "Boss Tweed and V. O. Key in Texas," in Miller and Sanders, *Urban Texas,* 58–74; Bridges, "Politics and Growth in Sunbelt Cities," in Mohl, *Searching for the Sunbelt,* 85–104; Bridges, "Winning the West to Municipal Reform," *Urban Affairs Quarterly* 47 (1992): 494–518; Bridges, "Creating Cultures of Reform," *Studies in American Political Development* 8 (1994): 1–23. For Dallas, see Hanson, *Civic Culture and Urban Change;* Rodriquez, "Disenfranchisement in

Dallas." See also Stephen Elkin, *City and Regime in the American Republic* (Chicago: University of Chicago Press, 1987).

4. Henry Tatum, "Dallas Could Use a Burst of Nostalgia," *Dallas Morning News*, June 5, 2002; Rena Pederson, "Build It; They Will Come," *Dallas Morning News*, September 1, 2001.

5. See Schutze, "Peep-Hole Power."

6. Wilson, "Metaphors, Growth Coalition Discourses and Black Poverty Neighborhoods," 91. See also Dear, *Postmodern Urban Condition;* Dear, *From Chicago to LA;* Dear, Shockman, and Hise, *Rethinking Los Angeles;* Beauregard, *Voices of Decline.*

7. I thank Grey Osterud for this formulation.

8. Jones, *Dallas,* 7.

9. Bainbridge, *Super-Americans,* 144–45.

10. Bill Porterfield, "The Dallas Way," *Dallas Times Herald,* November 15, 1987.

11. Tatum, "Dallas Could Use a Burst of Nostalgia."

12. A. C. Greene, "Power and Politics," in Oppenheimer and Porterfield, *Book of Dallas,* 233.

13. McCombs and Whyte, "The Dydamic Men of Dallas," 99.

14. Harold A. Stone, Don K. Price, and Kathryn H. Stone, *City Manager Government in Nine Cities* (Chicago: Published for the Committee on Public Administration of the Social Science Research Council by Public Administration Service, 1940), 263.

15. Ibid., 266.

16. Holmes and Saxon, *WPA Dallas Guide and History,* 11, 10. The *WPA Guide* continued: "apparently justifying the dictum of Adam Smith and the classical economists that the greatest good for the greatest number results from the spontaneous interaction of independent and unrestrained individual agents actuated only by intelligent self-interest."

17. Compare Fairbanks, *For the City as a Whole,* to Hill, *Dallas.* See also Black, "Empire of Consensus."

18. D'Eramo, *The Pig and the Skyscraper,* 142.

19. On the role of government spending during World War II in stimulating the growth of Sunbelt cities, see Abbott, *Metropolitan Frontier;* Bernard and Rice, *Sunbelt Cities;* Findlay, *Magic Lands;* Roger Lotchin, *Fortress California* (New York: Oxford University Press, 1992); Mohl, *Searching for the Sunbelt;* Rutheiser, *Imagineering Atlanta;* Soja, *Postmodern Geographies;* Sorkin, *Variations on a Theme Park;* Zukin, *Landscapes of Power.*

20. Elkin, *City and Regime;* Bridges, *Morning Glories.* Dallas's relatively informal and less than completely public political leaders constituted an active local state; see Monkkonen, *America Becomes Urban;* Stone, *Regime Politics.*

21. Dallas's racial-ethnic minority groups include Hispanic, Mexican, and Mexican American as well as African Americans. See Phillips, *White Metropolis;* Phillips, "The Fire This Time"; Hill, *Dallas;* Leslie, *Dallas Public and Private;* Cole, "Finding Race in Turn-of-the-Century Dallas"; Bridges, *Morning Glories;* and especially Schutze, *The Accommodation,* and efforts to suppress his book.

22. Smith, "How Business Failed Dallas," 158.

23. Ibid., 159. See also Stanley Marcus's ad after the Kennedy assassination, "What's Right With Dallas?" *Dallas Morning News,* January 1, 1964; Leslie, *Dallas Public and Private.*

24. On small group dominance, see Barta, "The *Dallas News*"; Thometz, *The Decision-Makers.* With respect to race, in addition to previous references, see Dulaney, "Whatever Happened to the Civil Rights Movement?"; Dulaney, "Progressive Voters League."

25. Only Hill's *Dallas* captures the challenges from below and conflicts within the elite during this period.

26. See "The Dallas Way" special section; Leslie, *Dallas Public and Private;* Hanson, *Civic Culture and Urban Change.*

27. See especially Phillips, *White Metropolis;* Hill, *Dallas;* Dulaney, "Whatever Happened to the Civil Rights Movement?"; Wilson, *Hamilton Park;* Schutze, *The Accommodation.*

28. Hanson, *Civic Culture and Urban Change;* Phillips, *White Metropolis;* Dulaney, "Whatever Happened to the Civil Rights Movement?"; Hill, *Dallas;* Schutze, *The Accommodation;* Leslie, *Dallas Public and Private;* Wright, *In the New World.*

29. "Bitter Racial Rift in Dallas Board Reflects Ills in Many Other Cities," *New York Times,* June 27, 1996; "Dallas Police Officer Is Held in Plot to Kill a Football Star," *Dallas Morning News,* June 28, 1996; "A Tough Home Crowd," *Dallas Morning News,* December 12, 1996; "Changes, Conflict: Year Had Its Violence, but Also Improvements," *Dallas Morning News,* December 29, 1996; Henry Tatum, "Dallas' Destiny No Longer Tied to Cowboys," *Dallas Morning News,* January 15, 1997; "Outlaw Cowboys," *New York Times,* August 6, 1997; "Switzer Arrest," *Dallas Morning News,* August 6, 1997.

30. Robert B. Bradley, "Goals for Dallas," in *Anticipatory Democracy: People in the Politics of the Future,* ed. Clement Bezold (New York: Random House, 1978), 58–97; see also Bridges, *Morning Glories.*

31. "The Dallas Way," special section. The film was made by Sam Bloom Advertising Agency for civic leaders, including the Dallas Citizens Council and Stanley Marcus. In *The Accommodation,* Schutze states: "Desegregation would be marketed. . . . 'We engaged Sam Bloom—a public relations sage,' [Stanley] Marcus said. . . . Bloom, a former newspaper ad salesman who had founded his own advertising agency . . . proposed making a movie . . . [and] achieved a master piece to stand the test of time" (128–29). By the 1980s, copies had disappeared from the Dallas Central Library. My students located a copy and had it reproduced and placed in several libraries. See Hanson, *Civic Culture and Urban Change;* also Morgan, *Governance by Decree;* "Desegregation," *Dallas Times Herald,* August 15, 1975; "A City Working for a 'Smooth Transition,'" special education supplement, *Dallas Times Herald,* August 15, 1975. Linden, *Desegregating Schools in Dallas,* is not a reliable guide; he gives a sense of the legal and judicial complications and some of the interests at work, but he overlooks the social context and the continuing plight of the still-segregated and deficient Dallas public schools. Compare

with Guadalupe San Miguel Jr., *Brown, Not White: School Integration and the Chicano Movement in Houston* (College Station: Texas A&M University Press, 2001).

32. Bridges, *Morning Glories*, 3. For a perverse take on the same phenomenon, see Fairbanks, *For the City as a Whole*. Despite its own claims that Dallas is different, it is like other southwestern cities. See Hill, *Dallas;* Dulaney, "Whatever Happened to the Civil Rights Movement?"; Schutze, *The Accommodation;* Barta, "The *Dallas News*"; Thometz, *The Decision-Makers;* Payne, *Big D.* This account depends on Amy Bridges's work because of the lack of local research.

33. Bridges, *Morning Glories*, 19.

34. Ibid., 20.

35. Ibid., 21. See Dulaney, "Whatever Happened to the Civil Rights Movement?"; Wilson, *Hamilton Park;* Schutze, *The Accommodation;* Michael L. Gillette, "The Rise of the NAACP in Texas," *Southwestern Historical Quarterly* 81 (1978): 393–46; Phillips, *White Metropolis;* Hanson, *Civic Culture and Urban Change.*

36. Bridges, *Morning Glories*, 24. See also Justin Kimball's school text; Marcus, "What's Right with Dallas?"; Leslie, *Dallas Public and Private;* and Fairbanks, *For the City as a Whole,* who evokes the city of Anglos.

37. Bridges, *Morning Glories*, 25–26, also 28, 29, 173.

38. Ibid., 29.

39. Ibid., 173, citing Arnold Hirsch, *Making the Second Ghetto: Race and Housing in Chicago, 1940–1960* (Cambridge: Cambridge University Press, 1983). For debates on the politics of growth, see Stone, *Regime Politics;* Elkin, *City and Regime;* Mollenkopf, *Contested City;* Logan and Molotch, *Urban Fortunes.*

40. Bridges, *Morning Glories*, 173.

41. Stone, Price, and Stone, *City Manager Government*, 280. See also Fairbanks, *For the City as a Whole;* Hill, *Dallas;* Stone, *Regime Politics;* Payne, *Big D.*

42. Stone, Price, and Stone, *City Manager Government*, 280, 281.

43. Ibid., 281, 287.

44. Ibid., 342. Huge questions about acquiescence remain; see Hill, *Dallas;* Hanson, *Civic Culture and Urban Change;* Leslie, *Dallas Public and Private;* Dulaney, "Whatever Happened to the Civil Rights Movement?"; Fairbanks, *For the City as a Whole;* Payne, *Big D.*

45. Thornton interview published in McCombs and Whyte, "Dydamic Men of Dallas," and quoted widely thereafter.

46. See Hill, *Dallas;* Stone, Price, and Stone, *City Manager Government;* Black, "Empire of Consensus"; Fairbanks, *For the City as a Whole;* Payne, *Big D.* On the Depression, see also "The Dallas Way"; Bridges, *Morning Glories;* Biles, "The New Deal in Dallas."

47. Hill, *Dallas,* xxviii. On these issues, compare Hill with Fairbanks, *For the City as a Whole,* and see Bridges, *Morning Glories;* Leslie, *Dallas Public and Private;* Barta, "The *Dallas News*"; Thometz, *The Decision-Makers.* See also Saul Friedman, "Tussle in Texas," *The Nation,* February 3, 1964; "Power in Dallas: Who Holds the Cards?" *D Magazine,* October 1974, 47–55; Jim Atkinson and John Merwin, "New Power: Starring

Bob Folsom, Dave Fox, Alex Bickley and (for a change) a Cast of Thousands," *D Magazine*, September 1977, 60–65, 111–13.

48. Quoted in "The Dallas Way."

49. Fairbanks, *For the City as a Whole*, muddles this unacceptably. Compare his views with Hill, *Dallas*, and Hanson, *Civic Culture and Urban Change*.

50. The selective, sympathetic readings and views in Fairbanks, *For the City as a Whole*, Hazel, *Dallas*, and Payne, *Big D*, contrast clearly with Hill, *Dallas*, Bridges, *Morning Glories*, and Phillips, *White Metropolis*.

51. See Hill, *Dallas*; Leslie, *Dallas Public and Private*; Enstam, *Women and the Creation of Urban Life*; Dulaney, "Whatever Happened to the Civil Rights Movement?"; Cole, "Finding Race in Turn-of-the-Century Dallas"; Schutze, *The Accommodation*. On the Dallas Way's strengths, see Fairbanks, *For the City as a Whole*; Hazel, *Dallas*; Payne, *Big D*. Fairbanks's uncritical approach to discourse and ideology obfuscates this lack of democratic representation, serving as an inadvertent object lesson in the Dallas Way's rhetorical effectiveness.

52. Bridges, *Morning Glories*, 12.

53. Compare Fullinwider, "Dallas: The City with No Limits?" with "The Dallas Way" and McCombs and Whyte, "Dydamic Men of Dallas."

54. "'The Dallas Citizens Council considered itself to be everybody's daddy,' says Peter Johnson, Dallas director of the Southern Christian Leadership Conference. 'They would say, "Well, this year we'll let them eat at the lunch counters downtown, and next year we'll integrate Fair Park for them."' . . . Erik Jonsson, who was then chairman of Texas Instruments and one of the Citizens Council's leaders, defends the council's work in race relations as 'reasonable, in light of what that time was like.' 'We had troubles. Everybody did, across the country. But the blacks in Dallas knew that the right people were working in good faith to solve our problems so when things got tough, Dallas didn't suffer like other cities.'" Dulaney, "Progressive Voters League," 32.

55. San Antonio, Houston, and Fort Worth all used Dallas as an example with which to criticize their own business elites; see Miller and Johnson, "Rise of Urban Texas." Outside Texas, see Rutheiser, *Imagineering Atlanta*; Frank, "Machine for Forgetting"; Mohl, *Searching for the Sunbelt*; Hirsch and Mohl, *Urban Policy in Twentieth Century America*.

56. Payne, *Big D*, 52, 48–52.

57. *Dallas Morning News*, September 11 and 12, 1934, quoted in Fairbanks, *For the City as a Whole*, 93.

58. *Dallas Morning News*, December 6, 1935, quoted in Fairbanks, *For the City as a Whole*, 94.

59. See Fairbanks, *For the City as a Whole*; Payne, *Big D*; Hill, *Dallas*; Ragsdale, *The Year America Discovered Texas*.

60. See Bridges, *Morning Glories*; Michael A. Pagano and Ann Bowman, *Cityscapes and Capital: The Politics of Urban Development* (Baltimore, Md.: Johns Hopkins University Press, 1995).

61. Fairbanks, *For the City as a Whole*, 93–94.

62. Wick Allison, "The Deion Principle," *D Magazine,* April 1996.

63. "Laura Miller's Choice," *D Magazine,* August 2002.

64. In another strange example of attempted purchase of culture, Perot proposed to purchase the National Museum of the American Indian in New York City and move it to Dallas. Not only was this federal institution not for sale, but Dallas had neither precedent for nor special interest in Native American studies.

65. See Hill, *Dallas;* Rodriquez, "Disenfranchisement in Dallas"; Schutze, *The Accommodation;* Phillips, *White Metropolis.*

66. On cities as polities, see Monkkonen, *America Becomes Urban.*

67. See Davis, *Spectacular Nature;* Findlay, *Magic Lands;* Gottdiener et al., *Theming of America;* Hannigan, *Fantasy City;* Gottdiener et al., *Las Vegas;* Rothman, *Devil's Bargains;* Rothman, *Neon Metropolis;* Rothman and Davis, *Grit Between the Glitter;* Judd and Fainstain, *Tourist City.*

68. Stone, Price, and Stone, *City Manager Government,* 266.

69. Holmes and Saxon, *WPA Dallas Guide and History,* 9, 10.

70. On planning, see Black, "Empire of Consensus"; Fairbanks, *For the City as a Whole;* Fairbanks, "Rethinking Urban Problems"; Wilson, *City Beautiful Movement;* Wilson, "Adapting to Growth"; Wilson, *Hamilton Park.*

71. See Daniel Bluestone, *Constructing Chicago* (New Haven, Conn.: Yale University Press, 1991); Mary Ryan, *Civic Wars: Democracy and Public Life in the American City During the Nineteenth Century* (Berkeley and Los Angeles: University of California Press, 1997); Ryan, "'A Laudable Pride in the Whole of Us': City Halls and Civic Materialism," *American Historical Review* 105 (2000): 1131–70.

72. On skyscrapers, see Carol Willis, *Form Follows Finance: Skyscrapers and Skylines in New York and Chicago* (Princeton, N.J.: Princeton Architectural Press, 1995); D'Eramo, *The Pig and the Skyscraper;* Carl Condit, *The Chicago School of Architecture: A History of Commercial and Public Building in the Chicago Area, 1875–1925* (Chicago: University of Chicago Press, 1998); Sarah Landau and Carl Condit, *Rise of the New York Skyscraper: 1865–1913* (New Haven, Conn.: Yale University Press, 1996); Roberta Moudry, ed., *The American Skyscraper: Cultural Histories* (Cambridge: Cambridge University Press, 2005). See also David Schuyler, *The New Urban Landscape* (Baltimore, Md.: Johns Hopkins University Press, 1986); Taylor, *In Pursuit of Gotham;* William R. Taylor, ed., *Inventing Times Square* (New York: Russell Sage Foundation, 1991); Mona Domosh, *Invented Cities: The Creation of Landscape in Nineteenth-Century New York and Boston* (New Haven, Conn.: Yale University Press, 1996); Boyer, *Dreaming the Rational City;* Mel Scott, *American City Planning* (Berkeley and Los Angeles: University of California Press, 1969); Richard Fogelsong, *Planning the Capitalist City* (Princeton, N.J.: Princeton University Press, 1986); Giorgio Ciucci et al., *The American City* (1973; repr., Cambridge, Mass.: MIT Press, 1983); Robert Fogelson, *Downtown: Its Rise and Fall, 1880–1950* (New Haven, Conn.: Yale University Press, 2003); Sies and Silver, *Planning the Twentieth-Century American City.*

73. Wilson, *City Beautiful Movement,* 257.

74. Bridges, Fairbanks, and probably Enstam would disagree with *The American Enterprise*'s claims for Dallas's exceptionality.

75. Michael Dear, "In the City, Time Becomes Visible: Intentionality and Urbanism in Los Angeles, 1781–1991," in *The City: Los Angeles and Urban Theory at the End of the Twentieth Century,* ed. Allen J. Scott and Edward W. Soja (Berkeley and Los Angeles: University of California Press, 1996), 77, 98.

5. TALES OF TWO CITIES, NORTH AND SOUTH, IN WHITE, BLACK, AND BROWN

1. Annual New Year's Editorial, *Dallas Morning News,* January 2, 2000. On residential segregation, see Hirsch, "With or Without Jim Crow"; Katz, *Price of Citizenship;* Michael B. Katz and Mark J. Stein, *One Nation Divisible: What America Was and What It Is Becoming* (New York: Russell Sage Foundation, 2006); Massey and Denton, *American Apartheid;* Zukin, *Landscapes of Power;* Levy, *New Dollars and Dream;* O'Connor, Tilly, and Bobo, *Urban Inequality;* Jargowsky, *Poverty and Place.*

2. To some observers, Dallas exhibits patterns that have seemed more southern, based on racial bifurcation, than western, with a triracial or multiracial system of social relations. To others, such patterns are associated with more liberal but still segregated cities like Boston or Chicago.

3. "Census Data Tell Tale of Two Cities: Gap between Northern, Southern Dallas Cited," *Dallas Morning News,* May 31, 1991.

4. Editorial, *Dallas Morning News,* November 19, 1997. See also Phillips, *White Metropolis;* Michael B. Katz, *The Undeserving Poor* (New York: Pantheon, 1990).

5. Zukin, *Landscapes of Power,* 22.

6. This chapter makes no pretense at being a history of African Americans or Mexican Americans in Dallas, although histories of these groups' experiences and perspectives are sorely needed.

7. J. McDonald Williams, "Tale of Two Cities: Dallas Must Revitalize Its Lagging Southern Sector," *Dallas Morning News,* March 8, 1998.

8. "Dallas at the Tipping Point" series, Part II: "Looking South," *Dallas Morning News,* December 12–16, 2004, esp. "Trust's Troubles Revealed: South Dallas/Fair Park Fund Overstated Revenue, Audit Shows," *Dallas Morning News,* December 14, 2004; "Broken Trust: S. Dallas/Fair Park Fund Seriously Lacks Results," *Dallas Morning News,* December 16, 2004. Compare to "Dallas Dinner Table: Let's Talk About Race, Economics and Geography," *Dallas Morning News,* January 2, 2005; "Study: 'Segregation Has Not Gone Away' in Schools," *Dallas Morning News,* February 15, 2005; "City Says Southern Dallas Economic Push Paying Off," *Dallas Morning News,* February 25, 2005. Also see "Public Housing Coming to Far N. Dallas: Legal Battle over Site in Far N. Dallas Seriously Delayed Development for 9 Years," *Dallas Morning News,* March 8, 2005.

9. In *One Nation Divisible,* Katz and Stein write: "Inequality among African Americans no longer grows out of a massive and mutually reinforcing, legal and extra-legal, public and private system of racial oppression. Rather, it is a subtler matter proceeding through a series of screens that filter blacks into more or less promising statuses,

progressively dividing them along lines full of implications for their economic futures" (87). For comparisons with Hispanics, see 115–20.

10. This gap persists also regardless of changes in income or suburbanization. See Massey and Denton, *American Apartheid,* 74–78; Michael B. Katz, ed., *The "Underclass" Debate: Views from History* (Princeton, N.J.: Princeton University Press, 1993); Roger Waldinger, *Still the Promised City: African-Americans and New Immigrants in Postindustrial New York* (Cambridge, Mass.: Harvard University Press, 1996); Hirsch, *Making the Second Ghetto;* Zukin, *Landscapes of Power;* Jargowsky, *Poverty and Place.* On Dallas, see Fairbanks, *For the City as a Whole;* Hill, *Dallas;* Dulaney, "Progressive Voters Leagues"; Dulaney, "Whatever Happened to the Civil Rights Movement?"; Gillette, "Rise of the NAACP in Texas"; Patricia E. Gower, "The Price of Exclusion: Dallas Municipal Policy and Its Impact on African Americans," *East Texas Historical Journal* 39 (2001): 43–54; Linden, *Desegregating Schools in Dallas;* Phillips, "White Violence, Hegemony, and Slave Rebellion"; Phillips, "The Fire This Time"; Phillips, *White Metropolis;* Dr. Robert Prince, *A History of Dallas from a Different Perspective* (Dallas: Sunbelt Media, 1993); Steven A. Reich, "Soldiers of Democracy: Black Texas and the Fight for Citizenship, 1917–1921," *Journal of American History* 82 (1996): 1478–1504; Larenda Lyles Roberts, *Dallas Uncovered* (Plano: Republic of Texas Press, 1995); Rumbley, *Unauthorized History of Dallas;* Schutze, *The Accommodation;* Roy H. Williams and Kevin J. Shay, *Time Change: An Alternative View of the History of Dallas* (Dallas: To Be Publishing, 1991); Wilson, "Private Planning for Black Housing in Dallas"; Wilson, "Desegregation of the Hamilton Park School"; Wilson, "Living in the Planned Community"; Wilson, "'This Negro Housing Matter'"; Wilson, *Hamilton Park.*

11. Katz, *Price of Citizenship,* 49; "Dallas at the Tipping Point" series, esp. "Broken Trust"; "Study: 'Segregation Has Not Gone Away' in Schools."

12. See Katz, *Price of Citizenship;* Zukin, *Landscapes of Power;* Sharon Zukin, "The Hollow Center: U.S. Cities in the Global Era," in *America at Century's End,* ed. Alan Wolfe (Berkeley and Los Angeles: University of California Press, 1991), 245–61, 526–28; Phillips, *White Metropolis.*

13. Shirley Achor, *Mexican Americans in a Dallas Barrio* (Tucson: University of Arizona Press, 1978; new preface, 1991); Fairbanks, *For the City as a Whole;* Fairbanks, "Public Housing for the City as a Whole"; see also "Public Housing Coming to Far N. Dallas."

14. William Julius Wilson, *When Work Disappears: The World of the New Urban Poor* (New York: Knopf, 1996); Wilson, *The Truly Disadvantaged: The Inner City, the Underclass, and Public Policy* (Chicago: University of Chicago Press, 1990); Katz, *"Underclass" Debate;* Jargowsky, *Poverty and Place;* Zukin, *Landscapes of Power.*

15. Deanna Sanchez and Harry Williams, "Environmental Justice in Dallas County, Texas: A Spatial Analysis of Hazardous Waste Site Locations," *Papers and Proceedings of Applied Geography Conferences* 24 (2001): 210–28.

16. See "Blacks Did It All," *Dallas Morning News,* February 11, 1996; "Playing a Big Role: Blacks' Part in Developing Dallas Economy Often Overlooked," *Dallas Morning*

News, February 1, 1996; "Mapping a Heritage: Records, Oral History Show Blacks' Huge Role in Shaping Dallas," *Dallas Morning News,* February 5, 1995.

17. "Blacks Did It All."

18. "History of Neglect Haunts West Dallas," editorial, first in "Forgotten Dallas" series, *Dallas Morning News,* August 30, 1992.

19. Compare Dulaney, "Whatever Happened to the Civil Rights Movement?" with Wilson, *Hamilton Park.*

20. See Schutze, *The Accommodation;* Phillips, *White Metropolis;* Phillips, "White Violence, Hegemony, and Slave Rebellion"; Dulaney, "Whatever Happened to the Civil Rights Movement?"; Fairbanks, *For the City as a Whole;* Hill, *Dallas.* See also data in Massey and Denton, *American Apartheid;* Hirsch, *Making the Second Ghetto.*

21. Dulaney, "Whatever Happened to the Civil Rights Movement?" 67–68, 69; see also Phillips, *White Metropolis;* Bridges, *Morning Glories.*

22. See "Forgotten Dallas" series, *Dallas Morning News,* August–September 1992; Achor, *Mexican Americans.* On police, see Hanson, *Civic Culture and Urban Change;* Phillips, *White Metropolis.*

23. *Handbook of Texas Online,* http://www.tsha.utexas.edu/handbook/online.

24. See William Brophy, "Active Acceptance—Active Containment," in *Southern Businessmen and Desegregation,* ed. Elizabeth Jacoway and David R. Colburn (Baton Rouge: Louisiana State University Press, 1982), 137–50; Stephanie Decker, "Women in the Civil Rights Movement: Juanita Craft Versus the Dallas Elite," *East Texas Historical Journal* 39 (2001): 33–42; Dulaney, "Whatever Happened to the Civil Rights Movement?"; Dulaney, "Progressive Voters League"; Gillette, "Rise of the NAACP in Texas"; Gower, "Price of Exclusion"; Hill, *Dallas;* Phillips, "White Violence, Hegemony, and Slave Rebellion"; Phillips, *White Metropolis;* Schutze, *The Accommodation;* William W. White, "The Texas Slave Insurrection of 1860," *Southwestern Historical Quarterly* 52 (1949): 259–85; Wilson, "Private Planning for Black Housing in Dallas"; Wilson, "Desegregation of the Hamilton Park School"; Wilson, "Living in the Planned Community"; Wilson, "'This Negro Housing Matter'"; Wilson, *Hamilton Park.*

25. Fairbanks, *For the City as a Whole,* 147; compare with Bridges, *Morning Glories,* Phillips, *White Metropolis,* and Hill, *Dallas.*

26. Fairbanks needs to read his sources more critically and contextually. An awareness of the role of ideology prevents the treatment of these sources as transparent statements to be taken at face value. Otherwise, the risks of circularity, reductionism, and exaggeration of the notion of "for the city as a whole" contribute to a striking sense of special pleading and apologetics. Why, for example, is the notion of what benefits the city "peculiar"? Although Fairbanks has a point, it is a limited one. To what "solutions" does he refer? Those proposed for housing or later for education could not "solve" the problems. Minorities, it seems, were sometimes part of the "city as a whole," but more often they were not.

27. Fairbanks, *For the City as a Whole,* 150, 154.

28. Ibid.

29. Quoted in ibid., 221. See Tanya Donaghey, "Earl Cabell and Transition in Dallas Politics" (master's thesis, Southern Methodist University, 1996).

30. Dulaney, "Whatever Happened to the Civil Rights Movement?" 75, 76.

31. Wilson, *Hamilton Park*, 11–12. For stories, see Schutze, *The Accommodation;* Phillips, *White Metropolis;* Dulaney, "Whatever Happened to the Civil Rights Movement?"; Hill, *Dallas.*

32. Wilson, *Hamilton Park,* 14–15. On African American suburbanization, see Bruce Haynes, *Red Lines, Black Spaces: The Politics of Race and Space in a Black Middle-Class Suburb* (New Haven, Conn.: Yale University Press, 2001); Andrew Wiese, *A Place of Their Own: African-American Suburbanization in the Twentieth Century* (Chicago: University of Chicago Press, 2004); Henry Louis Taylor, *Race and the City: Work, Community, and Protest in Cincinnati, 1820–1970* (Urbana: University of Illinois Press, 1993). On Hamilton Park, see also Wilson, "Private Planning for Black Housing in Dallas"; Wilson, "Desegregation of the Hamilton Park School"; Wilson, "Living in the Planned Community"; Wilson, "'This Negro Housing Matter.'"

33. Dulaney, "Whatever Happened to the Civil Rights Movement?" 75, 76; Dulaney, "Progressive Voters League." For more on Dallas, see Schutze, *The Accommodation;* Phillips, *White Metropolis;* Hill, *Dallas;* Hanson, *Civic Culture and Urban Change.*

34. See also Massey and Denton, *American Apartheid;* Hirsch, *Making the Second Ghetto;* Katz, *Price of Citizenship;* Thomas Sugrue, *The Origins of the Urban Crisis* (Princeton, N.J.: Princeton University Press, 1996).

35. Dulaney, "Whatever Happened to the Civil Rights Movement?" 77, 78.

36. C. A. Tatum, "To: Members of the Dallas Ministry," eight-page pamphlet (Dallas: Dallas Public Library, 1961). See also "Dallas at the Crossroads," a film made by Sam Bloom Advertising Agency for civic leaders, including the Dallas Citizens Council and Stanley Marcus. Questions beg for more in-depth treatment. For a beginning, see Hanson, *Civic Culture and Urban Change;* Hill, *Dallas;* Phillips, *White Metropolis;* compare with Linden, *Desegregating Schools in Dallas;* Morgan, *Governance by Decree;* Wilson, *Hamilton Park.*

37. Dulaney, "Whatever Happened to the Civil Rights Movement?" 77, 78.

38. Ibid., 82, 82–83. It is possible that in Dallas, as in other major cities, such as New York, Philadelphia, and Chicago, the split in the civil rights movement between those who focused on legal and institutional change and those who adopted direct action was more a matter of tactics than strategy and that this one-two punch strengthened rather than weakened the movement. There were instances in which conflicts among black leaders did get out of hand, but many cases in which the threat of militant action pushed whites to compromise with leaders perceived as more "moderate." However, as far as I can tell this tension does not seem to have been productive in Dallas.

39. The history of school desegregation in Dallas can be reconstructed through the newspapers: "Dallas Schools '76: New Goals, New Challenges," special education supplement, *Dallas Times Herald,* August 15, 1975; "Desegregation," special section, *Dallas Morning News,* August 15, 1976; "Integrated Dallas Still a Dream," *Dallas Times Herald,* April 3, 1988; "Forgotten Dallas" series; "A Vision Unfulfilled," *Dallas Morning*

News, April 7, 1993; "Civil Rights Sidelines: Dallas' African-Americans Saw Progress in the 1950s—but It Was on Television," *Dallas Morning News,* January 3, 1994; "'60s Rights Activists See Dallas Fight as Subdued, Profound," *Dallas Morning News,* February 6, 1994; "Breaking Through: Lawsuits Forced Shifting of Power during the 1970s," *Dallas Morning News,* February 13, 1994; "Road to Power: New Generation of Black Leaders Emerged in '80s," *Dallas Morning News,* February 20, 1994; "A Fair Share: Economics Moving to Forefront of Civil Rights Fight," *Dallas Morning News,* February 27, 1994; "Hispanic Boom Forcing the Dallas Independent School District to Reassess Needs," *Dallas Morning News,* November 5, 1995; "Hispanics See Chance for Progress Arising from Education Turmoil," *Dallas Morning News,* July 23, 1996; "Desegregation Came Slowly to Dallas Schools," *Dallas Morning News,* February 2, 1997; "One Father's Fight Led to Desegregation: Court Watch Still Needed, School Critics Say," *Dallas Morning News,* February 9, 1997; "Black Leaders Criticize Letter Targeting Minority Trustees," *Dallas Morning News,* July 23, 2002; "A New Day: Dallas Schools Ready to Move from Court Order," *Dallas Morning News,* August 11, 2002. On education, see Hanson, *Civic Culture and Urban Change;* Morgan, *Governance by Decree;* Schutze, *The Accommodation;* Linden, *Desegregating Schools in Dallas.*

40. See Bridges, *Morning Glories,* chapter 4.

41. See promotional materials, including films such as *The City as Enterprise,* a 1970s advertisement for Dallas designed to stimulate corporate as well as individual relocations. Recent city plans emphasize the physical and the aesthetic city. See James Pratt, "Dallas: Visions for Community: Toward a 21st-Century Urban Design," *Dallas Morning News,* November 19, 1990; Antonio Di Mambro, "The Global City: The Road Ahead for the Dallas-Forth Worth Metropolis in the 21st Century," with David Rusk, "Halfway Down the Road—to Decline," *Dallas Morning News,* March 4, 2001; *Dallas Morning News's* "Dallas at the Tipping Point" series.

42. Jim Henderson's article, "Democracy in Dallas," referred to "revolutionary" change and "profound metamorphosis"; *Dallas Times Herald,* August 23, 1987.

43. "Citizens Council Adapting to Its New Role in Dallas," *Dallas Morning News,* March 17, 1993; "The Dallas Way," special section commemorating the fiftieth anniversary of the Dallas Citizens Council, *Dallas Times Herald,* November 15, 1987; Jim Schutze, "Peep-Hole Power," *Dallas Observer,* November 5, 1998; Hanson, *Civic Culture and Urban Change;* Morgan, *Governance by Decree.*

44. See Massey and Denton, *American Apartheid;* Barbara M. Posadas, ed., *Race and Housing in Post World War II Chicago,* special issue, *Journal of the Illinois State Historical Society* 94 (Spring 2001); Hirsch, "With or Without Jim Crow"; Katz, *"Underclass" Debate;* Katz, *Price of Citizenship;* Katz, *Undeserving Poor;* Zukin, *Landscapes of Power;* Bridges, *Morning Glories.*

45. On reading cities, see Clay, *Close Up.* In contrast, studies of other cities find multiple cityscapes: Zukin identified five twentieth-century urban landscapes (Steeltown, Motown, Mill and Mall, Gentrified Downtown, Disney World), and John Findlay four western cityscapes (Disney Land, Stanford Industrial Park, Sun City, Seattle). Reyner Banham made his name critically and more popularly with his reading of

modern Los Angeles as "the architecture of four ecologies" (Surfurbia, Foothills, Plains of Id, Autopia). A quarter century later, geographer Richard Walker adapted that approach to identify "four ecologies of residence in the San Francisco area" (Victorian townhouse order, suburban ecotopian middle landscape, multiple unit housing, mass suburbia). See Zukin, *Landscapes of Power;* Findlay, *Magic Lands;* Banham, *Los Angeles;* Walker, "Landscapes and City Life." For a serious effort that is unintentionally humorous, see "Dallas Takes Off (In the Backyard of Bush and Cheney, the Sky's the Limit)," *The American Enterprise,* October–November 2000.

46. Ivins, *Molly Ivins Can't Say That, Can She?* 37, 38. See Massey and Denton, *American Apartheid;* Posadas, "Race and Housing in Post World War II Chicago."

47. Leslie, *Dallas Public and Private,* 28–29, 50.

48. Ibid., 33, 51. Leslie is more incomplete than inaccurate.

49. Sam Bass Warner, Jr., "The Management of Multiple Urban Images," in Fraser and Sutcliffe, *Pursuit of Urban History,* 383–94; Taylor, *In Pursuit of Gotham,* esp. chapters 1–3; Taylor, *Inventing Times Square.*

50. Phillips, *White Metropolis.* See also Massey and Denton, *American Apartheid;* Hirsch, *Making the Second Ghetto;* Katz, *Price of Citizenship;* Wilson, *The Truly Disadvantaged;* Jargowsky, *Poverty and Place.*

51. Stone, Price, and Stone, *City Manager Government,* 266.

52. Ibid., 265.

53. For critiques of images and assumptions about many immigrants' and migrants' inability to adapt to new environments, see the work of Charles Tilly, William Sewell Jr., Rudolf Vecoli, Virginia Yans McLaughlin, and Kathleen Conzen, summarized in Thomas Bender, *Community and Social Change in America* (New Brunswick, N.J.: Rutgers University Press, 1978).

54. Walter T. Watson, "Mexicans in Dallas," *Southwest Review* 22 (1937): 406.

55. Achor, *Mexican Americans,* 23.

56. Holmes and Saxon, *WPA Dallas Guide and History,* 306, 307. See also Achor, *Mexican Americans;* Watson, "Mexicans in Dallas"; Fairbanks, *For the City as a Whole.*

57. Holmes and Saxon, *WPA Dallas Guide and History,* 291, 292.

58. One dramatic example was a 1984 *National Geographic* issue coincident with the Dallas Republican Party Convention.

59. "Report on Minorities Due Next Month," *Dallas Times Herald,* January 24, 1988. See also "Report Gives Dallas a Goal to Achieve," *Dallas Times Herald,* January 25, 1988; "Forgotten Dallas" series.

60. See "Southern Dallas: The *Morning News* Hopes to Be a Catalyst," *Dallas Morning News,* November 3, 1995.

61. "Southern Dallas: City Should End the Economic Polarization," *Dallas Morning News,* November 19, 1997.

62. See Frances Fox Piven and Richard Cloward, *Poor People's Movements: Why They Succeed, How They Fail* (New York: Vintage, 1978); Katz, *Price of Citizenship.*

63. Henry Tatum, "Blacks and Hispanics Must Head Off Potential Conflicts," *Dallas Morning News,* March 21, 2001; Hanson, *Civic Culture and Urban Change.*

64. "West Dallas Isn't 'Forgotten' Anymore: Housing Construction Brings Hope to Once Neglected Area," *Dallas Morning News,* January 3, 2002; "West Dallas Is Making Progress," *Dallas Morning News,* December 4, 2000; "A New Look, a New Way of Life," *Dallas Morning News,* August 30, 2001; "Southern Dallas to Get Movie Complex: Mayor Hopes Cinemark Theater Is Preview of Things to Come for Area," *Dallas Morning News,* October 10, 2001; "Hopes High for S. Dallas Businesses," *Dallas Morning News,* December 27, 2001; "South Dallas: Neighborhood around Fair Park Is Improving," *Dallas Morning News,* April 28, 2002; "South Dallas: Legal Pressure Brings Improvement," *Dallas Morning News,* April 29, 2002; "Development Helps Transform Area of South Dallas," *Dallas Morning News,* May 2, 2002.

65. "Embattled S. Dallas Apartment Complex Closing; Many See Nowhere to Go," *Dallas Morning News,* April 23, 2002; "Room for Disagreement: Passions Collide on Developing Southern Dallas," *Dallas Morning News,* March 17, 2002; "Cadillac Heights: City Must Address Chronic Neighborhood Problems," *Dallas Morning News,* June 22, 2001; "Cadillac Heights: Is It Livable?," *Dallas Morning News,* June 21, 2001; "Affordable Housing: It's Time to Get Results from Funds," *Dallas Morning News,* January 24, 2001; "Southern Half of Dallas Still Awaits Housing Boom," *Dallas Morning News,* January 17, 2001; "Toxic Housing: Low-Income Residents Shouldn't Be Placed in Jeopardy," *Dallas Morning News,* October 10, 2000.

66. "Pizza Delivery Problem Targeted: City Official Planning to Address 'Redlining' Complaints in S. Dallas," *Dallas Morning News,* May 6, 1997.

67. In the Dallas Way, but also in protest and judicial responses, there is a strong tendency to imitate approaches that seemed to succeed and avoid those that seemed to fail elsewhere. The Dallas Way is obsessive about images and representations of the city, not only about law and order but also economic opportunities.

68. "Profitable Prospecting: Ignoring Southern Dallas Means Ignoring Opportunities," *Dallas Morning News,* November 23, 1997; "Economic Analysis Finds Area Poised for Investment," *Dallas Morning News,* November 19, 1997; "Southern Dallas: City Should End the Economic Polarization."

69. "Southern Dallas: The Place to Be," South Dallas Development Corp., advertising supplement, *Dallas Morning News,* October 25, 1992.

70. "Southern Dallas: This Is a Critical Time for Economic Strategies," *Dallas Morning News,* December 28, 1995. See also Henry Tatum, "Timing Right for New Southern Dallas Push," *Dallas Morning News,* November 20, 1996; Dallas Working Together, the Southern Sector Initiative, including a study by McKinsey and Co., 1997; periodic reports of the South Dallas Development Corp.; Williams, "Tale of Two Cities"; "Dallas at the Tipping Point" series.

71. Williams, "Tale of Two Cities."

72. Ibid. Williams was recognized and honored as a "hero" in Dallas and by the *Dallas Morning News.*

73. "Profitable Prospecting."

74. "West Dallas Says Yes to Wal-Mart," *Dallas Morning News,* June 27, 2002.

75. "Room for Disagreement."

76. Ibid.

77. "Majority Sees No Change in Dallas Race Relations: Most in Poll Say 14–1 Council Hasn't Helped," *Dallas Morning News,* April 28, 1997.

78. "Denied by White House, Lawyer Says Dallas Called Racial 'Mess,'" *Dallas Morning News,* December 12, 1997.

79. "Church Coalition 'Acts Out' Against Dallas at Meeting," *Dallas Morning News,* October 24, 1997. See Schutze, *The Accommodation;* Phillips, *White Metropolis;* Dulaney, "Whatever Happened to the Civil Rights Movement?"

80. See Massey and Denton, *American Apartheid;* Katz, *Price of Citizenship;* Katz and Stern, *One Nation Divisible;* W. J. Wilson, *When Work Disappears.*

6. MIMETIC AND MONUMENTAL DEVELOPMENT

1. *Souvenir Guide of Dallas,* 5–7.

2. Holmes and Saxon, *WPA Dallas Guide and History,* 3.

3. Oppenheimer and Porterfield, *Book of Dallas,* 257.

4. "Architect: Dallas Downtown Is Heart of Urban Problems," *Dallas Morning News,* May 4, 2002. For anxious commentaries on the downtown skyline, see *Dallas Morning News* editorial series on downtown, February 2002; Rena Pederson, "Build It; They Will Come," *Dallas Morning News,* September 1, 2001; "Building the New Dallas," *Dallas Business,* May 1998; Pederson, "The Skyline of Tomorrow," *Dallas Morning News,* August 3, 1997; "Downtown Dallas: Now Is the Time to Spotlight 'Big D,'" editorial, *Dallas Morning News,* April 5, 1995; "Downtown's Decline: It's Time for Aggressive Action," editorial, *Dallas Morning News,* March 15, 1994; "Downtown's Pivotal Decade: The State of the City" series, *Dallas Morning News,* December 1991; "The New Skyline," *Dallas Morning News,* December 13, 1987; "A New Vision for the City," *Dallas Morning News,* January 11, 1987.

5. D'Eramo, *The Pig and the Skyscraper,* 142.

6. Steve Blow, "Dallas Blind to Rich Past, Historian Says," *Dallas Morning News,* October 13, 1991.

7. Zukin, *Landscapes of Power,* 19.

8. For a different story of destroying the past, see Max Page, *The Creative Destruction of Manhattan, 1900–1940* (Chicago: University of Chicago Press, 2001).

9. Zukin, *Landscapes of Power,* 22, 20; see also Sorkin, *Variations on a Theme Park.*

10. On architecture and planning, see Boyer, *Dreaming the Rational City;* Scott, *American City Planning;* Fogelsong, *Planning the Capitalist City;* John Reps, *The Making of Urban America* (Princeton, N.J.: Princeton University Press, 1965); Giorgio Ciucci et al., *The American City* (1973; repr. Cambridge, Mass.: MIT Press, 1983); Donald Krueckeberg, ed., *An Introduction to Planning History* (New Brunswick, N.J.: Center for Urban Policy Research, Rutgers University Press, 1983); Sies and Silver, *Planning the Twentieth-Century American City;* Wilson, *City Beautiful Movement;* David Handlin, *The American Home* (New York: Little, Brown, 1982). On downtown, see Fogelson, *Downtown;* Larry R. Ford, *Cities and Buildings: Skyscrapers, Skid Rows, and Suburbs* (Baltimore, Md.: Johns Hopkins University Press, 1994); David M. Scobey, *Empire*

City: The Making and Meaning of the New York City Landscape (Philadelphia: Temple University Press, 2002); Alison Isenberg, *Downtown America: A History of the Place and the People Who Made It* (Chicago: University of Chicago Press, 2004).

11. See Donald J. Olsen, *The City as a Work of Art* (New Haven, Conn.: Yale University Press, 1986); Taylor, *In Pursuit of Gotham;* Page, *Creative Destruction;* Bluestone, *Constructing Chicago;* Mona Domosh, *The Creation of Landscape in Nineteenth Century New York and Boston* (New Haven, Conn.: Yale University Press, 1996).

12. Walter G. Dahlberg, "Growth, Planning, and the CBD," in *Dallasights: An Anthology of Architecture and Open Spaces* (Dallas: American Institute of Architects, Dallas Chapter, 1978), 22, 26.

13. McDonald, *Dallas Rediscovered,* 84. It is now an apartment building.

14. See Wade, *Urban Frontier;* Taylor, *In Pursuit of Gotham;* Wilson, *City Beautiful Movement;* Black, "Empire of Consensus." See also Mary P. Ryan, "Civil Society as Democratic Practice: North American Cities during the Nineteenth Century," *Journal of Interdisciplinary History* 29 (1999): 559–84; Ryan, *Civic Wars;* Ryan, "'A Laudable Pride in the Whole of Us.'"

15. Warner, "Management of Multiple Urban Images."

16. Kessler's route to Dallas went through St. Louis and Kansas City, where he developed plans and specific areas of the cities. Kessler was also influenced by Chicago and architect Daniel Burnham's Chicago Plan. Dallas and its subsequent planners continue to return to Kessler's plan and his development of Oak Cliff as a touchstone.

17. Wilson, *City Beautiful Movement,* 254.

18. Fairbanks, *For the City as a Whole,* 11.

19. Wilson, *City Beautiful Movement,* 255.

20. Ibid., 256.

21. Ibid., 257. Other treatments of Dallas planning attend to politics but seldom to building and architecture: Black, "Empire of Consensus"; Fairbanks, *For the City as a Whole;* Wilson, *City Beautiful Movement.* Fairbanks misreads profoundly; compare with McDonald, *Dallas Rediscovered;* American Institute of Architects, Dallas Chapter, *Dallasights; Dallas Architecture 1936–1986,* photographs by Doug Tomlinson, text by David Dillon (Austin: Texas Monthly Press, 1985).

22. Large-scale benefits are at least shared by the private sector, or private defined as public; see Fairbanks, *For the City as a Whole;* Black, "Empire of Consensus." On Kessler, see especially Wilson, *City Beautiful Movement.* A convenient list of plans is in Chris Kelley, "Developing Dallas," *Dallas Morning News,* April 21, 1996.

23. Alfred Koetter, "Monumentality and the American City," *Harvard Architectural Review* 4 (1984): 167. Olsen, *City as a Work of Art,* shows the importance of central city redevelopment even before the City Beautiful Movement. See also Taylor, *In Pursuit of Gotham;* Bender, *Toward an Urban Vision.* For useful comparisons, see Wilson, *City Beautiful Movement;* Domosh, *Invented Cities;* Bluestone, *Constructing Chicago;* architectural historian Carl Condit's many books on Chicago; Page, *Creative Destruction;* Peter Hall, *Cities of Tomorrow: An Intellectual History of Urban Planning and Design in the Twentieth Century* (Oxford: Blackwell, 1988); Ellin, *Postmodern Urbanism.*

24. Koetter, "Monumentality," 167, 167–68.

25. Zukin, *Landscapes of Power,* 19.

26. Enstam, *Women and the Creation of Urban Life;* McElhaney, *Pauline Periwinkle;* Hill, *Dallas;* Fairbanks, *For the City as a Whole;* Wilson, *City Beautiful Movement;* Black, "Empire of Consensus"; Hanson, *Civic Culture and Urban Change;* Bridges, *Morning Glories.*

27. Koetter, "Monumentality," 167, 168. For Dallas, see Fairbanks, *For the City as a Whole;* Wilson, *City Beautiful Movement;* Black, "Empire of Consensus"; Hanson, *Civic Culture and Urban Change.* On gender and the public sphere, see Mary Ryan, "Gender and Public Access: Women's Politics in Nineteenth-Century America," in *Habermas and the Public Sphere,* ed. Craig Calhoun (Cambridge, Mass.: MIT Press, 1992), 259–88; Ryan, *Women in Public: Between Banners and Ballots, 1825–1880* (Baltimore, Md.: Johns Hopkins University Press, 1990); Ryan, *Civic Wars;* Sarah Deutsch, *Women and the City: Gender, Space, and Power in Boston, 1870–1940* (New York: Oxford University Press, 2000); Deutsch, "Reconceiving the City: Women, Space, and Power in Boston, 1870–1910," *Gender & History* 6 (August 1994): 202–23; Maureen A. Flanagan, "The City Profitable, the City Livable: Environmental Policy, Gender, and Power in Chicago in the 1910s," *Journal of Urban History* 22 (1996): 163–90; Hazel V. Carby, "Policing the Black Woman's Body in an Urban Culture," *Critical Inquiry* 18 (1992): 738–55. On the public sphere more generally, see Davis, *City of Quartz;* Katz, *Price of Citizenship;* Katz, *"Underclass" Debate;* Sam Bass Warner, Jr., "The Public Invasion of Private Space and the Private Engrossment of Public Space," in *Growth and Transformation of the Modern City* (Stockholm: Swedish Council for Building, 1979), 171–80; Calhoun, *Habermas and the Public Sphere;* Nancy Fraser, "Rethinking the Public Sphere," *Social Text* 25/26 (1990): 56–80; Fraser, "Public Space: Urbanity, Streets, Costs," *Dissent,* Fall 1986, 470–94; Fraser, "Whatever Became of the Public Square," *Harpers,* July 1990, 49–60; Gerald Frug, *City Making: Building Communities Without Building Walls* (Princeton, N.J.: Princeton University Press, 1999).

28. Koetter, "Monumentality," 168, 169.

29. David Dillon, "City Hall Turns 20, and You Can't Beat It," *Dallas Morning News,* March 12, 1998.

30. See William H. Whyte, *The Social Life of Small Urban Spaces* (New York: The Conservation Foundation, 1980).

31. Ibid., 60, 60–61. There has been ongoing panic in Dallas about a visible homeless population downtown. See Lyn Lofland, *A World of Strangers* (Long Grove, Ill.: Waveland Press, 1985); Eric Monkkonen, *The Dangerous Class* (Cambridge, Mass.: Harvard University Press, 1975); Monkkonen, *Police in Urban America* (Cambridge: Cambridge University Press, 1980); John Schneider, *Detroit and the Problem of Order* (Lincoln: University of Nebraska Press, 1980).

32. See Greene, *Dallas U.S.A.;* Hanson, *Civic Culture and Urban Change;* Hill, *Dallas;* Leslie, *Dallas Public and Private;* Payne, *Big D.*

33. See, for example, the February 2002 *Dallas Morning News* series "Visions for

Downtown" and "Go Dallas"; the series of editorials on downtown retail, summer 2002; "Heart of City Is Still Beating," August 25, 2002.

34. See Dallas Plan; architect James Pratt's "Dallas: Visions for Community: Toward a 21st-Century Urban Design," *Dallas Morning News,* November 19, 1990. Di Mambro's concern about more green space downtown and elsewhere was expressed in *Dallas Morning News.*

35. "Panhandler Problem: It's Time for City to Restrict Street Solicitations," *Dallas Morning News,* July 11, 2002; "Group to Investigate City's Homeless Rules," *Dallas Morning News,* July 23, 2002.

36. On "selling" cities, see Kearns and Philo, *Selling Places;* Sorkin, *Variations on a Theme Park;* Mele, *Selling the Lower East Side;* Zukin, *Landscapes of Power.*

37. See Bernard Weinstein, "Texas Growth Hasn't Brought Prosperity," *Dallas Morning News,* January 31, 1997.

38. The *AIA Guide* calls Barnes's Dallas Museum of Art "the pivotal component of the Arts District." "In plan, the museum is a collection of simple volumes and courtyards organized around an internal circulation spine longer than the Grand Galerie of the Louvre. This gently sloping hallway connects pedestrian and vehicular entrances at opposite ends with a ceremonial entrance in the middle. The building's trademark barrel vault aligns with Flora Street at this location. The permanent collection galleries are arranged on four descending trays on the west side of the spine, with other museum spaces ingeniously tucked underneath. . . . At the DMA, Barnes has achieved a work of great simplicity, integrity, and elegance." Fuller, *American Institute of Architects, Guide to Dallas Architecture,* 32.

39. See Leslie, *Dallas Public and Private,* chapter 8; Francine Carraro, *Jerry Bywaters: A Life in Art* (Austin: University of Texas Press, 1994). More generally, see Lawrence Levine, *Highbrow/Lowbrow: The Emergence of Cultural Hierarchy in America* (Cambridge, Mass.: Harvard University Press, 1988); Michael Kammen, *Visual Shock: A History of Art Controversies in American Culture* (New York: Knopf, 2006).

40. Paul Goldberger, "Dallas Celebrates Art Museum by Edward Larrabee Barnes," *New York Times,* January 24, 1984.

41. Janet Kutner, "Dallas Museum of Art Hasn't Met Expectations Raised by Its Expansion," *Dallas Morning News,* June 11, 1995; see also Kutner, "Dallas–Fort Worth's Art Scene Stands at a Crossroad," *Dallas Morning News,* May 26, 1991.

42. Advertising flyer in support of the new concert hall. See Porter Anderson, "Is Elitism Killing the Arts?" *Dallas Magazine,* September 1992; Michael Berryhill, "Museums on the Make: The DMFA and the Kimbell Move into the Big Time," *Dallas Magazine,* December 1981; George Rodrique, "The Arts District," *Dallas Magazine,* May 1982; Peter Papademetriou, "Dallas Museum of Art: Extending the Modernist Tradition of E. L. Barnes," *Texas Architect,* January–February 1985; David Dillon, "The Dallas Arts District: Can It Deliver?" *Texas Architect,* January–February 1985; Skip Hollandsworth, "A Funny Thing Happened on the Way to the Symphony," *Dallas Magazine,* September 1986; Janet Kutner, "A Wing and a Prayer: DMA's Ambitious Expansion Comes at an Awkward Time," *Dallas Morning News,* November 11, 1990;

Kutner, "Dallas-Fort Worth's Art Scene Stands at a Crossroads"; Jerome Weeks, "Laughing at Dallas Again: Reactions to Stage Nudity and Interracial Kiss Provoke the Snickers," *Dallas Morning News*, November 14, 1993; Craig McDaniel, "Arts District: More Must Be Done to Bolster This Asset," *Dallas Morning News*, June 19, 1994; "Arts Funding," editorial, *Dallas Morning News*, August 26, 1994; "The Furor over Ethnic Arts Funding," *Dallas Morning News*, June 19, 1994; "Science Place: City's Funding Squabble Has Hurt Plans," editorial, *Dallas Morning News*, August 30, 1994; Kutner, "Dallas Museum of Art Hasn't Met Expectations Raised by Its Expansion"; Dillon, "The Show That Never Ends: The Theming of America," *Dallas Morning News*, August 27, 1995; "Old Red Museum: Here's a Way to Bring Dallas History to Life," editorial, *Dallas Morning News*, January 2, 1996; "Performing Arts: Plans for Center Are Gaining Momentum," editorial, *Dallas Morning News*, April 8, 1996; Kutner, "Dallas May Land Nasher Art Collection," *Dallas Morning News*, August 13, 1996; Philip Seib, "Dallas Needs to Make Decisions about Performing Arts Center," *Dallas Morning News*, January 19, 1997; Kutner, "City Offers Art Garden Proposal," *Dallas Morning News*, January 30, 1997; Mary Brown Malouf, "MAC-inations: The McKinney Avenue Contemporary Has Survived a Turbulent Birth, but Its Artistic Mission Remains More Confused Than Cutting-Edge," *Dallas Observer*, February 20–26, 1997; Martin Filler, "The Courting of a Sculpture Collection," *New York Times*, March 16, 1997; Kutner, "Nasher to Build Garden Downtown for Sculptures: Noted Museums Had Sought Works," *Dallas Morning News*, April 8, 1997; "Coveted Sculptures Are Going to Dallas," *New York Times*, April 8, 1997; "Sculpture Garden to Boost Economy, City Leaders Say: Nasher Collection Could Lure New Visitors, Create Jobs," *Dallas Morning News*, April 9, 1997; Kutner, "Benefits Flow from Nasher's Work of Heart," *Dallas Morning News*, April 13, 1997; Calvin Tomkins, "The Art World: Dallas," *The New Yorker*, June 13, 1983; "Latino Cultural Center: Facility Will Represent the Changing Face of Dallas," editorial, *Dallas Morning News*, December 14, 2000; Dillon, "Designing Woman: The Unknown Architect Inspired Immediate Confidence," *Dallas Morning News*, September 24, 2000; Dillon, "Making History: Dallas' New Women's Museum Is a Landmark Achievement," *Dallas Morning News*, September 24, 2000; "Nasher Center: Today's Ceremony Begins to Turn a Dream into Reality," editorial, *Dallas Morning News*, January 22, 2001; Dillon, "Renowned Architect Enlisted: Gehry to Design Downtown Museum," *Dallas Morning News*, March 13, 2001; "Bold Direction: New Natural History Museum Would Boost Downtown," editorial, *Dallas Morning News*, March 16, 2001; "Meadows Museum: It's a Jewel of Spanish Art," editorial, *Dallas Morning News*, March 22, 2001; Dillon, "Performing Arts Center to Have European Flair," *Dallas Morning News*, September 27, 2001; "About the Architects $250 Million Dallas Center for the Performing Arts, Norman Foster, Rem Koolhaas," *Dallas Morning News*, December 7, 2001; "Architects Selected for Arts Center Lauded," *Dallas Morning News*, December 7, 2001; "Arts District: Performance Hall Will Add Sizzle," *Dallas Morning News*, December 7, 2001; Kutner, "Local Museums and Galleries Flourish as Others Face Struggles," *Dallas Morning News*, December 26, 2001; Dillon, "Culture Unbowed: Cities Embrace Performance Venues as Catalysts of Growth,"

Dallas Morning News, December 28, 2001; "Museum Growing Beyond JFK: Sixth Floor Hopes New Exhibit Space Attracts More Local Visitors," *Dallas Morning News,* January 8, 2002; "Museum [Natural History] Eager to Join Arts District," *Dallas Morning News,* February 6, 2002; "Arts Group to Plan Latino Center's Exhibit," *Dallas Morning News,* March 23, 2002; "$42 Million Pledged for Arts Center: Winspear Contribution Is One of the Biggest in Dallas History," *Dallas Morning News,* May 14, 2002.

43. "The elegiac 1980s ended on a high note in Dallas with the opening of the Myerson Symphony Center, which provided the Arts District with the critical mass and architectural distinction it needed to be recognized as a viable entity. I. M. Pei rotated the shoebox form of the concert hall 26 [degrees] off the surrounding street grid and embraced it on three sides by a circular glass lobby topped by skylight lenses. This rotation opened the building toward the downtown skyline, while simultaneously acknowledging the Dallas Museum of Art at the opposite end of Flora Street. The curvilinear forms evident on the exterior have an even more dramatic impact inside, where Pei softened his usual rigid geometry with sinuous curves and complex, free-flowing spaces. By exploiting the Late Baroque as a general stylistic source, Pei achieved a space of Piranesian grandeur: mysterious, sensual and infinite. By contrast, the Eugene McDermott Concert Hall interior is a warm and richly detailed room notable for its gymnastic acoustical devices, including the suspended movable canopy over the stage and ceiling-level reverberation chambers": Fuller, *American Institute of Architects, Guide to Dallas Architecture,* 33.

44. "Donation to Arts Center Is Applauded," *Dallas Morning News,* May 15, 2002.

45. Anne Midgette, "With a Texas-Sized Ambition," *New York Times,* March 5, 2000. See also R. W. Apple, Jr., "Dallas, that 10-Gallon Place with Dreams to Match," *New York Times,* December 17, 1999.

46. Lee Cullum, "What 'World Class' Means for Dallas," *Dallas Morning News,* May 14, 2002.

47. "Dreher and Hicks Read 'World Class' as 'a Tacit Sign of Galloping Insecurity,'" *Dallas Morning News,* June 18, 2004.

48. Kutner, "Nasher to Build Garden Downtown for Sculptures"; "Coveted Sculptures Are Going to Dallas."

49. "Sculpture Garden to Boost Economy, City Leaders Say."

50. Apple, "Dallas, that 10-Gallon Place with Dreams to Match."

51. Dillon, "Dallas Arts District."

52. Ibid., 56–59; Sharon Zukin, *The Culture of Cities* (Oxford: Blackwell, 1995).

53. Dillon, "Dallas Arts District."

54. Chicago's Uptown took its name from the Uptown Theatre, built in 1925 with "an acre of seats"; by the early 1960s it was inhabited mostly by poor white people from Appalachia. Minneapolis, Winnipeg, Kansas City, and Houston also have Uptowns. City Place is also found in Chicago, St. Louis, West Palm Beach, Fort Worth, and naturally, Kansas City.

55. "Creating an Urban Dallas Neighborhood," *New York Times,* July 16, 1995.

56. See Findlay, *Magic Lands;* Gottdiener et al., *Las Vegas;* Hannigan, *Fantasy City;*

Judd and Fainstain, *Tourist City;* Rothman, *Devil's Bargains;* Rothman, *Neon Metropolis;* Rothman and Davis, *Grit Between the Glitter.*

57. Wilson, *City Beautiful Movement,* 254–55; see also Bridges, *Morning Glories;* Fairbanks, *For the City as a Whole.* On urban environments, see Martin V. Melosi, *The Sanitary City: Urban Infrastructure in America from Colonial Times to the Present* (Baltimore, Md.: Johns Hopkins University Press, 1999); Samuel P. Hays, *Beauty, Health, and Permanence: Environmental Politics in the United States, 1955–1985* (Cambridge: Cambridge University Press, 1989); Joel A. Tarr, *The Search for the Ultimate Sink: Urban Pollution in Historical Perspective* (Akron, Ohio: University of Akron Press, 1996).

58. See Harvey Molotch, "The City as a Growth Machine," *American Journal of Sociology* 82 (1976): 309–32; Logan and Molotch, *Urban Fortunes;* Mollenkopf, *Contested City;* Stone, *Regime Politics;* Stone and Sanders, *Politics of Urban Development.*

59. One example is Fullinwinder, "Dallas: The City with No Limits"; see also Jim Schutze's articles in the *Dallas Times Herald* and *Dallas Observer.*

60. Hanson, *Civic Culture and Urban Change;* see also Katz, *Price of Citizenship.*

61. See Hanson, *Civic Culture and Urban Change;* Katz, *Price of Citizenship;* John Mollenkopf, Peter Dreier, and Todd Swanstrom, *Place Matters: Metropolitics for the Twenty-First Century,* 2nd rev. ed. (Lawrence: University of Kansas Press, 2005). For a theoretical perspective, see Harvey, *Social Justice and the City;* Harvey, *Urbanization of Capital;* Harvey, *Consciousness and the Urban Experience;* Harvey, *Condition of Postmodernity;* Harvey, *Spaces of Capital.*

62. For a summary, see Kelley, "Developing Dallas." See also Fairbanks, *For the City as a Whole;* Wilson, *City Beautiful Movement;* Black, "Empire of Consensus"; Hanson, *Civic Culture and Urban Change.*

63. On Kessler, see Wilson, *City Beautiful Movement;* William S. Worley, "Kansas City Architects George Kessler, Henry Wright, and Sid and Herbert Hare," *Kansas History* 20 (1997): 192–205. See also Dillon and Tomlinson, *Dallas Architecture;* American Institute of Architects, Dallas Chapter, *Dallasights;* Hanson, *Civic Culture and Urban Change;* Richard Longstreth, "J. C. Nichols, the Country Club Plaza, and Notions of Modernity," *Harvard Architectural Review* 5 (1986): 121–37.

64. Quotation from Wilson, *City Beautiful Movement,* 257. Note earlier limits on Kessler's development of a civic center. On Goals for Dallas, see Bradley, "Goals for Dallas"; Fairbanks, *For the City as a Whole;* Black, "Empire of Consensus"; Hanson, *Civic Culture and Urban Change.*

65. Kelley, "Developing Dallas."

66. See Dillon and Tomlinson, *Dallas Architecture,* 119–24.

67. Kelley, "Developing Dallas."

68. Wilson, *City Beautiful Movement,* 265–66, chapter 12.

69. David Dillon, "The New Skyline," *Dallas Morning News,* December 13, 1987.

70. Dahlberg, "Growth, Planning, and the CBD," 28.

71. Ibid.

72. David Dillon, "Plaza Remains Urban Treasure: Fountain Place Unique in U.S.," *Dallas Morning News,* December 1, 1996.

73. Apple, "Dallas, that 10-Gallon Place with Dreams to Match," likes Pei's Myerson Hall. "But his Brutalist City Hall, built in 1978, already looks dated." See Dillon and others, "Downtown's Pivotal Decade" series; Dillon, "The New Skyline"; David Dillon, "Urban Enclaves," *Dallas Morning News,* December 22, 1991; Dillon "Plaza Remains Urban Treasure"; "A Reworked Plaza for Privacy," *Dallas Morning News,* September 16, 1992; "Downtown May Lose a Golden Chance: Cotton Building Could Be Housing," *Dallas Morning News,* December 22, 1991; "Is New Plaza Enough to Rescue Downtown?" *Dallas Morning News,* December 29, 1991; "Missing Pieces," *Dallas Morning News,* December 4, 1994; "David Dillon's Top 10 Architectural Events," *Dallas Morning News,* December 28, 2001. See also Paul Goldberger, "'Prima Donna' Buildings—Some Thoughts on Downtown's Skyline," *Dallas Downtown News,* February 17–23, 1986; Goldberger, "Interview," *Dallas Morning News,* October 29, 1995; Chris Kelley, "Past Provides a View of Dallas' Future: City Looks to Its Roots to Develop a More Authentic Sense of Place," *Dallas Morning News,* January 24, 1999; Smith, "Dallas: The Urge for Cosmetic Surgery"; Lee Cullum, "Architecture and Rodeo Driving of Dallas: Editor's Page," *Dallas Magazine,* December 1984; Cullum, "The Crescent, ARCO and Underground Dallas: Editor's Page," *Dallas Magazine,* March 1985; "Soul of a New City" *Dallas Magazine,* November 1988; Sally Giddens, "Will Anybody Come: What If the City Spent $95 Million and Opened a Downtown Mall," *Dallas Magazine,* January 1990; Mark Donald, "The Houses that David Built," *Dallas Observer,* April 14–20, 1994; Linda Jones, "Tower of Power: From any Angle, the Reunion Ball Makes its Mark on the Dallas Skyline," *Dallas Morning News,* April 28, 1996; Gregory Curtis, "Hanging on in the Akard Street Canyon," *Texas Monthly,* July 1985; Bill Marvel, "A New Vision for the City: Can Downtown Be More Than a Place to Work?" *Dallas Morning News,* January 11, 1987; "Projects Aim to Revitalize Housing," *Dallas Morning News,* June 3, 1994; Miriam Rozen, "Early Thaw: Hope Is Renewed for Four Downtown Housing Projects," *Dallas Observer,* December 1–7, 1994; "Downtown Upsurge: Big D Is Coming Back to Life," editorial, *Dallas Morning News,* December 14, 1994; "Downtown Dallas: Now Is the Time to Spotlight 'Big D'"; "Increment Districts: Here's a Way to Rev Up Downtown Dallas," editorial, *Dallas Morning News,* April 3, 1996; Jennifer Nagorka, "Bolstering Downtown: Taxing District Would Benefit Central City," *Dallas Morning News,* May 4, 1996; "Breaking Boundaries: Developers Spread Downtown Beyond Central Business District," *Dallas Morning News,* June 28, 1995; "Downtown Living: Housing Plans Should Reshape the City's Center," *Dallas Morning News,* August 31, 1996; Robert Miller, "Dallas City Center Group Detail Plans to Revitalize Downtown," *Dallas Morning News,* September 22, 1996; Chris Kelley, "3 Dallas Buildings Set for Face Lifts: U.S. Official Announces $25 Million Renovation Plan," *Dallas Morning News,* October 1, 1996; "Downtown Revival: Companies Are Smart to See the Potential," editorial, *Dallas Morning News,* October 8, 1996; "Things are Looking Up Downtown: Dallas's Core Office Market Rebounds," *Dallas Morning News,* October 25, 1996; Rena Pederson, "Downtown Is Buzzing," *Dallas Morning News,* January 2, 1997; Stanley Marcus, "Many Factors Make a City Cosmopolitan," *Dallas Morning News,* April 1, 1997; "Liftoff in the Lofts," *Dallas Morning*

News, May 2, 1997; "Dallas Tomorrow," editorial, *Dallas Morning News,* August 27, 2000; "Downtown Shopping," editorial, *Dallas Morning News,* September 24, 2000; "Downtown Walking: A Lost and Found Art," editorial, *Dallas Morning News,* November 24, 2000; "Main Street Retail," editorial, *Dallas Morning News,* February 7, 2001; "City Council Backs Mercantile Complex Renovations," *Dallas Morning News,* February 8, 2001; "Historic Downtown Buildings to Be Restored," *Dallas Morning News,* February 21, 2001; Henry Tatum, "Downtown Has to Capture Imaginations to Complete Revitalization," *Dallas Morning News,* February 28, 2001; "Global Dallas: Convention Center Hotel Is Vital," editorial, *Dallas Morning News,* April 2, 2001; "Making Dallas 24/7: More Downtown Improvements Are a Must," editorial, *Dallas Morning News,* June 17, 2001; "Dallas Tomorrow," editorial, *Dallas Morning News,* June 29, 2001; "Saving Downtown Dallas: Move Noxious Buses Off Main Street," editorial, *Dallas Morning News,* August 7, 2001; "Uniting to Boost City's Center: Summit Will Address Retail District, Other Ideas for Downtown," *Dallas Morning News,* August 29, 2001; "Greening Dallas: City Needs Better Park Funding," editorial, *Dallas Morning News,* April 14, 2002; "Apartment Conversion May Help Transform Downtown," *Dallas Morning News,* April 26, 2002; "Downtown Dallas Is Looking Alive Again," *Dallas Morning News,* June 18, 2002; "Downtown Parks: City Needs to Fill the Void," editorial, *Dallas Morning News,* August 12, 2002; "City Will Give to Victory," *Dallas Morning News,* October 12, 2002.

74. Dillon, "The New Skyline." Compare Paul Goldberger, "Dallas Punches a Hole in the Heart of Its Skyline," *New York Times,* February 14, 1988, to Apple, "Dallas, that 10-Gallon Place with Dreams to Match."

75. Dillon and Tomlinson, *Dallas Architecture,* 162.

76. Ibid., 199.

77. See summary in Kelley, "Developing Dallas"; also Fairbanks, *For the City as a Whole;* Wilson, *City Beautiful Movement;* Black, "Empire of Consensus"; Hanson, *Civic Culture and Urban Change.*

78. David Rusk, "Dallas: Halfway Down the Road—to Decline," with Antonio Di Mambro, "The Global City: The Road Ahead for the Dallas-Forth Worth Metropolis in the 21st Century," *Dallas Morning News,* March 4, 2001. Rusk refers to Neal Peirce's 1991 report on the city's future. Projecting a decade forward, the report was self-consciously alarmist.

79. Di Mambro, "The Global City."

80. "Architect: Dallas Downtown Is Heart of Urban Problems." "Larry Good, an architect and past chairman of the Central Dallas Association, proposed transforming Mr. Di Mambro's 'noose' into an 'emerald necklace' of linked parkland." Other ideas included a subway line, a centralized valet parking service, major city park, and a grocery store. "I do not believe that downtown wants to be an office park," said Dr. Gail Thomas.

81. A Texas city joke, and a question for another day: Dallas has a comprehensive set of zoning regulations, while Houston has remarkably and comparatively few. Yet the two cities share many spatial characteristics and in a number of ways appear to resemble each other. Why?

82. Bluestone, *Constructing Chicago,* 205, 206; see also Domosh, *Invented Cities.* For another, more recent Chicago comparison, see Timothy J. Gilfoyle, *Millennium Park: Creating a Chicago Landmark* (Chicago: University of Chicago Press, in Association with the Chicago History Museum, 2006).

7. A CITY AT THE CROSSROADS

1. Antonio Di Mambro, "The Global City: The Road Ahead for the Dallas-Forth Worth Metropolis in the 21st Century," *Dallas Morning News,* March 4, 2001. See also David Rusk, "Halfway Down the Road—to Decline," *Dallas Morning News,* March 4, 2001, which follows up on the report by Neil Peirce in 1991. The original report, which was also commissioned by the *Dallas Morning News,* is included in Neal R. Peirce, with Curtis W. Johnson and John Stuart Hall, *Citistates: How Urban America Can Prosper in a Competitive World* (Santa Ana, Calif.: Seven Locks Press, 1993).

2. Di Mambro, "The Global City."

3. See Henry Tatum, "Forget That Thermometer! Hell *Has* Frozen over: Two Old D/FW Rivals Join to Tackle Transportation Problem," *Dallas Morning News,* July 30, 2003; "It's Time for Region to Unite for Transport," editorial, *Dallas Morning News,* July 25, 2003; "Worst of Two Worlds: Region Faces Pollution *and* Sanctions," editorial, *Dallas Morning News,* June 11, 2003; "City-County Cooperation: Entire Area Has a Stake in Downtown Dallas," editorial, *Dallas Morning News,* November 24, 2003; "Ending Gridlock: The Region Needs a Unified Transit Agency," editorial, *Dallas Morning News,* November 10, 2002; Tatum, "Regional Transit Is Next Step," *Dallas Morning News,* November 6, 2002; "Regional Leaders: Time Right for More Cooperation. Population Growth, Economy, Technology Are Common Issues," *Dallas Morning News,* November 5, 2002; "The New Era: Dallas, Fort Worth Councils Wise to Cooperate," editorial, *Dallas Morning News,* November 1, 2002; "Big City Muscle: Dallas and Houston Could Help Each Other," editorial, *Dallas Morning News,* October 17, 2002; "Dallas, Fort Worth Find a Common Brand," *Dallas Morning News,* October 13, 2002. More recently, see "Forward Dallas," special supplement, *Dallas Morning News,* May 7, 2006.

4. Booz Allen Hamilton Consulting Web site: http://www.boozallen.com/publications/article/9734634?lpid66005.

5. "Dallas at the Tipping Point," special supplement, *Dallas Morning News,* April 18, 2004. Quotations following are also from this piece.

6. David Dillon, "Community," in "Dallas at the Tipping Point."

7. "Forward Dallas." See also David McAttee, "City Leaders Should Back the 'People's Comprehensive Plan,'" *Dallas Morning News,* June 12, 2006; "It's Not Backward Dallas: Don't Be Hasty about Changing City Plan," editorial, *Dallas Morning News,* June 12, 2006; "City with a Plan," editorial, *Dallas Morning News,* June 18, 2006. The Forward Dallas plan was passed by the City Council with a 12–2 vote. See Robert Bruegmann, *Sprawl: A Compact History* (Chicago: University of Chicago Press, 2005).

8. Hanson, *Civic Culture and Urban Change,* 74–75. See also profile in Peter J. Boyer, "The New Texan: Why George Bush Is Scared of Ron Kirk," *The New Yorker,* August 8, 2002.

9. Henry Tatum, "Kirk Broke through Old Stereotypes: Yet Big Projects Over-shadowed His Role as First Minority Mayor," *Dallas Morning News,* November 7, 2001; "Mayor Kirk: Eloquent Advocate Will Be Tough to Replace," editorial, *Dallas Morning News,* November 8, 2001; "As Mayor, Kirk One of a Kind: He Represented Several Firsts, but Evokes His Predecessors," *Dallas Morning News,* November 7, 2001.

10. "Kirk Touts City's Progress as He Launches Re-Election Bid: He Says Schools, Streets, Blighted Areas Need Attention," *Dallas Morning News,* February 6, 1999.

11. "The Streak: Mavericks Give Dallas a Psychological Boost," editorial, *Dallas Morning News,* November 21, 2002.

12. Among others: "A Dallas Bounce: Mavs Can Have Impact on City's Psyche," *Dallas Morning News,* May 21, 2003; "Wait until Next Year: Mavs Lifted Our Spirits, Established an Era," *Dallas Morning News,* May 31, 2003. In July 2003, on the death of Cowboys president and general manager Tex Schramm, obituaries, interviews, and articles stressed his role in rehabilitating Dallas: "Mr. Schramm helped pull this city out of its darkest period by providing the world a different view of Dallas. With Dallas still struggling to overcome its 'city of hate' image following the assassination of John F. Kennedy, Mr. Schramm already was on course to make the Cowboys 'America's Team.'" "Tex Schramm: He Brought Pride Back to Dallas," *Dallas Morning News,* July 16, 2003.

13. See Danielson, *Home Team;* Noll and Zimbalist, *Sports, Jobs and Taxes.*

14. See Dallas Together Forum South Sector Committee, "The Southern Sector Initiative: Dallas Working Together," November 1997; "Southern Dallas: City Should End the Economic Polarization," *Dallas Morning News,* November 19, 1997; "Dallas 'a Tale of Two Cities,' Study of Southern Half Says," *Dallas Morning News,* November 19, 1997; "Profitable Prospecting: Ignoring Southern Dallas Means Ignoring Opportunities," *Dallas Morning News,* November 23, 1997; "Housing Summit: Attendees Try to Prod Dallas toward Greatness," *Dallas Morning News,* February 3, 1998.

15. Danielson, *Home Team;* Noll and Zimbalist, *Sports, Jobs and Taxes.*

16. "Sports Challenge: Dallas Must Remain a Major Sports Town," editorial, *Dallas Morning News,* June 15, 1994.

17. "Church Coalition 'Acts Out' Against Dallas at Meeting," *Dallas Morning News,* October 24, 1997. See Schutze, *The Accommodation;* Phillips, *White Metropolis;* Dulaney, "Whatever Happened to the Civil Rights Movement?"

18. "City Will Give to Victory," *Dallas Morning News,* October 12, 2002.

19. "Arena Vote: Turnout, Results Deliver Key Message," *Dallas Morning News,* January 21, 1998.

20. "Arena Victory: Voters Give Dallas a Vital Lift," *Dallas Morning News,* January 19, 1998. The Belo Corporation, which owns the *Dallas Morning News,* stood to gain financially if Americans Airlines Center was built. Apparently, the newspaper failed to disclose this fact even as they supported the arena's construction, another illustration of the blurring between public and private interests in Dallas. See, for example, "Belo Sells Interest in Dallas Mavericks, American Airlines Center," News Release, Belo Corporation, January 30, 2002; "Dallas Gets First Look at Arena Model: Designers, Officials Say Style Fits with Historic West End," *Dallas Morning News,* July 29, 1999.

21. "Arena Vote"; Henry Tatum, "Arena Holds Lessons . . ." *Dallas Morning News,* January 21, 1998.

22. Philip Seib, ". . . About Power Shift," *Dallas Morning News,* January 21, 1998.

23. "American Airlines Center: Sky's the Limit," *Dallas Morning News,* July 22, 2001. See also "'Spectacular Year' for American Airlines Center: New Arena Not Without Its Controversy," *Dallas Morning News,* July 28, 2002; "Thinking Ahead: Downtown Must Have Plan If Victory Falters," editorial, *Dallas Morning News,* February 1, 2003; "West End Developers Push Ahead Despite Slump," *Dallas Morning News,* February 28, 2003; "Victory Developer Bows Out: City Leaders Frustrated, but Hillwood Says It'll Continue Arena Project," *Dallas Morning News,* March 14, 2003; "Not Everyone's Buying into Retail Plan," *Dallas Morning News,* April 13, 2003. More recently, see "5 Years on, AAC Gleams, Development Digs In," *Dallas Morning News,* July 29, 2006; "Once in Middle of It All, Reunion Now Out of It," *Dallas Morning News,* July 30, 2006.

24. See, for example, "American's Executive Packages Draw Fire: Airline's Plans Are Disclosed Amid Voting on Union Concessions," *New York Times,* April 18, 2003; "AMR CEO's To-Do List: Gain Trust, Sever Ties to Carty," *Dallas Morning News,* April 25, 2003; "American Gambles in Departing from Image: Some Brands Thrive, Others Don't After Repositioning," *Dallas Morning News,* May 25, 2003; "4 Officers to Receive AMR Stock Options: But CEO and Chairman Will Forego Bonuses As Pledged Previously," *Dallas Morning News,* July 24, 2003.

25. Editorial, *Dallas Morning News,* March 23, 2001.

26. "Chicago: It's Boeing's Kind of Town. Texas Backers Disappointed with Decision," *Dallas Morning News,* May 11, 2001.

27. "Boeing Fight Was Lost Downtown," *Dallas Morning News,* June 1, 2001. For more attempts at humor, see Larry Powell, "Boeing on Downtown: If You'd Filled It, We'd Have Come," *Dallas Morning News,* June 14, 2001; James Ragland, "As a Date, Dallas Fails to Take Office," *Dallas Morning News,* May 15, 2001; Powell, "The View from Here: Boeing . . . Boeing . . . Gone," *Dallas Morning News,* May 11, 2001. See also Henry Tatum, "North Texas Must Sell Boeing on Its People," *Dallas Morning News,* April 4, 2001.

28. "Boeing Fight Was Lost Downtown."

29. "Boeing Decision: Dallas Can Learn from This Experience," *Dallas Morning News,* May 11, 2002; Ray Perryman, "Culture Enriches Economy," *Dallas Morning News,* April 29, 2003.

30. "Learning from Losing," *Dallas Morning News,* May 13, 2001.

31. "Dallas Olympic Bid Touted as a Winner: 2012 Plan Submitted to U.S. Committee" *Dallas Morning News,* December 15, 2000; "Benefits of the Dallas 2012 Olympic Bid," *Dallas Morning News,* June 17, 2001.

32. "USOC Visit Major Hurdle for Dallas: Local Organizers Say Games' Payoffs Could Be Spectacular," *Dallas Morning News,* June 17, 2001; "No Euphoria, Just a Good Impression," *Dallas Morning News,* June 22, 2001; "No Time for Play Planning Games: Confident Dallas 2012 Leaders Not Resting in Bid for Olympics," *Dallas Morning News,* July 3, 2001.

33. "Council May Call Olympic Tax Vote: Referendum Could Make or Break Bid," *Dallas Morning News,* July 26, 2001.

34. "Olympic Vote May Be Fight: Sides Gearing Up to Lobby Public," *Dallas Morning News,* August 4, 2001; "Olympic Vote Will Be Nov. 6: Tempers Flair during Debate, but Bulk of Council Backs Plan," *Dallas Morning News,* August 9, 2001.

35. "Olympic Funding: Vote Will Show Dallas Wants to Compete," *Dallas Morning News,* October 10, 2001; "Kirk Wants All Eyes on 2012 Bid: Mayor Says Arena Development Tax Issue Detracts from Olympics," *Dallas Morning News,* October 20, 2001; Lee Jackson, "Voting 'Yes' to Dallas 2012 Plan Wouldn't Divert Money from Other Projects," *Dallas Morning News,* October 21, 2001; "2012 Trust Fund Focus of Debate," *Dallas Morning News,* October 26, 2001.

36. Henry Tatum, "Going for Gold: Public Still Hasn't Spoken on North Texas' Bid for Olympics," *Dallas Morning News,* August 1, 2001.

37. "Vote 'Yes': Olympics Would Revive Our 'Can Do' Spirit," *Dallas Morning News,* October 22, 2001.

38. "Backers Groan, Then Vow to Try Again for Games: Proponents Cite New Cooperation; Foes Say They'll Press Issues," *Dallas Morning News,* October 27, 2001.

39. "Dallas Out of Olympic Race: Fiscal Issues, Fears of Commercialism Cited; Houston, SF, NY, DC Are Finalists," *Dallas Morning News,* October 27, 2001. Less than two weeks later, the tax fund referendum, now meaningless, was defeated by a ratio of three to one by roughly 5 percent of registered voters; see "Olympics Fund, Already Irrelevant, Gets a Thumbs-Down from Voters," *Dallas Morning News,* November 7, 2001.

40. "Olympic Loss Is Blamed on USOC Mindset. Dallas 2012 Leader: 'International Character' Was Panel's Key Issue," *Dallas Morning News,* October 30, 2001.

41. "2012 Olympics: Dallas, North Texas Tried—and Should Learn," editorial, *Dallas Morning News,* October 27, 2001.

42. "Street Life: Dallas Needs to Solve Panhandling Problem," *Dallas Morning News,* February 11, 2003.

43. Henry Tatum, "Budget Turns Dallas Dream into Nightmare: The City's Bubbling Optimism Hits a Fiscal Brick Wall," *Dallas Morning News,* August 14, 2002; see also "Dallas Bond Issue: City Should Bite Bullet for Needed Work," editorial, *Dallas Morning News,* December 5, 2002.

44. See Beauregard, *Voices of Decline.*

45. Tatum, "Budget Turns Dallas Dream into Nightmare."

46. Di Mambro, "The Global City."

47. Recall Amy Bridges's important lessons about the selective activism and expansiveness of putatively limited polities in *Morning Glories.* See also Hanson, *Civic Culture and Urban Change.*

48. Gromer Jeffers Jr., "Fantasy Mayoral Fight: Miller vs. Kirk," *Dallas Morning News,* December 24, 2002.

49. "Mayoral Strongholds Break Mold: Miller's Sweep of North Dallas Defies Traditional Outcomes," *Dallas Morning News,* January 27, 2002.

50. Tatum, "Budget Turns Dallas Dream into Nightmare."

51. "Mayor Has Done Better Than We Expected," *Dallas Morning News,* February 14, 2003; "Miller Doesn't Stop Pushing Agenda When Council Disagrees," *Dallas Morning News,* April 11, 2003; "Dallas Agenda: Here Are Issues City Must Address," *Dallas Morning News,* June 9, 2003.

52. "Miller Pledges 'No Slowing Up': Homeless, Jobless, Trinity on Her Agenda as She Takes Oath Today," *Dallas Morning News,* June 9, 2003; "Miller Envisions City Makeover: As Mayor's First Full Term Begins, Colleagues Agree Plans Are Ambitious," *Dallas Morning News,* June 10, 2003.

53. Hanson, *Civic Culture and Urban Change;* Morgan, *Governance by Decree.*

54. Hanson, *Civic Culture and Urban Change;* for example, "The New Dallas: District Plan Won't Match Hispanic Growth," *Dallas Morning News,* August 24, 2001.

55. "3 Large Cities Seeking New Managers," *Dallas Morning News,* September 19, 2004, in which I am quoted: "'These are Texas cities that are almost obsolete in trying to maintain a form of government that has been rejected by most [big cities] across the country.' . . . Dallas adopted the council-manager system of government in 1930, Dr. Graff said—part of a 'fad' among cities to put professional experts at the helm. But with the rise of single-member districts, he said, competing interests, political differences, and racial and ethnic clashes have left little wiggle room for the manager. 'It's central to governance problems. . . . As these groups collide on city councils, the job of the manager is made that much more difficult.'"

56. "Rethinking City Hall: Strong-Mayor Concept Is Worth Consideration," editorial, *Dallas Morning News,* September 10, 2002. See also "Charter Review: Commission Would Remove Politics from Debate," editorial, *Dallas Morning News,* January 9, 1997; Henry Tatum, "Council-Manager System Is Off Track: It No Longer Is Being Operated as Originally Intended Decades Ago," *Dallas Morning News,* January 9, 2002; "Strong Mayor: Dallas Needs to Change Form of Government," editorial, *Dallas Morning News,* April 7, 2002; "Council Seeks Feedback on How Dallas Is Governed," *Dallas Morning News,* April 8, 2002; "Thinking Anew: Despite Fears, City Needs Charter Review," editorial, *Dallas Morning News,* April 10, 2002; "Change the Charter? It's Time to Tweak Council-Manager Format," editorial, *Dallas Morning News,* May 3, 2002; Tatum, "Some in Minority Community Wary of Mayor: Miller's Desire for Strong-Mayor System Is Viewed with Suspicion," *Dallas Morning News,* September 25, 2002; "Charter Changes: Panel Should Not Rule Out Strong-Mayor Option," editorial, *Dallas Morning News,* October 3, 2002; Lee Cullum, "Does Dallas Need Strong Mayor?" *Dallas Morning News,* October 6, 2002; "Poll Shows Mayor Is Preferred Leader: Answers Run Counter to Charter Review Hearings Favoring City Manager," *Dallas Morning News,* October 15, 2002; "Charter Review Talk Focuses on Race Issue: Mayor Surprised by Anxieties over Possible Reallocation of Power," *Dallas Morning News,* November 13, 2002; "Stronger City Council Proposed: Charter Review Panel's Preliminary Draft Seeks More Accountability," *Dallas Morning News,* February 2, 2003; "Charter Review Evokes Praise, Disappointment," *Dallas Morning News,* June 19, 2003. See Hanson, *Civic Culture and Urban Change,* esp. chapter 11.

57. "Strong Mayor Trounced: Turnout Unexpectedly High as Proposal Unites South Side, Splits North," *Dallas Morning News,* May 8, 2005.

58. See Hanson, *Civic Culture and Urban Change;* compare to Payne, *Big D,* and Fairbanks, *For the City as a Whole.* See also Morgan, *Governance by Decree.*

59. "Dallas Agenda: Big D Could Be the Millennium City," *Dallas Morning News,* January 1, 1999.

60. See also "Race and Class in Schools: An On the Record Special," broadcast in January 2003 by KERA-TV, *Dallas Magazine,* KTVT-Channel 11.

61. "Schools," in "Dallas at the Tipping Point."

62. DISD superintendent Mike Moses, former state educational commissioner, petitioned the federal courts to remove controls that had been in place under a series of orders since 1971, following court decisions ordering integration from 1960. See "Ruling Gives Dallas Independent School District 'Psychological Life': Moses Says District Can Drop Defensive Mode, Focus on Achievement," *Dallas Morning News,* June 7, 2003; "Dallas Independent School District Officials Aren't Surprised at Lagging Scores: Dallas Independent School District Prepares to Launch Massive Building Program," *Dallas Morning News,* May 21, 2003; Jim Schutze, "Segregation Forever: How Dallas Got What It Wanted," *Dallas Observer,* May 15, 2003; "As Dallas Independent School District Grows, So Does Anger over School Zones," *Dallas Morning News,* May 8, 2003; "Moses Testifies on Desegregation Order: Dallas Independent School District Ready to Function without Oversight, He Tells Federal Judge," *Dallas Morning News,* March 25, 2003; "Resegregation: Study May Help Guide Dallas Schools," editorial, *Dallas Morning News,* January 27, 2003; "Has Dallas Independent School District Met Desegregation Orders," *Dallas Morning News,* January 24, 2003; "Latinos Join Call to End Dallas Independent School District Court Order," *Dallas Morning News,* January 18, 2003; "Dallas Independent School District Asks Judge to Consider Release from Desegregation Order," *Dallas Morning News,* January 10, 2003.

63. "Steering the Schools: Presidency Shouldn't Derail Progress," editorial, *Dallas Morning News,* August 30, 2002.

64. Edward Rincon, "Dallas Schools Not Out of Federal Woods Yet: Lack of Improvement Argues for Continued Supervision," *Dallas Morning News,* December 2, 2002.

65. "Judge Ends Decades of Oversight; Moses Pledges Fairness for All," *Dallas Morning News,* June 6, 2003, includes a useful timeline. See "Black Leaders Criticize Letter Targeting Minority Trustees," *Dallas Morning News,* July 23, 2002; "A New Day: Dallas Schools Ready to Move from Court Order," *Dallas Morning News,* August 11, 2002; "Dallas Independent School District President Hangs on to Post: With Zornes Win, Minorities Narrowly Miss Chance to Lead," *Dallas Morning News,* August 29, 2002; "Dallas Independent School District Hasn't Given Enough Data on Desegregation, Monitor Says: Compliance Problems Also Noted; Moses Says He'll Seek Hearing," *Dallas Morning News,* October 17, 2002; "School Desegregation: It's Time to Free Dallas from Federal Control," editorial, *Dallas Morning News,* October 18, 2002; "Court Should End Oversight of Dallas Independent School District," *Dallas Morning*

News, October 28, 2002; "Moses Hopes Timing Right for End to Desegregation Order: Is Dallas Independent School District Ready to Move On?" *Dallas Morning News,* October 31, 2002; "Dallas Independent School District Moves Toward Hearing," *Dallas Morning News,* November 6, 2002; "Desegregation Points Approved: Trustees Endorse Commitments as Step toward End of Order," *Dallas Morning News,* November 8, 2002; "Dallas Independent School District Seeks Court Date on Desegregation: Federal Judge Will Be Asked to End Oversight of Order," *Dallas Morning News,* November 14, 2002; "Will Whites Come Back to Dallas Independent School District? District Hopes End to Desegregation Suit Will Reverse Trend," *Dallas Morning News,* December 4, 2002; "Trying to Blend Dallas Independent School District Schools: Desegregated Decades Ago, Some Campuses Remain Divided Within," *Dallas Morning News,* December 17, 2002. See also Hanson, *Civic Culture and Urban Change;* Morgan, *Governance by Decree.*

66. "A New Beginning: End of Deseg Order Should Improve Schools," editorial, *Dallas Morning News,* June 8, 2003; "Dallas Independent School District Is Ruled Desegregated," *Dallas Morning News,* June 6, 2003.

67. "Will Whites Come Back to Dallas Independent School District?"

68. "Dallas Schools Need to Lure Anglos Back: White Students Have Become an Endangered Species in City," *Dallas Morning News,* October 23, 2002.

69. "Dallas Independent School District Again Tops List of Low-Rated Schools: Students at 41 Campuses May Transfer under State Choice Law," *Dallas Morning News,* November 8, 2002.

70. "Moses Calls on Business Leaders to Get Involved: Chief Will Take 'Help in Just About Any Way,'" *Dallas Morning News,* September 29, 2002; "Dallas Schools: Business Community Can Do More to Help," editorial, *Dallas Morning News,* May 28, 1996.

71. Superintendents were Chad Woolery (1993–96); Yvonne Gonzalez (1997, eight months); James Hughey (1998–99); Waldemar "Bill" Rojas (1999–2000); Mike Moses (2001–4); Larry Groppel (2004–5); Michael Hinojosa (2005–). On the desegregation of public education, see Linden, *Desegregating Schools in Dallas;* Payne, *Big D;* Schutze, *The Accommodation;* "Dallas Schools '76: New Goals, New Challenges," special education supplement, *Dallas Times Herald,* August 15, 1975; "Desegregation," special section, *Dallas Morning News,* August 15, 1976; Tatum, "To: Members of the Dallas Ministry"; "Dallas Schools: Business Community Can Do More to Help"; Hanson, *Civic Culture and Urban Change;* Morgan, *Governance by Decree.* See also San Miguel, *Brown, Not White.*

72. "FBI Expands Dallas Independent School District Inquiry to Credit Cards," *Dallas Morning News,* July 31, 2006.

73. Ironically, the most serious starts in South Dallas were made by Texas A&M University and now by the University of North Texas, not Dallas institutions. See "State College: Veto Doesn't Kill Southern Dallas Proposal," editorial, *Dallas Morning News,* June 30, 1997; "Plea Made for Another University," *Dallas Morning News,* March 25, 1998; "Perry Gives Green Light to UNT-Dallas: It Would Become City's

First Public University," *Dallas Morning News*, May 5, 2001; "UNT Center Struggling to Grow: They Can't Build It Until the Students Come," *Dallas Morning News*, July 29, 2002.

74. Franklyn Jenifer, "UTD Poised to Become Research Power: North Texas Needs a Nationally Respected Research Institution," *Dallas Morning News*, February 16, 2003.

75. "Dallas Moves to Become Biotech Center: UT Southwestern, City Designate Land for Incubator Facility," *Dallas Morning News*, November 31, 2002; "Biotechnology: Dallas Has a Chance to Bolster This Industry," *Dallas Morning News*, November 10, 2002.

76. Metroplex Higher Education Benchmarking Study and Enhancement Strategy, prepared by SRI International for Dallas Citizens Council Education Committee, September 2002. Donald A. Hicks, "The Evolving Dallas/Fort Worth Metroplex Economy: Performance and Prospects," report to the North Texas Future Fund, 2003; "Economic Engine: Research Replaces Location for North Texas," *Dallas Morning News*, February 21, 2003.

77. Margaret O'Mara, *Cities of Knowledge: Cold War Science and the Search for the Next Silicon Valley* (Princeton, N.J.: Princeton University Press, 2004).

78. "Dallas Agenda: Big D Could Be the Millennium City," *Dallas Morning News*, January 1, 1999.

79. Metroplex Higher Education Benchmarking Study and Enhancement Strategy; Hicks, "Evolving Dallas/Fort Worth Metroplex Economy"; "Economic Engine."

80. "D/FW's University System Critiqued: Planning Could Bring More Funds for Area Schools, Experts Say," *Dallas Morning News*, September 21, 2002; "Big Goal for UTD Research: Officials Say Top Status Attainable, but Some Question One-School Focus," *Dallas Morning News*, December 12, 2002.

81. "Patience Urged for UTD Plan: Partnership with TI Expected to Make Big Splash—Eventually," *Dallas Morning News*, July 2, 2003; "A World-Class UTD Is on New Dean's List: Helms Vows to Attract $50 Million Research Budget, More Doctorates," *Dallas Morning News*, May 12, 2003; "TI Deal to Aid UTD: Tech Firm Would Expand Presence If State OKs $50 Million for Research," *Dallas Morning News*, June 6, 2003; "TI Ties Plant to UTD: Perry's Research Grant to College Sways Plans for $3 Billion Chip Factory," *Dallas Morning News*, June 28, 2003; "TI, State Join Up in UTD Windfall," *Dallas Morning News*, July 1, 2003; "UTD Expects Prominence with TI Deal: Plan Propels School's Goal of Being Engineering Powerhouse," *Dallas Morning News*, July 1, 2003.

82. "The Choice Is Ours: Collaboration Can Lift North Texas Colleges," *Dallas Morning News*, September 24, 2002.

83. "Brainpower: UT Regents, State Should Invest in North Texas," *Dallas Morning News*, December 16, 2002.

84. "The Choice Is Ours." See also "Panel: Dallas Lags in Nurturing Start-Ups," *Dallas Morning News*, January 29, 2006.

85. Dr. Lloyd V. Berkner, "Renaissance in the Southwest: Science Brews New Respect for the Intellect on a By-passed Frontier," *Saturday Review*, June 3, 1961; see

also Berkner, "Graduate Education in the Southwest: A Development Plan for the Graduate Research Center of the Southwest. A Preliminary Study, Mar. 29, 1961," *Journal of the Graduate Research Center* 29 (May 1961). See also Allan Neede, *Science, Cold War and the American State: Lloyd V. Berkner and the Balance of Professional Ideals* (Washington, D.C.: Smithsonian Institution and Harwood Academic Publishers, 2000).

86. Stuart W. Leslie and Robert H. Kargon, "Selling Silicon Valley: Frederick Terman's Model for Regional Advantage," *Business History Review* 70 (1996): 453–54.

87. Ibid., 453–54, 455, 456.

88. Ibid., 456. Compare the earlier dream to the discussion of higher education in "Dallas at the Tipping Point." See also O'Mara, *Cities of Knowledge.*

89. Henry Tatum, "Trinity Gives Dallas another Chance to Think Big," *Dallas Morning News,* February 5, 2003.

90. Ibid.: "This isn't about just resolving flood control problems that should have been handled decades ago or taking some traffic out of the clogged downtown freeways"; "Rollin' on a River: Let's Embrace a Bold Trinity Plan," *Dallas Morning News,* March 6, 2003; "Council Members Say Trinity Plan Short on Cash, Facts," *Dallas Morning News,* June 24, 2003. See also recent Dallas Plans, including Di Mambro, "The Global City."

91. David Dillon, "Simple, Elegant Design Could Help Define Dallas," *Dallas Morning News,* June 4, 2003; see also "Dallas Bridge Model Unveiled," *Dallas Morning News,* June 4, 2003; Henry Tatum, "Dallas Still Can Set a Good Example: Second Signature Bridge Doesn't Have to Be a Dead Idea," *Dallas Morning News,* January 30, 2002; "Bridges to the Future," *Dallas Morning News,* January 28, 2002. Ironically, for reasons of public safety, San Francisco and other cities are reducing foot and cycle traffic on bridges.

92. Compare Di Mambro with James Pratt's "Dallas: Visions for Community: Toward a 21st-Century Urban Design," *Dallas Morning News,* November 19, 1990; see also reports from Dallas Institute. The Forward Dallas plan that followed in 2006 represents a step backward.

93. "Dallas Is Just Beginning to Evolve into a Great City," *Dallas Morning News,* February 2, 2002.

94. Henry Tatum, "Dallas Now Must Decide What It Wants: We Already Have Heard Too Much of What Residents Don't Want," *Dallas Morning News,* December 26, 2001; "Planning Ahead: What Does Dallas Want to Be?" editorial, *Dallas Morning News,* May 1, 2002. Compare "Dallas at the Tipping Point" asking "who is Dallas?" to Tatum asking "what does Dallas want?"

95. "Dallas Bond Issue"; "Build a Better Dallas, City Can't Afford to Be Timid," *Dallas Morning News,* January 12, 2003. More recently, see "Dallas' Growing To-Do List," *Dallas Morning News,* June 28, 2006.

96. "Miller Says Time Not Right to Raise Taxes," *Dallas Morning News,* December 13, 2002.

97. "Build a Better Dallas, City Can't Afford to Be Timid." Dallas's bond rating did drop on Moody's from AAA to Aa1. "Rating Firm Lowers City's Bond Score,"

Dallas Morning News, June 17, 2003; "Lower Dallas Rating Isn't Really Bad News," *Dallas Morning News,* June 24, 2003.

98. The *Dallas Morning News* outlined its own role as providing community leadership, promoting a forum for debate, listening to and getting new voices on commentary pages, engaging readers and increasing readership, as in the old days of promoting planning; "Why a Bigger Bond Package," January 12, 2003.

99. Henry Tatum, "Dallas Could Use a Burst of Nostalgia," *Dallas Morning News,* June 5, 2002; "Crossroads of the Americas: It's a Proud Title That Dallas Should Seek," editorial, *Dallas Morning News,* January 5, 2003. See also Tatum, "Dallas Area Learned to Sell Itself 40 Years Ago," *Dallas Morning News,* August 8, 2001; "Build a Better Dallas: Half-Measure Bond Issue Won't Cut It," *Dallas Morning News,* January 7, 2003.

100. Henry Tatum, *Dallas Morning News,* January 7, 2003; "Getting the Message: Council Hears the Call for Adequate Bond Issue," *Dallas Morning News,* January 18, 2003; Bert Holmes, "Where's Council's Nerve," *Dallas Morning News,* January 23, 2003; "Open Letter: Council, Let's Make a Deal," *Dallas Morning News,* February 5, 2003.

101. *Dallas Morning News* editorials took aim: "Northeast Particularly Vulnerable to Suburbs" (January 8, 2003); "Southeast Needs a Bigger Bond Issue" (January 9); "Northwest Children Need Access to Libraries" (January 10); "Problems Are Obvious in Southwest" (January 11); "Disparities Persist as Dallas Crafts Bond Plan: Some Districts May Get More Funds but a Lesser Share of What's Needed" (January 14).

102. "Miller, 'Potholes, Pools, Police Are Priorities,'" *Dallas Morning News,* February 5, 2003.

103. "A Whole New Bond Game for Dallas: 17 Propositions, 2 Tiers, Lack of Mayor's Full Support Are Unique," *Dallas Morning News,* February 7, 2003.

104. "$555 Million Dallas Bond Vote Set: Miller, Poss Won't Actively Back Full Plan Reached in Fiery Session," *Dallas Morning News,* February 6, 2003. Poss was Miller's opponent in the May mayoral election.

105. "Build a Better Dallas: 11 Courageous Council Members Choose to Lead," editorial, *Dallas Morning News,* February 7, 2003.

106. "Bond Backers: No-Frill Package Quick to Deliver," *Dallas Morning News,* March 7, 2003.

107. Henry Tatum, "Consider Dallas' Bond Proposals a Package Deal," *Dallas Morning News,* April 23, 2003. See also "Arts Backers Mean Business with Bond Campaign: Soft Early Support Spurs Energetic PR Effort," *Dallas Morning News,* April 26, 2003; Victoria Loe Hicks, "Many Improvements Riding on Bond Vote," *Dallas Morning News,* April 27, 2003. For similar tactics in 2006, see "Dallas' Growing To-Do List"; "The New Can-Do City: At 150, Dallas Is Rebounding, but It Needs Help," *Dallas Morning News,* January 29, 2006.

108. "'Priority' Projects Getting Pushed Back by City Hall," *Dallas Morning News,* March 9, 2003. Hicks soon conceded that many of the separate bond issues did affect downtown; Hicks, "Many Improvements Riding on Bond Vote."

109. "All Bond Propositions OK'd, Funding Roads, Libraries, Parks," *Dallas Morning News,* May 4, 2003.

110. Sherry Jacobson, "Big D Is Becoming Dig Divide," *Dallas Morning News,* June 29, 2006; Victoria Loe Hicks, "The Lost Middle Class," *Dallas Morning News,* July 7, 2006. See Jason C. Booza, Jackie Cutsinger, and George Galster, "Where Did They Go? The Decline of Middle-Income Neighborhoods in Metropolitan America," Brookings Institution, Living Cities Census Series, June 2006.

111. On the proposed shift to a strong mayor system, see, for example, "Is System at Fault for Dallas' Woe? Some Say Other Top Cities Work Well under Council-Manager," *Dallas Morning News,* March 26, 2005; "Tight Race for Strong Mayor: Exclusive: Poll for *The News* Shows City Evenly Split on Proposal," *Dallas Morning News,* March 27, 2005; "Business Leaders Divided on Dallas Mayor's Power: Backers Point to Efficiency, Critics Fear Corruption," *Dallas Morning News,* February 19, 2005; "How Strong Is Too Strong? This Much Power Could Lead to Corruption," *Dallas Morning News,* February 26, 2005; "The Mayor Needs More Authority So City Hall Can Get Things Done," *Dallas Morning News,* February 26, 2005.

112. "The New Can-Do City."

113. "Defining Dallas: Citywide Efforts Forge Ties," *Dallas Morning News,* September 18, 2002.

114. See "Dallas Takes Off." For pretense of history, see Payne, *Big D.*

115. "Recession Strikes Texas, Too, But Not in Old Oil-Bust Way," *New York Times,* December 1, 2002. See also Allen R. Myerson, "A New Breed of Wildcatter for the 90s: With Ideas as Their Grub Stakes, Texans Are Striking Silicon Gold," *New York Times,* November 30, 1997; Bernard Weinstein, "Texas Growth Hasn't Brought Prosperity," op-ed, *Dallas Morning News,* January 31, 1997; "Corruption May Not Blemish City's Images: Prosperity, JFK, Sports Loom Larger, Some Say," *Dallas Morning News,* February 6, 2000; Bruce J. Shulman, "Is the Business of America Business?" op-ed, *New York Times,* May 13, 2001.

116. Mimi Swartz, "Deep in the Myths of Texas," *New York Times,* February 9, 2003.

117. For an unintended object lesson on the poverty of mimetic urbanism, see Steve Blow, "Determining Dallas's Top Seven Treasures," *Dallas Morning News,* April 6, 2003. Sometimes seriously, sometimes not, but always with an eye to other prominent cities' attractions, Blow includes Turtle Creek Boulevard, Dallas/Fort Worth International Airport, Houston Street Viaduct, NorthPark Center, Fort Worth, North Central Expressway, and the skyline.

118. Payne, *Big D;* Fairbanks, *For the City as a Whole;* Hazel, *Dallas;* Enstam, *Women and the Creation of Urban Life.*

119. Hanson, *Civic Culture and Urban Change,* 387–88.

INDEX

Harvey J. Graff is Ohio Eminent Scholar in Literacy Studies and professor of English and history at The Ohio State University. He is the author of numerous books on urban studies, literacy, and the history of children and adolescence, including *The Legacies of Literacy: Continuities and Contradictions in Western Culture and Society, The Labyrinths of Literacy: Reflections on Literacy Past and Present,* and *Conflicting Paths: Growing Up in America.*